# Protests as Events

# Protests as Events

## *Politics, Activism and Leisure*

Edited by Ian R. Lamond and Karl Spracklen

ROWMAN & LITTLEFIELD
INTERNATIONAL

London • New York

Published by Rowman & Littlefield International, Ltd.
Unit A, Whitacre Mews, 26-34 Stannary Street, London SE11 4AB
www.rowmaninternational.com

Rowman & Littlefield International, Ltd. is an affiliate of Rowman & Littlefield
4501 Forbes Boulevard, Suite 200, Lanham, Maryland 20706, USA
With additional offices in Boulder, New York, Toronto (Canada), and Plymouth (UK)
www.rowman.com

**British Library Cataloguing in Publication Information Available**
A catalogue record for this book is available from the British Library

ISBN: HB 978-1-78348-076-0
ISBN: PB 978-1-78348-077-7

**Library of Congress Cataloging-in-Publication Data**

Protests as events : politics, activism and leisure / edited by Ian R. Lamond and Karl Spracklen.
pages cm
Includes bibliographical references and index.
ISBN 978-1-78348-076-0 (cloth : alk. paper) — ISBN 978-1-78348-077-7 (pbk. : alk. paper) —
ISBN 978-1-78348-078-4 (electronic)
1. Political participation. 2. Protest movements. 3. Leisure—Political aspects. 4. Special events—
Management—Political aspects. I. Lamond, Ian R. II. Spracklen, Karl.
JF799.P765 2015
322.4'4—dc23
2014023957

∞™ The paper used in this publication meets the minimum requirements of American
National Standard for Information Sciences Permanence of Paper for Printed Library
Materials, ANSI/NISO Z39.48-1992.

Printed in the United States of America

# Contents

# Introduction

## Ian R. Lamond and Karl Spracklen

Within events management, events are commonly categorized along two axes—scale and content. Along the scale axis events range from the small-scale and local, through major events, which garner greater media interest, to internationally significant hallmark and mega-events, such as the Edinburgh Festival and the Tour de France. Content is frequently divided into three forms—culture, sport or business. Such a typology is a helpful heuristic for the interpretation and analysis of events within a commercial paradigm. However, such frameworks overlook and depoliticize a significant variety of events, those more accurately construed as protest.

The acknowledgement that events are political leads to intriguing possibilities within events management theory and practice. Can instances such as the procession of large numbers along a pre-arranged route, the festival feel of Pride parades and concerts such as Live 8, the raves that took place to celebrate the death of Margaret Thatcher, the occupation and reclamation of specific spaces by the Occupy movement, and local campaigns for change from group mobilization to lone acts of personal resistance, be understood as events within an events management framework? If these and other similar activities can be read as managed events, what does admitting them into the scope of the field mean for our understanding of them and how the study of events management is to be conceptualized? Similarly, how are we to conceptualize the activity of the individuals that participate as activists in such events? Stebbins's typology[1] of leisure activity, divided into three broad groups, can help here. When considering his distinctions of casual leisure, project-based leisure and serious leisure, it is the latter framework that seems best equipped to facilitate our understanding of activism.[2] How can we best interpret protests as events and activism as leisure?

It is such questions that led to the editors' convening of a symposium, Protests as Events/Events as Protests, at Leeds Metropolitan University in June 2013. This proved to be a highly successful one-day event. It drew together a trans-disciplinary group of around seventy academic researchers, activists and academic/activists. Participants came from seven countries, travelling from four continents, resulting in multiple fascinating and thought-provoking conversations. The symposium's purpose was to ascertain how protest and activism could be conceptualized, supported and sustained if it were viewed through the lens of a critical events management studies. The papers presented combined rigorous scholarship, hands-on workshops, plenty of fascinating debate and some laughter. This book develops and enhances the conversations begun that day and moves them on. It collects together the insights from some of the most exciting and challenging contributors to that event; giving them an opportunity to explore the ideas they introduced there in greater depth.

Our introduction and conclusion form key chapters that set out the book's critical dialogue, as well as articulating the scope for future research and action. The chapters are broken down into three sections: "Mediatization and Media Spectacle"; "Identity, Embodiment and Categorization"; and "Events as Dissent". Although the three parts frame the individual chapters they have much commonality between them. All the chapters exist in dialogue with one another, and all the chapters reflect, to a greater or lesser degree, on the themes of the three parts of the book.

This edited collection fits our publisher Rowman & Littlefield's strong interest in politics, globalization, cultural studies and the growing body of research associated with protest movements. The chapters address issues of individual and collective identity, relations between protests and social structures, theoretical reflections on the significance of social movements, spatiality and affective constructions of protest identities and embodiment in activism research.

The connections between politics, protest studies and cultural, social and political protest and events studies–events management studies–leisure studies represent an underdeveloped area of research and scholarship. It is an area ripe for development, though it needs increased encouragement. Nascent fields of critical events management studies and critical leisure studies, and their convergence around questions relevant to the study of protest and social movements, offer a new dynamic that can supplement and enhance the interdisciplinarity of politics and protest studies. This collection would indicate that the opportunities arising from drawing events management and leisure studies into research interested in politics and protest studies is alive and kicking. From the diversity of contributions presented here it would seem that, as a research domain, it is full of potential and ready for expansion and development.

As far as we are aware, this is the first book to consciously explore activism as leisure and protest as event. Through the acknowledgement that events are political, and seizing some of the intriguing possibilities that such a move opens up, this book brings together new research, from around the world, that explores the idea of protest as events, and activism as serious leisure. In so doing, it supports the development of a new critical politics of events and leisure.

## THEORIZING PROTEST AS EVENTS

Events management, as an academic subject, is situated firmly in the neo-liberal marketization of higher education. Events management courses teach students how to become efficient workers in the corporate events "industry", making their strong links with that "industry" a key part of their marketing and their curriculum. Events management researchers commonly work alongside corporations and policymakers, doing impact studies and cost-benefit analyses that conveniently come up with conclusions that help those corporations make more money. In this book we are making what might seem to be an impossible connection between social movement studies, political studies and events management. Social movement studies and radical political studies are critical in their analyses of capitalism and modernity. For researchers in social movement studies, what is at stake is the agency, and the limits of that agency, in the networks and groups that form new social movements, most of which are aligned on a radical political position against global capitalism, hegemony, governmentality, patriarchy, neo-liberalism and structural power in general. Radical political studies researchers and theorists seek to use their (relative) academic freedom, as well as their skills and knowledge, to critique political structures and systems that work against equality and social justice, such as global capitalism.

So how can these subject fields meet events management? It could be argued that the only thing these subject fields may have to offer events management is an instrumental understanding of how informal social networks might operate. That, potentially, could be of use to some events corporation looking to make profit from such networks. Looking at the discourse the other way, we suggest that many of the spaces and activities that surround social movements and activism might best be understood as events, or at the very least activities shaped by the corporate events against which people are protesting. Protests are events, and events are sites of protest. If nothing else, we would hope that our critical friends in social movement studies and political studies recognize that the idea of events is a useful analytical lens. But we want to go further than that. We want events management to actually learn from social movement studies and political studies. Our suggestion here is that events management, as it is currently constructed and constituted, as a curriculum, a university course and as a subject field, is in need of radical reform and overhaul. At a university level, students need to develop skills of critical thinking. Academics need to do critical research, and be ethical beings. That is why we are proposing to develop a subject field related to events management which we are calling critical events management studies. This rejects the notion of management as training for "industry"; instead, it locates events in the context of politics, and in social and cultural struggles against injustice and inequality. Of course, this is what has already happened in tourism and leisure, in which the dominant paradigm of management has been critiqued and partly replaced with critical tourism studies and leisure studies.

## ACTIVISM AS LEISURE

This book is situated in the wider critical subject field of leisure studies. We contend that activism is a form of leisure activity and leisure lifestyle, and protests (and events) are leisure spaces. Leisure studies researchers and theorists have been more aware of wider sociological and cultural ideas about the state of modernity. Leisure studies as a subject field is still dominated by structural and post-structural discourses indebted to Marxism and feminism—although this too is in danger of being overshadowed by the rising tide of management and instrumentality, not least in the new curricula of university leisure courses. Following Habermas,[3] Spracklen[4] argues that as the world has become more and more commodified and commercialized, leisure has become more instrumental. But leisure still provides a small communicative space in which humans can work to resist the colonization of their Habermasian lifeworld. Activism as leisure, then, describes this communicative rationality and action, the resistance and counter-hegemonic struggle.

## FORMING A THEORETICAL FRAMEWORK THAT CAN ACCOMMODATE PROTESTS AS EVENTS

The acculturation of events management, as an activity that operates within a neo-liberal field, emerges from a commonly unquestioned assumption, one which suggests that the question "what is an event?" is one that has an economic solution within a neo-liberal frame of reference. In so doing, questions pertinent to event management become framed by the horizons of that paradigm. Issues of relevance to the analysis of events, what they are, how they are organized and their development, sustainability and so forth become ones that (whether implicitly or explicitly) support and promote the dominant political hegemony. Concerns around the instrumentalism of events and their commodification, such as the arguments developed by Rojek[5] and Andrews and Leopold,[6] while rightly generating critiques of that hegemonic position, rarely address the acculturated conceptualization of event within event management.

In developing a theoretical framework that is able to accommodate protest, we need to begin by contesting the dominant construal of "event" within the field. Such a project requires the exploration of several trajectories which can be begun here, but require a separate, and more extended, space for their complete development. Badiou and Žižek's conceptualization of *event* as radical rupture[7] offers us a way of developing an alternative perspective on events. Their construal of *event* can work to support a re-alignment of events management, one that can incorporate protest and acts of civil disobedience. A valuable co-current aspect of their theorization of event is its essential connection to identity and the subjectivization of the subject. Recognition that at the heart of re-configuring events management is a requirement to critically review processes of subjectification draws us into a further important step in developing a theoretical framework.

Adorno's critique of the culture industry[8] is still a powerful indictment of how capitalism commodifies the human subject while reproducing itself through a cultural lens. His critique of the mass reproduction of culture presents us with a further trajectory, along which we are able to theoretically re-frame one of the culture industry's most recent incarnations—the similarly named "events industry". It is the production of standardizing models within events management education that evokes the dominant hegemony, which either ignores protests as events or construes them as a risk to be mitigated.

Associated with the industrialization and commodification of events are the communicative practices, which augment the construction of the subject with an articulation of relationships of power, that constitute the prevailing colonization of events management discourse within neo-liberalist paradigms. The works of Habermas[9] and, in the English cultural studies tradition, Jim McGuigan[10] contribute substantially to how we may interrogate those discourses. McGuigan's formulation of Cool Capitalism in particular suggests a prism through which the elements of the events industry can be clearly diffracted and carefully assessed. His definition of Cool Capitalism as "the incorporation, and . . . neutralisation, of cultural criticism and anti-capitalism into the theory and practice of capitalism itself"[11] epitomizes how the de-politicization of events frames much of the events management literature.

A conceptualization of events that construes event as a contested referent, that critiques the commodification of the event industry, acknowledges and goes beyond Badiou and Žižek's formulation of event as rupture to encompass the event as a potential arena of dissensus.[12] Operating at a point of convergence between aesthetics and politics, events as protests, protests as events, radically reconfigures the ontology of event management, widens its reach and facilitates epistemological approaches that currently do not figure within the field.

In conclusion, the theoretical framework necessary to accommodate protests as a valid part of events management, and events studies research and scholarship, problematizes "events" and articulates a critique of the "events industry". In so doing, it locates an understanding of those two terms within a critical perspective, which challenges a neo-liberalist construal of them, framing them as a valid ground for the discussion of concerns regarding emancipation and oppression.

The remainder of this introduction will concentrate on presenting an overview of the book. Each of the three sections will be introduced and contextualized with a short essay by the authors.

## PART I: MEDIATIZATION AND MEDIA SPECTACLE

A major characteristic of event management is the use of spectacle and the media to construct an imaginary around the event. The function of that imaginary is to frame the discourses associated with the event and its purpose. In this section ideas of media and mediatization will be considered at the juncture between protests and events, and activism and leisure.

## Chapter 1: The Construction of Contested Public Spheres: Discourses of Protest and Identity in a British Campaigning Organization

Through debates about how to protest and how to use events as protest, campaigning organizations and their activist members attempt to construct public spheres that express a coherent internal logic which advocates an alternative discourse to that of the dominant political hegemony. This research focuses on what motivates activist members to identify with particular campaign organizations, what sustains them in their activism and how their activism is enacted in the wider public sphere. This chapter is based on new qualitative research, utilizing anonymous semi-structured interviews with local-national activists who are members of a well-known (but unnamed) British campaigning organization.

A critical analysis of the discourse articulated through the organization's website, selected campaign material and public discussion forums will be used to ascertain the construction of its "worldview". That organizational "worldview" will then be compared to those drawn from a similar analysis of interview transcripts. Lamond, Kilbride and Spracklen argue that activists use a number of strategies to articulate activist identities; protest and event are just two ways of constructing common leisure identities within the campaigning organization. They go on to suggest that what is at stake in protest is the construction of contested public spheres, different and potentially incommensurable ontological spaces in which the construction of a common ground between the organization and the dominant political hegemony may be impossible to achieve.

## Chapter 2: SlutWalk Hong Kong and the Media: Sharing Lessons Learned

The global SlutWalk movement, which began in Toronto in 2011 when a police officer announced that sexual assault could be avoided by women's refraining from dressing like "sluts", has spread to over 100 cities around the world. The SlutWalk movement aims to raise awareness around sexual violence and victim blaming. As part of that movement, SlutWalk Hong Kong (SWHK) has marched in both 2011 and 2012.

In order to reach the general public, it is important for protests to be covered by the media; however, what constructions the media chooses to convey to the public are decided by the media outlets themselves. There are many lessons to be learned by the way the local media has chosen to cover SWHK, and the difference in coverage between 2011 and 2012 also offers valuable insights for activists. This chapter explores these differences, drawing out some interesting conclusions about how the media construes protest as event, from the perspective of SWHK.

## Chapter 3: Lights, Camera, Direct Action: The Protest Spectacle as Media Opportunity and Message Carrier

In February 2008 five activists from the environmental direct action group Plane Stupid occupied the roof of the House of Commons. Calling into question the Labour government's policy on airport expansion, they unfurled a banner that read "BAA HQ". This happened at the same time as Prime Minister's Questions and on the final day of the government's consultation into airport expansion. Plane Stupid's action was timed to maximize the press and political impact of their protest.

This chapter examines the protest tactics and media strategy of the environmental direct-action group Plane Stupid, demonstrating how they have adapted their tactics to gain press attention and promote their messages with a professionalized media strategy through the use of controlled messages and media-trained spokespeople. Press relationships were a central consideration of the group's protest tactics; when direct action was used they always considered the potential costs and benefits to the group of engaging with the media. The argument put forth in this chapter is that Plane Stupid's symbolic direct action served as a message carrier; it attracted press attention and allowed activists a platform to unveil their messages.

A content analysis of UK national press coverage of the group illustrates that press reaction to Plane Stupid's attempts at media attention divided the newspapers along ideological lines. The press reaction often depended on the target of protest action. Plane Stupid adapted and exploited the press's fascination with events to their advantage. Doing that through the use of spectacle and well-constructed messaging, they were able to create a narrative that connected airport expansion to climate change.

## Chapter 4: Paving the Way for Anti-Militarism in Romania: Activists, Events and Public Authorities during the 2008 NATO Summit in Bucharest

This chapter analyses two highly mediatized events surrounding the NATO Summit 2008 in Bucharest: the counter-summits "Kiss Your Enemy—A Day of Creativity and Action" and the "Anti-NATO Days". While the first event had a more entertaining approach, with the purpose of "reaching the biggest number possible" via movie screenings, light discussions and so on, the second one took a more radical stance. Its objective was to "welcome NATO with our own means", intending to express a "militant critical voice", culminating in a riot-police raid on the convergence centre in Bucharest (Timpuri Noi). The author uses the findings from an online expert survey, interviews, and an analysis of press reports to argue that activities of the peace movement and the anti-globalization movement were the least visible types of mobilization in Romania. Due to that low visibility, combined with the overall positive reporting on Romania's achievement in attracting the NATO Summit, the organizational aspects of the preparation of these events, ideological alignments and the reaction of public authorities and the police are interrogated. Secondly, this chapter tries to identify personal grounds and motivations for mobilization of the activists and their individual involvement, ranging from "a way to say no to militarism" to "NATO is not always good". That is done from the activists' perspective of understanding their mission, and mechanisms of personal networking that were employed for mobilization purposes. The analysis of the "Anti-NATO Days" event also takes into account reports of a counter-movement which threatened the organization and the organizers in person.

## PART II: IDENTITY, EMBODIMENT AND CATEGORIZATION

The concepts of identity, embodiment and categorization play a substantial part in the conceptualization of cultural and sports events. This section will look at how those concepts can be applied to enrich our understanding of protests as events.

## Chapter 5: Academic-Activism(s) in Urban Resistances: Pioneers or Obstacles for a Common Ground

Urban regeneration projects in Istanbul have led to a new political identity, with different types of activism and organization appearing. One of the main determinant aspects of this has been the emergence of the academic-activist, engaged in urban oppositions while conducting (more than) his/her research. This chapter elaborates the interface between academics and activists through the case study of urban social oppositions in Istanbul. It will assess their effectiveness in constructing and shaping resistances at the grassroots through the use of various discursive constructions, apparent mainly in campaigns and protests, to break the silence and divisions and create a common *uncommon* ground for resistance. [13]

In this chapter it is the significance and pioneering role of individual actors, more than groups, as well as tensions between academic-activists and other activists, and within academic-activists in different respects, that take centre stage. Its focus is mainly related to the positions of academic-activists with other activists and to their conflicting views, practices and experiences of resistances. Methodologically, this chapter uses participatory solidarity action research, [14] incorporating a self-reflexive process as an activist-scholar, [15] and supported by in-depth interviews with other academic/activists. It will illustrate this issue from moments of protests, using international and local campaigns organized for an allied and effective movement in, for (against) and beyond Istanbul; incorporating different views of academic-activists at those protest events.

## Chapter 6: As Barriers Fall, Contingency Becomes Possibility: Protest Resisting and Escaping Containment and Categorization

This chapter argues that protest can be seen as a crystallization of "actually existing" societal discontent and antagonism, which is more or less visible in a specific time and place, becoming an event in the process. Protest as event is, in this sense, one in which barriers fall and the contingency of different agents—none more so, than those "in" and "outside" an (anti-)political milieu—are dissolved by collective action, communal endeavour, and the shared thrill of opposition and resistance. This conceptualization of protests as events/events as protests looks at how barriers, that may have existed between participants before involvement in an event can, and frequently do, fall as different subjectivities coalesce and experience is shared.

This chapter aims to sketch how such confluences create new possibilities for those engaged in them and how these can be seen as a form of resistance to, and escape from, strategies of containment and categorization mobilized by the powers operating against them. Indeed, the division of those engaged in protest into spurious categories based on their identifiable affiliations is the favoured tactic of the state and media. In doing so, its objective is to contain and isolate protestors within this same arbitrary categorization of the "protestor" who is politicized, but whose concerns and discontents are otherwise something completely separate from the general population. However, when protest becomes an event, in which barriers fall and common linkages are made, it becomes far more difficult for those involved to be isolated by categorization, contained and neutralized as harmless. Crucially, participation is opened up to all those previously "outside" (anti-)political activity, newly emboldened and "politicized" by their involvement; further dissolving former separations. Ultimately, this chapter's concern is to sketch how protest as event can enter an uncharted realm of event as protest, resisting categorization and escaping containment.

## Chapter 7: "It's a Beautiful Thing, the Destruction of Wor(l)ds": The Script

The singular compelling imagery of "occupying" as a form of resistance is its multiplicity of voices—the collective mobilization of the "multitude". Yet the force and urgency of a collective resistance lies in the individual untold stories of its proponents. Rather than glorify the movement as a faceless entity, this chapter draws on a paper/performance presented at the Protests as Events symposium which embraced the daily stories, struggles and wounds of occupation, through the use of photographs.

The resistant performances of the "outraged" in Athens have gathered momentum since 2011, transforming the fixed landscape of a city into a platform for negotiation and dialogue. Both forms are connected with existing social conditions: austerity measures, mass immigration and "crisis". In this chapter it is argued that resistance is a space of radical openness in which the self is re-imagined in relation to its landscape and, in turn, the landscape is remapped.

The chapter reflects the presentation format of the original paper, in that it takes the form of a dialogue/performance of collected stories of protesters from Athens. The authors attempt to resist discursive borders of social science and the arts by occupying both. The stories used evoke the urban remapping of a politically charged multitude (in squares and streets) alongside narratives of personal resistance. The common element is a view of resistance as embodied, with an aim to radically transform the spaces of domination and oppression perceived to be limiting the human rights of subjects.

The data arouse effects/affects of resistance by recalling images (photographs), interview testimonies and narratives of resisting bodies.

## Chapter 8: The Logic of Movement Practice:
## An Embodiment Approach to Activist Research

Investigating protests as events is an emerging field of research activity. This chapter seeks to contribute to a debate around methodology in that area. This is done through the development of an activist research methodology that breaks with a dichotomous understanding of theory and practice. That congruence is achieved through the application of an epistemological reading of Pierre Bourdieu's theory of practice to the analysis of embodied praxis in alter-globalization movements, which focuses on the example of the Clandestine Insurgent Rebel Clown Army (CIRCA).

The bodily expressions of that activist group educe emotions and experiences that aim to go beyond purely cognitive understandings of action. Bourdieu's sociology of embodiment constituting the link between the archetype of pure thought—academia—and the archetype of action—movement activism, this chapter follows the suggestion that during phases of abeyance movements do not cease to move; instead, they are actively engaged in the construction of meaning and identity. Hence, when activists have time to reflect and make sense of their realities, this constitutes a practice in itself. Research can only grasp the logic of movement practice when it can come to terms with those fluid borders between thought and action. With knowledge embodied through day-to-day involvement, the researcher cannot take the position of a passive external observer; rather, she needs to subject her role to examination. By adopting Bourdieun concepts such as "habitus" and "epistemic reflexivity", a departure from traditional research distinctions, such as those between object and subject or theory and practice is facilitated, and a move towards an activist research methodology which analyses theory as practice is enabled.

## PART III: EVENTS AS DISSENT

So far, in this introduction, we have concentrated on developing our understanding of an emerging research field, one that locates the conjunction of protest with events management and leisure studies by focusing on the ideas of protests as events. In this final section that juncture is reversed, as we consider how events can be construed as protests.

## Chapter 9: Sounds of Dissent: Music as Protest

Music has long been associated with social movements and protests. While this is most commonly associated with the civil rights movements in the 1960s it also, more recently, has been found to contribute to the activism of occupy groups, and the protests and social change that began in North Africa in earnest in 2011, and continues there still.

Thus far, most research in this area has been concerned with one of three aspects: first, a focus on the social activity which surrounds musical activity in such settings; second, the lyrical and semiotic content of protest songs; and third, musicological studies of the musical and lyrical content of protest songs, independent of the social interactions involved.

In this chapter, which builds on Christopher Small's concept of active musicking,[16] it is suggested that music can be seen as an act of protest in itself as well as a form of social control. Understood in this way, music as protest is dependent on specific contexts and a dynamic, reflexive relationship between musicking, memory, identity, emotion and belief.

Using research conducted in Bosnia, as well as Egypt, Tunisia, Libya and Morocco, this chapter will demonstrate those processes in terms of both a matrix of interdependent influences and how they influence social behaviour (positive as well as negative), and also suggest that music has a greater potential to improve conflicted social space than is currently generally utilized.

## Chapter 10: Rave Culture: Freeparty or Protest?

This chapter argues that rave culture can be classified as a form of protest. As a youth-oriented subculture, or "tribe", based around social ideas, music and art, raves emerged from the era of Thatcher's children. Its "cultural heroes came in the form of radical young entrepreneurs, who started up clubs and record labels, rather than the politicians and poets of yesteryear". Furlong[17] views raves as "a mix of hedonism, consumerism and escapism", a sanctuary away from education and work, in which participants are free from boundaries and controls, in an environment that involves active protest and the consumption of drugs. The "grassroots organized, anti-establishment" rave in which "drug use is portrayed as the defining characteristic" is examined through the lens of protest. Despite a perception that raves are only subversive because they are an illegal trespass (under the Criminal Justice and Public Order Act 1994), Alwakeel[18] argues that "a specific political currency lies precisely in its very persistence in the face of regulation". Meanwhile, Tepper[19] notes the construction of "a 'cultural frame' that links an activity . . . to a lifestyle, a category of people, and a social problem, thereby constructing notions of deviance and harm in the public's imagination".

The research presented in this chapter suggests that, having been treated historically as forms of symbolic protest, raves have evolved into "freeparties". In examining criteria that might shed light onto this discussion, we compare and contrast two sets of primary research: the first undertaken with rave participants and organizers, and the second with a discrete church community, which explicitly identifies itself as functioning within the realm of protest and social justice. In exploring those two narratives, we may find parallels in the elements of shared values, activities and motivations.

## Chapter 11: Events of Emancipation and Spectacles of Discontent: How the Tea Party and Occupy Wall Street "Happened"

In conceptualizing protest as events one is confronted with an ambivalence, one that can be illustrated by contrasting two ways the concept of the "event" can be framed within the critical social sciences and political philosophy. On the one hand, it is conceptualized as a point of rupture and irreducible freedom, allowing for the transcendence of a given socio-political setting.[20] On the other hand, the event as festival is understood as inherent to the cultural logic of late capitalism, thereby constituting a feature of the given socio-political structure.[21] This chapter draws on research undertaken on Occupy Wall Street. One thing that comes across most strikingly from that research is the vocabulary employed by interviewees, which sometimes verges on the sacralizing when referring to their first encounter with the respective protests. Nearly all of them perceived that encounter as something that lifted them above the routines and grievances of the everyday. That consistency did not extend to their ex-post accounts of the subsequent developments, which diverged dramatically, the difference mirroring the ambivalence of the concept "event" as tension in their own accounts.

Methodologically, this chapter grasps that phenomenon through the concept of the habitus in crisis. As a dispositional structure, habitus is at once contributing to the discontent and framing its articulation in the respective protests. Through analysing that structural tension by reconstructing the interviewees' trajectory and position in social space, it is contrasted with their own sense-making, as manifested in the interviews, and re-embeds it in developments in and around political mobilizations. It is argued that a "structural potential"[22] for an opening can be identified. Nevertheless, in most cases, the event relapses into a carnivalesque outburst, which, albeit temporally disburdening, in the long run stabilizes the situation that caused the underlying discontent.

## Chapter 12: Emotional Construction of Identities in Protest Spaces

The production of protest spaces is considered in this chapter as a case of emotional framing by movement networks and other public actors. A relational and action-oriented concept of space, influenced by a structuration approach, is applied in order to study how collective identities are (re)created with regard to space. The field research at the heart of this chapter focuses on political sites of the radical left-wing scene in Berlin and, more specifically, on the protest events influenced by it. Using Goffman's concept of social occasion,[23] the transfer of meanings between different aspects of such complex events is studied. In so doing, this contribution asks how certain protest spaces allow the whole event to be considered as political.

Through protest practices, participants bring together symbolic and material/physical aspects of spaces; constructing discrete and relational "non-landscapes" of meanings. Further, the interactional spatial orders (such as "bloc" or "chain") are subjects of emotional framing in their own right. The embodied and emotional character of protest events makes these mechanisms of identity construction particularly effective. In protest spaces symbolic relations and oppositions can be experienced not only on the cognitive but also on the emotional and bodily levels simultaneously, suggesting that protest routines are spatial routines and emotional routines as well.

## CONCLUSION: SETTING THE AGENDA FOR CRITICAL EVENTS STUDIES

The conclusion will draw together the key themes and set out the important ontological, epistemological, political and ethical issues for activists and academics as activists. The conclusion will then map out the agenda for a new subject field, critical events studies, showing how this might engage with other disciplines to challenge the hegemony of neo-liberalism in the teaching and research of events management.

## REFERENCES

Adorno, Theodor W. *The Culture Industry.* London: Routledge, 2005 [1991].
Alwakeel, Ramzy. "The Aesthetics of Protest in UK Rave". *Dancecult: Journal of Electronic Dance Music Culture* 1, no. 2 (2010). Accessed 31 May 2013. https://dj.dancecult.net/index.php/dancecult/article/view/287/264.
Andrews, Hazel, and Teresa Leopold. *Events and the Social Sciences.* Abingdon: Routledge, 2013.
Badiou, Alain. *Philosophy and the Event.* Translated by Louise Burchill. Cambridge: Polity, 2013.
Bertuzzo, Eliza, Eszter B.Ganter, Heike Oevermann, and J. Niewohner, eds. *Kontrolle offentlicher Raume: Unterstutzen Unterdrucken Unterhalten Unterwandern.* Berlin: Lit Verlag, 2013.

Chatterton, P. "'Give Up Activism' and Change the World in Unknown Ways: Or, Learning to Walk with Others on Uncommon Ground". *Antipode* 38, no. 2 (2006): 259–81.
Chatterton, Paul, Duncan Fuller, and Paul Routledge. "Relating Action to Activism: Theoretical and Methodological Reflections". In *Participatory Action Research Approaches and Methods: Connecting People, Participation and Place*, edited by Sara Kindon, Rachel Pain, and Mike Kesby. Routledge Studies in Human Geography. London: Routledge, 2007.
Debord, Guy. *The Society of the Spectacle*. Translated by Donald Nicholson-Smith. New York: Zone Books, 1999.
Furlong, Andy. *Youth Studies: An Introduction*. Oxford: Routledge, 2013.
Goffman, Erving. *Behaviour in Public Places: Notes on the Social Organisation of Gatherings*. New York: Free Press, 1985.
Gordon, Uri. "Anarchist Geographies and Revolutionary Strategies". *Antipode* 44, no. 5 (2012): 1742–51.
Habermas, Jürgen. *The Theory of Communicative Action, Vol. 1: Reason and the Rationalization of Society*. Cambridge: Polity, 1986.
Habermas, Jürgen. *The Theory of Communicative Action, Vol. 2: Lifeworld and System: A Critique of Functional Reason*. Cambridge: Polity, 1992.
Jameson, Fredric. *The Political Unconscious: Narrative as a Socially Symbolic Act*. Ithaca, NY: Cornell University Press, 1981.
McGuigan, Jim. *Cool Capitalism*. London: Pluto Press, 2009.
Pain, Rachel. "Social Geography: On Action-Orientated Research". *Progress in Human Geography* 27, no. 5 (2003): 649–58.
Ranciere, Jacques. *Dissensus: On Politics and Aesthetics*. Translated by Steven Corcoran. London: Continuum International Publishing, 2010.
Rojek, Chris. *Event Power: How Global Events Manage and Manipulate*. London: Sage, 2013.
Small, Christopher. *Musicking: The Meaning of Performing and Listening*. London: Wesleyan University Press, 1998.
Spracklen, Karl. *The Meaning and Purpose of Leisure: Habermas and Leisure at the End of Modernity*. Basingstoke, UK: Palgrave, 2009.
Stebbins, Robert A. "A Leisure-Based Theoretic Typology of Volunteers and Volunteering". *Leisure Studies Association Newsletter*, no.78 (2007): 9–12.
Stebbins, Robert A. *Amateurs, Professionals and Serious Leisure*. Montreal, Quebec: McGill-Queen's University Press, 1992.
Stebbins, Robert A. "Serious Leisure: A Conceptual Statement". *Pacific Sociological Review* 25, no. 2 (1982): 251–72.
Tepper, Steven J. "Stop the Beat: Quiet Regulation and Cultural Conflict". *Sociological Forum* 24, no. 2 (2009): 276–306.
Žižek, Slavoj. *Event: Philosophy in Transit*. London: Penguin, 2014.
Žižek, Slavoj. *The Year of Dreaming Dangerously*. London: Verso, 2012.

## NOTES

1. Robert A. Stebbins, *Amateurs, Professionals and Serious Leisure* (Montreal, Quebec: McGill-Queen's University Press, 1992), and "A Leisure-Based Theoretic Typology of Volunteers and Volunteering", *Leisure Studies Association Newsletter*, no. 78 (2007): 9–12.

2. See, for example, Stebbins, *Amateurs, Professionals and Serious Leisure*.

3. Jürgen Habermas, *The Theory of Communicative Action, Vol. 1: Reason and the Rationalization of Society* (Cambridge: Polity, 1986), and *The Theory of Communicative Action, Vol. 2: Lifeworld and System: A Critique of Functional Reason* (Cambridge: Polity, 1992).

4. Karl Spracklen, *The Meaning and Purpose of Leisure: Habermas and Leisure at the End of Modernity* (Basingstoke, UK: Palgrave, 2009).

5. Chris Rojek, *Event Power: How Global Events Manage and Manipulate* (London: Sage, 2013).

6. Hazel Andrews and Teresa Leopold, *Events and the Social Sciences* (Abingdon: Routledge, 2013).

7. See, for example, Alain Badiou, *Philosophy and the Event,* trans. Louise Burchill (Cambridge: Polity, 2013); Slavoj Žižek, *Event: Philosophy in Transit* (London: Penguin, 2014).

8. Theodor W. Adorno, *The Culture Industry* (London: Routledge, 2005 [1991]).

9. Habermas, *The Theory of Communicative Action, Vol. 2.*

10. Jim McGuigan, *Cool Capitalism* (London: Pluto Press, 2009).

11. Ibid., 38.

12. Jacques Ranciere, *Dissensus: On Politics and Aesthetics*, trans. Steven Corcoran (London: Continuum International Publishing, 2010).

13. P. Chatterton, "'Give Up Activism' and Change the World in Unknown Ways: Or, Learning to Walk with Others on Uncommon Ground", *Antipode* 38, no. 2 (2006): 259–81.

14. See, for example, Rachel Pain, "Social Geography: On Action-Orientated Research", *Progress in Human Geography* 27, no. 5 (2003): 649–58; and Paul Chatterton, Duncan Fuller, and Paul Routledge, "Relating Action to Activism: Theoretical and Methodological Reflections", in *Participatory Action Research Approaches and Methods: Connecting People, Participation and Place*, ed. Sara Kindon, Rachel Pain, and Mike Kesby, Routledge Studies in Human Geography (London: Routledge, 2007).

15. Such as Uri Gordon, "Anarchist Geographies and Revolutionary Strategies", *Antipode* 44, no. 5 (2012): 1742–51.

16. Christopher Small, *Musicking: The Meaning of Performing and Listening* (London: Wesleyan University Press, 1998).

17. Andy Furlong, *Youth Studies: An Introduction* (Oxford: Routledge, 2013).

18. Ramzy Alwakeel, "The Aesthetics of Protest in UK Rave", *Dancecult: Journal of Electronic Dance Music Culture* 1, no. 2 (2010), accessed 31 May 2013, https://dj.dancecult.net/index.php/dancecult/article/view/287/264.

19. Steven J. Tepper, "Stop the Beat: Quiet Regulation and Cultural Conflict", *Sociological Forum* 24, no. 2 (2009): 276–306.

20. Badiou, *Philosophy and the Event*; Žižek, *Event: Philosophy in Transit.*

21. For example, Fredric Jameson, *The Political Unconscious: Narrative as a Socially Symbolic Act* (Ithaca, NY: Cornell University Press, 1981), and Guy Debord, *The Society of the Spectacle*, trans. Donald Nicholson-Smith (New York: Zone Books, 1999).

22. Eliza Bertuzzo, Eszter B. Ganter, Heike Oevermann, and J. Niewohner, eds., *Kontrolle offentlicher Raume: Unterstutzen Unterdrucken Unterhalten Unterwandern* (Berlin: Lit Verlag, 2013).

23. Erving Goffman, *Behaviour in Public Places: Notes on the Social Organisation of Gatherings* (New York: Free Press, 1985).

*Part I*

# Mediatization and Media Spectacle

A major characteristic of event management is the use of spectacle and the media to construct an imaginary around the event that attempts to shape the discourses associated with the event and its purpose. Event management serves the purpose of controlling subaltern groups, counter-hegemonic movements and individual acts of agency. The imaginary is the sleight-of-hand that removes from sight the actual levers of hegemony and control. To be immersed in an event as spectacle, one becomes lost in the mythmaking that surrounds it and yet somehow one believes the myths to be true. Events are believed to bring people together, to help people make connections, to entertain and give pleasure. They are also sold to us as entire ethical frameworks that define our lives and the perfect life of the people at the event (the other spectators and the participants). The Olympics represent such an imaginary, with the myth of how Olympianism takes us above politics, and teaches us how to be decent human beings. The imaginary is the spectacle of the opening ceremonies, the passion of the fans, the feats of the medal winners, the heartwarming tales of athletes struggling to represent their country over incredible levels of adversity. But the imaginary masks the truth of these mega-events. For example, in the run-up to the Olympics in London in 2012, the International Olympic Committee ensured that they and their sponsors had complete subjugation of free spaces around the event, as well as complete control of the private spaces of the event. [1] That is, they made sure that advertising promoting corporations not sponsoring the event, advertising that used the Olympics, or campaigning organizations trying to use the Olympics as spaces of resistance were all targeted, controlled and ultimately removed from inside and outside the buildings where the event was held. The IOC or its partners took over roads, closed down businesses, destroyed houses and made people homeless, demanded huge sums of money and supressed dissent. Not only that, but the IOC also insisted that the UK government create new legislation that gave the IOC's repressive practices the veneer of legitimacy and respectability.

Mediatization is the way in which such imaginaries and myths are normalized. The growth of popular culture and the media industries in Europe and North America have been noted and critiqued by Adorno and others.[2] By the rise of modernity in Europe and North America at the turn of the twentieth century, newspapers and magazines constructed popular imaginations and provided ways of indoctrination and control for governments and the elites that dominated them. A shared imaginary called the West appeared as a "normal" source of identity for the bourgeoisie and the working classes in those parts of the world that were closely linked to America and America's homogenizing popular culture. New technologies emerged by the middle of the twentieth century that made the hegemonic imaginary more directly a spectacle: the rise of radio, cinema and television constructed hegemonic cultures and national identities, and perpetuated gender orders and stereotypes. In our brave new world, mega-events have become key ways in which active participation in sports, leisure and culture become transformed into passive consumption of programmes and news reports. Every sports competition sells itself as the best one ever, the biggest one, the one with the strongest or the fastest. Every music festival sells itself as the one you have to watch on television to be cool. Mediatization of events changes the way we think about our agency, our tastes and preferences, and our place in the social web of significance. And the rise of the Internet and social media online make the pressure of mediatization more acute. Now we are constantly negotiating our way through the instrumental products of global capitalism, working our way past adverts that tell us that the next soccer World Cup is happening soon and we can only see all the action live if we give our money and our personal details to some corporation.

If mega-events and the imaginary are part of the tool-box of hegemonic mediatization, the media agency of activists is at work in more radical ways. Protest is a form of event, and activism is a form of leisure, as we have argued in the introduction to this book. Individuals and radical campaigning groups have the agency to do the "serious leisure" of activist work. That is, they can use their agency to use the structures, systems and technologies of mediatization for their own purposes. Activists can interact with each other through the Internet, and through capturing events and demonstrations to perform their own spectacles. Activists can get their messages across as if they are selling the latest soft drink or faith, hijacking mainstream media and subverting it in displays of Debordian bravado. Campaigning organizations can become media savvy in how they use all kinds of technologies and strategies associated with marketing, capitalism and instrumentality. Of course, this then has the potential to reduce campaigning organizations to the campaign story, and not the morality or politics at the heart of the campaign. There is thus a danger in the reification of campaigning, the pursuit of members, donations, subscriptions, headlines and "likes" on social media, over effecting real change in the world. This juxtaposition between politics by instrumental marketing and politics by feeling is at the centre of the chapters here. In this section ideas of media and mediatization will be considered at the junction between protests and events and activism and leisure. Each chapter demonstrates in different ways how activists and campaigning organizations can use the media to create new public spaces and spheres in which their messages can be heard. With the growth of the Internet and alternative media spaces, there are possibilities to circumvent the hegemonic control of the mainstream press and news channels. But the mainstream media is still important for activists and organizations who try to turn events into protest, and those who wish to subvert the mainstream's imaginary.

## REFERENCES

Adorno, Theodor W. *Prisms*. London: Neville Spearman, 1967.
Graham, Stephen. "Olympics 2012 Security: Welcome to Lockdown London". *City* 16, no. 4 (2012): 446–51.

## NOTES

1. Stephen Graham, "Olympics 2012 Security: Welcome to Lockdown London", *City* 16, no. 4 (2012): 446–51.
2. Theodor W. Adorno, *Prisms* (London: Neville Spearman, 1967).

*Chapter One*

# The Construction of Contested Public Spheres

*Discourses of Protest and Identity in a British Campaigning Organization*

Ian R. Lamond, Cassandra Kilbride
and Karl Spracklen

Jürgen Habermas' ideal of the public sphere, founded on the bourgeois revolution of the Enlightenment, the development of democratic constitutions, and the creation of a free press, assumes individuals can (and do) meet as free and equal citizens.[1] In this account of politics and political action, free agents transcend hegemonic power to discuss and decide policy in a communicatively rational manner. In this chapter, we want to outline ways in which the public sphere is contested by different agents and powers. We are interested in how, in this late modern society, the communicative freedom of the public sphere is at risk, as Habermas himself suggests, of being wiped out by the instrumental rationality that controls transnational structures and systems. In his work on the meaning and purpose of leisure, Spracklen[2] has suggested that spaces associated with such activities might be the last communicative remnants of the Habermasian lifeworld. That is, as global capitalism and state controls exert enormously limiting power on the spaces and forms of work and of popular culture, leisure time becomes the only time when it becomes possible to resist the hegemonies in other parts of everyday life. So, with the ideal public sphere of the lifeworld swamped by instrumentality, the only way to organize resistance and protest is through volunteering, volunteer activism, protest on the margins and counter-hegemonic spectacle.[3] Thus, protest becomes a form of communicative leisure, the only space and practice where counter-hegemonic resistance becomes possible, and new public spheres are potentially constructed.

Instances of protest become events that present a public articulation of such potential. Following Badiou[4] and Žižek,[5] the protest event can thus be construed as "a change of the very frame through which we perceive the world and engage with it"[6]; it is a reframing, a break (or rupture) with how the world is conceived. It confronts what the prevailing hegemony fabricates as the mundane by presenting us with an alternative to how it is currently shaped. The protest event opens a space of potentiality, a liminal space in which language, relationships, and the symbolic order of actions and interactions, pertinent to daily life, can be other than they currently are. It is not, simply, that such events offer us the prospect of an alternative way of orientating ourselves to the world; rather, it presents us with the possibility of completely reconstituting that symbolic order, redefining what the world is and that deep rootedness in it which constitutes our identity as part of it. By challenging the consensual frame of the dominant hegemonic worldview the protesting subject becomes defined, through participation, as contrary to the discourses of that dominant hegemony. It is through the articulation of communicative leisure that the protesting subject becomes self othered, or as Ranciere expresses it in one of his ten theses on politics,[7] they become the "essence of politics" as the "manifestation of dissensus . . . the presence of two worlds in one".[8] It is through debates about how to protest, and how to use events as protest, that campaigning organizations, and their activist members, attempt to construct public spheres that express a coherent internal logic which advocate an alternative discourse to that of the dominant political *consensus*.

In our research, we are interested in what motivates activist members to identify with particular campaign organizations, what sustains them in their activism and how their activism is enacted in the wider public sphere. We are interested in how activists and workers in such organizations develop what Robert Stebbins calls a serious leisure project,[9] in which some individuals shape careers and work without any monetary reward, while others transform their leisure hobby into a paid job. The concept of serious leisure has been applied to sports participants and musicians, but also many other volunteers who become workers, such as committee members in social clubs and social enterprises.[10] In this chapter we are using serious leisure to map the motivations, webs of belonging, and social, moral and political discourses of political activists. In construing activism as serious leisure, protest becomes *communicative* leisure.

The discussion in this chapter is based on new qualitative research using anonymous semi-structured interviews with local-national activists, who are members of a well-known (but unnamed) radical, British, campaigning organization. While it could be argued that our framework of activism as serious leisure and protest as communicative leisure could be applied to any marginal political activity (such as the political activism of the far right), we believe that the nature of communicative rationality is such that it stands against ideologies that (knowingly or unknowingly) support and endorse hegemony. The activism of the far right is predicated on false ideologies of racialization, nationalism and hegemonic masculinity. Those false ideologies promote the interests, and maintain the power, of nation-states and transnational corporations, even if the far right articulates suspicions about some of the effects of that power.[11] So communicative activism and protest has to be radical, or left, fighting the power of people and institutions that actually control things, and not fighting phantoms of history such as "foreigners" or other *minority* groups.

Our research has concentrated on the constructions of identity and belonging in a radical-left campaigning organization. The organization's website, selected campaign material and public discussion forums were scrutinized using a combination of critical discourse analysis and a variation of Goffman's frame analysis.[12] Those approaches were used to ascertain the construction of the organization's "worldview", which was then compared to that drawn from a similar analysis of interview transcripts.

In this chapter, we will argue that activists use a number of strategies to articulate activist identities; protest and event are just two ways of constructing common leisure identities within the campaigning organization. We will also argue that what is at stake in protest is the articulation of contested public spheres: different and potentially incommensurable ontological spaces, in which the construction of a common ground between the organization and the dominant political hegemony may be impossible to achieve. That is, the power of the neo-liberal nation-state over the remains of the Habermasian public sphere may be so hegemonic that activists and campaigning organizations are limited to making their own spaces of activism, far removed from the "mainstream". Before we turn to our discussion, analysis and conclusions, we will discuss our theoretical framework and our methodological choices in a traditionally academic manner.

## LITERATURE REVIEW

The authors carried out an initial literature audit in early 2014. The basis upon which the literature was scanned focused on three areas within the study of serious leisure and events management, these were: protest and identity, political activism and the use of public spheres for protest. It was envisaged that by compiling a review on those areas, a convergence of theory aligning the study of serious leisure and event management, within the context of political activism, would begin to emerge. To date, that topic remains a largely unexplored territory.

In 2002 Mair concluded that "there remains a need to capture this leisure form [activism] and determine in what ways leisure theory can be strengthened".[13] Since her paper on exploring the relationship between leisure, activism and social change, in which she makes that conclusion, only a handful of other research papers have been published that address the issue. Where there are discussions of contested public spheres, discourses of protest and identity, from a serious leisure and event management perspective, event management scholars have exhibited a tendency to approach those topics from a socioeconomic perspective. Their research has focused on the social, political and economic *impacts* of large global events, such as the Olympics, Live Aid and Live 8, and, from a historical perspective, Woodstock,[14] with large- and small-scale protests being almost completely overlooked.

Mair's research has addressed many concerns raised in this chapter, including identity, motivation and the reclaiming of "discursive space". On the two former issues she describes the formation of "multi-issue coalitions", or the coming together of many small activist groups to attend large-scale high-profile protests such as those that follow world trade summits, the G8 and so forth. "Activists", she argues, "generally form large multi-issue coalitions and include workers, artists, feminists, environmentalists, religious leaders, academics and many others".[15] Drawing upon the work of others,[16] Mair suggests that it is more accurate to "describe these events as social gatherings of concerned people who are attempting to reframe the conditions within which economic, social and political decisions are made". Continuing, she points out that these events often include a range of activities that would commonly be found at conventional festivals such as "teach-ins, art, music, drama and policy meetings".[17]

Mair goes on to discuss, in some depth, how activism fits into the definition of serious leisure. "Serious leisure", she writes, "includes a characteristic of staying committed when confronting danger, undoubtedly an important ingredient, when differentiating serious from casual leisure", but also observes from her interviews with activists that "there are ways in which the notion of serious leisure does not completely capture the essence of what these data are indicating. First, regarding the motivations for attending these events, there is a sense of collective duty or citizenship that elicits a deeper commitment than serious leisure might suggest". She goes on to suggest that the risks involved in acts of protest and political activism are "arguably beyond the scope of serious leisure".[18]

One further interesting point Mair makes is that "the general tone of leisure research suggests the growth of commodified forms of leisure has led mainly to self-serving and consumptive behaviour, and lends little to the building of community or the encouragement of political engagement".[19]

That concept has not gone unnoticed by other serious leisure researchers.[20] Spracklen, Richter and Spracklen suggest that it is not just our leisure time that has become commercialized and consumptive. That commercialization has meant our towns, cities and public spaces have become ever more commodified. Using Leeds, a city in the north of England, as an example, they concluded that a consequence of local government cultural policies and city centre regeneration schemes has been to create city spaces that appeal only to the people who work in them or who go to such spaces to engage in commodified forms of leisure. While such leisure activities might encompass shopping, eating out, going to the theatre or nights out drinking, they have also actively reduced places where alternative groups would otherwise have congregated. In their case study, a key example is the decision to "transform" the city's quirky Corn Exchange, an unusual retail building full of independent and alternative shops, into a food quarter selling expensive and premium foods. Based on three distinctive and alternative subgroups, and the steady decline of alternative Leeds, the research concludes, "Successive decision makers and planners have minimized, then eliminated, alternative leisure spaces from the urban landscape, leaving alternative scenes on the margins of the city centre".[21] They go on to say that while "there are no fences stopping any alternative people entering the city centre . . . there is nothing designed to entice them in".[22] Although they found that the left-wing activists who took part in their research refused to surrender, "most accepted that the city centre of Leeds was an alien, gentrified, and eventized space".[23]

It could be argued that the example of one city isn't enough to prove a far-reaching trend towards gentrification. However, in her study of parks and public squares, and their comparison to online and offline protest spheres, Arora[24] came to a similar conclusion. She states:

> If we pay attention to the trajectory of urban parks across cultures and time, we see a similar and challenging trend. The transformation of park from relatively unregulated public space to currently corporatized, commercialized and semi privatized space should give us deep cause for concern. . . . Malls, gated-communities and corporate plazas have created controlled diversity whereby the masses are differentiated based on their consumption patterns, creating a dissipated or a pseudo public.[25]

In her paper, Arora historically contextualizes the creation and usage of parks and public space. Such spaces, she argues, were originally created to allow people from different classes and backgrounds to come together during leisure pursuits. The creation of spaces that appeal only to a limited subsection of society limits both their use and the interaction between those subsections, which, as Mair has pointed out,[26] is often the makeup of activist groups. One may thus conclude that activism is adversely affected by gentrification and eventization.

Gilchrist and Ravenscroft[27] address the contesting of public spheres in their discussion of the act of space hijacking, which they describe as a form of culture jamming. According to Gilchrist and Ravenscroft:

> Space hijackers are fundamentally aware of the formidable opposition posed by the state and market which necessarily provokes antagonism and conflict alongside pre-figurations of freedom born through the projects they deploy. Their projects aim to shed light on behaviours that are discouraged in the urban public realm, for example shifts in security, privatisation and laws of urban public space that make it easier to be monitored and policed. Projects are designed to draw out the ideological intent of the architect and their complicity in designing a built environment primarily for work and consumption. Some "projects" also challenge the narrow range of permissible activities by performing non-consumptive behaviours in direct contravention to consumerist norms governing parts of the city.[28]

Some activists have begun challenging the hijacking of public space by policy makers in a more subtle way; they have been called craftivists. So far only a handful of papers have been written on this emerging trend.[29]

Wallace's "study of craftivism and mobility" explains "craftivism" as a term coined by Betsy Greer in 2003 to signify the merging of crafting and activism. In her words, "craftivism is a way of looking at life where voicing opinions through creativity makes your voice stronger, your compassion deeper and your quest for justice more infinite". Combining a do-it-yourself ethic, the covert movement of street art, and needlework, craftivists bomb urban spaces and inanimate objects as a means of art and consciousness raising—sometimes political, sometimes humourous, sometimes dazzling, but always unexpected. In a similar vein, collective knit-ins juxtapose the act of knitting, which is "generally constructed as a feminine and domestic craft with its sheer out-of-placeness at protests, undermining accepted ideas of protesters as violent, and offering, what is seen, at least to knitters, as a constructive approach to activism that encourages interpersonal interaction and everyday resistance".[30] A quick Internet search of the term *craftivism* will bring up many examples of activism through craft, from campaigns by big activist organizations such as wool against weapons[31] to the Craftivist Collective,[32] which works on a multiple range of issues.

What the literature has shown is that while government policy and town planners have actively reduced spaces in which, at one time, protesters were able to occupy, gather and engage in protest, alternative forms of leisure as activism have emerged as a response. That leisure activism, which incorporates a wide variety of traditional leisure/craft activities, has arisen in order to reclaim those gentrified spaces, to make them places where leisure and event blur with activism and protest.

## METHODOLOGY — ETHICS AND POSITIONALITY

The research was approved through our university's research ethics process, in line with our university's research ethics policy. We believe it is ethical to give respondents the veil of anonymity and the promise of confidentiality. Those concerns are important because we are trying to establish what respondents think, privately, about their politics and motivations, and their relationships with others in the organization. Given that we were potentially asking respondents to be critical of the organization they support, and their colleagues in it, we needed to make sure respondents felt safe speaking with us. We have tried throughout this chapter to ensure the organization remains unnamed and respondents unidentifiable.

Our own personal politics leads the three of us to sympathize with the political aims of the organization. All the authors have supported the objectives of the organization chosen; one of us is still active within it. However, our support of its political aims does not mean we necessarily agree with how the organization is organized or how it, its members and its workers work with each other.

## INTERVIEWS

We interviewed ten activists involved in, or supporting, the national organization. Participants were identified through a process of prior knowledge and snowball sampling. That process was aided by two of the researchers knowing one key person involved in the organization, an activist and officer of the organization at the local, regional and national level. Through that person we were able to approach the local organization's membership and ask if they would be happy for us to interview them. Our contact gave us a list of local activists, and workers who he advised us would be willing to be interviewed. As it transpired, some of those people chose not to be involved in the project; ten, however, agreed. We decided that those offering to participate presented the research with enough diversity of background, and position within the local organization, to meet our aims. All interviews were recorded and the sound files were held securely. The data captured through the interviews was analysed using a constant comparative method.

## WEB DATA

The web data investigated in this chapter come from two primary sources. Of those, the first is the website, embedded social media feeds and campaign materials presented on the organization's official, national site. Second is a regional satellite website connected to that of the national organization but managed and maintained independently.

The rationale for selecting two sites was to ascertain the similarities and differences in the worldview articulated by the national and regional websites. It was anticipated that the national site would present a worldview that transcended local concerns, its operational raison d'être combining elements of nationally focused information sharing and the highlighting of national and international aspects of its campaigns. A key function of the site was expected to be the manifestation of itself as a national campaigning body, the construal of visitor identity, expressed by the national site, being one that focused on drawing people into participation in its national, and international, agenda. As a worldview, it was postulated that the overall message of the site would be one that concentrated on what you could do for the cause.

While it was expected that the regional site would also contain aspects of that visitor identity found in the national site, it was expected that there would be a greater focus on regional issues. In terms of the overall tone of the site, that would necessitate a shift in the orientation of the organization's worldview to one that was weighted more towards local information sharing and activism. A stronger connection to a more regionally focused communicative leisure is one that would, in turn, construe the site visitor as one of potential co-creator and collaborator (i.e., what we can do, collectively, to bring about change locally).

To identify the worldview of the two websites, associated social media feeds and campaign materials, a combination of critical discourse analysis and frame analysis was used. While critical discourse analysis (CDA) has no single, universally agreed methodological approach, Barbara Johnstone[33] has proposed a heuristic strategy that can serve as a toolkit for uncovering the discourse at work within a text. Johnstone's heuristic centres on using a set of basic questions. Those questions are set as prompts for the reader, helping them reflect text while reading it. To adapt her approach in a manner that suits the analysis presented in this chapter, her prompts became:

What is the text's purpose?
How is the relationship between the text and the rest of the world construed?
What forms of language are common to the text under investigation?
How does the text construe the relationship between itself and its reader?
What connections (if any) does the text make between itself and other texts?
Is there anything particular to the media being examined that might be contributing to the articulation of any of the above?

The questions of this heuristic are intended to be neither sequential nor exclusive: the analysis they are intended to provoke frequently mixes them up and uses them in an overlapping manner. As a tool, however, the heuristic is most effective when handling words; a different, though connected, approach is required when considering the imagery used. Recently Eeva Luhtakallio adapted Goffman's frame analysis for the analysis of the imagery. She has applied her approach to great effect in her analysis of protest, as articulated by regional media and social movements in Lyon and Helsinki.[34] Her approach applies Goffman's ideas of alignment and keys to the interpretation of image-based data. Combining Luhtakallio's technique of semiotic frame analysis with Johnstone's heuristic approach to the analysis of discourse helped highlight how the web content was used to both consolidate a social movement's worldview and provoke a response from the site visitor.

## DISCUSSION AND ANALYSIS

### Discussion—Interview Respondents

Our respondents were naturally self-selecting for their commitment and motivation to the politics and ethics of the organization; they would not have been activists if their own politics and ethics had not aligned with the values and aims of the national campaigning organization. All were members of the organization because they supported what it was trying to achieve in local, national and transnational politics. They were involved in campaigns at a local and national level, participating in discussions around politics and activism at meetings and online. Their participation in the organization included the design of leaflets, banners and websites and the organization of fund-raising events, such as walks, dances, and cycling events, while some had stood for election for officer positions within the organization, locally, regionally and nationally. They contributed to conferences, seminars and committee meetings; lobbied local and national politicians; and went on marches and became involved in nonviolent direct action. Some of the interviewees had been arrested at demonstrations and actions. All were continually active, and their continued activism demonstrated a belief in how, through their own agency, the world could be changed for better. Each of them clearly believed that what they did—as a volunteer, a marcher, a worker or a committee member—contributed to the aim of changing the mainstream public sphere. Theirs was not a "lazy" activism of clicking on petitions or donating money only, though they did those things as well.

As well as their active engagement with the work of the organization that formed the basis of our research, some of our respondents were also involved in "passive" support for other radical political groups and ethical causes. Their active engagement was not restricted to the local; most were also involved in fund-raising and "cheerleading" for the national campaigning organization as well. None of them saw a distinction or paradox between their radical beliefs about politics and global capitalism, and the need to raise funds to pay bills and the salaries of paid campaigners and organizers. The campaigning organization exists in this society, in this economy, and at this moment in late modernity. It cannot function without making compromises with the instrumental rules and systems of Western, neo-liberal democracy. It has to be part of the mainstream public sphere for its voice to be heard. As one explained, "We need to be realistic about what we can and cannot do. We can't exist without fund-raising; we need that money from membership, from donations, from campaigns . . . to campaign".

Their own life histories demonstrated a number of common themes that drew them into supporting, then working and campaigning for the organization. Each respondent described an epiphany at which they realized the world had to change, and the policies that the organization campaigns against needed to be challenged and overturned. That recounting of an epiphany may of course be mere post hoc rationalization of a long journey to radical politics and activism. But for each of our respondents there was a strong need to justify their commitment to their politics and ethics through such an awakening. For one of our respondents, the process occurred at an early age when talking politics with his parents, who were Labour Party members. For others, the moment came at university, when studying certain subjects or getting involved in student politics opened the door to the specific ethical issues that the national campaigning organization strives to resolve. Finally, the idea of epiphany seems particularly suited to describe the narratives of the two respondents who identified their religious beliefs as drivers in becoming activists. One explained to us how he was brought up a Christian with mainstream, conservative politics and ethics; it was his dissatisfaction with this worldview that led him to the deep conviction that the message of Jesus was radical, anti-capitalist and anti-hegemony.

Two of our respondents were heavily involved in working inside the organization. One was a former regional and current national officer with many years of experience serving on various committees and officer posts. He supported many other radical political organizations, but his time away from his paid work was completely taken up with activism for the national organization. Some of this involved lobbying and networking, but a large part of his activist career was concentrated on making sure the organization's internal processes worked, attending meetings and being closely involved in decision making. For this respondent, activism seemed at times to be "work", a job of balancing the commitment to democracy inside the organization and managing potentially chaotic meetings. He evidently managed to retain his passion and belief in the organization's ethics, despite the instrumental rationality that transformed his activism into bureaucracy.

The other respondent held a paid post as a manager for a regional office. He described his work as "definitely blurring the lines" between fulfilling the mundane objectives of his job description and the voluntarism associated with direct action and activism. He recognized that the work he did was necessary to help the campaign retain members and raise money, but he was suspicious of the way campaigning organizations in general became modern, professional lobbying groups. He preferred that his agency to be used in shaping a new, alternative, public sphere for activists against capitalism and hegemonic power. The "serious leisure" nature of his work made this respondent excited to be doing something morally "correct"; nevertheless, he was clearly struggling to match his own ethics with the routine processes and tasks of the paid work. He was keen to stress that he had had a rewarding and worthwhile time working for the organization and a good working relationship with the national office—at the same time, he was leaving the job to go travel and work overseas.

All our respondents had radical-left politics, but the type of politics and commitment varied. For some, party politics (and the British political system) had failed, and they expressed anarchist views. But others were involved in party politics, or had been involved—the Green Party being the one that most frequently appeared. One of our respondents was heavily involved in the Green Party locally, and had stood for both election and being an agent. Interviewees commonly expressed the same kinds of activism present in their party politics as in their activism for the national campaigning organization.

As well as paying subscriptions as members, our respondents gave much of their free (leisure) time to campaigning and direct action. Work for most of our respondents was fairly irrelevant to their self-identity and their agency as activists. Work gave them money to be able to be members, campaigners and activists. Work was something they did that did not crush their motivation and commitment. Some of our respondents did work in jobs that were more morally focused and bound to their personal politics and ethics. In all cases, the activism for the national campaigning organization, their identity as activist, and the serious leisure of activism dictated who they were, what they did in their free time and what they thought about at work.

## Discussion—Web Data

For the analysis that follows, the home pages of two websites have been considered. Both home pages are from the same anti-war campaigning organization; however, one page is that of the organization's national body, while the other is produced by a regional branch. In this chapter it was decided to focus on the home page of each of these groups, as it is that page which forms the hub through which all of a site's other pages are connected. The hub character of a home page privileges it as a point of access; it acts as a setter of the tone for the site and all the pages accessible from it. That *tone setting* frames visitors' expectations, which are then supported, developed or, occasionally, challenged by other pages on the site, or sites to which it is linked. To maintain the group's anonymity in this analysis, the organization's national home page will be referred to as ~N, while ~R will be used to refer to the regional home page.

On first viewing ~N and ~R there are a number of striking visual differences, differences that we find are consonant with the page's content. The background of ~N is a light colour, split into distinct sections; it has a light grey tone background and the page uses a series of frames, headings and subheadings reminiscent of newspapers and web-based news pages. There is a very subtle contrast between the background and the contained text boxes. Consequently, while each box is discrete, there is a suggestion that the transition from one box to another is fluid.

Unlike ~N, ~R has a distinctive blue background, with all the text contained within one large box. Its text box is white, which is a strong contrast to its surround; this highlights its central text, bringing it strikingly into the foreground. The regional home page looks like a basic blog, and it is in fact produced using a template from a popular online low-cost/free blog and webpage building provider. As for the overall impression conveyed by the ~R page, it is that of an e-newsletter.

Although the navigation tabs on both pages are similar, the layout of each home page is very different. On ~N, below the organization's banner and navigation tabs, there is a large panel promoting three ongoing campaigns. Each of these is active—in that clicking on one of the campaigns opens up information pertinent to how each campaign is progressing—offering various opportunities for participation. Adjacent to that box are two smaller boxes: one seeking funding support (through either membership or donation), and the other asking people to sign up for e-mail updates on the organization's campaigns.

~R also leads with a campaign banner, which in this instance precedes the navigation tabs; this, however, is a relatively passive link. If one clicks on the large banner, which appears on all the site's pages, one is linked back to ~R's home page. The visitor can therefore use the banner for orientation around the site, but not deeper engagement with the issue it raises.

Following the campaign banner, ~R has a large central post which forms the main focus of attention on the home page. The text begins by setting out the context of the organization's perspective on its core campaign objective, concentrating on a focused range of central, long-running, national issues, before drawing out local threads that show the connection those concerns have with its home region. There are three images incorporated into the text. The images are not attributed to a source; one looks like a stock image while the other two could have easily been taken by members of the group.

To the right of that central text there are a number of subheadings, two of which are followed by bullet-pointed links. The first subheading is a general in-site search box, which is followed by a list of the five most recent posts to the site. Each post connects to a short item of news about activity in the geographic region covered by the organization's branch. The next two subheadings offer an opportunity to follow the group's activity on Facebook and Twitter, with the latter showing the three most recent Tweets. Scrolling down the page, we come to the last two subheadings, which offer opportunities to subscribe to the site's e-mail list and to donate to support their work. The forms of engagement presented on the ~R home page are campaign neutral, in that the invitations to *participate* do not connect to active engagement in specific campaigns; instead, they are invitations to "follow", "subscribe", "get involved" and "support"/"donate". The page offers up to the visitor a worldview in which it is the group that is presented as active and effective: new groups are shown as forming; existing groups, we are informed, are coordinating events; and the successes of previous events are commented upon.

In the main body of the page, the discourse ~R articulates is around the forms of debate in which it is engaged. Values are explicitly stated in terms such as "we oppose", "we believe", "we campaign for", but this "we" is left deictically without context, so readers are left unclear as to whether or not they can be placed within its reach. Those values are reinforced when the text goes on to tell us that money spent on the military budget could be "better used on . . . the things people really need", or implied by the use of scare quotes around the term "defence" (preferring the expression to be "an offensive system"), and arguing that existing military systems are resulting in an expansion rather than reduction in the production of weapons of mass destruction. The main body of the page is a strong declaration of the axiological space the group occupies; it is a statement of where they stand, setting out a framework of what is to count as rational discussion around the issue with which it is concerned. It is a declaration of a public sphere, rather than an invitation to participate in it. Visitors, for the most part, have the option of agreeing, disagreeing or finding out more. The forms of engagement the site presents are akin to ones that might be found in a newsletter. The reader is construed as an outsider, looking in. If she likes what she sees, there are opportunities to learn more and, at some point in the future, extend her participation, but at the moment the main thing she can do is either put some coppers in the collection tin, ask someone if she can get the newsletter next time it comes out or dismiss it as not her thing.

~N has no central body text. The lighter contrast between the text boxes means the focus is on colour and image rather than text. While graphic elements on the page are, as with ~R, not attributed, they do feel as though they have been produced specifically for the page. The use of colour and image on the page is interesting, and hints at deeper connections and associations that may be working to reinforce many of the messages articulated by the text. An association with environmental issues is suggested by the use of green at a number of points on the page; it is in the organization's logo, the calls for visitor action associated with each of the three campaigns highlighted in the heading banner area, the font for the latest news on the general secretary's blog, and the links at the end of the page that take you deeper into the site.

The campaign that (at the time of the analysis) appears as default in the banner section, when you first access ~N's home page, uses several bands of colour. A rainbow is suggested—even if it is not directly referenced. By not representing a rainbow while suggesting it, the striking use of so much colour, in a relatively confined space, suggest a multiplicity of possible readings. The most direct of those is the environmentalist and peace movements' symbolic use of the rainbow to suggest global concern, collective action and the possibility for international cooperation. That referent itself, arguably, draws on a religious connotation. In a number of sacred texts the rainbow is associated with humanity's peace with the divine, following a global catastrophe. Whether deliberate or not, the use of banded colour also hints at its symbolic use by the LGBT community. More subtly, especially as the campaign was running on the lead-up to the 2014 elections to the European Parliament, the colours also suggest a variety of political positions. At least five of the colours used in the graphic echo those associated with the Labour Party, Conservatives, Liberal Democrats, UKIP and Green Party. There is the suggestion of consensus expressed in this compilation of colours. The welcome to engage with the debate on which the organization is focused is declared open to all.

The balance of the page is weighted much less towards imparting news, and much more concerned with presenting opportunities for the visitor to become directly involved in the organization's cause. ~R asks the visitor to "Support our work", with a "Donate" hyperlink. ~N makes a similar request of the visitor, but the tone of that request is rather different: "We're funded entirely by our members and supporters. People like you", which is followed by a link with the more inclusive "Support us". ~N orientates the reader as someone who is being drawn towards participation; it is seeking confederates to work within their number. ~R suggests the donator is still, to some extent, external to the group; there is no hint of the donator being, in any deeper sense, an actor in the organization's wider activities. Those differences are subtle, but they resonate with how both ~N and ~R articulate engagement elsewhere on the home page.

Below its campaign banner section ~N splits into three columns. Each column addresses a different level of potential engagement. On the left, where the eye of a reader of English would fall, is the heading "Take Action". The heading is preceded by two chevrons, suggesting movement, and a silhouette image of a demonstration. As a message, it seems to clearly suggest that the area is one where you can directly participate in some of the issues that concern the organization. There is a construal of the reader as activist, it is a space that suggests your leisurely visit to the site could have a real impact—now. In the section are links to activities that ask you to support campaigns, sign petitions or write to your MP.

The central column is for news updates. It is divided into a section of reports, submitted by members, on local, national and international news, and a blog from the organization's general secretary. The officer's position is, however, not referred to. Instead, the blog postings use the person's name; in so doing, an impression of familiarity with the writer is suggested. Posts become messages from a person, one you may get to know, and not from the general secretary of a nationally and internationally active organization.

In the final column are the latest feeds from the group's Twitter and Facebook accounts. That, again, creates a sense of things happening in the present. Whether correct or not, the suggestion is of a live update on events, not a report posted in retrospect to inform you of things that have already happened. The sense of getting the news as it happens is reinforced by a link to a podcast, which immediately follows the two feeds, offering an alternative means of keeping up to date with the organization's perspective on national and global issues.

So far, all the forms of engagement presented on ~N's home page have focused on activity the visitor can, arguably, engage in with a degree of privacy—that is, can be enacted from the relative comfort of their chair. Such *clicktivism* has a greater connection with casual leisure, rather than a more identity-driven activity that could be associated with "project-based" or "serious leisure". However, at the foot of the page, the opportunities for visitors to publicly show their support for the organization's objectives are widened. In that space, links are presented that enable visitors to acquire resources to publicize their support and to engage in more public forms of demonstrating their involvement. Posters, books, clothing, badges and more form a foundation from which individuals can articulate their identity as part of the wider organization's purpose.

~N offers the visitor multiple forms of engagement, with varying levels of commitment; it is this that most strikingly differentiates it from ~R. ~N and ~R have, understandably, a consonant worldview. However, the suggestions for how a casual visitor may participate in that view are different. ~R construes the visitor as someone who already has a commitment to the organization's objectives, and who wants to be kept informed. The only opportunity open to a casual or curious visitor is to offer some financial support as a means of showing they are in broad agreement with its agenda. It is only by consciously digging deeper into the site, in an act consistent with project-based leisure that more involved levels of participation are exposed. ~N presents the visitor with a greater range of opportunities to engage with the organization's concerns immediately. Its primary aim is not simply to inform but to involve people there and then. Some of that difference will be a product of organizational capacity. The budget for a national site is, and ought to be, greater than that for a local one. With a greater budget the organization is able to employ a workforce that can participate in debate at a national and international level. Those working for the organization at this level are more likely to be operating at the interface between serious leisure and paid employment. At a regional office level, the proportion of volunteers will be higher. As volunteers, they will have to balance work, family and leisure more carefully. The interface here is thus more likely to be between project-based and serious leisure. Those active in a region are more likely to engage in debates at a personal and local level. While contributing to national initiatives, they will predominantly concentrate on how the national and global are impacting the local. That difference is not a criticism of either group; the differences are as they should be. Regional groups need to focus on regional issues if they are to build support and effect change at a local level. Similarly, while national organizations support regional groups, any greater involvement would, justifiably, be seen as external interference. However, those differences appear to have an impact on how the regional and the national organization articulate their communicative relationships and present the public sphere in which they engage in debate.

Whatever the reasons, the scope for rational debate in ~R appears focused on the construction of a communicative community bound by its existing practices. The scope for rational debate in ~N seems much broader: enabling people to engage at many differing levels of commitment, while still feeling they are involved with the ultimate objectives of the organization. That difference, in turn, has an impact on the form activism as leisure can take. With its wider range in level of commitment and depth of engagement ~N is more easily able to accommodate visitors prepared to engage at different levels of leisure involvement; casual, project-based and serious. ~R, however, is geared more towards those who are more inclined to pursue their activism as a project-based or serious leisure activity.

## CONCLUSIONS

Through the interviews with active members and a consideration of the presence of the campaigning organization online, incorporating an analysis of its national home page and the equivalent page for one of its regional branches, we have found a wide variety of forms of activism articulated and supported. Those interviewed are, or have been, active in their participation for a number of years. The ultimate objectives of the organization, for them, form an intrinsic element in their identity. A sense of epiphany was common to them all. Epiphany, a sudden awakening, encountering a manifestation of how the world should be, resonates strongly with the idea of event in Badiou and Žižek that was presented earlier in the chapter. The protest event is one that does not just change our orientation to the world but also changes "the very frame through which we perceive the world and engage with it".[35] It is a consequence of that change to the frame through which we engage with the world that our communicative relationships also, necessarily, alter: deterrents become weapons, defence becomes aggression and so forth. The horizon of rationality within such a communicative structure works to reinforce the group's cohesion. However, if the organization's core objective is to change the world to one where those supportive communicative relationships become a universal, there is a potential problem. The public sphere constituted from the epiphanic worldview of those participating in the organization at the level of serious leisure risks placing barriers to the entry of those currently located outside. The gap between public spheres constituting antagonistic worldviews, or those of people who have a casual leisure interest in the concerns of the organization and those of the serious-leisure activist, may be too great.

In the analysis of ~R those potential barriers were clearly discernible in its language and structure. ~R worked best as a conduit for information sharing and conferring cohesion to the work of the organization at a local level—that is, for those already participating in the organization at a project-based or serious-leisure level. As a site, it worked less well as a point of entry for those who were, as yet, unprepared to engage with the objectives of the organization at such a level of commitment. ~N, however, was much more open to the casual activist, or what some may call clicktivist. The varieties of contestation with a prevailing discourse were much more fluid in ~N. To some extent this is understandable. ~N has a much larger potential pool of membership and visitorship than ~R. The drifting in and out of casual activists at a national level has a lesser impact on overall group cohesion than it would regionally. A hint of that was observable in the response of some interviewees to one of the regional group's core members moving to work overseas. That relocation, even though the individual's ideological perspective had not altered, was forcing structural changes within the local group. If a similar situation were to occur within the national group, it would be unlikely to have quite so profound an impact.

While maintaining a tighter grip on the construal of participation presents regional groups with a risk of disintegration, it also provides a much firmer foundation for internal support and a clearer voice when advocating change. Nationally, working to mitigate disintegration requires a continuous process of translating casual activism into project-based and serious leisure. The varying levels of engagement presented on ~N's home page is indicative of that process at work. Read this news clip; sign that petition; follow that blog; like this page; buy that badge; come on that march—all building up to draw the clicktivist from a point of casual leisure/activism to one that is more project based or serious.

Both ~R and ~N have lessons that can be learnt from each other. The former needs to be more open to the casual visitor, while the latter needs to develop strategies for enhancing group cohesion; both should work on strengthening how they convert the clicktivist to becoming more of an activist. It is through increased awareness of those engaged in casual leisure/ activism that those visitors can be drawn into the communicative relationships which lie at the heart of the public sphere constituted by identification with the organization's core objectives.

This chapter has worked with interview material gathered from ten participants and an analysis of two websites; clearly more work is needed to develop these ideas further. It has, however, highlighted a number of areas that enhance our understanding of the relationship between the contested public spheres of a campaigning organization, both within itself and with that of a dominant political hegemony. Through widening our interpretation of the concept of "event" to incorporate protest and leisure in activism, we are able to gain a clearer view of how communicative relationships and their associated public spheres are constructed and contested.

## REFERENCES

Arora, Payal A. "Usurping Public Leisure Space for Protest: Social Activism in the Digital and Material Commons". *Space & Culture* (2013): 1–26.

Badiou, Alain. *Being and Event*. Translated by Oliver Feltham. London: Continuum, 2007.

Cameron, David R., and Janice G. Stein. *Street Protests and Fantasy Parks: Globalization, Culture and the State*. Vancouver: University of British Columbia Press, 2002.

Debord, Guy. *The Society of the Spectacle*. Translated by Donald Nicholson-Smith. New York: Zone Books, 1999 [1967].

della Porta, Donatella, and Sidney Tarrow, eds. *Transnational Protest and Global Activism: People, Passions and Power*. Washington, DC: Rowman & Littlefield, 2004.

Eaton, Marc. "Manufacturing Community in an Online Activist Organization". *Information, Communication & Society* 13, no. 2 (2010): 174–92.

Gilchrist, Paul, and Neil Ravenscroft. "Space Hijacking and the Anarcho-Politics of Leisure". *Leisure Studies* 32, no. 1 (2013): 49–68.

Habermas, Jürgen. *The Structural Transformation of the Public Sphere*. Cambridge: Polity, 2005 [1989].

Johnstone, Barbara. *Discourse Analysis*. 2nd ed. Oxford: Blackwell, 2007.

Kohl-Arenas, Erica, Myrna M. Nateras, and Johanna Taylor. "Cultural Organizing as Critical Praxis: Tamejavi Builds Immigrant Voice, Belonging, and Power". *Journal of Poverty* 18, no. 1 (2014): 5–24.

Lenskyj, Helen J. *Inside the Olympic Industry: Power, Politics and Activism*. Albany: State University of New York Press, 2000.

Low, Setha M., Dana H. Taplin, and Mike Lamb. "Battery Park City: An Ethnographic Field Study of the Community Impact of 9/11". *Urban Affairs Review* 40, no. 5 (2005): 655–82.

Luhtakallio, Eeva. *Practicing Democracy: Local Activism and Politics in France and Finland.* Basingstoke, UK: Palgrave Macmillan, 2012.

Mair, Heather. "Civil Leisure? Exploring the Relationship between Leisure, Activism and Social Change". *Leisure/Loisir* 27, nos. 3–4 (2002): 213–37.

Picard, David, and Mike Robinson, eds. *Festivals, Tourism and Social Change: Remaking Worlds.* Clevedon, UK: Channel View Publications, 2006.

Ranciere, Jacques. *Dissensus: On Politics and Aesthetics.* Translated by Steven Corcoran. London: Continuum International Publishing, 2010.

Sandlin, Jennifer A. "Netnography as Consumer Education Research Tool". *International Journal of Consumer Studies* 31, no. 3 (2007): 288–94.

Spracklen, Karl. *The Meaning and Purpose of Leisure: Habermas and Leisure at the End of Modernity.* Basingstoke, UK: Palgrave Macmillan, 2009.

Spracklen, Karl. *Whiteness and Leisure.* Basingstoke, UK: Palgrave Macmillan, 2013.

Spracklen, Karl, Anna Richter, and Beverley Spracklen. "The Eventization of Leisure and the Strange Death of Alternative Leeds". *City: Analysis of Urban Trends, Culture, Theory, Policy, Action* 17, no. 2 (2013): 164–78.

Stebbins, Robert A. "Serious Leisure, Volunteerism and Quality of Life". In *Work and Leisure,* edited by John T. Haworth and Anthony J. Veal. Hove, UK: Routledge, 2004.

Stebbins, Robert A. *Serious Leisure: A Perspective for Our Time.* New Brunswick, NJ: Transaction, 2006.

Waitt, Gordon. "Urban Festivals: Geographies of Hype, Helplessness and Hope". *Geography Compass* 2, no. 2 (2008): 513–37.

Wallace, Jacqueline. "Yarn Bombing, Knit Graffiti and Underground Brigades: A Study of Craftivism and Mobility". *Journal of Mobile Media.* Special Issue: *Mobile Cultures* 6, no. 3 (2012).

Waterman, Stanley. "Carnivals for Elites? The Cultural Politics of Arts Festivals". *Progress in Human Geography* 22, no. 1 (1998): 54–74.

Žižek, Slavoj. *The Year of Dreaming Dangerously.* London: Verso, 2012.

Žižek, Slavoj. *Event: Philosophy in Transit.* London: Penguin, 2014.

# NOTES

1. See, for example, Jürgen Habermas, *The Structural Transformation of the Public Sphere* (Cambridge: Polity, 2005 [1989]).

2. Karl Spracklen, *The Meaning and Purpose of Leisure: Habermas and Leisure at the End of Modernity* (Basingstoke, UK: Palgrave Macmillan, 2009).

3. Guy Debord, *The Society of the Spectacle,* trans. Donald Nicholson-Smith (New York: Zone Books, 1999 [1967]).

4. Alain Badiou, *Being and Event,* trans. Oliver Feltham (London: Continuum, 2007).

5. Slavoj Žižek, *The Year of Dreaming Dangerously* (London, Verso, 2012).

6. Slavoj Žižek, *Event: Philosophy in Transit* (London: Penguin, 2014), 10.

7. Jacques Ranciere, *Dissensus: On Politics and Aesthetics,* trans. Steven Corcoran (London: Continuum International Publishing, 2010).

8. Ibid., 37.

9. Robert A. Stebbins, *Serious Leisure: A Perspective for Our Time* (New Brunswick, NJ: Transaction, 2006).

10. Robert A. Stebbins, "Serious Leisure, Volunteerism and Quality of Life", in *Work and Leisure,* ed. John T. Haworth and Anthony J. Veal (Hove, UK: Routledge, 2004).

11. Karl Spracklen, *Whiteness and Leisure* (Basingstoke, UK: Palgrave Macmillan, 2013).

12. As developed in Eeva Luhtakallio, *Practicing Democracy: Local Activism and Politics in France and Finland* (Basingstoke, UK: Palgrave Macmillan, 2012).

13. Heather Mair, "Civil Leisure? Exploring the Relationship between Leisure, Activism and Social Change", *Leisure/Loisir* 27, nos. 3–4 (2002): 213–37.

14. See, for example, Stanley Waterman, "Carnivals for Elites? The Cultural Politics of Arts Festivals", *Progress in Human Geography* 22, no. 1 (1998): 54–74; Helen J. Lenskyj, *Inside*

*the Olympic Industry: Power, Politics and Activism* (Albany: State University of New York Press, 2000); Donatella della Porta and Sidney Tarrow, eds., *Transnational Protest and Global Activism: People, Passions and Power* (Washington, DC: Rowman & Littlefield, 2004); David Picard and Mike Robinson, eds., *Festivals, Tourism and Social Change: Remaking Worlds* (Clevedon, UK: Channel View Publications, 2006); Gordon Waitt, "Urban Festivals: Geographies of Hype, Helplessness and Hope", *Geography Compass* 2, no. 2 (2008): 513–37; and Erica Kohl-Arenas, Myrna M. Nateras, and Johanna Taylor, "Cultural Organizing as Critical Praxis: Tamejavi Builds Immigrant Voice, Belonging, and Power", *Journal of Poverty* 18, no. 1 (2014): 5–24.

15. Mair, "Civil Leisure?" 218.

16. In particular, she cites C. E. Clark, "Differences between Public Relations and Corporate Social Responsibility", *Public Relations Review* 26, no. 3 (2000): 363–80; H. Friedmann, "The World Social Forum at Porto Alegre and the People's Summit at Quebex Coty: A View from the Ground", *Studies in Political Economy* 66 (2001); and J. Grundy and A. Howell, "Negotiation the Culture of Resistance: A Critical Assessment of Protest Politics", *Studies in Political Economy* 66 (2001).

17. Mair, "Civil Leisure?" 218.

18. Ibid., 226–27.

19. Ibid., 214.

20. Among others this has been noted by Jennifer A. Sandlin, "Netnography as Consumer Education Research Tool", *International Journal of Consumer Studies* 31, no. 3 (2007): 288–94; and Karl Spracklen, Anna Richter and Beverley Spracklen, "The Eventization of Leisure and the Strange Death of Alternative Leeds", *City: Analysis of Urban Trends, Culture, Theory, Policy, Action* 17, no. 2 (2013): 164–78.

21. Spracklen, Richter and Spracklen, "The Eventization of Leisure", 174.

22. Ibid.

23. Ibid.

24. Payal A. Arora, "Usurping Public Leisure Space for Protest: Social Activism in the Digital and Material Commons", *Space & Culture* (2013): 1–26.

25. Ibid., 17. See also David R. Cameron and Janice G. Stein, *Street Protests and Fantasy Parks: Globalization, Culture and the State* (Vancouver: University of British Columbia Press, 2002); and Setha M. Low, Dana H. Taplin and Mike Lamb, "Battery Park City: An Ethnographic Field Study of the Community Impact of 9/11", *Urban Affairs Review* 40, no. 5 (2005): 655–82.

26. Mair, "Civil Leisure?"

27. Paul Gilchrist and Neil Ravenscroft, "Space Hijacking and the Anarcho-Politics of Leisure", *Leisure Studies* 32, no. 1 (2013): 49–68.

28. Ibid., 58.

29. Jacqueline Wallace, "Yarn Bombing, Knit Graffiti and Underground Brigades: A Study of Craftivism and Mobility", *Journal of Mobile Media*, Special Issue: *Mobile Cultures* 6, no. 3 (2012). In particular, she cites Ricia A. Chansky, "A Stitch in Time: Third-Wave Feminist Reclamation of Needled Imagery", *Journal of Popular Culture* 43, no. 4 (2010): 681–700.

30. Wallace, "Yarn Bombing"; she cites Kirsty Robertson, "Rebellious Doilies and Subversive Stitches: Writing a Craftivist History", in *Extra/Ordinary: Craft and Contemporary Art*, ed. Maria E. Buszek (Durham, NC: Duke University Press, 2010).

31. http://www.woolagainstweapons.co.uk/.

32. http://craftivist-collective.com/.

33. Barbara Johnstone, *Discourse Analysis*, 2nd ed. (Oxford: Blackwell, 2007).

34. Luhtakallio, *Practicing Democracy*.

35. Žižek, *Event: Philosophy in Transit*, 10.

*Chapter Two*

# SlutWalk Hong Kong and the Media

*Sharing Lessons Learned*

Angie Ng

The SlutWalk movement was founded in Canada by Heather Jarvis and Sonya J. F. Barnett in 2011.[1] It began in response to the instructions given by a representative of the Toronto Police Service during a safety presentation at York University, whose advice was that "women should avoid dressing like sluts in order to not be victimised".[2] Fed up with the use of the historically negative term "slut", which places responsibility for the crime on victims rather than perpetrators at a cultural and institutional level, blaming victims and making it difficult for victims to talk about or report the crimes, Slut-Walk was initiated.[3]

This chapter presents an analysis of the local media coverage of SlutWalk Hong Kong. It uses this analysis as a starting point for a discussion on how to handle media situations related not only to SlutWalk events but also, potentially, to others. Perhaps this discussion can serve as a springboard for others to reflect upon their own practice as activists or organizers of activist events.

Although SlutWalk was originally aimed at Toronto, people from other cities started contacting the organizers, wanting to take up the cause in their own locations.[4] In the first year, more than a hundred local SlutWalks were initiated around the world.[5] This shows not only that rape culture, a culture in which society itself normalizes rape and perpetuates rape myths, exists around the globe but also that both men and women in various locations were fed up with this fact. The global spread of the movement, as of the end of 2011, stretched from North America to all the other continents except for Antarctica.[6]

It was as part of this outrage against rape culture, and with the wish to raise awareness and prompt social change, that SlutWalk Hong Kong was first held on 4 December 2011. Around three hundred men and women, from a variety of age groups, ethnic backgrounds and social classes, came together to say that they, too, had had enough of victim blaming. Various groups such as the Women's Coalition (which is an LGBT organization), United Filipinos in Hong Kong (a migrant workers' rights group), Socialist Action and the League of Social Democrats came out to support the cause. Professor Sam Winter of Hong Kong University, a transgender activist and lecturer, sent a speech supporting SlutWalk to be read at the rally. Dr Yau Ching, a sexuality expert at Lingnan University, also came to speak at the event.

An in-depth discussion on the relevant gender issues is beyond the scope of this chapter, but it is necessary to briefly establish what is meant by *rape myths* if we are to understand victim blaming. Rape myths are beliefs about sexual assault that do not match actual reality, and they concern not just rape victims but also rapists and rape itself.[7] Such myths are generally widely held within any given society, constituting "rape cultures", in which sexual assault is legitimized, ignored and/or blamed on victims.[8] Even the very seriousness and nature of sexual assault is subverted by mainstream society, with the word "rape" being used casually or "humorously" in conversations.[9] Meanwhile, rape myths put victims under scrutiny and suspicion, excluding various categories of women from being legitimate victims; these include, for example, those who are perceived as sexually "available", or who were "asking for it", and those who are not considered sexually attractive by mainstream standards.[10] In cases that make it to trial, these incorrect stereotypes and views, which may be conscious or subconscious, influence juries to acquit. In Canada, where the SlutWalk movement was born, sexual assault cases are less likely than other violent crimes to result in sentencing.[11] Rape myths also serve to excuse various categories of perpetrator from being recognized as such, including husbands, partners and other men who are known to the victims; men considered sexually attractive by conventional standards; and basically men who are not deranged.[12] These rape myths exist within a larger context of gender oppression and patriarchal ideology,[13] especially around the sexual control and objectification of women.

Within the Hong Kong context, victim blaming is part of the dominant discourse.[14] Re-traumatization of victims via insensitive attitudes and victim blaming, also known as secondary traumatization or secondary victimization, is systemic, involving the judicial system, schools, law enforcement and the medical system.[15] In May 2013, Hong Kong's Security Chief, Lai Tung-Kwok, recommended that "young ladies" not "drink too much" to avoid being sexually assaulted.[16] Such comments show that even at the highest levels, government institutions, which should actually serve to protect victims, there is an acceptance of rape myths. In fact, it is known that even local institutions such as the Equal Opportunities Commission are sources of secondary victimization.[17] The mainstream media in Hong Kong are also known to be a source of secondary trauma.[18] Not only are the local media known to reveal victims' identities and exaggerate the details, but they also spread falsities which serve to blame victims[19] (for example, that the victim is involved in "compensated dating").

In terms of coverage by the popular press, SlutWalk has been disadvantaged on three levels. It is a grassroots, progressive movement; it is part of the larger women's movement; and it is also about sexual violence against women. The following paragraphs discuss how these are problematic in terms of coverage by the popular press.

Regarding mass media in general, it is important to keep in mind Gramsci's radical criticism of mainstream media, that the "current bourgeois control of society, while certainly manifest in material modes of production, is culturally embedded and naturalized in the minds of the people via its hegemony over discourse".[20] The mass media's purpose is both to provide the general public with entertainment and information and to condition them with attitudes and beliefs in line with the status quo, defending the agenda of privileged, dominant groups.[21] The elite are able to determine which news is "newsworthy", fit to be printed or broadcast. In that way "news" can be deployed to diminish resistance, enabling government and dominant private interests to communicate their messages to the public.[22] Those elites do that via direct ownership of media outlets, having close business relationships with them, acting as sources of advertising revenue, and delivering a constant flow of information that can be made into news. Their position of power gives the authorities the ability to punish the media for negative coverage through a variety of forms of penalty, such as costly litigation.[23]

Around the world, the press in general is controlled by men, and it continues to perpetuate attitudes and beliefs in line with the interests of both male power and class dominance.[24] As senior editors and others with decision-making powers are predominantly male, it is men who get to decide which stories are covered, and from what angle.[25] Within that context, it is not surprising that the women's movement in general is marginalized by the popular press.[26] Coverage has been sparse, and the tone has usually been light and/or humorous,[27] as if women's movements were not to be considered worthy of being "real" news. Just as the mass media portray those harmed by enemy states as true victims and exclude from such a category those treated in the same way by friendly governments,[28] the mainstream media also divide women harmed by male violence into worthy and unworthy victims. They also divide this type of violence into "real", which is that perpetrated by strangers, and "normal", which is that committed within private relationships and homes.[29] There is also a tendency for coverage to serve as a warning to women and girls against leaving their "proper place in society".[30] It is no surprise, therefore, that there is a tendency for male journalists to identify with the men in cases of male violence against women and children,[31] and to be more in tune with the claims of male perpetrators than those of their victims.[32] Together, these false dichotomies of worthy versus unworthy victims, and real violence versus normal violence, support the aforementioned rape myths.

Although some may view the appearance of stories about SlutWalk within mass media as a sign of progress, it is necessary to remember that in order to support the illusion of media neutrality some amount of dissent and progressive protesting must be covered.[33] Naturally, the stories are always in line with the dominant masculinized ideology's goals, which in this case would be to maintain the prevailing gendered hierarchy and rape culture. Manufactured corporate social movements, who have cleverly hidden business interests, can obtain supportive coverage.[34] In 2000, for example, the core organizers of the Serbian youth movement Optor, which toppled the nationalistic communist government of Serbia, in turn leading to the country's transition into a neo-liberal economic model, were connected to, and funded by, the U.S. government.[35] Meanwhile, progressive social movements are marginalized to prevent interference with the elite's agenda.[36] If genuine grassroots protests are covered in the media at all, various techniques are employed to belittle movements and take away their perceived legitimacy. Such techniques use what Chan and Lee term the "journalistic paradigm" or "protest paradigm", which directs where, and for what, journalists should or should not look.[37]

The tactics of the "protest paradigm" include "othering", in which the mass media focus on certain features to make it difficult for the public to relate to protestors and their movements.[38] There is also a focus on activities and appearances rather than objectives.[39] That, in turn, serves news outlets' goal of grabbing the interest of readers and viewers with sensationalist pieces, rather than raise awareness on the issues at hand. Additionally, there is a reliance on "official" sources, and a focus on protester confrontation with authority.

Another common tactic used to delegitimize an event is to downplay its size.[40] Stories about events can also be hidden in areas of a publication that have a low readership, such as those towards the back of a paper.[41] At the same time, events are sometimes not covered at all, as news of any resistance against the system can potentially stimulate further resistance.[42] Despite the use of the aforementioned "protest paradigm", if news of a protest reaches the public, there is always a chance that others will join in, in solidarity, or start similar movements to confront the status quo.

This chapter uses as its data the media coverage of SlutWalk Hong Kong in both 2011 and 2012. That data was not initially collected for this study; instead, it was gathered in order to post relevant news stories for 2011 and 2012 on SlutWalk Hong Kong's website, and also to allow reflection for the sake of improving the campaign. The analysis presented here serves as a springboard for a discussion of how to better deal with the media situation surrounding SlutWalk events.

## DIFFERENCE IN MEDIA COVERAGE

The type of press coverage the Hong Kong SlutWalk received in 2011 differed dramatically from that of 2012. In 2011, SlutWalk Hong Kong received much attention from the local media. We were invited to do interviews on radio shows, film video for HK Broadband, take part in a photoshoot and interview for a multipage story for a magazine. The day of the event, more than a dozen photographers, videographers and journalists were on-site to cover the march. One of the two local television channels even covered the event in their English-language evening news segment. That evening, I was awakened in the middle of the night by a telephone call from a reporter hoping to get firsthand information on the march.

Now contrast this to the low level of media interest received in 2012. Only one media outlet which had covered the march in 2011 was still interested in covering it in 2012; this media outlet was *Hong Kong* magazine, a local magazine targeting trendy, affluent expatriates. Aside from that, only two local, online sources mentioned the event. A positive note is that the local English-language newspaper, *South China Morning Post* (*SCMP*), produced three articles related to the march, in addition to one editorial belittling it and one op-ed response from myself. Three international outlets covered the event—*China Daily*'s international site and two progressive websites: Jezebel and Minerva.

Before discussing the media in general, it is important to highlight the difference in coverage that was noticeable between individual journalists and editors. In 2011, a news presenter from TVB Pearl, Philippa Stewart, was very supportive and interested in our story, successfully selling it to those deciding what gets covered and what does not. In 2012, as Ms Stewart had moved away from Hong Kong, all she could do was recommend the story to a former colleague, who perhaps was not as interested in this type of event.

In 2011 there was no one interested in covering the event for *SCMP*, but in 2012 a progressive journalist had started working with them and was enthusiastic about the movement in general—hence the multiple articles on the event (I will discuss this again in the section "Insights on Dealing with the Mainstream Media"). As for *Hong Kong* magazine, there was a progressive journalist, who supported the movement by writing pieces in 2011 as well as 2012; that was the only media outlet to cover SlutWalk Hong Kong both years.

As for the local media in general, the difference in coverage illustrates a couple of main points. It shows the media's dual purpose of entertaining the public and acting as a tool of control and maintenance of the status quo. As other social activists, such as Sally from Socialist Action, commented, it is expected that the media lose interest after the first year, because they are always chasing after newer stories in order to entertain viewers/readers. In the case of coverage of social activism, with the exception of sympathetic journalists and/or editors, the goal in general is neither to inform the public in any great depth nor to spark social change. Instead, it is to use selected events as news fodder and belittle social activists in general and other groups, such as "sluts".

## DIFFERENCES IN COVERAGE CONTENT

Not only was the media coverage of the event noticeably different between 2011 and 2012, but the content and way in which it was covered also differed dramatically. That difference is obvious from the photos used to accompany the articles. Although the event was popular with the media in 2011, the coverage was largely in line with the "protest paradigm" mentioned above.[43] It used "othering", depicting organizers and supporters as what locals would consider "sluts" and "outsiders". The movement was portrayed as a "Western" phenomenon. Coverage largely revolved around my experience as a foreign-educated person who had been raped while frequenting bars and nightclubs in an area popular with foreigners. This is a form of "othering", as having a foreign education within the Hong Kong context denotes "Western", while going out drinking matches one local construction of "slut". In terms of media selection of imagery, one of our volunteers was very popular with news outlets and had numerous photos appear in the media. That foreign exchange student attended the event as a drag queen in a Santa's helper outfit; photographs of him undoubtedly supported a meme of "Western" and "slut". The media also used the local stereotypes of mainland Chinese women as sexual predators/"sluts". A supporter from mainland China who was working in Hong Kong was featured multiple times in photographs despite being neither an organizer nor a volunteer. As someone from mainland China, she would be considered an outsider by local Hong Kong Chinese. So media coverage "othered" the protestors and participants as "outsiders", whether this was a non-Asian, a foreign-educated Chinese, or a mainland Chinese woman working in Hong Kong, making it more difficult for locals to identify with the movement. Also, in order to distance the largely sexually conservative general public from the movement, media sources used popular, local constructions of "sluts".

Before moving on, it is also important to discuss the much-covered story of my being victimized after going on a night out. Aside from playing into local constructions of "slut", it also matched popular rape myths stating that rape is perpetrated by strangers and that women who drink alcohol deserve to be raped. As previously noted, stories of sexual violence in the mainstream media tend to involve male strangers as perpetrators and are used as warnings to women and girls to not step outside of socially accepted boundaries. In this case, the implied warnings would be against going out late, going out drinking and talking to strangers. So although the story was shared to show other survivors that it is not their fault, and that they should not be the ones feeling ashamed, it was framed in a way that served to support rape myths and the sexual control of women.

Another type of "othering" was the portrayal of SlutWalk Hong Kong as an event for "privileged" women. For example, although an article in the English-language newspaper the *Standard*, which is of lower quality than *SCMP*, seems innocuous on the surface,[44] its title of "Sex Message for the Urbane" suggests that the movement was composed of "privileged" urbanites who had a message for other such "privileged" urbanites. Also, although reportage of my being a PhD student in Europe may have added some legitimacy to the movement, it may also have served to distance the general public because, in Hong Kong, having a foreign education is seen as a sign of privilege.

Also to distance the public from the movement, many reports suggested that only women, or mainly women, supported SlutWalk Hong Kong. An example of this is the aforementioned article in the *Standard*.[45] In fact, some supporters reported that there were actually more men attending the march in 2011 than women. Reports in line with that representation of attendance make it appear to the public as if the issue were women versus men; that is a misrepresentation, as the issue is actually a social one: everyone, regardless of gender, needs to be part of the solution.

As is typically the case with grassroots social movements, the mainstream media also downplayed the number of supporters that attended the event. The numbers were reported at around one hundred,[46] even though participants estimated that there were almost three hundred people. This also strikes at the perceived legitimacy of the movement and the local relevance of its message.

Missing from the media coverage was any mention of the academics, nongovernmental organizations and others that attended and/or supported the movement. The large variety of individuals and groups which came together in 2011 to show that the message of SlutWalk was applicable to different communities within Hong Kong was ignored by the mainstream media. This omission contributed to the ongoing challenge made by the popular media regarding the relevance and legitimacy of the movement.

Of course, "sexy" clothing was also an important theme in 2011. Not only were there numerous mentions of supporters wearing "sexy" clothing, but that aspect of the movement caught so much attention that a tabloid magazine wanted to do a centrefold photoshoot, for which they wanted me to pose in "sexy clothing" in the aforementioned bar and nightclub area. The reporter revealed that the male editor wanted photos of me sitting in a smoky bar, holding a cigarette and glass of wine. They believed that photos like that would help raise awareness about our "cause", whatever he perceived that to be. However, as we thought this would play more into the aforementioned stereotypes than send out the message of SlutWalk, I did not go through with the shoot.

In line with this, some coverage seemed to suggest that the primary message of SlutWalk was about fighting for women's right to dress or be "sexy". For example, *Metro Hong Kong*'s article was titled "蕩婦遊行 性感無罪", which translates into "SlutWalk, Being Sexy Is Not a Crime".[47] Beyond that, within the first paragraph, it clearly states that the event's message was that being sexy is not a crime. Another example is the article in the *Sun*, which was titled "蕩婦遊行' 捍衞性感", which translates into "'SlutWalk', Defending the Right to Be Sexy". Although the main message of SlutWalk is that victims should not be blamed for being victimized, it seems that fighting for the right to "be sexy" was considered more interesting to report. This matches previous research, which suggests that the women's movement in general is portrayed more as entertainment, or "soft news", than real news.[48]

As for 2012, although there was much less coverage, the stories that did appear focused more on the issues than the organizers. Instead of focusing on "sexy" clothing, my rape story or "othering" themes from 2011, stories dealt with the issues. Photographs depicted a group of supporters ironically dressed in "Power Ranger"–esque outfits, with a sign bearing the question "Does my outfit make you feel like a rapist?" The message was that no type of clothing can protect one against sexual violence, because (1) sexual violence is not about clothing to begin with, and (2) only rapists can choose to rape. That difference is because the movement was covered by supportive journalists and other progressive channels, rather than journalists out for sensationalist news fodder.

Although a supportive journalist wrote helpful articles for *SCMP*, one of the editors felt the need to pen an editorial titled "SlutWalk Protests Need to Consider Common Sense".[49] The editorial attributed sexual assault to "bad people among us", thus supporting the rape myths that sexual assault is perpetrated by strangers or "crazy" men, while framing rape within a law enforcement paradigm. That being said, it is a positive note that they published my op-ed response to this editorial, which they titled "No Skirting around Sexual Violence Issue".[50]

## INSIGHTS ON DEALING WITH THE MAINSTREAM MEDIA

There are various guides available on how social movements should deal with the media; for example, *Recipes for Disaster: An Anarchist Cookbook, a Moveable Feast* features a whole section on the mainstream media.[51] Listed below are some suggestions for dealing with the mainstream media based on the experiences of SlutWalk Hong Kong from 2011 and 2012:

> Catch the media off guard.
> Be friendly and seek out sympathetic journalists and editors.
> Lower expectations of what the mainstream media can do for movements.
> Be aware of frames that may be used.
> Avoid providing material that may be used against the movement or oneself.
> Use gimmicks to "sell" the story to outlets.

It appears that the advice to move quickly and catch the media off guard[52] may be quite useful, especially when holding an event for the first time. In 2011, journalists were scrambling to get a piece of the story; since SlutWalk was a fresh face in the activist circle in Hong Kong, and the event was also new to the city, the media didn't know what to expect.

The advice to be friendly is also useful, and it seems productive to cultivate relationships with supportive journalists. As previously mentioned, SlutWalk Hong Kong owes some of its coverage to media personnel who are sympathetic with the movement and its message. In Hong Kong, the high turnover within media outlets is problematic, so perhaps the advice here would be that there is always the potential to find sympathetic reporters and editors.

At the same time, it is necessary to lower expectations, both when trying to contact the media and after interviews. Grassroots movements cannot expect mainstream media outlets to actually be interested in their movement's progressive messages. It is the nature of the media to maintain, not change, the status quo. Even if they are keen on producing a story, it is not possible to control how their stories are reported, or if they will be reported at all. In the end, other decision makers, higher up the news hierarchy, will always have the ability to change stories to be in line with the protest paradigm, or make them disappear completely.

Related to this is the need to be aware of the techniques the media may use to frame a "story", such as those that portray protestors as deviants,[53] and avoid playing into those frames. For example, in 2011 the media made much use of the "sluts" in "sexy" clothing label, reporting on supporters' appearance—a common technique used to delegitimize.[54] Then, in 2012, a group of volunteers decided to combat this using their unisex Power Ranger–esque outfits. Of course, it is also necessary to keep in mind that, even if one is very careful, the press may still spin the story in some way to marginalize and belittle movements, framing the articulation of activism in line with the "protest paradigm".

Keeping in mind that the mainstream media cannot be controlled by the social movement, there is the need to avoid providing any material that one does not want in the public domain. This tip was originally conveyed to me by Helen, a friend and fellow SlutWalk volunteer who helped organize the march in 2011. It was she who advised against cooperating with a tabloid magazine in its proposal for a "sexy" photoshoot. Reflecting on 2011's media coverage, it would have been better if I had just shared that I was a rape survivor, instead of revealing a larger context. In divulging that bigger picture, the story was used to support problems the movement was trying to fight—namely, rape myths and the sexual control of women. Anything one says in the presence of a reporter, or any footage one allows photographers and videographers to take, can always be used not only against oneself but also against the entire movement.

Before discussing alternatives to using mainstream media, knowing the nature of such media outlets, it is worth mentioning the use of gimmicks to attract attention and appear to them to have high entertainment value. Aside from progressive journalists, and editors who are supportive of the movement, other media personnel are just interested in receiving news fodder which will entertain their readers and viewers. It is important to remember this because without a high level of readership and viewership, a media outlet will not be attractive to advertisers. Without revenue from advertisers, the media outlet will not be profitable. In the case of issues related to women, whether or not they are covered, and how they are covered, depends on the perceptions that senior decision-making staff have about "what the reader wants", which is itself influenced by the dominant masculine hegemony.[55] Media outlets are businesses; even sympathetic journalists must sell their stories to their editors. If progressive social movements wish to have coverage, they must have some "selling points".

## ALTERNATIVES

The discussion above dealt with how to deal with the mainstream media. There is a tendency for social movements, including SlutWalk Hong Kong, to follow the mainstream media. This is because it has traditionally served as the primary route for reaching the general public. However, there are those who point to the pitfalls of focusing on the popular press. As mentioned in the introduction, those with power in mainstream media organizations are interested in maintaining the current oppressive relationships of power, whether in terms of class dominance or gender dominance. They are not concerned about encouraging radical social change. That is not to say that movements should completely ignore the mainstream media. However, there is a danger in allowing media response to define a movement's actions.[56] It is important to remember that the mainstream media are actually just one of many avenues which can be used to reach the public. Below is a list of some alternatives to mainstream media:

Reach the public directly.
Seek out alternative, independent, media outlets.
Use the Internet and social media.
Spread the word within other progressive circles.

Instead of pursuing "product placement" within media, it is suggested that social movements should reach the public directly.[57] Examples of this approach could include informal public discussion events and workshops, which can serve to allow people to identify with protestors, mitigating the "othering" employed by the mainstream media. Such events can also allow for a focus on the real issues, which the "protest paradigm" avoids. Direct engagement might also include participation in other civil society events and the provision of free services to the public.

It has also been suggested that social movements seek out alternative media in a creative manner.[58] Referring back to the media coverage of Slut-Walk Hong Kong in 2012, two of the international outlets and one of the local ones were alternative, progressive websites. Where the mainstream press serves the goals of the dominant hegemony, these alternative sources are actually the ones who hold goals in common with progressive social movements and share a similar point of view. Because they may have a narrower audience of progressive people, the way they report on a movement's event may more accurately portray both the movement and its message. In this information age, it is also possible for members of the general public who hear about a movement in the mainstream media to search for additional information on the Internet and find those progressive articles.

Along similar lines, it is necessary to use the Internet and social media, making sure your group has such things as a website and a Facebook page. This is not only for communicating with supporters but also to provide information about a movement directly to members of the public who may be looking online to learn more about an event or its organizers. In addition, the use of social media allows movements to reach members of the public more directly, bypassing the mainstream media; this can be done using social media advertisements, or posts and invitations shared by supporters.

Another important task is spreading the word to other progressive organizations within activist circles. As people within these organizations already have a more egalitarian perspective, it is easier to gain their support and have them spark discussions both within their own groups and with others.

# CONCLUSION

SlutWalk Hong Kong has marched yearly in Hong Kong since 2011, when the SlutWalk movement began in Toronto. The movement began in response to a Canadian law enforcement officer's advice to university students not to dress like "sluts" if they wanted to avoid becoming a victim of sexual assault. Since then, over one hundred separate, local SlutWalks have been initiated all over the world protesting against rape culture and rape myths that normalize rape, blame victims and excuse perpetrators. As gender inequality, which dichotomizes gender roles, is harmful to people of all genders, women and men have marched together in SlutWalks around the world, raising awareness and seeking a change in social attitudes. Similar to other locations, the blaming of victims of sexual violence is widespread in Hong Kong, and the mainstream media are known to be problematic.

The purpose of the popular press is to preserve the interests of the dominant class and gender hegemony; it should not be a surprise that they have goals which oppose the egalitarian ones belonging to progressive social movements. Although the media may try to maintain an illusion of neutrality by covering some protests, when such events are covered, they are framed within a "protest paradigm" that belittles grassroots movements, takes away their perceived legitimacy and "others" protestors. In acting in that way they operate as a mechanism for distancing the general public from those movements. Similarly, although the women's movement does not receive much coverage, when it does, it is generally portrayed as light entertainment rather than serious news. Reporting on sexual violence, in particular, tends to focus on cases that fit a rape myth, portraying a sexual attack as one that is perpetrated by strangers who assault deserving victims. That portrayal articulates a message that argues women should control their movements and actions in line with patriarchal standards. In terms of mainstream media coverage, Slut-Walk has been disadvantaged on a number of different levels; it is a grassroots, progressive movement, part of the women's movement, and one that recognizes sexual violence is commonly committed by men against women.

In 2011, when the event was considered a novelty, mainstream media outlets of all types scrambled to cover the story. Most stories used the "protest paradigm" to distance the general public from the movement; portraying activists as containing the local stereotypes of "sluts", "outsiders", "Westerners" and "privileged" women wearing "sexy" clothing. The number of supporters was downplayed and the wide variety of marchers and speakers omitted. This suggested that the message of the movement had little to no local relevance. The purpose of SlutWalk Hong Kong was distorted into fighting for women's right to be "sexy", construing sexual violence as a secondary concern.

In contrast, had it not been for journalists sympathetic to SlutWalk's cause, there would have been a local media blackout in 2012. This, in addition to coverage by some local and international alternative websites, known to be progressive, allowed the movement's message to come through more clearly.

In dealing with the mainstream media, it may be useful to consider some of the points learned from SlutWalk Hong Kong's media experience. It is helpful to use an element of surprise so that the mainstream media are caught off guard, not knowing what to expect. It is wise to seek out sympathetic journalists and editors and develop relationships with them. That being said, it is imperative to remember the mass media's purpose and whose interests they serve; it cannot be controlled by grassroots social movements. Expectations towards traditional media must be lowered, and much caution must be used to avoid playing into their frames of reference, providing material that could be used to support those frames. As the popular press, in general, operates on a for-profit business model, it is not interested in egalitarian messages for their intrinsic value; gimmicks may therefore be useful in attracting their attention.

Although the mainstream media should not be ignored or rebuffed, it is important to remember that they are not the only avenue by which movements can reach the general public. Instead of purely focusing on traditional media, and pursuing coverage, it is possible to hold, or participate in, events that directly engage the public while also contacting alternative media sources. In an information age, online news sources, along with a movement's own website and social media pages, can provide information to those who wish to learn about the movement. Networking with like-minded groups and individuals can help spread a movement's message, sparking discussion within those other circles, which can also be helpful.

Regarding the mass media, it is important to keep in mind that it is their nature to act as a tool for social control of the masses in the service of the goals of the elite. This makes it an unreliable resource for any genuine grassroots movement with a progressive message, which includes the women's movement. Aside from sympathetic journalists or editors, unless a movement is a manufactured, corporate one, the popular press in general are not interested in helping spread a movement's message. They are businesses that care about advertising revenue and serving the elite's goal of keeping the public complacent within the current system through entertainment. Whether organizing a movement's event or consuming mainstream media products, it is always necessary to be wary of disinformation. As in everything, always question what messages are being sent, and ask yourself: Whose interests are being served?

# REFERENCES

Ashley, Laura, and Beth Olson. "Constructing Reality: Print Media's Framing of the Women's Movement, 1966 to 1986". *Journalism & Mass Communication Quarterly* 7, no. 4 (1998): 263–77.

Association Concerning Sexual Violence Against Women and Department of Social Work, Hong Kong Baptist University. "A Research Report on Help Seeking Experiences of Sexual Violence Victims in Hong Kong: Community Responses and Second Victimization". Hong Kong: Author, 2011.

Barker, Michael. "Mass Media and Social Movements: A Critical Examination of the Relation between the Mainstream Media and Social Movements". Accessed April 22, 2008. www.globalresearch.ca/mass-media-and-social-movements/8761.

Burt, Martha R. "Rape Myths". In *Confronting Rape and Sexual Assault*, edited by Mary E. Oden and Jody Clay-Warner, chap. 11. Oxford: Scholarly Resources Inc., 1998. Kindle edition.

Carter, Cynthia. "When the 'Extraordinary' Becomes 'Ordinary': Everyday News of Sexual Violence". In *News, Gender and Power*, edited by Cynthia Carter, Gill Branston, and Stuart Allan, ch. 13. London: Routledge, 2002. Kindle edition.

Chan, Joseph M., and Chi-Chuan Lee. "The Journalistic Paradigm on Civil Protests: A Case Study of Hong Kong". In *The News Media in National and International Conflict*, edited by Andrew Arno and Wimal Dissanayake, 183–202. Boulder, CO: Westview, 1984.

CrimethInc. *Recipes for Disaster: An Anarchist Cookbook, a Moveable Feast*. 2nd ed. Salem, OR: CrimethInc., 2012.

CrimethInc. Workers' Collective. "Demonstrating Resistance: Mass Action and Autonomous Action in the Election Year". Accessed February 5, 2013. www.crimethinc.com/texts/atoz/demonstrating.php.

Davidson, Katie. "Media as Direct Action". *Tidal* 2 (March 2012): 26–27. Accessed February 4, 2013. http://tidalmag.org/issue-2-spring-is-coming/.

Garrett, Daniel, and Angie Ng. "Visualizing SlutWalk: Participants, the Public and the Media". Paper presented at the 2nd International Sociological Association's Forum of Sociology: Social Justice and Democratization, Buenos Aires, Argentina, August 1–4, 2012.

Herman, Edward S., and Noam Chomsky. *Manufacturing Consent: The Political Economy of the Mass Media*. London: The Bodley Head, 2008. Kindle edition.

Hung, Suet-Lin. "A Study on Help Seeking Experiences of Sexual Violence in Hong Kong: Community Responses and Second Victimization". Paper presented at the Hong Kong Women's NGO Forum: Working with CEDAW, Hong Kong, May 7, 2011.

Ip, Kelly. "Rapes Soar 60pc in First Quarter". *Standard*, May 15, 2013. Accessed October 7, 2013. http://www.thestandard.com.hk/news_detail.asp?pp_cat=11&art_id=133749&sid=39663661&con_type=1.

Kitzinger, Jenny. "The Gender-Politics of News Production: Silenced Voices and False Memories". In *News, Gender and Power*, edited by Cynthia Carter, Gill Branston, and Stuart Allan, ch. 11. London: Routledge, 2002. Kindle edition.

Luttwak, Edward. *Coup d'état: A Practical Handbook*. Cambridge, MA: Harvard University Press, 1979.

Major, Ashley. "Rape and Sexual Assault Myths: Examining Their Prevalence in the Criminal Justice System and Greater Society". *Slaw*, March 2, 2012. Accessed March 2, 2014. www.slaw.ca/2012/03/02/rape-and-sexual-assault-myths/.

*Metro Hong Kong*. "蕩婦遊行 性感無罪". December 5, 2011. Accessed January 2, 2014. www.metrohk.com.hk/index.php?cmd=detail&id=176277&search=1.

Ng, Angie. "No Skirting around Sexual Violence Issue". *South China Morning Post*, December 5, 2012. Accessed January 2, 2014. www.scmp.com/comment/letters/article/1097620/letters-editor-december-5-2012.

*Occupied Times*. "Editorial". October 15, 2012. Accessed February 5, 2014. http://theoccupiedtimes.org/?p=7297.

Romito, Patrizia. *A Deafening Silence: Hidden Violence against Women and Children*. Bristol, UK: Policy Press, 2008.

SlutWalk Toronto. "Why". SlutWalk Toronto. Accessed January 3, 2014. http://www. slutwalktoronto.com.

*South China Morning Post.* "SlutWalk Needs to Consider Common Sense". November 29, 2012. Accessed January 1, 2014. www.scmp.com/comment/insight-opinion/article/109 3326/slutwalk-protests-need-consider-common-sense.

*Standard.* "Sex Message for the Urbane". December 5, 2011. Accessed 29 May 2013. www. thestandard.com.hk/news_detail.asp?pp_cat=21&art_id=117673&sid=34666801&con_ type=1&d_str=20111205&sear_year=2011.

Theobald, John. "The Intellectual Tradition of Radical Mass Media Criticism: A Framework". *Fifth-Estate-Online: The International Journal of Radical Mass Media Criticism*, October 2005. Accessed April 3, 2014. www.fifth-estate-online.co.uk/criticsm/TheobaldFifthEstate. pdf.

Traven, B. "Serbia: Fake Revolutions, Real Struggles". CrimethInc. Workers' Collective, October 14, 2010. Accessed April 2, 2014. www.crimethinc.com/blog/2010/10/14/serbia-fake-revolutions-real-struggles/.

# NOTES

1. "Why", SlutWalk Toronto, last accessed January 3, 2014, www.slutwalktoronto.com.
2. Ibid.
3. Ibid.
4. Ibid.
5. Daniel Garrett and Angie Ng, "Visualizing SlutWalk: Participants, the Public and the Media", paper presented at the 2nd International Sociological Association's Forum of Sociology: Social Justice and Democratization, Buenos Aires, Argentina, August 1–4, 2012.
6. Ibid.
7. Martha R. Burt, "Rape Myths", in *Confronting Rape and Sexual Assault*, ed. Mary E. Oden and Jody Clay-Warner (Oxford: Scholarly Resources Inc., 1998), Kindle edition, first page of chapter 11.
8. Ashley Major, "Rape and Sexual Assault Myths: Examining Their Prevalence in the Criminal Justice System and Greater Society", *Slaw*, March 2, 2012, last accessed March 2, 2014, www.slaw.ca/2012/03/02/rape-and-sexual-assault-myths/.
9. Ibid.
10. Burt, "Rape Myths".
11. Major, "Rape and Sexual Assault Myths".
12. Burt, "Rape Myths".
13. Ibid.
14. Association Concerning Sexual Violence Against Women and Department of Social Work, Hong Kong Baptist University, "A Research Report on Help Seeking Experiences of Sexual Violence Victims in Hong Kong: Community Responses and Second Victimization" (Hong Kong: Author, 2011), 15, last accessed May 14, 2014 www.rainlily.org.hk/en.
15. Ibid., 12.
16. Kelly Ip, "Rapes Soar 60pc in First Quarter", *Standard*, May 15, 2013, last accessed October 7, 2013, http://www.thestandard.com.hk/news_detail.asp?pp_cat=11&art_id=133749 &sid=39663661&con_type=1.
17. Association Concerning Sexual Violence Against Women and Department of Social Work, Hong Kong Baptist University, "A Research Report", 12; Suet-Lin Hung, "A Study on Help Seeking Experiences of Sexual Violence in Hong Kong: Community Responses and Second Victimization", paper presented at the Hong Kong Women's NGO Forum: Working with CEDAW, Hong Kong, May 7, 2011.
18. Hung, "A Study on Help Seeking Experiences of Sexual Violence in Hong Kong".
19. Association Concerning Sexual Violence Against Women and Department of Social Work, Hong Kong Baptist University, "A Research Report", 92.
20. John Theobald, "The Intellectual Tradition of Radical Mass Media Criticism: A Framework", *Fifth-Estate-Online: The International Journal of Radical Mass Media Criticism*, Octo-

ber 2005, last accessed April 3, 2014, http://www.fifth-estate-online.co.uk/criticsm/ TheobaldFifthEstate.

21. Edward S. Herman and Noam Chomsky, *Manufacturing Consent: The Political Economy of the Mass Media* (London: The Bodley Head, 2008 [Kindle edition]), ch. 1.

22. Ibid.

23. Ibid.

24. Jenny Kitzinger, "The Gender-Politics of News Production: Silenced Voices and False Memories", in *News, Gender and Power*, ed. Cynthia Carter et al. (London: Routledge, 2002 [Kindle edition]).

25. Ibid.

26. Laura Ashley and Beth Olson, "Constructing Reality: Print Media's Framing of the Women's Movement, 1966 to 1986", *Journalism & Mass Communication Quarterly* 75, no. 2 (1998): 263–77.

27. Ibid., 272.

28. Herman and Chomsky, *Manufacturing Consent*, ch. 2.

29. Cynthia Carter, "When the 'Extraordinary' Becomes 'Ordinary': Everyday News of Sexual Violence", in *News, Gender and Power*, ed. Cynthia Carter et al. (London: Routledge, 2002).

30. Ibid.

31. Kitzinger, "The Gender-Politics of News Production".

32. Patrizia Romito, *A Deafening Silence: Hidden Violence against Women and Children* Bristol, UK: Policy Press, 2008), 136.

33. Herman and Chomsky, *Manufacturing Consent*, ch.1.

34. Michael Barker, "Mass Media and Social Movements: A Critical Examination of the Relation between the Mainstream Media and Social Movements", April 22, 2008, last accessed May 14, 2014, http://www.globalresearch.ca/mass-media-and-social-movements/8761.

35. B. Traven, "Serbia: Fake Revolutions, Real Struggles", CrimethInc. Workers' Collective, October 14, 2010, last accessed April 2, 2014, www.crimethinc.com/blog/2010/10/14/serbia-fake-revolutions-real-struggles/.

36. Barker, "Mass Media and Social Movements".

37. Joseph M. Chan and Chi-Chuan Lee, "The Journalistic Paradigm on Civil Protests: A Case Study of Hong Kong", in *The News Media in National and International Conflict*, ed. Andrew Arno and Wimal Dissanayake (Boulder, CO: Westview, 1984), 187.

38. Barker, "Mass Media and Social Movements".

39. Ibid.

40. Ibid.

41. Ashley and Olson, "Constructing Reality", 267.

42. Edward Luttwak, *Coup d'état: A Practical Handbook* (Cambridge, MA: Harvard University Press, 1979), 58.

43. Barker, "Mass Media and Social Movements".

44. "Sex Message for the Urbane", *Standard*, December 5, 2011, last accessed May 29, 2013, www.thestandard.com.hk/news_detail.asp?pp_cat=21&art_id=117673&sid=34666801&con_type=1&d_str=20111205&sear_year=2011.

45. Ibid.

46. Ibid.

47. "蕩婦遊行 性感無罪", *Metro Hong Kong*, December 5, 2011, last accessed January 2, 2014, www.metrohk.com.hk/index.php?cmd=detail&id=176277&search=1.

48. Ashley and Olson, "Constructing Reality", 267.

49. "SlutWalk Needs to Consider Common Sense", *South China Morning Post*, November 29, 2012, last accessed January 1, 2014, www.scmp.com/comment/insight-opinion/article/1093326/slutwalk-protests-need-consider-common-sense.

50. Angie Ng, "No Skirting around Sexual Violence Issue", *South China Morning Post*, December 5, 2012, last accessed January 2, 2014, www.scmp.com/comment/letters/article/1097620/letters-editor-december-5-2012.

51. CrimethInc., *Recipes for Disaster: An Anarchist Cookbook, a Moveable Feast*, 2nd ed. (Salem, OR: CrimethInc., 2012).

52. CrimethInc. Workers' Collective, "Demonstrating Resistance: Mass Action and Autonomous Action in the Election Year", accessed February 5, 2013, www.crimethinc.com/texts/atoz/demonstrating.php.

53. Ashley and Olson, "Constructing Reality", 268.

54. Ashley and Olson, "Constructing Reality", 268.

55. Kitzinger, "The Gender-Politics of News Production".

56. Katie Davidson, "Media as Direct Action", *Tidal* 2 (March 2012): 26–27, accessed February 4, 2013, http://tidalmag.org/issue-2-spring-is-coming/; "Editorial", *Occupied Times*, October 15, 2012, last accessed February 5, 2014, http://theoccupiedtimes.com.

57. "Editorial", *Occupied Times*.

58. CrimethInc. Workers Collective, "Demonstrating Resistance".

## Chapter Three

# Lights, Camera, Direct Action

*The Protest Spectacle as Media Opportunity
and Message Carrier*

## Jonathan Cable

In February 2008 five activists from the environmental direct action group Plane Stupid occupied the roof of the House of Commons in London. They unfurled a banner reading "BAA HQ", calling into question the Labour government's policy on airport expansion. This happened at the same time as Prime Minister's Questions and on the final day of the government's consultation into airport expansion.[1] The action was timed to maximize the press and political impact of the protest. This chapter will examine the protest tactics and media strategy of environmental direct action group Plane Stupid. It will demonstrate how they adapted their tactics to gain press attention and promote their messages. In doing so, this chapter utilizes data from in-depth interviews with activists from Plane Stupid to uncover how, and why, they used a professionalized media strategy, incorporating controlled messages and media-trained spokespeople. It will be argued that Plane Stupid's symbolic direct action worked as a message carrier, attracting press attention and allowing activists a platform to unveil their messages. A content analysis of UK national press coverage examines how these messages penetrated the reporting of their protest actions, and the ways in which Plane Stupid tried to adapt and exploit the event-based nature of the press. This raises two important questions: (1) Why does a group like Plane Stupid use symbolic direct action and professionalized media strategies? (2) What difference does this make to the press coverage they receive? Before this chapter addresses these questions, however, a brief theoretical background to the research is presented so as to situate it within the broader context of academic debate.

## BACKGROUND THEORY AND METHODS

Groups like Plane Stupid are involved in championing causes and highlighting politically contentious issues. Those politically contentious issues cover many different topics, ranging from complex identity politics to single-issue protest. The issues, it is argued, take their origin from the "structural conflicts of interest" which exist in society.[2] The point where "structural conflict" exists is at the point where protest groups, the press and protest targets meet to contest and put forth their definition of issues. However, and importantly for this chapter, a protest group's visibility and impact on the public consciousness often follows protest activity. Protest action, in this sense, is able to attract publicity and, as a consequence, highlight an issue. Lipsky provides a helpful definition of protest activity which encapsulates these dynamics:

> Protest activity is defined as a mode of political action oriented toward objection to one or more policies or conditions, characterized by showmanship or display of an unconventional nature.[3]

Building on Lipsky's definition, Eisinger talks about protest as "collective manifestations", which attempt to provide "relatively powerless people with bargaining leverage in the political process".[4] However, in the case of contentious politics, it is protest activity that causes conflict between those protesting and those being protested against and the relative power of each group to define an issue. It follows that protest activity occurs in one of three ways: it is "demonstrative, confrontative or violent".[5] Furthermore, Kriesi et al. go on to describe five broad forms of protest action within these three types of protest activity:

1. Direct democratic events (such as a vote)
2. Demonstrative events (such as petitions and demonstrations)
3. Confrontational events (such as blockades and occupations)
4. Events of light violence (such as violent demonstrations and limited damage to objects)
5. Heavy violence (bombings, arson and violence against persons)[6]

Where protest activity lies in relation to these different types of protest action has consistently impacted upon the nature and tone of mainstream media. The nature of the coverage received, and the relative success and failure of protest action is predicated upon the prevailing political and media opportunities available to a protest group. This chapter will now explain what this means in theory and underline the reality of the political and media opportunities which were available to Plane Stupid.

## POLITICAL AND MEDIA OPPORTUNITIES

The term *political opportunities* is used here to mean "the institutional and political factors that shape social movement options".[7] The "options" referred to in the quote correspond to the media strategies, protest tactics, and the relationship between a protest group and the protest target. However, the idea of political opportunities underplays the influence of quite possibly the most important variable of all, the media. Behr and Iyengar go as far to argue that changes in the media agenda have a substantial influence over the public agenda.[8] A protest group's decision of how and when to act upon media and political opportunities further aids in defining the outcomes of protest action, and the nature of media coverage. For instance, timing a protest activity to coincide with another high-profile event, or drawing upon a pre-existing public attitude, results in protest groups generating their own political opportunities. This is where an effective use of communications strategies and protest tactics by groups enters more prominently into the argument. Those groups who are able to get their message highlighted by the media can help prompt debate and provoke a reaction from dominant institutions, thereby creating further gaps in institutional arguments and debates, which produce additional space for protest groups to promote their view of the world. For Plane Stupid, their actions against the expansion of Heathrow Airport, in particular, happened against a backdrop of political opposition at both a local level, with the council disagreeing with airport expansion,[9] and the national level, with the Liberal Democrat and Conservative parties' opinion conflicting with the ruling Labour government's proposals for Heathrow.[10] How such debates are depicted and shaped, and how the issues are defined, is more specifically about media and protest framing.

## MEDIA AND PROTESTER FRAMING

The importance of framing in the context of protest actions is due to the impact of protest and media tactics on the representation of a protest group's messages; the media may select an issue to cover, thereby elevating its salience over a myriad of other issues. Consequently, media framing provides one perspective, or narrow view, on an issue, and it acts as a "thought organizer".[11] To quote Gamson, the media is acting as a "picture frame":

> It puts a border around something, distinguishing it from what is around it. A frame spotlights certain events and their underlying causes and consequences, and directs our attention away from others.[12]

This picture frame, however, is not entirely neutral, because of the preferential attention that is paid to one issue to the detriment of others. This is what Entman calls an "imprint of power".[13] More accurately the framing of issues has three important elements; he argues frames: (1) diagnose causes; (2) make moral judgements; and (3) suggest solutions to issues.[14] Media frames in particular originate from the ideological viewpoint of a media outlet. This is not to say that a dominant perspective, or master frame, does not exist. It is just that frames are neither monolithic nor impenetrable; there are discrepancies in how issues are defined, and, as already mentioned, it is within those gaps in definition that protest groups operate.

The media are not the only ones to utilize frames. Referred to as "collective action frames" by Snow and Benford, this type of frame has, as the name suggests, a more collective element to it. These frames are the shared coming together of a protest group's viewpoints, and collective experiences, in a "relatively unified and meaningful fashion".[15] They are, however, independent of political opportunities and exist within the groups themselves. In order to become public, and transition beyond the confines of a protest group, favourable media and political opportunities are required. What these types of frame are attempting to do is to define an issue and the arguments from the viewpoints of the protest group. However, those frames will be in competition with other social actors who are trying to have their own frames publicized, including those of dominant institutions and the media. It is the perspectives contained within frames that try to point towards how issues should be thought about, and what the preferred solution/solutions should be. Before entering into a discussion of Plane Stupid's media and protest tactics, the methods used and the materials gathered and analysed (which provide the empirical backing to this chapter) will be detailed.

## METHODS AND MATERIALS USED

In order to fully investigate Plane Stupid's collective action frames, tactics, and the reactions of the UK national press to their protest actions, a number of different empirical methods were deployed. First, Plane Stupid's official website and social media presence was examined. This was carried out in order to uncover the key issues at the heart of their campaign: who they blamed for the issues arising, suggested solutions and why they chose those particular times to act (or, to put it another way, how they framed protest opportunities). It is those elements that are seen to be at the centre of what constitutes collective action framing.[16] By following messages and reactions to the group in the press, using a content analysis of UK national newspapers, it was possible to build a detailed picture of media response. The debates around issues which protest provokes, Wahl-Jorgenson suggests, reveal "strategies of power or strategies for defining the rational and the common-sensical".[17]

The newspaper samples were taken from February 2008 until May 2009 and covered the full range of newspapers from tabloids to broadsheets and left- and right-wing ideologies. The online newspaper database Nexis was utilized to collect the reports, with the search focused on the name of the group, Plane Stupid, and the names of the seven most high-profile activists taking part in the campaign. The rationale for this approach helped to broaden the range of publications which could be included, and meant that Plane Stupid's methods and messages could be focused upon. Sampling in this way was able to yield 207 articles within the timeframe. To explore the press coverage fully, physical copies of the newspapers were obtained with the goal of analysing the imagery used to accompany each article and ascertain how this complemented or contrasted with the item's content. Through interrogating the interrelationship between image and text, a broader view of the dominant framing of protest events was obtained. This chapter will now detail the results of these empirical methods, and the implications of the findings for protest groups.

## SYMBOLIC DIRECT ACTION AND THE SPECTACLE OF PROTEST

The specific type of protest action used by Plane Stupid was symbolic nonviolent direct action; this includes tactics such as occupying or blockading a space—for example, an airport runway. In addition to direct action, Plane Stupid used a tactic which they referred to as "direct intervention". The difference between intervention and action is that direct intervention has the benefit of having a measurable impact. By shutting down an airport runway, planes will not be able to take off and land; this will result in a reduction in the amount of carbon dioxide and other pollutants released into the atmosphere. The key indicator here is "you can materially measure the success, or the impacts of your action".[18] Their rationale behind the use of these particular tactics is similar to a cost-benefit analysis. Plane Stupid was aware of the effect that its protest actions might have on the press and its coverage; this was an active consideration in determining what the protest targets were, and what particular style of action would be used. The way this worked in practice can be found in a quote by one Plane Stupid activist:

> We don't break the law lightly. . . . We are aware that our disturbances cause people distress and we don't like doing that, but we do need to get our message across. We have genuine concerns.[19]

What this quote shows is that the activist has acknowledged the extent to which direct action causes disruption, while maintaining that it is these types of tactics that are required to highlight the issues. Taken further, the quote recognizes that protest groups do not carry out actions without reason. It is this awareness which meant that Plane Stupid was able to identify and exploit the underlying news values of the press by playing to what Gamson and Mayer argued as the primary news value of protest:

> Spectacle means drama and confrontation, emotional events with people who have fire in the belly, who are extravagant and unpredictable. This puts a high premium on novelty, on costume, and on confrontation. [20]

These visual requirements are met by the presence of protest spectacle and are enhanced through the use of "showmanship or display of an unconventional nature". [21] The lines between political expression and media spectacle in this context are thus blurred, but the main goal of Plane Stupid's direct action was to "critique through spectacle, not critique versus spectacle". [22]

To think of the group another way is to consider them as protest opportunists, looking for and planning their actions to correspond with other events, and further exploiting press attention. Each action will be slightly different, but the key messages will remain the same—namely, airport expansion and climate change. This helps to create a continuing political narrative through a direct action campaign and aids in avoiding being delegitimized as "mindless". This is what one activist referred to as planning actions "according to key dates", tailoring the messages to the protest action, and linking explicitly to these external events. [23] The argument at the heart of Plane Stupid's protest tactics was to generate news coverage of the issues; it did not matter to the activists what tone the reporting took because the "more media attention the better, even bad press generates dialogue". [24] To Plane Stupid, the most important point was that the issues were being discussed and debated. As one activist put it, their role was to "force the issue into the open". [25] Direct action in this case is being used to carry a message, and the use of spectacular events, driven by direct action, is to capture the press's attention; once activists enter the press, as sources, they highlight the issues. [26]

Plane Stupid fully recognized the political opportunity the expansion of Heathrow Airport presented had a "strong policy rationale", and that direct action was the strategy best suited to changing government policy. [27] One activist went so far as to say that direct action was one of the reasons for the increased debate about the issue, and that Plane Stupid had acted as a catalyst for political change. [28] Plane Stupid was fully aware of the media and political context within which it was campaigning, using it as a platform upon which to build its campaign. Furthermore, with that campaign taking place a year to two years before a general election, Plane Stupid recognized that the issues around Heathrow's expansion would become an electoral issue, and that politicians could be pressured through the threat of losing votes.

What this section has done is detail the type of protest tactics that Plane Stupid utilized, and the rationale behind the choice of said tactics; what will now be discussed is how the press in Britain reacted to Plane Stupid's protest events.

## PRESS COVERAGE OF PLANE STUPID

The importance of the press to Plane Stupid, in publicizing their message, cannot be underestimated, and it is summed up in the following activist quote: "Before we do an action we try to visualise what the front page of the newspaper will be".[29] This led to Plane Stupid attempting to manage the media as part of its planning and preparation for their protests. The rationale for this is cited as the importance of the press's reach compared to that of a protest group, and this led to one activist presenting the following stark choice:

> We cannot put out hundreds of thousands of newspapers; we cannot make a broadcast and get millions of people to see it. It is the media that does that. We have to work with them or are forced to.[30]

In doing so Plane Stupid was very successful in gaining press coverage. Its actions generated 207 articles over a fifteen-month period. What is interesting, however, is the thematic breakdown of the press coverage and where its attention was most regularly concentrated. The reporting of Plane Stupid's actions was predominantly about aspects of law and order and the spectacle of protest. Across the sample the content analysis found there were 188 references (present in 43 percent of articles) relating to law and order. This included the talk of arrests and subsequent trials of activists, any disruption caused to the public, and police and security concerns over the ramifications stemming from, for example, the occupation of an airport runway. The impact of the press's fixation on law and order shifts the status of a protest from one of democratic expression and transforms it into an act of criminality. The spectacle of protest, however, occurred 172 times (present in 38 percent of articles) and included the structure of the protest action—that is, the people taking part and other logistical details, references to similar historical protests, and highlighting the personal information and background of activists. Taken together, the prevalence of law and order and the spectacle of protest serve to distract from the issues under protest and decontextualize why activists are carrying out their actions.

To give an example of how law and order and the spectacle of protest manifest themselves, the coverage of the first major protest action from the newspaper sample is used to show how those story elements interact. The occupation of the roof of the House of Commons was covered by 42 of the

207 articles (or 20 percent of the total). The protest action prompted a lot of newspaper talk around security issues relating to parliament, with police and security concerns being voiced in 11 of the 42 articles (or 26 percent). Direct action, by its very nature, is disruptive to targets, and this often leads to discussion about the security of sensitive locations and the legality of protest. These then become the focus of the coverage and not the issues. The following comment was found in relation to the House of Commons action, which the *Daily Mirror* reported as "Shout it from the rooftops: our security is a shambles".[31] However, as mentioned previously, these kinds of press angles are fully recognized by members of Plane Stupid. In a quote by one of the activists, given from the roof of the House of Commons, they acknowledge the security implications of their actions by saying they had "exposed a huge security flaw".[32]

Another story angle which would appear prominently throughout the coverage of Plane Stupid, from the House of Commons action onwards, was an evocation of historical protests, and the protesters who carried them out, a much more personalized and individually focused kind of reporting. The protester who was mentioned most often was the 1990 anti-roads activist "Swampy". In April 1997 Swampy gained prominence, and even a level of celebrity, after he, together with a number of other campaigners, was involved in tunnelling and living beneath the roads around Manchester Airport. Their actions, and the press reporting they provoked, has meant that "Swampy" became a by-word for environmental direct action.[33] The presence of past protests was evident in twenty-four of the newspaper articles (12 percent), in which Plane Stupid was talked about, with the group being referred to as the heirs to Swampy. In one particular example, found in the *Daily Mail* on 1 March 2008, the headline simply read "Move Over Swampy".[34] However, the article does make a distinction between Plane Stupid and Swampy, which includes some ingrained stereotypes and the personal history and background of the activists. Plane Stupid are said to be beyond the old stereotypes of so-called crusty activists, with the focus placed on the novelty of the tactics and personalities involved. The following passage is taken from the already mentioned *Daily Mail* article in which often-repeated stereotypes are used to argue that Plane Stupid are a "new breed" of protester:

> This new breed of protester is a world away from the likes of the infamous Swampy, and the usual raggle-taggle of jobless drop-outs that are so often associated with the eco-warrior cause.[35]

The *Guardian* declared that Plane Stupid had learnt "lessons from Swampy" and they were hailed as a "new wave (of) protesters" that "target airport expansion".[36] This narrative of celebrity protests is nowhere more evident than in the following quote: "A decade after Swampy defied Britain's road building programme and invented the eco-protester as national celebrity".[37] This kind of personalization and elevation of the individuals involved was a regularly occurring theme in the press coverage, in which activists' backgrounds appeared in thirty-two articles (15 percent of total) across the sample. This is no more evident example than in this strapline about the House of Commons protest: "A Baronet's granddaughter, a philosophy graduate, and an MP's grandson, the oh-so smart backgrounds of this week's Commons invaders".[38] This information was used to deflect attention away from the issues, with some members of Plane Stupid having a perceived privileged background prompting the tabloids to refer to them as "upper crusties".[39] A consequence of being open with the press is that activists are left open to having their personal and private lives exposed. The information is then used to deflect attention away from the rationale for the protest. When activists become bigger than the group they represent they also attract all of the attention, consequently side-lining the issues.

In this respect the group did more than just highlight the issues; they were also challenging the ingrained perceptions of direct action activists. They were effectively attempting to "reframe" the press coverage in the direction of their narrative, and as a consequence, how the issues were being defined. The process by which this happened was through their meticulously planned protest actions and finely tuned messaging. This is the very basis of what they were doing: using a protest event as a spectacle to draw the press's attention and then unveil their message, an approach one activist referred to as a "Trojan Horse":

> If you are clever and you understand how the [media] game works then you can actually use spectacular actions as a kind of Trojan Horse which you leave outside the gates of the big media corporations, and they are like ooh we like the look of that, then they bring the horse in, then you jump out with your radical message.[40]

In doing so the connection between Plane Stupid's actions, messages and protest targets was made explicit, fully exploiting the protest and media opportunities the actions created. Such tactics helped to achieve their aim of having airport expansion debated in public. In this section it has been shown how Plane Stupid's actions were generally covered by the media. The next section will demonstrate how diverse protest targets and tactics generate different tones in how they are reported.

## DIFFERENT PROTEST TARGETS, DIFFERENT COVERAGE

The two examples below will demonstrate the influence the choice of protest tactics has on media opportunities and press coverage. The first of the two examples took place on 6 March 2009 when a Plane Stupid activist, Leila Deen, threw a canister of green custard over the government's business secretary, Lord Mandelson. This action was timed to coincide with a government launch of a summit concerning the low-carbon economy.[41] Personality certainly plays its part in the resultant coverage of the action, but this time the focus is more on how the newspapers felt about Peter Mandelson, as the following selection of headlines suggests:

1. *Daily Mail*—Lord Mandy Gets His Just Desserts![42]
2. *The Express*—The Slime Minister[43]
3. *Daily Star*—I Am Discustard with You, Mandy[44]
4. *Daily Mirror*—Lord C'stard[45]

To illustrate this further, the presence of Peter Mandelson is also a reflection of the political ideologies of the newspapers that reported the action. There were eighteen articles (9 percent of total) which covered the protest, but there is a clear right-wing bias in the coverage. The left-wing newspapers only produced four articles, while the right-wing press printed fourteen reports relating to the action. This is, perhaps, more representative of the press's opinion of Peter Mandelson rather than the protest itself.

The media coverage of this event is somewhat different from that of Plane Stupid's occupation of the runway at Stansted Airport, which took place on 9 December 2008. A significant difference between the two actions is that in the Stansted protest it was the public who were disrupted by the protest, not a single individual. That difference can be seen in the much more negative reporting of the Stansted action, which is reflected in the headlines that appeared the following day:

1. *Daily Star*—Plane Mean![46]
2. *The Independent*—Stansted Brought to Standstill by Plane Stupid Protesters[47]
3. *Daily Mail*—Three Days of Chaos after Airport Invasion[48]
4. *Daily Mirror*—Could They Stop Air Terrorists?[49]

The focus is very much on the actions of the protesters and debates about their choice of target and tactics. The first article in the list describes the protests as selfish, because the protest took place in the run-up to Christmas.[50] This aspect of the action became the focal point for the *Daily Star*, which led with the headline "Protesters Play Scrooge". It was framed as the disruption of "HUNDREDS of kids on their way to see Father Christmas [who] had their flights cancelled yesterday as protesters stormed Stansted Airport".[51] The second report brings the activists' background into the story mentioning that the action was carried out by "middle class militants".[52] This is a form of exclusion by inclusion, in which protesters are included in press coverage only to be discredited and delegitimized, because they are posing a challenge to the political consensus. The final two examples attempt to de-politicize the issue by turning their focus on the security implications of shutting down the airport, and the disruption thus caused to the public.[53] All of these themes are reflected in the published reports. In terms of press coverage, this was Plane Stupid's most covered protest. The occupation of Stansted Airport generated forty-eight articles in total (18 percent of total articles) across the UK's national newspapers. Unlike the coverage of the Mandelson action, the airport protest was covered in a similar fashion in the majority of media; this is demonstrated by the appearance of an equal amount of articles (twenty-four in each) in both left- and right-wing news-papers, respectively.

The targeting of an airport, and the disruption to the public it caused, was by far the most focused aspect of the action occurring in twenty-four of the forty-eight articles (50 percent of Stansted-related articles). This demon-strates that the action of the protesters was at the forefront of press coverage. But it is important to note that the gaining of press coverage is not solely dependent upon spectacular events, as the next section will demonstrate that having a prominent profile, and a positive relationship with journalists, leads to alternative routes of press attention.

## ACTIVIST/PRESS RELATIONS

The maintaining of press attention is one of the biggest challenges for a protest group. The sample of newspaper articles contained thirty-nine (19 percent of total) which were not directly related to a specific protest action by Plane Stupid. The subject matter of these articles was highly varied, ranging from Plane Stupid's inclusion in a profile about environmental activist John Stewart,[54] and offering comments in an article about the introduction of showers onto planes.[55] This demonstrates the level of credibility and per-ceived authority Plane Stupid developed, during their campaign, to comment on such issues in the press. As well as this, the group used their relationships with select journalists to aid in generating newspaper stories. Those addition-al stories, beyond the protest action, are all part of maintaining publicity for the group and ensuring that the narrative around airport expansion is as prominent as possible. Essentially, this should be viewed as the use of media opportunities to make sure that political opportunities remain open. The higher the profile of an issue being debated in the press, the greater the likelihood that the government, or other protest targets, will not be able to ignore it.

The use of that relationship is evident in the coverage of the events surrounding the unveiling of a corporate spy within the group, and attempts by Strathclyde Police to turn one activist into an informant. The incidents were framed by the group in two different ways, but the goal of going public with these stories was to protect activists from future infiltration. Taking the corporate spy story first, one activist discussed how they worked closely with a journalist at the *Times,* and how the relationship was used to cultivate the story and have it told from Plane Stupid's point of view. In the activist's words, "We felt that we were working with journalists in order to tell a story in the way that we wanted to".[56] The spy, as it turned out, was fairly incompetent; for this reason, the choice of framing for the story was one of humour, and the group chose to portray him as "a bit Austin Powers".[57] This humorous angle was then reflected in the press coverage.

The act of self-preservation was a more prominent part of the framing around Strathclyde Police attempts to turn one of the Plane Stupid activists into an informant. The very serious nature of this incident was not viewed lightly by the group and was dealt with in a much more sombre tone. The activists believed that the whole episode would be a massive news story and pitched the idea for an article to a journalist at the *Guardian.*[58] The other activists agreed with this assessment, with one referring to the use of the event to create press coverage as "a real propaganda coup".[59] Another stated that it was "pretty much all a media stunt".[60] The press reacted to Plane Stupid's framing of the story and reported it as a very serious matter, with substantial civil liberties implications.

The intended goal of that particular media strategy was to protect activists and to highlight issues around public order policing. This demonstrates the ways in which Plane Stupid exploited the media opportunities presented to them, and shows how successful they were at doing so. Their attempts at press coverage played into a constant, and consistent, endeavour of keeping their messages as high profile as possible. This was independent of what was being discussed, it always all coming back to the underlying narratives around the issues. The group's aptitude in generating press stories, and ability to frame them from their perspective, demonstrates the size of the media opportunity they had created for themselves. Cultivating relationships with the press, and offering compelling news stories, meant that the probability of their action being covered would increase.

## CONCLUSION

In closing, it is worth reflecting on the overall impact of Plane Stupid's media and protest strategies. If the group had not existed it is unlikely that the issue of airport expansion would have been covered so heavily. The spectacle of direct action feeds the media's need for entertainment, as it provides dramatic images that can be reported on in a relatively simplified manner. Spectacle, such as shutting down an airport, creates an event which can cross a press threshold; you either gain attention or remain unreported. In addition, their professional and press-focused approach meant that the group was able to advance their viewpoints and exploit press attention. The more incredible and spectacular the protest, the greater the amount of press coverage received. Despite the breadth of the different tactics used, the group maintained a consistent message across their actions, which connected each protest together to create a coherent narrative: using direct action as a platform for media messages to be transmitted. The power of that message was only disrupted by a fixation on the backgrounds of the activists, a focal point that provided a distraction to the issues. The intrinsic use of theatre turns protesters into actors on the media stage and leads to an increasing need for activists to "stay in character" or risk losing media interest. However, for Plane Stupid, it was not a consideration of spectacle over debate; rather, it was an approach centred on using the spectacle to prompt debate. Accepting the rules of the press game also meant that they had accepted the associated risks.

## REFERENCES

Activist 1. Telephone Interview. 2010.
Activist 2. Telephone Interview. 2010.
Activist 3. Telephone Interview. 2010.
Anderson, Alison. "Environmental Activism and News Media". In *News, Public Relations and Power*, edited by Simon Cottle, 117–32. London: Sage, 2003.
Anonymous. "The Mile-High Shower Club". *Sunday Times*, 23 March 2008, 2.
Behr, Roy L., and Shanto Iyengar. "Television News, Real-World Cues, and Changes in the Public Agenda". *Public Opinion Quarterly* 49, no. 1 (1985): 38–57.
Caesar, Ed. "Fort Granny to Defy Heathrow Bulldozers; Resistance Pensioners Are Preparing to Barricade Their Threatened Homes in the Fight to Halt the Third Runway". *Sunday Times*, 29 May 2009, 10.
Cameron, Lucinda. "Police Tried to Bribe Me". *Sunday Mirror*, 26 April 2009, 8.
DeLuca, Kevin M. *Image Politics: The New Rhetoric of Environmental Activism*. New York: Guilford Press, 1999.
Eisinger, Peter K. "The Conditions of Protest Behaviour in American Cities". *American Political Science Review* 67, no. 1 (1973): 11–28.
Entman, Robert M. "Framing: Toward Clarification of a Fractured Paradigm". *Journal of Communication* 43, no. 4 (1993): 51–58.
Gamson, William A. *Bystanders, Public Opinion, and the Media*. Oxford: Blackwell, 2003. http://www.blackwellreference.com/subscriber/tocnode?id=g9780631226697_chunk_g978

063122669712.

Gamson, William A., and David S. Meyer. "Framing Political Opportunity". In *Comparative Perspectives on Social Movements: Political Opportunities, Mobilising Structures, and Cultural Framings*, edited by Doug McAdam, John D. McCarthy and Mayer N. Zald, 275–90. New York: Cambridge University Press, 1996.

Gaunt, John. "It Took the Police the Best Part". *Sun*, 12 December 2008, 35.

Glass, Dan. "The Media Is the Message". Bournemouth University, http://blogs.bournemouth. ac.uk/environmental-change/category/podcast/.

Greenhill, Sam. "Lord Mandy Gets His Just Desserts!" *Daily Mail*, 7 March 2009, 5.

Hannah, Ciran. "Cops Facing Spy Storm". *Sunday Star*, 26 April 2009, 2.

Harris, Gillian. "Better a Whistleblower Than a Spy; Tilly Gifford the Climate Change Activist Has Won Praise and Censure for Going Public with a Covert Police Attempt to Recruit Her as an Informant". *Sunday Times*, 3 May 2009, 9.

Hounslow Council. "Heathrow Expansion". London Borough of Hounslow, www.hounslow. gov.uk/index/heathrow.htm.

Fisher, Kimberly. "Locating Frames in the Discursive Universe". *Sociological Research Online* 2, no. 3 (1997). www.socresonline.org.uk/2/3/4.html.

Kerr, Jimmy. Telephone Interview. 2010.

Klandermans, Bert. "New Social Movements and Resource Mobilization: The European and American Approach". *International Journal of Mass Emergencies and Disasters* 4, no. 2 (1986): 13–37.

Knight, Kathryn. "Move Over Swampy: A Baronet's Granddaughter, a Philosophy Graduate, and an MP's Grandson, the Oh-So Smart Backgrounds of This Week's Commons Invaders". *Daily Mail*, 1 March 2008, 65.

Kriesi, Hanspeter, Ruud Koopmans, Jan Willem Duyvendak, and Marco G. Giugni. "New Social Movements and Political Opportunities in Western Europe". *European Journal of Political Research* 22, no. 2 (1992): 219–44.

Levy, Andrew, and Tom Kelly. "Three Days of Chaos after Airport Invasion". *Daily Mail*, 9 December 2008, 9.

Lipsky, Michael. "Protest as a Political Resource". *American Political Science Review* 62, no. 4 (1968): 1144–58.

McGurran, Aidan. "Could They Stop Air Terrorists? Flight Security Fears as Protesters Close Stansted". *Daily Mirror*, 9 December 2008, 17.

Meyer, David S. "Protest Cycles and Political Process: American Peace Movements in the Nuclear Age". *Political Research Quarterly* 46, no. 3 (1993): 451–79.

Milmo, Dan, and Owen Bowcott. "New Wave Protesters Target Airport Expansion". *Guardian*, 1 March 2008, 13.

Milmo, Dan, and Haroon Siddique. "Airport Protesters Take to Parliament Roof". *Guardian*, 28 February 2008, 4.

Milne, Meg. "Pressure on over Police Spies Claims". *Sunday Express*, 26 April 2009, 12.

Moreton, Cole. "A One-Man Eco-Industry". *Sunday Times*, 12 October 2008, 30.

Murray, Leo. Telephone Interview. 2010.

Perry, Ryan. "Shout It from the Rooftops: Our Security Is a Shambles". *Daily Mirror*, 28 February 2008, 35.

Plane Stupid. "Climate Campaigners Hang 'No 3rd Runway' Banner before PMQs—27th February 2008". Plane Stupid, http://www.planestupid.com/content/plane-stupid-scales-parliament-27th-february-2008.

Reynolds, Mark. "The Slime Minister". *Daily Express*, 7 March 2009, 14.

Roberts, Bob. "Lord C'stard". *Daily Mirror*, 7 March 2009, 7.

Scott, David. "Protesters Play Scrooge". *Daily Star*, 9 December 2008, 4.

Sireau, Nicolas. *Make Poverty History: Political Communication in Action*. London: Palgrave Macmillan, 2009.

Snow, David A., and Robert D. Benford. "Master Frames and Cycles of Protest". In *Frontiers in Social Movement Theory*, edited by A. D. Morris and C. M. Mueller, 133–55. New York: Vali-Ballou Press, 1992.

Taylor, Jerome. "Stansted Brought to Standstill by Plane Stupid Protesters". *Independent*, 9 December 2008, 10.

Wahl-Jorgensen, Karin. "Speaking Out against the Incitement to Silence: The British Press and the 2001 May Day Protests". In *Representing Resistance: Media Civil Disobedience, and the Global Justice Movement*, edited by Andy Opel and Donnalyn Pompper, 130–48. Wesport, CT: Praeger, 2003.

Wall, Emma. "I Am Discustard with You, Mandy". *Daily Star*, 7 March 2009, 9.

Wheatley, Gemma. "Plane Mean!" *Daily Star*, 9 December 2008, 4.

# NOTES

1. Plane Stupid, "Climate Campaigners Hang 'No 3rd Runway' Banner before PMQs—27th February 2008", Plane Stupid, www.planestupid.com/content/plane-stupid-scales-parliament-27th-february-2008.

2. Bert Klandermans, "New Social Movements and Resource Mobilization: The European and American Approach", *International Journal of Mass Emergencies and Disasters* 4, no. 2 (1986): 19.

3. Michael Lipsky, "Protest as a Political Resource", *American Political Science Review* 62, no. 4 (1968): 1145.

4. Peter K. Eisinger, "The Conditions of Protest Behaviour in American Cities", *American Political Science Review* 67, no. 1 (1973): 13.

5. Hanspeter Kriesi et al., "New Social Movements and Political Opportunities in Western Europe", *European Journal of Political Research* 22, no. 2 (1992): 221.

6. Ibid., 228.

7. David S. Meyer, "Protest Cycles and Political Process: American Peace Movements in the Nuclear Age", *Political Research Quarterly* 46, no. 3 (1993): 455.

8. Roy L. Behr and Shanto Iyengar, "Television News, Real-World Cues, and Changes in the Public Agenda", *Public Opinion Quarterly* 49, no. 1 (1985): 38.

9. Hounslow Council, "Heathrow Expansion", London Borough of Hounslow, www.hounslow.gov.uk/index/heathrow.htm.

10. Ed Caesar, "Fort Granny to Defy Heathrow Bulldozers; Resistance Pensioners Are Preparing to Barricade Their Threatened Homes in the Fight to Halt the Third Runway", *Sunday Times*, 29 May 2009, 10.

11. This connects to Erving Goffman's original concept of framing as the process by which a society produces meaning.

12. William A. Gamson, *Bystanders, Public Opinion, and the Media* (Oxford: Blackwell, 2003), http://www.blackwellreference.com/subscriber/tocnode?id=g9780631226697_chunk_g978063122669712. online. para 21.

13. Robert M. Entman, "Framing: Toward Clarification of a Fractured Paradigm", *Journal of Communication* 43, no. 4 (1993): 55.

14. Ibid., 52.

15. David A. Snow and Robert D. Benford, "Master Frames and Cycles of Protest", in *Frontiers in Social Movement Theory*, ed. A. D. Morris and C. M. Mueller (New York: Vali-Ballou Press, 1992).

16. Nicolas Sireau, *Make Poverty History: Political Communication in Action* (London: Palgrave Macmillan, 2009), 136–37, 162; William A. Gamson and David S. Meyer, "Framing Political Opportunity", in *Comparative Perspectives on Social Movements: Political Opportunities, Mobilising Structures, and Cultural Framings*, ed. Doug McAdam, John D. McCarthy, and Mayer N. Zald (New York: Cambridge University Press, 1996), 286.

17. Karin Wahl-Jorgensen, "Speaking Out against the Incitement to Silence: The British Press and the 2001 May Day Protests", in *Representing Resistance: Media Civil Disobedience, and the Global Justice Movement*, ed. Andy Opel and Donnalyn Pompper (Wesport, CT: Praeger, 2003), 133–34.

18. Dan Glass, "The Media Is the Message", Bournemouth University, http://blogs.bournemouth.ac.uk/environmental-change/category/podcast/.

19. Activist 2, Telephone Interview (2010).

20. Gamson and Meyer, "Framing Political Opportunity", 288.

21. Lipsky, "Protest as a Political Resource", 1145.

22. Kevin M. DeLuca, *Image Politics: The New Rhetoric of Environmental Activism* (New York: Guilford Press, 1999), 22.

23. Activist 2, Telephone Interview.

24. Activist 3, Telephone Interview (2010).

25. Activist 1, Telephone Interview (2010).

26. Ibid.

27. Ibid.

28. Ibid.

29. Glass, "The Media Is the Message".

30. Activist 3, Telephone Interview.

31. Ryan Perry, "Shout It from the Rooftops: Our Security Is a Shambles", *Daily Mirror*, 28 February 2008, 35.

32. Dan Milmo and Haroon Siddique, "Airport Protesters Take to Parliament Roof", *Guardian*, 28 February 2008, 4.

33. Alison Anderson, "Environmental Activism and News Media", in *News, Public Relations and Power*, ed. Simon Cottle (London: Sage, 2003).

34. Kathryn Knight, "Move Over Swampy: A Baronet's Granddaughter, a Philosophy Graduate, and an MP's Grandson, the Oh-So Smart Backgrounds of This Week's Commons Invaders", *Daily Mail*, 1 March 2008, 65.

35. Ibid., 65.

36. Dan Milmo and Owen Bowcott, "New Wave Protesters Target Airport Expansion", *Guardian*, 1 March 2008, 13.

37. Ibid., 13.

38. Knight, "Move Over Swampy", 65.

39. John Gaunt, "It Took the Police the Best Part", *Sun*, 12 December 2008, 35.

40. Activist 1, Telephone Interview.

41. Mark Reynolds, "The Slime Minister", *Daily Express*, 7 March 2009, 14.

42. Sam Greenhill, "Lord Mandy Gets His Just Desserts!" *Daily Mail*, 7 March 2009, 5.

43. Reynolds, "The Slime Minister", 14.

44. Emma Wall, "I Am Discustard with You, Mandy", *Daily Star*, 7 March 2009, 9.

45. Bob Roberts, "Lord C'stard", *Daily Mirror*, 7 March 2009, 7.

46. Gemma Wheatley, "Plane Mean!" *Daily Star*, 9 December 2008, 4.

47. Jerome Taylor, "Stansted Brought to Standstill by Plane Stupid Protesters", *Independent*, 9 December 2008, 12.

48. Andrew Levy and Tom Kelly, "Three Days of Chaos after Airport Invasion", *Daily Mail*, 9 December 2008, 9.

49. Aidan McGurran, "Could They Stop Air Terrorists? Flight Security Fears as Protesters Close Stansted", *Daily Mirror*, 9 December 2008, 17.

50. Wheatley, "Plane Mean!", 4.

51. David Scott, "Protesters Play Scrooge", *Daily Star*, 9 December 2008, 4.

52. Taylor, "Stansted Brought to Standstill", 10.

53. Levy and Kelly, "Three Days of Chaos after Airport Invasion", 9; McGurran, "Could They Stop Air Terrorists?" 17.

54. Cole Moreton, "A One-Man Eco-Industry", *Sunday Times*, 12 October 2008, 30.

55. Anonymous, "The Mile-High Shower Club", *Sunday Times*, 23 March 2008, 2.

56. Activist 1, Telephone Interview.

57. Ibid.

58. Ibid.

59. Activist 3, Telephone Interview.

60. Activist 2, Telephone Interview.

*Chapter Four*

# Paving the Way for Anti-Militarism in Romania

*Activists, Events and Public Authorities during the 2008 NATO Summit in Bucharest*

Henry Rammelt

In April 2008, Romania's capital, Bucharest, hosted the twentieth NATO Summit—the largest summit in NATO's history.[1] Considered by Romanian authorities as the main foreign policy event organized by Romania, and widely celebrated as a major achievement in Romania's foreign affairs by large parts of Romania's mainstream media, the Summit also provided a platform for (small-scale) social mobilization. Activists, foreign and domestic, issued from different spheres of militantism, especially anti-war and anti-globalization, calls for political protest. The mere suggestion of possible protests during that event received much attention from national media, and public authorities, with the issuing of warnings about "foreign anarchists coming to Romania" and "domestic troublemakers". That discourse led to a situation characterized by the Romanian Press Monitoring Agency "Active-Watch" as a collaboration between certain media outlets and the authorities, the purpose of which was to create an image in which all protesters were to be associated with violence and extremism.[2] Activists and media analysts perceived the media campaign as a "demonization of left-wing-militants and anarchists [that was] obviously preparing the ground for repression during the NATO event",[3] or at least discouraging people from making use of their right to free expression.[4] However, given that the media coverage was not limited to the Summit itself, but rather expanded gradually to include issues related to protests and protesters in general, the mobilization benefited partially from it.

The media attention, together with the high (or unusual) degree of repression, is understood to be the main reasons for the dynamics of mobilization and network creation before, during and after the Summit. The events gathered a pool of Romanian militants, which the author considers to be the first generation of post-revolution activists.[5]

In this chapter, I argue that the protests around the 2008 NATO Summit were a crucial moment in the creation of a militant network as well as in the transformation of the public attitude/discourse. Following della Porta, both might be considered to be the "effects of eventful protests",[6] or, as Giugni has put it, "unintended consequences of social movements".[7] To demonstrate the dynamics of mobilization, and especially its identity/solidarity component, we will analyse two events that were meant to provide a platform for alternative interpretations of NATO's role in world politics, and the social function of militarism in society. These are the two counter-summits "Kiss Your Enemy—A Day of Creativity and Action" and the "Anti-NATO Days". The first event had a more entertaining approach, with the purpose of "reaching the biggest number possible"[8] via movie screenings, light discussions and so on. The second event took a more radical stance, with the objective to "welcome NATO through our own means",[9] intending to express a "militant critical voice". Initially these two events were not intended to constitute a common platform, but rather to be in opposition to each other; however, a deep interaction between the two developed during the Summit, resulting in synergy effects for both.

Inspired by authors working on "the effects of protest on the social movement itself",[10] mainly using della Porta's and Giugni's perspective, we will focus on elements of the 2008 protests that can provide the basis for further militant activity. Some key elements in the scientific debate on consequences of protest, especially on the cultural and symbolic dimensions of social movement activity, were noticeable in the 2008 protests. We consider the following outcomes as being the most influential: the first two on a personal/meso level, the third on a macro level:

1. The accumulation of social capital, both relational and cognitive social capital,[11] the first resulting in the creation of a militant network, via an accumulation of contacts, the second resulting in the creation/strengthening of a collective identity and internal solidarity.
2. The accumulation of protest specific knowledge/know-how.
3. The transformation of the public discourse.

## THEORETICAL FRAMEWORK

As the author acknowledges, the growing tendency in the discipline of social movement studies towards becoming a multi-centric subfield, benefiting from a diversity of analytical angles,[12] the present chapter distances itself from single-paradigm approaches to social movements. Its purpose is to thus contribute to the stimulating dialogue on the use of multiple theoretical avenues, drawing on a wide range of theoretical directions. In order to familiarize the reader with the protests' environment, major lines of argumentation, stemming from the three *classical schools on social movements*—"opportunity structures", "framing" and "resource mobilization"—will be employed. Such an endeavour seems suitable for the present analysis, even though its main focus is not a social movement, *stricto sensu*, but the events/counter-summits and especially their participants and the activist network bearing the protests.

By "opportunity structures" we refer to the degree to which groups are able to gain access to power and to influence political decision making, as defined by McAdam,[13] and that describes the social environment that sets the basic conditions for social mobilization. The main focus will lie within two of the four dimensions proposed by that author,[14] "repression" and the "availability of elite-allies", while somewhat neglecting the "relative openness of the political system" and the "stability of elite alignments". In this respect, it appears to be important to underline that those basic parameters for collective action should not be understood as objective "opportunity structures", but rather as *ex-post* analytical tools for the understanding of the actors' preferences. The degree to which those structures influence their decisions depends on how opportunities are perceived as such, or recognized as menace.[15] Consequently, we focus on the activists' perception of opportunities, instead of pursuing an assessment based on objective data or determined by the point of view of analysts. As briefly mentioned in the introduction, the media, or at least the way in which the participants perceived media reporting, had a substantial impact on the identity construction of the activist group. Therefore, as suggested by Balme and Chabanet[16] and others, we also include the media in the "opportunity structures". Mobilization efforts will be analysed via aspects included in the conception of "framing", underlining the importance of the attribution of meaning to social action, whereas its channels and structures will be dealt with under the umbrella of "resource mobilization", focusing on the rational component of collective action. Concerning the approach to "framing", the author will draw, at this point, on the three classic frames:[17] the "diagnostic frame", defining and scandalizing the perceived problem; the "identity frame", creating feelings of togetherness; and the "prognostic frame", articulating goals and perspectives to solve the identified problem.

Our main analytical focus lies within the construction of identity and the creation of an activist network (or "networking in action" to use della Porta's term[18]) during the events; hence, we direct our attention towards *the accumulation of social capital and know-how*. According to Bob Edwards,[19] social capital is a quintessential "sociological concept that has long been identified as both an important resource facilitating social movement mobilization and a significant outcome produced by social movement activities". Following Nahapiet and Ghoshal, we consider social capital to comprise three main components: a structural component, being effective especially on a macro level; a relational component, on a micro level; and a cognitive component, localized on a meso level. For the present analysis, we understand cognitive and relational social capital as an important resource for future mobilization, produced during the events surrounding the NATO Summit in Bucharest and, henceforth, being a self-reinforcing outcome of the protests. The specific literature on symbolic dimensions of outcomes of social movements, which we are locating within the topic of cognitive social capital, encompasses the strengthening of internal solidarity and identity[20] and the creation of new collective identities among members of the activist circle,[21] as well as the importance, for the consolidation of activist groups, of individual and collective experiences during protests. Concerning the latter, Tilly has argued that it is important that groups present themselves as having a (longer) history of actions.[22] The dissemination of stories/narratives about repression and the police, combined with a type of "hero worship", appears to serve mobilization purposes in this regard tremendously. It spurs moral outrage and constitutes, therefore, what Gamson et al. call "injustice frames",[23] often resulting in even more emotionally charged discussions, putting "fire in the belly and iron in the soul".[24] The injustice frame appears to be more effective the more severe the repression,[25] or at least the high(er) the *perceived* degree of repression. Della Porta observes the use of such injustice frames especially during transnational demonstrations, in which the "arrogance of a power that violates the very principle of democracy"—manifesting in the rejection of demonstrators at borders, no-protest zones and so on—is blamed.[26] With their focus on a major international summit, expanded movement restrictions (in Bucharest as well as at the borders), and a (low) number of international participants, the events under analysis clearly qualify for such circumstances. The author considers the accumulation of relational social capital—notably contacts, social ties and access—to be a result/by-product of protests, where large numbers of individuals, often belonging to multiple circles of activists, interact with each other.

From a more interactionist learning theory point of view, we take into account that participants also acquire protest-specific knowledge/know-how during collective actions. Protest participants get to know how to carry out protests, register them, how to demonstrate; thus they gain organizational skills, or they learn how to file complaints against the police or local authorities. The accumulation of social capital and of protest-specific knowledge results in "militant biographies" of people, bound together by common goals and feelings of solidarity, for which protest becomes a part of their daily life. We will demonstrate the evolution of such a militant network during the NATO Summit in Bucharest in the analytical part of the chapter.

As argued above, the media also hold an important role in the dissemination of injustice frames, effective on the meso level, but they also contribute to the *transformation of the public discourse*. Protests often provoke debates, not only about the issue brought forward by the protesters but also about the protest itself,[27] or on even broader subjects such as the right to free expression, the right to protest and so forth.[28] Discussions, whether they depict the protest or the respective mobilization issue in a positive or a negative manner, always increase the visibility, and sometimes even the salience, of collective action or the goals of mobilization. Participation in social mobilization depends on the value the society accords to it,[29] mainly because "collective identities require ratification or affirmation from the outside".[30] How important this outside affirmation was for the "coming of age" of the Bucharest protesters' militant consciousness, for their consolidation as a group and for the development of their *radical habitus* will be covered in the analytical part of this chapter.

## METHODOLOGICAL CONSIDERATIONS

The diversity of analytical angles, briefly introduced in the theoretical part, finds its equivalent in the discussion of method as well: in the absence of methodological dogmatism, in the diversity of research approaches and in the high degree of innovation (even re-invention) of empirical methods.[31] In the widely discussed manual on methods in social movement research, edited by Klandermans and Staggenborg, several authors manifest their appreciation for empirical triangulation of both sources and techniques. Blee and Taylor observe and welcome a growing trend towards combining several data collection techniques,[32] Klandermans and Staggenborg indicate multi-method approaches as the desirable research design for the analysis of social movements,[33] and Snow and Trom promote the usefulness of triangulation of methods.[34] That discussion is not limited to the field of social movement research, with arguments recurring in almost all areas of social sciences.[35] Starting from a critique of the positivist paradigm, most authors claim that triangulation enables the researcher to obtain a better (and deeper) understanding of the analysed case,[36] mainly because the reality is too complex and manifold to be grasped with one single method.[37] The research design of the present study is conceived as a *multi-method design*, using several investigative approaches and multiple data collection techniques. The author draws on the following data sources, all of which were qualitatively interpreted and analysed in a hermeneutic manner: fifteen semi-structured interviews[38] with activists/participants and organizers of the two events were conducted in the summer of 2012; mainstream media content was monitored, including a multitude of militant productions, such as flyers and blogs,[39] as well as a documentary,[40] starring ten crucial participants, most of whom are also included in the interview sample.

## CONTEXT AND EVENTS

To understand the importance of the 2008 protests for the Romanian mobilization environment, one has to take into account the societal conditions for collective action at the time. Nineteen years after the end of the Ceauşescu regime, the political culture is still widely influenced, or even shaped, by communism, resulting in low rates of participation, low social capital indicators and low social mobilization. The 2008 NATO Summit in Romania took place in a social context characterized by very low interest for politics; the European Value Survey (EVS) 2006, for instance, lists Romania as one of the European countries with the highest percentage of respondents (41.3 percent) that are "not at all" interested in politics, and a total of 74.8 percent of the population that is not interested in politics.[41] Especially among young people, the percentage of those who manifested an interest in politics, during a Gallup Romania study, was fairly low: 22 percent.[42] This low preoccupation with politics can also be observed in the frequency of interpersonal discussions having political topics: according to Gallup Romania's Public Opinion Barometer, over 70 percent of the respondents are rarely or never talking about politics.[43]

Concerning civic engagement, studies prior to, or published in, 2008 report a weakness of *social capital indicators* (volunteering, associational membership, trust and bridging ties) in Romania compared to other former communist countries. Lower rates in "unconventional political participation" such as signing petitions, contacting politicians or participating in rallies[44] were also found. Mungiu-Pippidi argues that Romania's political culture is strongly influenced by residual communist attitudes, characteristic for modernization delays.[45]

In regard to *social mobilization*, analysts attest lower levels of political involvement, arguing there is a negative influence from a "non-participatory culture".[46] Consequently, Romania is often considered to be an archetypical example of the scarcity of the civil society in former communist countries.[47] As a result of the destruction of the civic spirit under communism, the high degree of repression that hampered all independent/autonomous activities[48] and the lack of social cohesion after the end of communism, political claim-making reaches very low levels in Romania.[49] Additionally, as in most other post-communist countries, Romania has also witnessed waves of institution-alization and demobilization of protest.[50] The two events to be analysed took place in a societal environment that was far from beneficial for social mobil-ization; instead, the conditions were hostile for anti-militarism, as one orga-nizer of the "Kiss Your Enemy" event states:

> Being a soldier here is something with high status; there are boys from poor places and they want to become soldiers; it is not compulsory here to go to the army, so people go to have a career, a lot of money, you are a hero. Nobody ever said, here, that fighting a war or being a soldier is bad; it is not a public discussion here. . . . And then it doesn't concern us directly; we are not in open conflict with anyone. Why do I care that people die somewhere else?[51]

The main message that both events were carrying, was, accordingly, to put into question the idea of militarism/militarization of contemporary soci-eties. The "Kiss Your Enemy" event aimed to investigate the possibilities for "peaceful alternatives to solve the political and economic tensions in the context of today's world. The key goal of this event was raising aware-ness . . . and encouraging debate on the subject, especially among young people".[52] The focus of the "Anti-NATO Days" was on "questioning Roma-nia's legitimacy to organise the largest NATO summit in history".[53] For the latter one, the emphasis was put on the gap between "the luxury of heads of state and generals" (and their safety) and the costs and lives for/of "the poor people".[54]

The "Kiss Your Enemy" event took place in a big old factory, trans-formed into a club. It had a more entertaining character, offering a music festival, a diversity of workshops, public readings and parties, and it was run by fifteen people; excluding the night party, the event attracted around 250 people. Mainly due to movement restrictions by the police, the "Anti-NATO Days" event was limited to the convergence centre, also an old factory, in the Timpuri Noi neighbourhood. According to activists, this event counted al-most fifty organizers[55] and reached, at its peak, 250 people. The foreign and domestic activists most invested in the cause, who stayed at the centre over-night, numbered around one hundred people. Their main activities, during the day, were the distribution of flyers and small-scale attempts to organize rallies.

As presented in the theoretical framework, in this chapter we borrow from the classical approaches to structure our argumentation on the events. It is necessary to underline that all considerations are from the point of view of the participants, especially for *opportunity structures*, which depend, as argued above, even more on the perspective of those who are involved and on their perception.

The "Kiss Your Enemy" festival managed to reach several elite allies, including NGOs (beyond the organizing NGO, Komunitas), individual members of Parliament, several artists and musicians and even a photographer from the *Times*, who was taking photos of the event. They encountered no repression by state authorities whatsoever, even though, as one of the organizers stated, "There is always some stress if the city hall is involved".[56] The "Anti-NATO Days" organizers indicated a complete absence of elite allies, although some individual members of NGOs participated sporadically because "the event was organised by anarchist groups. So we would look suspicious to any political group or organised structure".[57] One NGO, the Romanian branch of the Helsinki Committee, Apador CH, got involved later, providing some sort of legal aid and advising on issues of access to justice. This event encountered severe repression, in the sense of physical surveillance and wiretapping, culminating in physical aggression and a violent police raid on the convergence centre. The degree of surveillance and the campaign in the media reminded some of the activists of pre-democratic times:

> I was feeling like being back in Soviet Union times, before the police raid, there was propaganda in the press, about anarchists coming from Germany to Bucharest to burn cars etc. I was watching this, and then also later when things happened, I always thought, "that is not possible", nothing of this should have happened; maybe they wanted to set a precedent.[58]

> I never lived under the illusion of a post-89 democracy, but I never imagined that things would remain so unchanged.[59]

The overall situation involving both the media and public authorities was characterized by the director of the Romanian Press Monitoring Agency as an attempt to attack the right to free expression and assembly:

> The video excesses of militia, combined with the unconscious campaign led by politicians and the press, are terrorist acts: They are terrifying every citizen who wants to speak freely against NATO.[60]

Media coverage about Romania's achievement of attracting the NATO Summit, and the disruptive force of "anarchists" threatening it, was impressive. Whether the motivations were political or economic, mainstream media intended to create an image of a very hostile environment, exaggerating the expected threats to public order. Accordingly, the more entertaining event, "Kiss Your Enemy", was almost ignored. Except for some announcements on the radio concerning the musical festival, the event did not happen in the media: no journalists (of the traditional media) attended the final press conference. On the other hand, the more radical activists, the so-called anarchists, were scrutinized closely, especially by mainstream TV stations: for example, there was twenty-four-hour live coverage from the entrance door of the convergence centre on national television. Some activists suspected a media/Secret Service conspiracy: "It was very clear that there were actually people from the secret services, very involved in the editorial teams". [61]

Organizers and activists of both events underline the fact that there is no critical voice in Romania, especially concerning external affairs and militarism. It is the absence of independent media, and the collaboration of media power holders, that we identify as the main *diagnostic frame*:

> In Romania, we don't have any critical voice. When Romania joined the EU, there was not one critical voice, when Romania joined the NATO, when it was proposed that the American radar will be stationed here, there was no critical voice. [62]

> The discourse was: "Wow, they come, the presidents of all countries, they come here, it is great, and they come with nice cars". Bush was here and everybody loved him, there was a rainbow the day he arrived. [63]

As mentioned in the introduction, the two events were not meant to interact. The "Kiss Your Enemy" festival even formulated its character, more or less *ex-negativo*, to the "Anti-NATO Days", constituting its *identity frame* as

> a group that organised something in an abandoned factory and it was with fights and arrests, and we said, we don't want this; we want to reach as many people as possible and to transmit our message. [64]

> And when they organised the anti-NATO event, they didn't call us. And I really wanted to participate and I was like frustrated that they didn't contact us, we were excluded because we were like an NGO and they didn't want to work together with NGOs for such an event. . . . I wanted to get involved because I was active in different scenes and this movement was a completely new area, like anti-militarism, and we had a history together with these groups [the "Anti-NATO Days" organizers], but they didn't include us anymore. . . . And then, me and my colleague, [F] . . . because we were so frustrated that they left us aside, we decided to organise our own event, in parallel with the anarchist protest. [65]

The "Anti-NATO Days" organizers underlined the effects of an entirely hostile environment, focusing on the media, a counter-movement, and especially the interaction with the police, as a base for their collective identity:

> It became very common, five, six days before the NATO Summit, that you would spread leaflets, and the police would just pick you up, with force, and take you to the police station. And you stay there for a few hours, and then they would let you go, no charges, nothing. So it was really weird, if you know that ten of your friends are spreading leaflets, you know that at least five of

them would be at the police station. So for us, this was the big motivation, that we don't agree, that we don't want to have this.[66]

Some people of the far right started a website, called ANTIFA.ro, and they were using this website to name politically active people in Romania; it is a tactic of the right wing in Romania. They were also doing this with Indymedia; they bought the Indymedia.ro domain, and they tried to discredit the actual Indymedia. . . . This website was used to highlight some people that were known as being active, many of them from Indymedia Romania, I was one of them, and then the press, the mainstream press, was actually taking information, personal data from this website, around the anti-NATO events, making names public, spreading false information, like real bullshit, and the idea was that the kids who were attacked by the authorities, were just "troublemakers".[67]

Resulting from the existing problems identified by the activists of both events, the "what to do", or the *prognostic frame*, was oriented towards providing such a critical voice, inspiring others and demonstrating that mobilization against more than simply militarism is possible, even in the most unlikely places:

My motivation was, then, to show those countries that there is actually a mobilization against this, even in Romania, even in Romania, which is part of the countries that are perceived as not so active. . . . I had a chance to see activism in different countries, there is a very big difference between Romania and countries like Germany, Greece, France, Italy, where you have high rates of activism, whereas in post-communist countries activism is not so popular, and that's the reason why the political elites can easily manipulate the people. They just create one image, and there are no people who say "it can be different".[68]

The hope that others will mobilise to organise similar actions. We need events that make us think for a moment and to encourage us to think critically constructive.[69]

With regard to "resource mobilization" big differences between the two events can be observed. One, a professionally organized event, also involving a cultural festival organizer (Yazee), managed to mobilize substantial financial means, thanks to revenues from ticket sales, fund-raising activities and its proximity to the civil society sector. Work relations were professional and formal. The other, "Anti-NATO Days", was largely financed by personal means, most of which were used to pay the rent for the convergence centre.[70] There was no formal organization: most of the discussions were held online, decisions were taken horizontally, based on consensus, organizing capacities were partially provided by international (especially German) activist networks. While for the "Kiss Your Enemy" event we are able to clearly identify the main organizers, who also took many decisions on their own, it is almost impossible to find such persons for the "Anti-NATO Days", even though there are, of course, different degrees of involvement noticeable. Informal organization, inclusiveness and openness were the modalities of coordination: "We tried to make it as legal and open as possible. . . . It was not conceived as something for a closed group; it was not closed at all".[71]

Briefly, the unintended combination of entertainment (movie screenings, concerts, etc.) with political activism (workshops, debates, rallies), combined with the media campaign and the high degree of repression, made two small and isolated events a successful and influential political mobilization.

## FINDINGS

One of the most obvious outcomes of the events surrounding the NATO Summit and the protest was the *evolution of cooperation*, which we consider to be the empirical counterpart to "the accumulation of relational capital". On a group, or meso, level, the growing involvement of the human rights NGO Apador-CH was remarkable. Especially after the police raid of the convergence centre, ties between the "Anti-NATO Days" activist network and Apador-CH grew very quickly:

> Apador-CH, the Romanian branch of the Helsinki Committee, were pretty much involved; they had everyday people coming to them [the arrested], and they made it public, and they said: OK, we will help you by showing you how to file a complaint, to go to court against the fines you received, against the concerned institution, police, gendarmerie etc.[72]

This legal aid, or at least the legal advice provided by this NGO, also took place in the framework of the "Kiss Your Enemy" event, which was used as a platform for this cooperation:

> Talks took place between the people who were arrested and Human Rights advocates . . . S. and M. [S. being one of the most involved "Anti-NATO Days" activists, and M. one of the Komunitas and "Kiss Your Enemy" organizers] both knew some of the people who were arrested. . . . There were also foreigners arrested, who came especially for the event. And we organised the talk after they were free, and they called this lawyer from a Human Rights NGO, Helsinki Committee, she is also a journalist, working with the press monitoring agency [another NGO], they were also a contact of ours.[73]

The two events, and the two groups behind the events—the participants— were mutually encouraging each other, showing support for each other, and, most importantly, surpassing their apparent isolation in an environment that was perceived as hostile, illegitimate and threatening. Thus, the intersections, personal and thematic, between the two presented events increased, resulting in synergy effects for both: The number of spectators and participants at the "Kiss Your Enemy" festival increased due to the high media coverage about the "anarchists", especially after the police raid on the convergence centre. However, the "Anti-NATO Days" activists benefited from the platform provided by the entertaining event, giving them the opportunity to share their stories and to make their voices heard in front of an audience other than the already mobilized participants. On a micro level, the accumulation of contacts and network access was impressive. The total number of activists was (and still is) very low in Romania, and most of the militant activists knew each other prior to the events, as the following quotes of "Anti-NATO Days" activists exemplify:

> Some of us, we knew each other from several protest activities, from concerts or Internet forums dealing with issues we are all interested in. [74]

> Most of it is based on friendship and on relations with friends. Kind of friendship relation . . . so I would say it was mainly friendship based, but the common theme was that everybody was against militarism, we were there because we were against war. [75]

Those friendship relations intensified due to the growing in-group solidarity, even though S. "wouldn't go to grab a beer or talk about her personal problems with most of the people". But the accumulation of relational social capital was not limited to bonding ties; the circle and the diversity of contacts increased (or networked access to personal resources), leading to an overall expansion of the activist network:

> The thing is, we know each other, we have mutual activities, but we don't know each other as friends. . . . And it is with many people like this, the activist scene is just starting to gather up, but we don't really know each other. The next step for me is to build some bridges among groups, and to create a bigger scene. [76]

Also, it is worth mentioning the short-term internationalization of the protest network. The accumulation of relational social capital benefited tremendously from the accumulation of *cognitive social capital*; that aspect demonstrates how self-reinforcing social capital can be. The most crucial element, therefore, is the "injustice frame" employed by the activists; its effectiveness in the construction of collective identity and the strengthening of solidarity, combined with della Porta's "arrogance of power". The fact that the border controls were tightened, that foreign activists were returned at the borders, and that civil rights did not apply anymore in the inner city centre illustrated for the activists a state of hypocrisy in which the ruler does not comply with the ideals they are promoting. This value/practice contradiction bolstered up the militants' perception of an ignorant, arrogant and unjust state of affairs:

> For us, who lived in Bucharest at this time, it was really weird, before the NATO Summit, because Bucharest changed completely, so it was weeks before, it was horrible. They were announcing it like the end of the world. You had to be checked all the time at bigger squares, like Unirii, Casa Poporului, etc. It was like real terror, it was like you couldn't live in your own city. And we thought, "OK, this is really too much".[77]

> I was shocked by the atmosphere in the city. . . . Flags everywhere, Romanian flags, NATO flags, flags of other NATO countries, and the streets deserted, empty of people, empty of cars. What disgusted me the most was the mood of the city—all those preparations and rehearsals. It was as if a theatre play was being staged. It reminded me of Gorbachev's last visit to Romania in 1987— I was a child back then—when people weren't allowed to stroll casually on the streets.[78]

> During the Summit, it felt like I was living in a detention camp, in a police state: police at every fifty metres. A cop would stop me; ID me for fifteen minutes, and then another one a hundred metres later. I was afraid to go out on the streets.[79]

Most of the activists had similar experiences, often together, spurring stories of what actually happened, and "myths" based on personal perception of the events. Especially after the police raid on the convergence centre, repression and police violence became the most important element of the creation/accumulation of cognitive social capital:

> It was really unbelievable. Those who came to the place were kept at a distance by the police, with heads to the wall. . . . *The police had weapons, weapons I have never seen in Bucharest*, guns anyway. The people that were inside, they put them with their faces on the ground, they beat them, they distributed them to five or four police stations, so they separated them, and they kept them for the whole day, and then they were released one by one.[80]

> They started hitting us; they put us to the ground and sprayed us with tear gas. When on the ground, they handcuffed us and continued beating us. It lasted around one hour.[81]

The exaggerated surveillance of activists during the events contributed crucially to the construction of feelings of togetherness, or "us" vs. "them":

> Well you cannot be sure, but I know that we were followed, discreetly. We were also followed afterward, and openly—cars, people following us on the

streets. The phones: for example, the phones had a weird echo. And a lot of people around us had this, and *we all had this feeling.*[82]

The experience of violent police forces had long-term effects, not only on the activists' behaviour but also on their collective identity, strengthening internal solidarity via collective experiences:

> The fear of being followed and spied on continued for many months. Those things we wanted to keep secret, we never said out loud. *We whispered to each other even when we were alone in the room.*

> I was whispering to *those people I knew and trusted.* We weren't conspiring, we had no secrets, but it was a way of controlling our surroundings. . . . I searched for certainty, trying to discern who was sincere, which made everyone vulnerable, but, on the same hand, *some proved to be people I could depend on* and would have the duty to protect.[83]

Apart from the protest/repression-related experiences that were shared, *protest-specific knowledge* was also acquired. The police violence triggered an increased reconsideration towards civil rights and legal requirements for the police. The legal advice provided by Apador-CH led to a wave of complaints against the police and public authorities; the experience of the struggle with them enhanced the activists' understanding of the adversaries' tactics (during the protests, "actual police work", as well as after the protests how authorities try to avoid consequences) and of militant tactics (how to register a rally, how to avoid arrest, etc.). Addressing the public became an important means to deal with the perceived brutality, notably by filming the scenes:

> Some of the cops were sued for their attitude afterward, a lot of people got beaten up, YouTube is full of such videos; they were randomly collecting people in order to bring a group to the police station.[84]

The role of the media before and during the protests cannot be overestimated. The news coverage on the issue, and the fact that certain journalists "bow to the secret services",[85] provoked outrage, especially among activist circles (and in other circles as well). Further intensifying collective solidarity and strengthening conviction to the cause, it likewise led to a *partial transformation of public opinion.* The mere fact that the activist networks were presented to a larger public brought national visibility for the first time and contributed to a discussion about social mobilization in Romania, seldom witnessed before. At the same time, the images of repression led to an increase of the number of participants, and most probably to an increase of potentially mobilizable individuals—that is, those who started to get interested in issues of social activism for the first time:

In December 2007, part of the press began a *manipulation campaign* to create panic, announcing that anarchist groups would be coming during the NATO Summit, and they would manifest themselves through violent actions.

[In order to] challenge the link made by the media between protests and violence, we decided to make a peaceful protest that was connected to every-day gestures.

The general climate was obviously induced by somebody. There were articles in newspapers with names of people who were involved, and it was almost personal harassment, and everything was done with one single purpose: to frighten people and to reduce activism. Actually, partially, they did manage to do it, because we weren't that many in Bucharest. *There were more people joining after the police intervened.*[86]

In sum, the accumulation of social capital and of protest-specific know-how, together with the new social acknowledgement of militant activity and protest, providing an increased social valorization of militantism, resulted in the development of "militant biographies". Those narratives, nourished by "hero profiles" of those who were active, or even got beaten up, constituted the base for a network of activists, with multiple political affiliations, for whom militant political activity is part of their everyday life and of their self-conception—a network of activists that is close to what Crossley calls a "radical habitus".[87]

## CONCLUSION

The three main outcomes of the 2008 events, identified in this chapter, ena-bled the protesters to constitute themselves as the "first generation of post-revolution activists". To quote F. of Komunitas, "There was nobody before. There are no older anarchists". If Romania is considered a country that is still located in a transition period, so is the status of social mobilization.

Sometimes you can fight for a common cause, but your points of view are completely different. But that's Romania right now, we are all looking to find our way, things are not very clear in this moment. The (activist) scene is very small, I mean it appeared in the past few years. . . . In many ways, *we were like pioneers*, like we were opening doors in various areas of activism, always doing the first event or protest on all types of what we perceived as problemat-ic issues in Romania.[88]

One of the NGOs that is really big now was a very small group of people from Rosia, Montana, that got politicised, and they did a lot of pure activism, direct actions even at that time. But I would say that this kind of more informal group, alternative group, completely non-institutional, *this is a newer phenomenon, of this present generation.*[89]

In this chapter we have argued that the NATO Summit in Bucharest was a turning point in social mobilization in Romania. According to an online expert survey, conducted by the author, anti-militarism is the least visible militant activity in Romania. The answer to the question raised in the title of this chapter, whether the protests were paving the way for anti-militarism, is clearly "no". They did, however, pave the way for future social mobilization in Romania. The three most crucial outcomes of the protests, and the situation of increased mobilization, constitute the beginning of *sustained* interactions of an activist network in Romania. The impact of those activist networks was still visible several years later, during the anti-austerity protests in 2012 and the mobilization of the "Salvati Rosia Montana" movement, in which *all* actors of both of the events analysed here participated.

## REFERENCES

Amenta, Edwin, and Michael P. Young. "Making an Impact: Conceptual and Methodological Implications of the Collective Goods Criterion". In *How Social Movements Matter*, edited by Marco Giugni, Doug McAdam, and Charles Tilly, 22–41. Minneapolis: University of Minnesota Press, 1999.

Badescu, Gabriel, Paul E. Sum, and Eric M. Uslaner. "Civil Society Development and Democratic Values in Romania and Moldova". *East European Politics & Societies* 18, no. 2 (2004): 316–41.

Balme, Richard, and Didier Chabanet. *European Governance and Democracy: Power and Protest in the EU.* Lanham, MD: Rowman & Littlefield, 2008.

Blee, Kathleen M., and Verta Taylor. "Semi-Structured Interviewing in Social Movement Research". In *Methods of Social Movement Research*, edited by Bert Klandermans and Suzanne Staggenborg. Minneapolis: University of Minnesota Press, 2002.

Chazel, François. *Du pouvoir à la contestation.* Paris: Librairie Générale de Droit et de Jurisprudence, 2003.

Crossley, Nick. "From Reproduction to Transformation: Social Movement Fields and the Radical Habitus". *Theory, Culture and Society* 20, no. 6 (2003): 43–68.

Crowther, William. "Romania". In *The Handbook of Political Change in Eastern Europe*, edited by Sten Berglund, Joakim Ekman, and Frank H. Aarebrot, 363–415. Northampton, UK: Edward Elgar, 2004.

Denzin, Norman K., and Yvonna S. Lincoln. "Introduction: The Discipline and Practice of Qualitative Research". In *The Sage Handbook of Qualitative Research*, edited by Norman K. Denzin and Yvonna S. Lincoln, 1–32. Thousand Oaks, CA: Sage, 2011.

della Porta, Donatella. "Protest, Protesters, and Protest Policing: Public Discourses in Italy and Germany from the 1960s to the 1980s". In *How Social Movements Matter*, edited by Marco Giugni, Doug McAdam, and Charles Tilly, 66–96. Minneapolis: University of Minnesota Press, 1999.

della Porta, Donatella. "Eventful Protests, Global Conflicts". *Distinktion* 17 (2008): 27–56.

della Porta, Donatella, and Olivier Fillieule. "Policing Social Protest". In *The Blackwell Compendium to Social Movements*, edited by David A. Snow, Sarah A. Soule, and Hanspeter Kriesi, 221–41. Malden, MA: Blackwell, 2004.

Edwards, Bob. "Social Capital and Social Movements". In *The Wiley-Blackwell Encyclopaedia of Social and Political Movements*, edited by David Snow, Donatella della Porta, Bert Klandermans, and Doug McAdam, 1173–76. Oxford: Blackwell, 2013.

Fillieule, Olivier, Eric Agrikoliansky, and Isabelle Sommier. "Introduction". In *Penser les mouvements sociaux: Conflits sociaux et contestations dans les sociétés contemporaines*, edited by Olivier Fillieule, Eric Agrikoliansky, and Isabelle Sommier, 7–18. Paris: La Decouverte, 2010.

Fillieule, Olivier, and Bernard Pudal. "Sociologie du militantisme: Problématisation et déplacement des méthodes d'enquête". In *Penser les mouvements sociaux: Conflits sociaux et contéstations dans les sociétés contemporaines*, edited by Olivier Fillieule, Eric Agrikoliansky, and Isabelle Sommier, 163–84. Paris: La Decouverte, 2010.

The Gallup Organization Romania. *Being Young in Romania*, 2004. www.gallup.ro/english/poll/releases/pr050418/pr050418.html.

The Gallup Organization Romania. *Public Opinion Barometer*, 2006. www.gallup.ro/english/poll/releases/pr060705/pr060705.html.

Gamson, William A. *Talking Politics*. Cambridge: Cambridge University Press, 1992.

Gamson, William A., Bruce Fireman, and Steven Rytina. *Encounters with Unjust Authority.* Homewood, UK: Dorsey Press, 1982.

Giugni, Marco. "Introduction: How Social Movements Matter: Past Research, Present Problems, Future Developments". In *How Social Movements Matter*, edited by Marco Giugni, Doug McAdam, and Charles Tilly, xiii–xxxiii. Minneapolis: University of Minnesota Press, 1999.

Klandermans, Bert, and Suzanne Staggenborg. "Introduction". In *Methods of Social Movement Research*, edited by Bert Klandermans and Suzanne Staggenborg. Minneapolis: University of Minnesota Press, 2002.

Levy, Jack S. "Qualitative Methods and Cross-Method Dialogue in Political Science". *Comparative Political Studies* 40, no. 2 (2007): 196–214.

McAdam, Doug. "Conceptual Origins, Current Problems, Future Directions". In *Comparative Perspectives on Social Movements: Political Opportunities, Mobilizing Structures, and Cultural Framings*, edited by Doug McAdam, John D. McCarthy, and Mayer N. Zald, 23–40. Cambridge: Cambridge University Press, 1996.

McAdam, Doug, Sidney Tarrow, and Charles Tilly. *Dynamics of Contention*. Cambridge: Cambridge University Press, 2001.

Mondak, Jeffrey J., and Adam F. Gearing. "Civic Engagement in a Post-Communist State". *Political Psychology* 19, no. 3 (1998): 615–37.

Mungiu-Pippidi, Alina. "Deconstructing Balkan Particularism: The Ambiguous Social Capital of Southeastern Europe". *Southeast European and Black Sea Studies* 5, no. 1 (2005): 49–68.

Mungiu-Pippidi, Alina. "Romania: Fatalistic Political Cultures Revisited". In *Democracy and Political Culture in Eastern Europe*, edited by Hans-Dieter Klingenmann, Dieter Fuchs, and Jan Zielonka, 308–35. New York: Routledge, 2006.

Richardson, Joanne, and Nadia Len (Producers). *Reconstruction*. Documentary film. 2009. D Media, Anti-NATO Initiative 2008, and h.arta. http://subsol.c3.hu/joanne/video_reconstruction.html.

Rossi, Federico M. "From the Coup to the Escalation of Violence: The Transition to Democracy in Romania". COSMOS Working Papers 2012/2013. http://cosmos.eui.eu/Documents/Publications/WorkingPapers/2012WP13COSMOS.pdf.

Rucht, Dieter, and Friedhelm Neidhardt. "Soziale Bewegungen und kollektive Aktionen". In *Lehrbuch der Soziologie*, edited by Hans Joas, 533–56. Frankfurt/Main: Campus Verlag, 2001.

Sadowski, Christine M. "Autonomous Groups as Agents of Democratic Change in Communist and Post-Communist Eastern Europe". In *Political Culture and Democracy in Developing Countries*, edited by Larry Diamond, 155–87. Boulder, CO: Lynne Rienner, 1993.

Snow, David, and Leno Anderson. "Researching the Homeless: The Characteristic Features and Virtues of the Case Study". In *A Case for the Case Study*, edited by Joe R. Feagin, Anthony M. Orum, and Gideon Sjoberg, 148–73. Chapel Hill: University of North Carolina Press, 1991.

Snow, David A., and Danny Trom. "The Case Study and the Study of Social Movements". In *Methods of Social Movement Research*, edited by Bert Klandermans and Suzanne Staggenborg, 146–72. Minneapolis: University of Minnesota Press, 2002.

Tilly, Charles. "Conclusion: From Interactions to Outcomes in Social Movements". In *How Social Movements Matter*, edited by Marco Giugni, Doug McAdam, and Charles Tilly, 253–70. Minneapolis: University of Minnesota Press, 1999.

Voicu, Bogdan. "Riscurile politicilor de dezvoltare bazate pe formarea capitalului social". *Sociologie Românească* 1 (2008): 11–25.

Voicu, Bogdan, and Basina Tanja. "Social Capital and Civic Participation in Ukraine and Romania". In *Social Sciences Perspectives on the European Postcommunist Societies*, edited by Bogdan Voicu and Horatiu Rusu, 75–96. Sibiu, Romania: Psihomedia, 2005.

von Zweck, Claudia, Margo Paterson, and Wendy Pentland. "The Use of Hermeneutics in a Mixed Method Design". *Qualitative Report* 13, no. 1 (2008): 116–34.

# NOTES

1. According to the Romanian Ministry of External Affairs (www.mae.ro/en/node/2079).

2. ActiveWatch/Agentia de Monitorizare a Presei, *Freeex Program: Media Freedom in Romania*, 2008, p. 14. Please consult the whole document for a more detailed description of the politically charged media coverage on the subject and how it went hand in hand with public authorities' reactions (http://activewatch.ro/Assets/Upload/files/Freeexeng_2008_dtp(1).pdf).

3. R., a Romanian Anti-NATO activist in an interview conducted by the author in 2012.

4. Mircea Toma, director of ActiveWatch in an editorial on indymedia.org (http://admin. romania.indymedia.org/ro/2008/04/2519.shtml).

5. Leaving aside the Targu Jiu miners, especially known for the so-called mineriades in the early 1990s, a movement that cannot be considered to be "post-revolution" due to the continuity of its protest history (organizing a major strike in the 1977) and benefiting from their longstanding pre-1990s tradition of syndicalism.

6. Donatella della Porta, "Eventful Protests, Global Conflicts", *Distinktion* 17 (2008): 27–56.

7. Marco Giugni, "Introduction: How Social Movements Matter: Past Research, Present Problems, Future Developments", in *How Social Movements Matter*, ed. Marco Giugni, Doug McAdam, and Charles Tilly (Minneapolis: University of Minnesota Press, 1999), xiii–xxxiii.

8. F., an activist of the Romanian NGO Kommunitas, which provided organizational resources for the "Kiss Your Enemy—A Day of Creativity and Action" event, in an interview conducted by the author in 2012.

9. As the official banner, and several flyers stated (see, for instance, http://www.gipfelsoli. org/Home/Bukarest_2008/4955.html).

10. della Porta, "Eventful Protests", 29.

11. Van Stekelenburg and Klandermans argue that social capital is a crucial concept in the analysis of social embeddedness and, henceforth, of movement participation, because it enables the researcher to take the social context into account. Referring to Nahaphiet and Ghoshal (1998), they distinguish three components of participation-relevant social capital: a structural, a relational and a cognitive component. (See Jaquelien van Stekelenburg and Bert Klandermans, "The Social Psychology of Protest", in *sociopedia.isa*, 2010 (http://www.surrey.ac.uk/politics/ research/researchareasofstaff/isppsummeracademy/instructors/Social%20Psychology%20of% 20Protest,%20Van%20Stekelenburg%20%26%20Klandermans.pdf.) As argued below, under the topic "accumulation of social capital and know-how", the author considered the relational and the cognitive component of social capital to be the most conducive aspects for the purpose of this chapter.

12. Olivier Fillieule, Eric Agrikoliansky, and Isabelle Sommier, "Introduction", in *Penser les mouvements sociaux: Conflits sociaux et contestations dans les sociétés contemporaines*, ed. Olivier Fillieule, Eric Agrikoliansky, and Isabelle Sommier (Paris: La Decouverte, 2010), 8.

13. Doug McAdam, "Conceptual Origins, Current Problems, Future Directions", in *Comparative Perspectives on Social Movements: Political Opportunities, Mobilizing Structures, and Cultural Framings*, ed. Doug McAdam, John D. McCarthy, and Mayer N. Zald (Cambridge: Cambridge University Press, 1996), 23.

14. Ibid., 27.

15. Doug McAdam, Sidney Tarrow, and Charles Tilly, *Dynamics of Contention* (Cambridge: Cambridge University Press, 2001), 43; François Chazel, *Du pouvoir à la contestation* (Paris: Librairie Générale de Droit et de Jurisprudence, 2003), 124.

16. Richard Balme and Didier Chabanet, *European Governance and Democracy: Power and Protest in the EU* (Lanham, MD: Rowman & Littlefield, 2008), 31.

17. Dieter Rucht and Friedhelm Neidhardt, "Soziale Bewegungen und kollektive Aktionen", in *Lehrbuch der Soziologie*, ed. Hans Joas (Frankfurt/Main: Campus Verlag, 2001), 551. (They refer to Snow and Benford [1988] and Gamson [1999].)

18. della Porta, "Eventful Protests", 34.

19. Bob Edwards, "Social Capital and Social Movements", in *The Wiley-Blackwell Encyclopaedia of Social and Political Movements*, ed. David Snow, Donatella della Porta, Bert Klandermans, and Doug McAdam (Oxford: Blackwell, 2013), 1173. (Emphasis added.)

20. Giugni, "Introduction: How Social Movements Matter", xiii.

21. Edwin Amenta and Michael P. Young, "Making an Impact: Conceptual and Methodological Implications of the Collective Goods Criterion", in *How Social Movements Matter*, ed. Marco Giugni, Doug McAdam, and Charles Tilly (Minneapolis: University of Minnesota Press, 1999), 34ff.

22. Charles Tilly, "Conclusion: From Interactions to Outcomes in Social Movements", in *How Social Movements Matter*, ed. Marco Giugni, Doug McAdam, and Charles Tilly (Minneapolis: University of Minnesota Press, 1999), 263.

23. William A. Gamson, Bruce Fireman, and Steven Rytina, *Encounters with Unjust Authority* (Homewood, UK: Dorsey Press, 1982).

24. William A. Gamson, *Talking Politics* (Cambridge: Cambridge University Press), 32, cited in Sidney Tarrow, *Power in Movement: Social Movements and Contentious Politics*, 2nd ed. (Cambridge: Cambridge University Press, 1998), 111.

25. Donatella della Porta and Olivier Fillieule, "Policing Social Protest", in *The Blackwell Compendium to Social Movements*, ed. David A. Snow, Sarah A. Soule, and Hanspeter Kriesi (Malden, MA: Blackwell, 2004), 233.

26. della Porta, "Eventful Protests", 44.

27. Donatella della Porta, "Protest, Protesters, and Protest Policing: Public Discourses in Italy and Germany from the 1960s to the 1980s", in *How Social Movements Matter*, ed. Marco Giugni, Doug McAdam, and Charles Tilly (Minneapolis: University of Minnesota Press, 1999), 68.

28. Giugni, "Introduction: How Social Movements Matter", xxi.

29. Olivier Fillieule and Bernard Pudal, "Sociologie du militantisme: Problématisation et déplacement des méthodes d'enquête", in *Penser les mouvements sociaux: Conflits sociaux et contestations dans les sociétés contemporaines*, ed. Olivier Fillieule, Eric Agrikoliansky, and Isabelle Sommier (Paris: La Decouverte, 2010), 179.

30. Amenta and Young, "Making an Impact", 35.

31. Bert Klandermans and Suzanne Staggenborg, "Introduction", in *Methods of Social Movement Research*, ed. Bert Klandermans and Suzanne Staggenborg (Minneapolis: University of Minnesota Press, 2002), ix–xx.

32. Kathleen M. Blee and Verta Taylor, "Semi-Structured Interviewing in Social Movement Research", in Klandermans and Staggenborg, *Methods*, 111.

33. Klandermans and Staggenborg, "Introduction", xv.

34. David A. Snow and Danny Trom, "The Case Study and the Study of Social Movements", in Klandermans and Staggenborg, *Methods*, 147.

35. Jack S. Levy, "Qualitative Methods and Cross-Method Dialogue in Political Science", *Comparative Political Studies* 40, no. 2 (2007): 196f. Mahoney makes a similar observation for all subfields (hereby included social movement studies) of political science (James Mahoney, "Qualitative Methodology and Comparative Politics", *Comparative Political Studies* 40, no. 2 [2007]: 122f).

36. Norman K. Denzin and Yvonna S. Lincoln, "Introduction: The Discipline and Practice of Qualitative Research", in *The Sage Handbook of Qualitative Research*, ed. Norman K. Denzin and Yvonna S. Lincoln (Thousand Oaks, CA: Sage, 2011), 5f; Claudia von Zweck,

Margo Paterson, and Wendy Pentland, "The Use of Hermeneutics in a Mixed Method Design", *Qualitative Report* 13, no. 1 (2008): 116–34.

37. David Snow and Leno Anderson, "Researching the Homeless: The Characteristic Features and Virtues of the Case Study", in *A Case for the Case Study*, ed. Joe R. Feagin, Anthony M. Orum, and Gideon Sjoberg (Chapel Hill: University of North Carolina Press, 1991), 158.

38. One has to keep in mind that the militant scene in Romania was—and still is—very small, compared to other countries, encompassing a low number of activists in general. Consequently, the number of people actively involved in the organization of the events was limited.

39. Such as gipfelsoli, contradoxa and indymedia.

40. *Reconstruction*, documentary produced by Joanne Richardson and Nadia Len, a collaboration between D Media, Anti-NATO Initiative 2008 and h.arta, 2009 (http://subsol.c3.hu/joanne/video_reconstruction.html).

41. EVS, 2006; S. 11, zit. nach: www.gesis.org/EN/data_service/evs/ .

42. The Gallup Organization Romania, *Being Young in Romania*, 2004, www.gallup.ro/english/poll/releases/pr050418/pr050418.html, p. 12.

43. The Gallup Organization Romania, *Public Opinion Barometer*, 2006, www.gallup.ro/english/poll/releases/pr060705/pr060705.html, p. 56.

44. Jeffrey J. Mondak and Adam F. Gearing, "Civic Engagement in a Post-Communist State", *Political Psychology* 19, no. 3 (1998): 615–37; Alina Mungiu-Pippidi, "Deconstructing Balkan Particularism: The Ambiguous Social Capital of Southeastern Europe", *Southeast European and Black Sea Studies* 5, no. 1 (2005): 49–68; Gabriel Badescu, Paul E. Sum, and Eric M. Uslaner, "Civil Society Development and Democratic Values in Romania and Moldova", *East European Politics & Societies* 18, no. 2 (2004): 316–41; Bogdan Voicu, "Riscurile politicilor de dezvoltare bazate pe formarea capitalului social", *Sociologie Românească*, no. 1 (2008): 11–25.

45. Alina Mungiu-Pippidi, "Romania: Fatalistic Political Cultures Revisited", in *Democracy and Political Culture in Eastern Europe*, ed. Hans-Dieter Klingenmann, Dieter Fuchs, and Jan Zielonka (New York: Routledge, 2006), 316ff.

46. Bogdan Voicu and Tanja Basina, "Social Capital and Civic Participation in Ukraine and Romania", in *Social Sciences Perspectives on the European Postcommunist Societies*, ed. Bogdan Voicu and Horatiu Rusu (Sibiu, Romania: Psihomedia, 2005), 75–96.

47. William Crowther, "Romania", in *The Handbook of Political Change in Eastern Europe*, ed. Sten Berglund, Joakim Ekman, and Frank H. Aarebrot (Northampton, UK: Edward Elgar, 2004), 363.

48. Christine M. Sadowski, "Autonomous Groups as Agents of Democratic Change in Communist and Post-Communist Eastern Europe", in *Political Culture and Democracy in Developing Countries*, ed. Larry Diamond (Boulder, CO: Lynne Rienner, 1993), 155–87.

49. Tudor Pitulac, "Common Economic Challenges, Similar Political Solutions, Different Social Reactions in Times of Crises: Barriers against the Structured Social Movements in Romania", in *Anuarul Universitatii "Petre Andrei" din Iasi* (Yearbook "Petre Andrei" University of Iasi), *Fascicula: Asistenta Sociala, Sociologie, Psihologie* (Fascicle: social work, sociology, psychology), no. 7 (2011): 41–60; Sadowski, "Autonomous Groups", 155–87.

50. Frederico M. Rossi, "From the Coup to the Escalation of Violence: The Transition to Democracy in Romania", in COSMOS Working Papers 2012/2013, http://cosmos.eui.eu/Documents/Publications/WorkingPapers/2012WP13COSMOS.pdf, p. 18.

51. F., activist and organizer of the Romanian NGO Komunitas during an interview conducted in the summer of 2012.

52. From the "What We Want" section of the "Kiss Your Enemy" blog (http://www.kissyourenemy.blogspot.fr/).

53. From the "Purpose" section of one of the "Anti-NATO Days" blogs (http://contra-doxa.com).

54. Radu Salahoru (the self-proclaimed leader of the protests, who unfortunately rejected several invitations for an interview with the author) on http://contra-doxa.com.

55. Here as well, it is worth mentioning that the degree of involvement strongly differed from one activist to the other.

56. F., of Komunitas.

57. G., an Anti-NATO militant and active organizer of the "Anti-NATO Days" during an interview conducted in the summer of 2012.

58. Ibid.

59. Ro., an "Anti-NATO Days" activist in the documentary *Reconstruction*.

60. Mircea Toma, "Terorismul antiterorismului", April 2008, http://lists.indymedia.org/pipermail/imc-romania/2008-April/0401-io.html.

61. R., an "Anti-NATO Days" activist during an interview conducted in the summer of 2008. The involvement of members of the Romanian Secret Service (SRI) in the production of news is a broader discussion that is not limited to the 2008 events alone.

62. S., an "Anti-NATO Days" activist during an interview conducted in the summer of 2008.

63. F., of Kommunitas.

64. Ibid.

65. K., activist and organizer of the Romanian NGO Kommunitas during an interview conducted in the summer of 2012.

66. S., of the "Anti-NATO Days".

67. R., of the "Anti-NATO Days".

68. G., of the "Anti-NATO Days".

69. F., of Komunitas.

70. According to the Romanian press agency Mediafax, the rent amounted to 2,800 lei (approximately 750 euros) (http://www.mediafax.ro/english/anti-NATO-militants-lease-space-in-bucharest-factory-to-protest-security-intervenes-2509282).

71. S., of the "Anti-NATO Days".

72. Ibid.

73. F., of Komunitas.

74. R., in the documentary.

75. S., during the interview.

76. M., of Komunitas.

77. S., of the "Anti-NATO Days".

78. R.M., in the documentary.

79. R.S., in the documentary.

80. S., of the "Anti-NATO Days". All emphases in interview quotations added by the author to highlight aspects crucial for the argumentation.

81. G., in the documentary.

82. G., during the interview.

83. R. and M., in the documentary.

84. S., during the interview.

85. R.M., in the documentary

86. R.M., S. and G., in the documentary.

87. Nick Crossley, "From Reproduction to Transformation: Social Movement Fields and the Radical Habitus", *Theory, Culture and Society* 20, no. 6 (2003): 43–68.

88. M., of Komunitas.

89. R., of the "Anti-NATO Days", during the interview.

*Part II*

# Identity, Embodiment and Categorization

Identity work is central to our sense of agency, our sense of community, and the limits of both in the face of increasing Habermasian instrumentality.[1] We create our identities in the social webs that surround us (as Geertz[2] famously put it). There is no such thing as a self that exists untouched and unaltered by our social and cultural ties. As children, we learn the rules of identity in our cultures through our parents, others in our family or our teachers and elders. We believe the stories taught to us about what we are, which community is ours, what religion we believe, what is the "correct" way of being in terms of caste, class, gender, sexuality, ethnicity. As we grow older the mythology of our particular social-identity formation is lost, and we believe that who we are is a natural product of some internal construction of "mind".

As we become young adults we do identity work in two ways. First, we conform to what others around us do, so that we do not stand out of the crowd. That is, we embody norms and values that belong to our culture, community and society—and we enforce the boundaries of belonging that make others become the Other. Secondly, we might use our agency, or our perceived agency, to reject those norms and values to create identities that are sub-cultural, countercultural or counter-hegemonic. The first way of making social identity is ultimately one that is hegemonic, exclusionary and narrow. In modernity, such bonds of belonging and conformity are reduced to the role of creating pliant workers in a rationalized society. In this century, we can see that this form of identity making fits with the increasing commodification of culture, of leisure and of events: this is the identity making of flag waving and national anthems, of closing borders and limiting human rights. The second way of identity making is deliberately communicative and radical in its nature. To choose to stand against the norms and values of the mainstream is to challenge patriarchy, hegemony, nationalism and the power of elites, be they religious leaders, feudal landlords or transnational capitalists. This second way of identity making is seen in the decisions to become radical activists, the moral and political debates at work in turning events into forms of protest, and leisure into social activism. This is the identity work that is identified and articulated by postmodern and post-structural theorists such as Butler, Debord and Deleuze, the identity making of humans consciously rejecting the mainstream and transgressing borders. In both forms of identity making, embodiment and categorization are at work, making individuals and imaginary communities of belonging and exclusion.

The concepts of identity, embodiment and categorization, then, play a substantial part in the conceptualization of cultural, leisure and sports events. In this section the authors are exploring how events and protests can become the focus of a collective of people sharing similar worldviews and perceived backgrounds, creating an imaginary community that is the amalgam of perceived values within particular local and global spaces, and invented traditions based on present-centred readings of the various communities' "real" origins. How individual identity is expressed is defined by the boundaries of those imaginary communities, which are created by insiders privy to tacit knowledge. However, the imaginary community is dynamic, and the boundaries are contested and maintained by a constant tension of production and reaffirmation. In events and leisure, we can see that this identity making around imaginary communities is at the heart of struggles over the control of events, the commodification of leisure and the idea that events can be transformed through protest. Mega events such as the soccer World Cup reaffirm hegemonic masculinity, global capitalism and "traditional" nationalism, but campaigns against them, such as the protests in Brazil ahead of the 2014 World Cup, give activists a sense of purpose and a strong sense of belonging. Imaginary communities, like events, and like leisure, can be communicative, the product of agency and democratic discourse between equal agents, or they can be instrumental and hence exclusionary.

This section will look at how these concepts can be applied to enrich our understanding of protests as events, events as protest and activism as leisure. The chapters in this section draw on a broad range of events, spaces and campaigns to show how the struggle over being given an identity versus choosing an identity is at the heart of activism and radical agency. In events and leisure, we choose to be, we choose to act communicatively, while at the same time we are defined and constrained by hegemonic powers that use events and leisure to keep us under control. So activists may find true identity and belonging in the midst of actions and protests, a space and a web of significance that gives them meaning and purpose. But in wider society such political agency is defined as marginal, subversive and dangerous. So activists have their agency over their own identity making taken from them by government agencies, the mainstream media and transnational corporations. This can be seen in the news coverage surrounding any protest. For the people at the protest, there is a sense of solidarity and pride, a feeling one's agency is being put to good use to change the world. There is the identity work of being an activist, being a radical, surrounded by others who approve of our identity. But in the news coverage that follows such a protest, the collegiality of the march is replaced by the fear of the mob, the outrage from "decent citizens" about the "antisocial behaviour" of the anonymous rioters, and the only debate is between politicians and bureaucrats over how tough they want the police and the courts to be on the activists they have arrested.

## REFERENCES

Geertz, Clifford. "Thick description: Towards an Interpretive Theory of Culture". *The Interpretation of Cultures*, by Clifford Geertz. London: Hutchinson, 1975.

Habermas, Jürgen. *The Theory of Communicative Action, Vol. 1: Reason and the Rationalization of Society*. Cambridge: Polity, 1986.

Habermas, Jürgen. *The Theory of Communicative Action, Vol. 2: Lifeworld and System: A Critique of Functional Reason*. Cambridge: Polity, 1992.

## NOTES

1. Jürgen Habermas, *The Theory of Communicative Action, Vol. 1: Reason and the Rationalization of Society* (Cambridge: Polity, 1986), *The Theory of Communicative Action, Vol. 2: Lifeworld and System: A Critique of Functional Reason* (Cambridge: Polity, 1992).

2. Clifford Geertz, "Thick Description: Towards an Interpretive Theory of Culture", in *The Interpretation of Cultures*, by Clifford Geertz (London: Hutchinson, 1975), 3–30.

*Chapter Five*

# Academic-Activism(s) in Urban Resistances

*Pioneers or Obstacles for a Common Ground*

Nezihe Başak Ergin

Urbanism, an ideology of the state which gains the power of using the myth of technocracy, was mainly utilized in Istanbul in the 2000s for so-called "socio-spatial problems" and the "risk of earthquake".[1] Urban land decisions and related transformations in Istanbul have been marked by the drastic change from populist to neo-liberal practices.[2] This ideology is realized through demolition and dislocation in *gecekondu*,[3] historical and many other neighbourhoods, which results in new deprivations and dispossessions with an economic and social aggravation of existing inequalities. The geographical relocation of poverty as conceptualized by Kuyucu and Ünsal becomes principally a displacement and dispossession of largely the poor while Istanbul is branded with the expulsion and eradication of everyone or everything else which does not fit the brand,[4] such as the "European Capital of Culture", and projected as the centre of finance through "mega-projects". These policies transform the cities from "Spaces of Hope" to "Spaces of Hopelessness" for those who live and try to survive in the city.[5] Multiple claims against these projects but for urban commons[6] have challenged ways of doing politics. This chapter deals with the literature on academic-activisms and thoughts on different forms of involvement and engagement in Istanbul which form and affect the dynamics of the urban opposition in Istanbul. Leading and forming various ways of resistances, academic-activists in urban resistance in Istanbul still try to find effective forms of solidarities in urban oppositional groups and organizations and produce discourses and ways from various positions, objectives, changing organizational and tactical repertoires, and strategies. The study considers the significance and pioneering roles of academic-activists as well as tensions between them and other activists, in different respects mainly related to their positions and to their conflicting views and practices and experiences of resistances. The main problematic behind potentialities and obstacles of urban opposition in Istanbul rises from the fact that there are divisions along different groups of academics. On the other hand, they inform and also learn from each other, which in time leads to new types of organizations with different types of activisms including attempts of alternative plans, critical reports and statements or new organizations.

This research studies different views of academic-activists on these protest events from in-depth interviews[7] with academic-activists as well as intellectuals in urban opposition in Istanbul. The self-reflexive, political and academic concerns[8] of the study led to solidarity and participatory action research[9] to reveal commonalities and to ask what needed to be studied and written on. The study discusses ideas and experiences of the leading activist-academicians active in the urban opposition and their roles in grassroots oppositions as well as alliances in terms of common and conflicting positions that still keep changing with time.

## THOUGHTS ON PARTICIPATORY AND SOLIDARITY ACTION RESEARCH: AN INNER GUIDELINE ON THE PATH OF ACADEMIC-ACTIVISM(S)

Participatory action research with the potential to reduce the distance and co-develop emancipatory theory and action with active engagement could also result in "giving-up activism" on uncommon ground by making possible connections and extending places for the commons.[10] Activist-led research history dates back to the cultural and political turns of the 1990s.[11] On the other hand, according to the general and over-imposed political and scientific view, the academic's primary role is as the producer of knowledge, not as activist. On these grounds, the question Blomley[12] asks is crucial: How do academics interact with activists and be activists themselves?

Blomley also questions "spaces of activism" in which academic-activism occurs for the possibilities of radical politics based on dialogical connections and encounters with others. Blomley advocates for a "third space" located between academia and activism, which is in fact a space of continual flux and movement.[13] Routledge states that all these are attempts between theory and practice to make visible socio-spatial processes which reproduce inequalities.[14] The intellectual has dual and dueling agendas for Bourdieu, as cited in Cushman: the intellectual must belong to the autonomous intellectual world by using the competence gained from the intellectual field in the political action.[15] Yet, as a praxis research rather than an oppressive relationship between the researcher and those studied, activist research mainly advocates the notions of reciprocity and dialogue between scholars and those whom with knowledge is made.

By referring to Burawoy, Fuller considers another related concept, which is "public geographies" as a flexible and engaging entity whose meaning and success comes from its interactive and engaging characteristics.[16] For Burawoy, reflexive knowledge has its critical academic audience and an extra-academic audience: questions about "knowledge for whom?" and "knowledge for what?" define the main character of sociology as a discipline.[17] Activist, participatory and public geographies must be beyond the dualism of the academic as the "expert researcher" and activist as the "researched community".[18] To create change is only possible with activity and involvement in a self-evaluated and reflexive process about the positional issues.

Chatterton, Hodkinson, and Pickerill[19] propose "Autonomous Geographies" as virtual, local and translocal spaces which question the laws and social norms of society, and as a creative desire to constitute noncapitalist, collective forms of politics, identity, and citizenship in capitalist, individualized and consumption-oriented cities. They state, "We need to reject the false distinction between academia and wider society in conceptualisations of valid sites of struggle and knowledge production, and to find ways to research and engage collectively and politically, rather than individually".[20] Accordingly, "solidarity action research" for Chatterton, Hodkinson and Pickerill is an approach influenced by traditions of research militancy of the Italian and Argentinian autonomist aims to "work horizontally and in solidarity with groups, co-produce outputs relevant to the resistance movement and not to academia, funders or our careers".[21] Activist research implies a common identification of problems and desires through using research encounters for solidarity and direct forms of democracy in order to co-produce contextually relevant and useful knowledge: Solidarity Action Research.[22]

To create participation and collaborative research with and for the individuals from the bottom up as participatory geographies[23] and change the world with activity and involvement in a self-reflexive process could be cited as some of the principal objectives of this approach. Participatory research can be defined as research undertaken collaboratively with and for individuals, groups, and communities in order to create an emancipatory potential, especially for excluded groups. Askins says that the activist-academic must consider the role of experiences and emotions—more exactly "emotional becomings"—central in activism as well as in learning, teaching and doing research in a self-reflexive way.[24]

No research methods are inherently liberatory and reflexive; however, being an activist involved in an opposition movement makes it possible to raise all the research questions from the field. Participatory research must be held with priority in practice, rather than knowledge production distinguished by the aims of multiple participation, practical results, changes and related knowledge production. Mason emphasizes the formation of mutual solidarities, which is not a smooth process due to the antagonisms rising from differences as well as agreements and political determinations.[25] Chatterton, Fuller and Routledge caution that activism and Participatory Action Research are not the same thing: it is necessary to ask ourselves how we can create spaces and conversations extending past and beyond our research encounters and open up universities and academic research.[26]

## ACADEMIC-ACTIVISTS AND SOLIDARITIES AND TENSIONS IN, FOR AND BEYOND ISTANBUL?

This study was mainly based on a participatory action research attempt, which partly deals with academic-activists not only writing about but also struggling for urban issues in Istanbul.[27] One of the research objectives was to display commonalities, as well as tensions and obstacles. Urban politics gathered together many people and academicians who previously were not "activists" in the conventional sense. It is necessary to admit that there are some tensions based on political differences between academic-activists struggling in different groups and also between active neighbourhood residents.

The European Social Forum of July 2010 held in Istanbul was an opportunity to build locally what we can call a strategic alliance (namely, "Urban Movements Forum—Kent Hareketleri") of different activists from different groups and neighbourhood associations.[28] This was initiated by some academicians and intellectuals both from and outside the neighbourhoods and other professional and academic groups, in spite of differences and tensions, to build a connection at the local level and to get over the splits mainly between academic-activists, whose roles were considerable in terms of the relationship between theory and practice and related frame construction in urban oppositions. Before and after the European Social Forum, meetings were held to discuss different positions and to overcome tensions. A forum was organized and, at the end, a manifesto was written, mainly by academic-activists involved in the urban opposition of "active inhabitants"[29] from the neighbourhoods to be read in the meeting of the urban movements in the ESF. The main arguments of this statement concentrated on the claims of reappropriation of neighbourhoods, public spaces and historical heritage, with the emphasis on the use-value of the urban space. The right-to-the-city concept of the struggle emerged with the influence of international networks and, more importantly, academic-activists present and active in these struggles.

However, the local forum resulted in a return to existing tensions and cleavages. In time, this forum turned into a coordinator group which organized meetings and campaigns, particularly to provide information to the neighbourhoods and to generate solidarity. In the first meetings, it was underlined that information must be given without all the "academics" or, more exactly, "academic discourse discussions". Neighbourhood activists said they had already listened to too many theories, and it was necessary to express themselves in their own words and to create something useful for the purpose of resisting together. Even though the Social Forum could not create the desired alliance, it created a discussion milieu for different groups in the urban struggle in Istanbul. The international call before the European Social Forum initiated by actors and neighbourhood associations led to some alliances of actors and sharing of information to build solidarity, while new actors were brought in with the commonality of urban issues.

Some inhabitants of the neighbourhoods under the threat of demolition believed the academic-activists were filling a need for theoretical discourse, while for others, it was more important to discuss tensions and conflicts in order to abolish them, rather than engage in academic discussions. There was an urgent need for making something practical in terms of ways of resisting together, and in this respect the Forum was an opportunity for the urban opposition in Istanbul to be informed about other neighbourhoods' struggles and groups from other cities and all over the world experiencing similar processes. Even though groups came together and tried to pave and walk on a common path, this process led to new fragmentations and tensions. For many people from the neighbourhoods, the intellectuals could not get beyond the theoretical level with their "academic discourse and discussions", since they did not live in any demolition areas. The urban opposition in Istanbul, especially in the period before the European Social Forum, made apparent the significance and effect of actors from and outside the neighbourhoods in terms of discourse formation and the emergence of new dynamics and tensions. Two main groups of opposition to intellectuals emerged from the critique of the urban planning profession and its practices: İMECE[30] and Solidarity Studio[31] (Dayanışmacı Atölye). The groups differ mainly in terms of their focus points, such as legal, spatial, technical and systemic. However, academic-activists underline the importance of self-organization of the neighbourhood. The technical and academic language of groups outside the neighbourhoods is used and learnt by neighbourhood inhabitants, while, reciprocally, academicians and activist-intellectuals from outside are learning from the neighbourhoods.

This interest in reciprocal learning emerged and was accentuated in Sulukule, the Romani historical neighbourhood facing demolition, which was one of the first and most unique examples of solidarity among different neighbourhood organizations, including artistic groups and intellectuals. As a result, it took on the meaning of a turning point in the personal experiences of struggle for these various actors. Solidarity Studio,[32] comprising mainly urban planner academicians and students, proposed for the first time an alternative plan for Sulukule. As a voluntary and interdisciplinary working group, they emphasized the importance of mutual learning processes, supplying technical and international information as well as the everyday life support needed by the inhabitants. Solidarity Studio and its allies took various approaches, while keeping in mind the importance of the Romani "culture" of the most disadvantaged people in Sulukule.

However, there were some splits, mainly in terms of academicians' approaches to alternative planning, due to political and ideological standpoints, principles and methods of resistance, since alternative planning is considered to be negotiation with the authorities and acceptance of their criteria. Some of the academicians and intellectuals were against the alternative planning, especially the second phase, in that these plans turned out to be negotiations based on the defence of private property, the acceptance of need and the limiting of potential urban struggles in the neighbourhoods.

Gündoğdu says this urban planning project entailed controversies between private property and public interest in capitalist production.[33] Solidarity Studio admits their position was used and abused in a sense by the authorities in the Sulukule case. Neighbourhoods under threat of demolition and eviction admit that especially the technical support of the Studio played a crucial role in their resistance against demolitions in the neighbourhood. Yalçıntan argues that Solidarity Studio aimed to challenge hegemonies and to be present and write about the neighbourhood when the neighbourhood needed and permited it.[34] Yalçıntan and Çavuşoğlu underline the problem of coordination based on conflicts of interest and "chauvinism", the ambition of leadership.[35] The main problems are cited as lack of representation and inclusiveness due to the organization around three or five people and their ideas and preferences. There are inconsistent discourses, conflicts of interest, rivalry, personal ambitions and competition to be in the centre, with all involved avoiding taking the initiative to form common principles apart from campaigns signed by academicians, which start and end with the signature campaign.

İMECE—namely, People's Urbanism Movement—as an independent civil association, was founded in 2006. In their earlier period, they introduced themselves as urban planners supporting the working classes and labour resistance. By working side-by-side with people and critiquing urban planning practices in the crisis of professional ethics, this initiation was a reappropriation of urban planning against "professional specialization". In their principles, they underlined that they comprise people from different professions, students and academics, and, more crucially, they are open to neighbourhood dwellers, claiming, "The Urbanist is you!" They declared that planning is a process which everyone must participate in equally so as to attain public benefit. Even though they still mainly comprise urban planners, instead of proposing alternative projects, they emphasize the necessity of struggling with systemic problems, defining *neighbourhood* as meaning working-class neighbourhoods. In their principles, they declare that, being independent of any civil, political and professional organization, they are open to everyone. They emphasize that they are learning urbanism in the streets and state that they offer science in the service of solidarity. They use technical and academic knowledge to write critical reports and articles and to inform people not only technically but also "theoretically" on urban isssues. They support the idea that knowledge is a social fact and must be produced together. Their meetings and forums as well as e-mail groups, open to every-one, inform many people from and outside neighbourhoods and create an open, inclusive and common milieu. As they underline in their principles, it is a non-hierarchical group, with decisions being made collectively. Even though they are open to everyone and every urban and rural issue as a systemic problem, they preserve their position outside the neighbourhoods according to their principles and experiences. In time, new activists from different political and professional backgrounds joined or attended these meetings.

Hatice, an İMECE activist, underlined:

> İMECE does not go to any neighbourhoods to organise them. It is one of our principles. We do not concern ourselves with organising. . . . It is better to support the neighbourhood that is having problems. We support them but they have nourished us too—a type of opposition that we shape together. We have professional knowledge. We asked ourselves whether or not we are doing the right thing. Is it better to go and organise in the neighbourhoods? We are trying to remain at the same distance from every group as people coming from outside. It is important to wait and understand what is going on locally. . . . The alternative project for us is the mentality, philosophy, and how we might live better in the city and with which characteristics. What academic-activists are doing as an alternative could be accepted by the government and used and become a gun against you. . . . It impedes the struggle sometimes. You think that you have solved a problem . . . but if there is no opposition in the neighbourhood, you cannot do anything. . . . The academic view becomes day after day more closed and strict. There is an academy which follows the government and there are academicians outside this; they try to be with these platforms more indirectly. They could be criticised, but I won't be so harsh to them. The academy has a problem in its approach . . . its relations with capital and power.

Deniz Özgür, another crucial figure and activist from outside the neigh-bourhoods, spoke about his involvement in urban opposition and engagement with İMECE: "I followed meetings of İMECE every week. I began to love the people there. It was like a school. I read materials and tried to learn". He continued regarding İMECE and the position that they took:

> They were thinking that there must be a distance between them and the organ-isation of the neighbourhood. They believe that they cannot orient and organ-ise on behalf of neighbourhoods. Yes, they can share information, but I think they must play an active role in urban opposition by organising and orienting. If you have knowledge, you have to share this with people. You have to change it into a utilisable form and mobilise people. The sphere that we can organise is the "public sphere": the commons, public space. . . . There must be a mobilisation from a common and then appropriation of the neighbourhood. We have to appropriate what is public today. If we went to the neighbour-hoods, they would ask about property. We have to struggle in public space and then this must have a place in people's minds. . . . For instance, Taksim Square . . . Socialist organisations must appropriate it. We had a few people and became the protesters for some parties. It must be a mass movement. . . . We have to do something for Taksim. By the way, we have to relate struggles: ecological struggle, immigrant, labour, social. The intersection area is urban struggle. . . . The public square could accomplish this. We are a group of few people, planting a seed. We are trying to organise a group of commons with the involvement of other groups together.

Deniz underlined the necessity of forming linkages between the public sphere and neighbourhoods:

> The group İMECE agrees that we have to have an idea for the city as a whole and they struggle for that. They have a mission of carrying all this information to each other and to form bonds between the city, the public sphere and neighbourhood. It is difficult to form these linkages. . . . We have to build from the common space and this idea must have a meaning for people. It is impor-tant that people who come to our meetings share this with the neighbourhood. If we do not have any gains, it is difficult to mobilise. We have to share neighbourhood experiences and gains as well. . . . What I attach importance to is self-organisation in the neighbourhood.

He continued with a self-critique and argued:

> There are not many people in the urban opposition groups. İMECE puts impor-tance on neighbourhood information, on preparing documents that they need. I told them that I could do everything that they need. I did some film screen-ing. It is important to accomplish things that neighbourhood inhabitants need. . . . There must not be any separation: you do not have to say that you are from inside or not. It depends on the way that you associate. . . . I must emphasise that a neighbourhood can organise only in the neighbourhood. We cannot accomplish this outside.

In addition, he went on to say:

> I feel close to İMECE. It was like a school. They were teaching people from and outside of the neighbourhoods. When I participated, three years ago, there were only a few people who did not have this professional knowledge. . . . They do not like to speak on behalf of inhabitants and the neighbourhoods. They do not organise in the neighbourhoods. They are anti-capitalist; they do not compromise with any government. They do not negotiate on any issue with any municipality. They do not make the housing issue an exchange issue. They consider this as part of the whole neo-liberal damage. However, we see that it works differently in neighbourhoods. . . . We have to have and convey an idea about the whole city. We are connecting with people through films, articles. . . . We have to think about language too to break the alienation. Even I have problems with the academic language. I went for two years to meetings— like having courses. I went to all the forums. . . . We have to explain it in the simplest and most basic way. People are selling their houses. We have to explain this in a very easy way and in short time. We have to have a simple language.

İmre Azem, the director of the film *Ekümenopolis* and active in urban opposition, indicated, "Sure, it is useful to have a relationship with academicians and activists in terms of transferring information and sharing experience, in terms of issues which require expertise, in terms of international support. These are all important and none of them are mutually exclusive. . . . Capital attacks from everywhere, so we have to develop a defence and resistance from every possible front. . . . I think neighbourhoods have to be dominant. . . . There is a problem of representation".

About the vital necessity of activists from outside the neighbourhoods, Deniz added:

> I think people coming from outside is vital. . . . We went to neighbourhoods to do film screening. For instance, we saw a need for information in the neighbourhoods. [An active neighbourhood inhabitant] was collecting newspapers; he was reading everything that he found. He did not have any idea about plans and laws. He asked me to share our information with them. I said I wish I knew something about plans and laws. I felt so bad. . . . Intellectuals, academic-activists from outside cannot produce the spark and idea that mobilises people. . . . They do not aim to produce an alternative and they do not use academic knowledge to oppose. . . . They could not even appropriate their own university buildings. . . . I cannot accept this approach to be objective. . . . They could not play their role in urban opposition. Or they have little information about organisation.

Cihan, a pioneering urban activist who initated great international support, stated:

Every Monday, I was giving courses in the form of conversations as a volunteer. . . . In 2005 . . . I went to people's houses to inform and be informed, and they welcomed me with a warm hospitality even though it was very hard for them due to their economic conditions. . . . And nobody was interested in this. We were writing to our friends, groups, and calling the press. And at that time, I wrote to a . . . journalist and he put the entire letter in his column. We have produced cards on the articles of the Constitution and international agreements on the right of housing. . . . At the New Year 2007, I wrote an article about it. . . . Later I decided to write my thesis—to be announced and shared—on these rights violations.

Cihan continued with her efforts to inform international institutions about Ayazma to get support vis-à-vis the difficulties of neighbourhood organization: "Then I wrote . . . about human rights violations. . . . We formed a translation group. It was a horizontal solidarity group and everyone had a mission. . . . Even leftist groups could not accomplish that, since they do not speak the same language".

Çavuşoğlu, an activist-academician who produced alternative and solidarity urban knowledge from Solidarity Studio, stated in an interview that the support "instead of" and "in spite of" neighbourhood inhabitants is weird. So the role of the activists must be providing inspirational and encouraging support for the struggle, which must be led by local actors, and this must be realized without any hierarchy between intellectual and labourers. For international networking and support, even though they are not for the long term, Çavuşoğlu said that it is crucial that people in opposition share their experiences, especially for the visibility in local media. Çavuşoğlu made a presentation about roles, changing characteristics and types of intellectuals: indifferent, transformative and opposed.[36] The opposed have six main problems, which are Bonapartism (critical of the higher institutions of the state and the hierarchy and reward system), elitism (uneasy in *gecekondu* neighbourhoods and even insincere), orientalism (as an attitude against neighbourhoods based on characteristics and feelings such as specialization and pity), dogmatism (teaching according to limitations of leftist and academic knowledge), professionalism (as the producer of words and definitions and the owner of reality, sometimes accompanied by elitism and arrogance) and academism (characterized by rationalism, with society as research object, fetishizing the science and trivializing the life in neighbourhoods). These problems result in a genetically modified and domesticated intellectual. In this respect, we have to be aware of neighbourhoods' active inhabitants; these attempts at research have crucial meanings and in time these academic people became pioneering active figures for neighbourhoods. With his colleagues Çılgın and Strutz, Çavuşoğlu once again analysed actors in urban opposition. In this respect, the "academy-centred actors" can only contribute if they go to the streets.[37]

Erdoğan, a pioneer and significant intellectual from the neighbourhoods, underlines:

> What we do not have is academic qualifications. For this reason, we have opened our doors to academic productions about urban opposition. We have problems in producing a local language of the right-to-the-city discourse. The academy plays an important role in forming this bond between the local and urban opposition. There, culture and art institutions which produce alternative art have functions too. Here, the neighbourhood is not a field. Here is not an object. Not a laboratory. It is not a place that you come from outside of, do your research in and then leave. . . . We were expecting something, but they [academic-activists] left at the end. There is no continuation. . . . They did not forsee and intend this. If the study does not give any feedback to the neighbourhood, it remains only what researchers have taken. It is an alienation. . . . We live power relations everywhere, in every sphere of life. Urban planners expressed their power to us by saying "you will like this and that". . . . But we live here. We have to have our right to words and decisions about the future.

Regarding being from and outside of the neighbourhood and unequal conditions, Kumru, an important academic-activist from Solidarity Studio, argued:

> There is a huge difference between being from the neighbourhood and not; we have to reduce this difference as much as we can. . . . I do not see myself from outside. I could not live there, but if we give the feeling that we are from outside, it won't work. If you do this when you go there for the support, there will be a consideration that you have only come for the help. . . . The role of academicians and intellectuals is important and problematic in this respect. There is a need to support a neighbourhood without any benefit. Nobody must do something just to strengthen his/her status, and his/her place and to have a material benefit from something. These people must neutralise their own positions. Nobody has to go there as an intellectual or academician. . . . It is important that outside the neighbourhoods, academicians resist against their own roles. To guide, to form solidarities, and to give some advice . . . with their technical knowledge . . . these actors have to have a mission and principles. They have to be in neighbourhoods without gazing down from above . . . and not only come to conduct a project or write an article.

To overcome the impasses of urban oppositions and groups from outside, everyone and every group is needed in the opposition. Erdoğan, the active inhabitant for both his neighbourhood and all of Istanbul, suggested:

> We learnt a lot. The groups from outside must learn too. The universities and professors have more to learn. We have to develop learning and teaching dialectic. We have friends who are accused of thinking as a liberal. There are people who are thought to focus on resistance, not the future. We could show that both can be in the same opposition. A space can be created where all these

differences can build from the concept of the right to the city. . . . They must not think that they are weak and they need us. We could for sure walk together. . . . We need everybody who produces knowledge and contributes experiences, including the academy and chambers in this process. Since neighbourhood associations and urban movement groups have power up to a certain level . . . everybody who produces knowledge in this issue in the academy has a lot to contribute.

Ömer, a leading neighbourhood resident active in Urban Movements Forum, argued, "Academicians and intellectuals do play important roles. . . . It is an advantage to meet people who have knowledge. . . . These people—doctorate students, various institutions and people with an oppositional stance—are very important. Their contributions are very important to make our voice heard, to oppose in a country where social rights, basic human rights are ignored, where people do not believe in law. International institutions are important in this respect . . . people come to visit us and listen to engaged inhabitants' interests".

## CONCLUSION: ACADEMIC-ACTIVISTS AS PIONEERING AND PREVENTIVE (F)ACTORS

The distance between the academy and activism becoming a third space is one of the main aspects of resistance: academic-activists struggle to inform, listen, and not to talk over others; they must learn to walk together and to form real solidarity and engagement. This becomes a necessity when inhabitants claim their rights to the city are more and more marginalized by the authorities. Academic-activists as well as active inhabitants emphasize that neighbourhood self-organization alone can change the neighbourhoods. Different activists, including academic-activists, choose their "affinity groups"[38] according to their professional and academic relations, political stances and practices as well as different emotions, including amity. Even though differences between academic-activists and activists from outside neighbourhoods and neighbourhood associations are valid, the fragmentation between activists from "outside" affects mostly the struggle dynamics and the possibility of resisting together. The split in terms of politics, personal relations and past expriences do matter for activists outside neighbourhoods.

There is a changing relationship and tension between groups and actors from neighbourhoods and activist-academicians. While neighbourhoods expect support and guidance for their oppositions, the general idea is that neighbourhood oppositions must find their way by themselves. Neighbourhood active inhabitants sometimes consider academic-activists as people who do not understand their situation. Moreover, based on their experiences, they consider them as academic people in the neighbourhoods, present mainly for academic purposes, who will leave someday. According to some active inhabitants, the intellectuals are unable to pass beyond theoretical approaches and old discussions, which results in new fragmentations.

Critical professional or academic groups became both initiating and hindering actors and factors in different attempts at urban opposition in Istanbul including discursive constructions mainly in campaigns and protests: they sometimes declared that they have their "own principles for urban issues" and "political approaches that they would not relinquish". In this respect, the main proposed contradiction was the negotiation with municipalities in terms of property rights or alternative planning. The role of intellectuals was intended to be oriented to the formation of a "law commission" or an "alternative technical group" responsible for writing reports, while those neighbourhood inhabitants directly affected by urban regeneration projects must do the talking.

Intellectuals and academicians must follow this line and form the ground beyond their fragmentations as well as beyond Istanbul. More than groups and associations, the actors and intellectuals and their affinity groups must be elaborated in the framework of multiple agents of urban learning.[39] In this respect intellectual figures play crucial roles in overcoming these impasses, shaping the discourse and forming another language. It is necessary to recognize the importance of the intellectuals in both urban oppositions and their alignments. However, one of the main issues is the inclusion and exclusion of emotions,[40] and mutual expectations between groups to understand the dynamics and to think about the effectiveness of urban oppositions. Few people in these associations can change their flexible affiliations and leave their group. Lived experiences and perceptions of the activists sometimes lead to tensions between affiliated groups. One of the main cleavages emanates from tensions between groups of academicians, intellectuals and neighbourhood associations.

For some inhabitants, being from outside and inside the neighbourhoods does matter in terms of direct effect and related involvement. Moreover, there is a changing relationship between groups of actors from neighbourhoods and outside. While neighbourhoods expect support and guidance for their oppositions, some of the actors prefer that neighbourhood resistance finds its own way and organizes self-sufficiently. On the other hand, there is a need and desire for the support from intellectuals and academicians outside the neighbourhoods. Urban opposition groups and activists organize in a non-hierarchical way and form new grassroots associations, criticize existing ones and search for alternative solutions. The technical and academic positions and knowledge-related social distance between actors from neighbourhoods and outside neighbourhoods is both reduced and increased in the struggle. People and groups from outside diverge in terms of support and their approach to the meaning of resistance. Even though groups outside the neighbourhoods might not come together and form coalitions, activists always underline that the togetherness of local groups and activists is absolutely necessary. Differences in terms of political and strategic points of view matter. Consequently, neighbourhoods in general contacted and worked together with different groups and tried their methods of resistance. Some groups started to act and mobilize with other groups formed by the same activists. International campaigns initiated by some activists created a motive for neighbourhood activists to speak, to be informed and to know each other. However, here, it is necessary to underline that when campaigns and protests became "the aim" in the process of urban commoning, the result was disappointment and loss of energy at the end of the event, and the whole process considered as a "failure".

Some inhabitants believed that some academicians exluded some leftist activists due to their "politics". Local activists from some neighbourhoods and in some instances considered actors and intellectuals outside the neighbourhoods as people who could not understand their situation, or "academic people" who were in the neighbourhoods for academic purposes and would leave some day soon. The organization of meetings and conferences that included neighbourhood dwellers in some respect (in terms of openness, speaker or just a participant) resulted in commoning and use of "academic" and "technical" language. Even though different meetings included different groups and actors for possible alliances, most of the groups, especially those which were not neighbourhood organizations, like alternative professional or academic groups, became both initiating and hindering (f)actors. They declared that they had their "own principles for urban issues" and "political approaches that they would not relinquish". The main actors defined urban regeneration projects as the "common" enemy and the reason why the neighbourhood associations formed. The limits of the groups in neighbourhoods must be open to a broad and meticulous discussion: the orientation to particular issues or the academic language, their presence and distance vis-à-vis neighbourhoods. It is necessary to underline that people try to propose and practice the method that they find the best. However, academic-activists must not insist on practicing a particular method or approach, but instead work to find the common agenda. We are witnessing a period of an urban commoning not only in/beyond Istanbul but all over the country after the Gezi Park uprising; the underestimation and indifference towards urban resistances have become over-interest since Gezi Park and the self-organization of "ordinary" people in the streets. However, this also created a tension within academics due to the popularity and the abrupt and immediate publications about the urban protests in Turkey. However, the oligopoly of some academics and academic milieus who previously were not engaged academically or practically in "urban oppositions" both criticized and wrote on this issue. The Gezi Park uprising had initiated the politicization and involvement of ordinary people from the urban space through the practices of urban commoning[41] beyond party politics. The uncommon common ground is still being formed by grassroots and academic-activists who define and think critically about characteristics but more crucially their positions.

## REFERENCES

Askins, Kye. "'That's Just What I Do': Placing Emotion in Academic Activism". *Emotion, Space and Society* 2, no. 1 (2009): 4–13. http://dx.doi.org/10.1016/j.emospa.2009.03.005.

Aslan, Şükrü. *1 Mayıs Mahallesi: 1980 Öncesi Toplumsal Mücadeleler ve Kent*. Istanbul: İletişim Yayınları, 2004.

Aslan, Şükrü, and Besime Şen. "Politik kimliğin temsil edici mekanları: Çayan Mahallesi". *Toplum ve Bilim* 120 (2011): 109–32.

Blomley, Nicholas K. "Activism and the Academy". *Environment and Planning D: Society and Space* (1994): 383–85. doi: 10.1068/d120383.

Blomley, Nicholas K. "Activism and the Academy". In *Critical Geographies: A Collection of Readings*, edited by Harald Bauder and Salvatore Engel-Di Mauro. Praxis (e)Press Critical Topographies Series. Kelowna, BC: Praxis (e)Press, 2008.

Bookchin, Murray. *The Ecology of Freedom: The Emergence and Dissolution of Hierarchy*. Palo Alto, CA: Cheshire Books, 1982.

Burawoy, Michael. "For Public Sociology". *American Sociological Review* 70, no. 1 (2005): 4–28. doi: 10.1177/000312240507000102.

Çavuşoğlu, Erbatur. "Kentsel Muhalefetin Akademik ve Aydın Aktörlerinin Değerleri ve Kapasite Sorunları". Planlama.org, October 2011. http://www.planlama.org/index.php/haberler/59-planlamaorg-yazlar/erbatur-cavuolu/2693-kentsel-muhalefetin-akademik-ve-aydn-aktoerlerinin-deerleri-ve-kapasite-sorunlar.

Çavuşoğlu, Erbatur, Kumru Çılgın, and Julia Strutz. "Kentsel Dönüşüm Baskısı Altındaki Mahallelerdeki Güç İlişkilerinin Bourdieucu Bir Okuması". Paper presented at the 7th Urbanism Congress, YTÜ, Istanbul, November 2011. www.academia.edu/6265664/Kentsel_Donusum_Baskisi_Altindaki_Mahallelerdeki_Guc_Iliskilerinin_Bourdieucu_Bir_Okumasi.

Chatterton, Paul. "'Give Up Activism' and Change the World in Unknown Ways: Or, Learning to Walk with Others on Uncommon Ground". *Antipode* 38, no. 2 (2006): 259–81. doi: 10.1111/j.1467-8330.2006.00579.x.

Chatterton, Paul. "Demand the Possible: Journeys in Changing Our World as a Public Activist-Scholar". *Antipode* 40, no. 3 (2008): 421–27. doi: 10.1111/j.1467-8330.2008.00609.x.

Chatterton, Paul. "The Urban Impossible: A Eulogy for the Unfinished City". *City* 14, no. 3 (2010a): 234–44. doi: 10.1080/13604813.2010.482272.

Chatterton, Paul. "Seeking the Urban Common: Furthering the Debate on Spatial Justice". *City* 14, no. 6 (2010b): 625–28. doi: 10.1080/13604813.2010.525304.

Chatterton, Paul, Duncan Fuller, and Paul Routledge. "Relating Action to Activism: Theoretical and Methodological Reflections". In *Participatory Action Research Approaches and Methods: Connecting People, Participation and Place*, edited by Sara Kindon, Rachel Pain, and Mike Kesby. Routledge Studies in Human Geography. London: Routledge, 2007.

Chatterton, Paul, Stuart Hodkinson, and Jenny Pickerill. "Beyond Scholar Activism: Making Strategic Interventions Inside and Outside the Neoliberal University". *Acme* 9, no. 2 (2010): 245–75. http://www.acme-journal.org/vol9/AGC10.pdf.

Clark, John P. *The Anarchist Moment: Reflections on Culture, Nature, and Power*. Montreal: Black Rose Books, 1984.

Clough, Nathan L. "Emotion at the Center of Radical Politics: On the Affective Structures of Rebellion and Control". *Antipode* 44, no. 5 (2012): 1667–86. doi: 10.1111/j.1467-8330.2012.01035.x.

Cushman, E. "The Public Intellectual, Service Learning, and Activist Research". *College English* 61, no. 3 (1999): 328–36.

Elden, Stuart. *Understanding Henri Lefebvre: Theory and the Possible*. London: Continuum International Publishing Group, 2004.

Erman, Tahire. "The Politics of Squatter (Gecekondu) Studies in Turkey: The Changing Representations of Rural Migrants in the Academic Discourse". *Urban Studies* 38, no. 7 (2001): 983–1002. doi: 10.1080/00420980120080131.

Erman, Tahire. "Gecekondu Çalışmalarında *'Öteki' Olarak Gecekondulu Kurguları*". *European Journal of Turkish Studies Thematic Issue Gecekondu*, no. 1 (2004). http://ejts.revues. org/85.

Fuller, Duncan. "Public Geographies: Taking Stock". *Progress in Human Geography* 32, no. 6 (2008): 834–44. doi: 10.1177/0309132507086884.

Fuller, Duncan, and Rob Kitchin. *Radical Theory/Critical Praxis: Academic Geography beyond the Academy?* Kelowna, BC: Praxis (e)Press, 2004. www.praxis-epress.org/rtcp/ RTCP_Whole.pdf.

Goodwin, Jeff, and James M. Jasper. *The Social Movements Reader: Cases and Concepts*. Oxford: Blackwell, 2009.

Gordon, Uri. "Anarchist Geographies and Revolutionary Strategies". *Antipode* 44, no. 5 (2012): 1742–51. doi: 10.1111/j.1467-8330.2012.01036.x.

Gündoğdu, İbrahim. "Sosyalist-Sol Yerel Strateji? Yerellikler, Kent Planlama ve Sulukule Atölyesi". In *Tarih, Sınıflar ve Kent*, edited by Besime Şen and Ali Ekber Doğan. Ankara: Dipnot Yayınları, 2010.

Harvey, David. *Rebel Cities: From the Right to the City to the Urban Revolution*. London: Verso Books, 2012.

Hodkinson, Stuart. "The New Urban Enclosures". *City* 16, no. 5 (2012): 500–518. doi:10.1080/ 13604813.2012.709403.

Kuyucu, Tuna, and Özlem Ünsal. "'Urban Transformation' as State-Led Property Transfer: An Analysis of Two Cases of Urban Renewal in Istanbul". *Urban Studies* 47, no. 7 (2010): 1479–99. doi: 10.1177/0042098009353629.

Mason, Kelvin. "Academics and Social Movements: Knowing Our Place, Making Our Space". *Acme* 12, no. 1 (2013): 23–43. www.acme-journal.org/vol12/Mason2013.pdf.

McFarlane, Colin. *Learning the City: Knowledge and Translocal Assemblage*. London: Wiley-Blackwell, 2011.

Pérouse, Jean-François. "Les tribulations du terme gecekondu (1947–2004): Une lente perte de substance. Pour une clarification terminologique". *European Journal of Turkish Studies: Social Sciences on Contemporary Turkey* no. 1 (2004). http://ejts.revues.org/117.

Purcell, Mark. "Excavating Lefebvre: The Right to the City and Its Urban Politics of the Inhabitant". *GeoJournal* 58, nos. 2–3 (2002): 99–108. doi: 10.1023/B:GEJO. 0000010829.62237.8f.

Routledge, Paul. "Transnational Resistance: Global Justice Networks and Spaces of Convergence". *Geography Compass* 3 (2009): 1881–1901. doi: 10.1111/j.1749-8198.2009. 00261.x.

The Trapese Collective. *Do It Yourself: A Handbook for Changing Our World*. London: Pluto Press, 2007.

Türkmen, Hade. "Debates on Right to the City in Istanbul". Paper presented at the International RC21 Conference, Amsterdam. July 2011. www.rc21.org/conferences/amsterdam2011/ edocs2/Session%2018/RT18-2-Turkmen.pdf.

Türkün, Asuman. "Urban Regeneration and Hegemonic Power Relationships". *International Planning Studies* 16, no. 1 (2011): 61–72. doi: 10.1080/13563475.2011.552473.

Ünsal, Özlem, and Tuna Kuyucu. "Challenging the Neoliberal Urban Regime: Regeneration and Resistance in Başıbüyük and Tarlabaşı". In *Orienting Istanbul: Cultural Capital of Europe*, edited by Deniz Göktürk, Levent Soysal, and İpek Türeli, 52–70. London: Routledge, 2010.

Ward, Kevin. "Geography and Public Policy: Towards Public Geographies". *Progress in Human Geography* 30, no. 4 (2006): 495–503. doi: 10.1177/0309132507078955.

Ward, Kevin. "'Public Intellectuals', Geography, Its Representations and Its Publics". *Geoforum* 38 (2007): 1058–64. doi: 10.1016/j.geoforum.2006.11.021.

Yalçıntan, Murat C. "Kentsel Muhalefetin Halleri ve Halsizlikleri", Planlama.org, February 2009. http://www.planlama.org/index.php/planlamaorg-yazlar6/planlamaorg-yazlar/57-plan lamaorg-yazlar/murat-cemal-yalcintan/489-kentsel-muhalefetin-halleri-ve-halsizlikleri.

Yalçıntan, Murat C. and Erbatur Çavuşoğlu. "Kentsel Dönüşümü ve Kentsel Muhalefeti Kent Hakkı Üzerinden Düşünmek". In *Kentsel Dönüşüm ve İnsan Hakları*, edited by Senem Zeybekoğlu Sadri, Mustafa Ökmen, Kıvılcım Akkoyunlu Ertan, Birol Ertan, Hossein Sadri, Murat Cemal Yalçıntan, Erbatur Çavuşoğlu, Dikmen Bezmez, Sibel Yardımcı, Ayten Alkan, and Ezgi Tuncer Gürkaş, 87–106. Istanbul: İstanbul Bilgi Üniversitesi Yayınları, 2013.

## NOTES

1. Stuart Elden, *Understanding Henri Lefebvre: Theory and the Possible* (London: Continuum International Publishing Group, 2004), 145.

2. Tuna Kuyucu and Özlem Ünsal, "'Urban Transformation' as State-Led Property Transfer: An Analysis of Two Cases of Urban Renewal in Istanbul", *Urban Studies* 47, no. 7 (2010a): 1479–99, doi: 10.1177/0042098009353629.

3. *Gecekondu* is a type of spontaneous, self-constructed housing as a popular urgent solution for state inability to construct social housing for migrated people since the 1940s, the early industrialization period. Considering that there are different neighbourhoods with different characteristics, *gecekondu* neighbourhoods have been changed in time by spatial and popular interventions as well as changing legalizations and discourses. Urban regeneration projects in this respect represent another break for its "illegalization". The studies of Aslan (2004) and Aslan and Şen (2011), of Erman (2001, 2004) and of Pérouse (2004) are strongly recommended in order to understand *gecekondu* neighbourhoods, their struggles as well as their stigmatizations and criminalization in urban and state policies and discourses.

4. David Harvey, *Rebel Cities: From the Right to the City to the Urban Revolution* (London: Verso Books, 2012), 104–8.

5. Asuman Türkün, "Urban Regeneration and Hegemonic Power Relationships", *International Planning Studies* 16, no. 1 (2011): 61–72, doi: 10.1080/13563475.2011.552473, p. 64.

6. Paul Chatterton, "Seeking the Urban Common: Furthering the Debate on Spatial Justice", *City* 14, no. 6 (2010b): 625–28, doi: 10.1080/13604813.2010.525304; Stuart Hodkinson, "The New Urban Enclosures", *City* 16, no. 5 (2012): 500–518, doi:10.1080/136048 13.2012.709403.

7. Some related questions posed during the interviews are as follows: "What are you thinking about support from outside the neighbourhoods?" "Do you think that there is a difference between being from or outside the neighbourhood?" "What are you thinking about the roles of the academicians and intellectuals?"

8. Paul Chatterton, "Demand the Possible: Journeys in Changing our World as a Public Activist-Scholar", *Antipode* 40, no. 3 (2008): 421–27, doi: 10.1111/j.1467–8330.2008.00609.x; Uri Gordon, "Anarchist Geographies and Revolutionary Strategies", *Antipode* 44, no. 5 (2012): 1742–51, doi: 10.1111/j.1467–8330.2012.01036.x.

9. Paul Chatterton, Duncan Fuller, and Paul Routledge, "Relating Action to Activism: Theoretical and Methodological Reflections", in *Participatory Action Research Approaches and Methods: Connecting People, Participation and Place*, ed. Sara Kindon, Rachel Pain, and Mike Kesby, Routledge Studies in Human Geography (London: Routledge, 2007).

10. Paul Chatterton, "'Give Up Activism' and Change the World in Unknown Ways: Or, Learning to Walk with Others on Uncommon Ground", *Antipode* 38, no. 2 (2006): 259–81, doi: 10.1111/j.1467–8330.2006.00579.x.

11. Duncan Fuller and Rob Kitchin, *Radical Theory/Critical Praxis: Academic Geography beyond the Academy?* (Kelowna, BC: Praxis (e)Press, 2004), http://www.praxis-epress.org/rtcp/RTCP_Whole.pdf.

12. Nicholas K. Blomley, "Activism and the Academy", *Environment and Planning D: Society and Space* (1994): 383–85, doi: 10.1068/d120383.

13. Nicholas K. Blomley, "Activism and the Academy", in *Critical Geographies: A Collection of Readings,* ed. Harald Bauder and Salvatore Engel-Di Mauro, Praxis (e)Press Critical Topographies Series (Kelowna, BC: Praxis (e)Press, 2008).

14. Paul Routledge, "Transnational Resistance: Global Justice Networks and Spaces of Convergence", *Geography Compass* 3 (2009): 1881–1901, doi: 10.1111/j.1749-8198. 2009.00261.x.

15. E. Cushman, "The Public Intellectual, Service Learning, and Activist Research", *College English* 61, no. 3 (1991): 328–36.

16. Duncan Fuller, "Public Geographies: Taking Stock", *Progress in Human Geography* 32, no. 6 (2008): 834–44, doi: 10.1177/0309132507086884.

17. Michael Burawoy, "For Public Sociology", *American Sociological Review* 70, no. 1 (2005): 4–28, doi: 10.1177/000312240507000102. See especially page 11.

18. Kevin Ward, "'Public Intellectuals', Geography, Its Representations and Its Publics", *Geoforum* 38 (2007): 1058–64, doi: 10.1016/j.geoforum.2006.11.021.

19. Paul Chatterton, Stuart Hodkinson, and Jenny Pickerill, "Beyond Scholar Activism: Making Strategic Interventions Inside and Outside the Neoliberal University", *Acme* 9, no. 2 (2010): 245–75, http://www.acme-journal.org/vol9/AGC10.pdf.

20. Ibid., 243.

21. Ibid., 252.

22. Chatterton, Fuller, and Routledge, "Relating Action to Activism".

23. Kevin Ward, "Geography and Public Policy: Towards Public Geographies", *Progress in Human Geography* 30, no. 4 (2006): 495–503, doi: 10.1177/0309132507078955.

24. Kye Askins, "'That's Just What I Do': Placing Emotion in Academic Activism", *Emotion, Space and Society* 2, no. 1 (2009): 4–13. http://dx.doi.org/10.1016/j.emospa.2009.03.005.

25. Kelvin Mason, "Academics and Social Movements: Knowing Our Place, Making Our Space", *Acme* 12, no. 1 (2013): 23–43. www.acme-journal.org/vol12/Mason2013.pdf.

26. Chatterton, Fuller, and Routledge, "Relating Action to Activism".

27. For the formulation of "in, for, and beyond" Istanbul, I must refer to Chatterton's studies (2010a, 2010b): Chatterton (2010a, 236) argued that the urban impossible is being simultaneously within, against and beyond the current urban condition. Chatterton (2010b, 628) stated that rebellions in the city are not only in the city but also against the city.

28. Hade Türkmen, "Debates on Right to the City in Istanbul", paper presented at the International RC21 Conference, Amsterdam, July 2011, www.rc21.org/conferences/amsterdam2011/edocs2/Session%2018/RT18-2-Turkmen.pdf.

29. Mark Purcell, "Excavating Lefebvre: The Right to the City and Its Urban Politics of the Inhabitant", *GeoJournal* 58, nos. 2–3 (2002): 99–108, doi: 10.1023/B:GEJO. 0000010829.62237.8f.

30. İMECE, People's Urbanism Movement, Toplumun Şehircilik Hareketi, http://www. toplumunsehircilikhareketi.org/.

31. Dayanışmacı Atölye, Solidarity Studio, http://www.dayanismaciatolye.org/.

32. Here is a part of the statement about Solidarity Studio: "We are not people who walk in front of neighbourhood dwellers with whom we are working together or who teach and talk on behalf of them. We believe in mutual learning and co-producing. We support both within ourselves, as well as in the neighbourhoods that we are walking together, methods which oversee the implementation of the equal sharing of information and stand for the truth of the interaction with each other. To produce information, collect and share without any professional or academic pursuits via field studies and case studies on urban injustice and inequalities. We are producing together and share legal, administrative and scientific knowledge against interventions which ignore the city's ecological and social values to facilitate getting together those who are victims of these interventions. We are trying to develop together decision-making mechanisms so that the victims feel themselves stronger and that they exist and they are made visible. . . . So far, we have not stopped learning, knowing and seeing. We have to be side by side with people who are ignored and whose lives are victimized for rent aspirations. And still we continue on".

33. İbrahim Gündoğdu, "Sosyalist-Sol Yerel Strateji? Yerellikler, Kent Planlama ve Sulukule Atölyesi", in *Tarih, Sınıflar ve Kent*, ed. Besime Şen and Ali Ekber Doğan (Ankara: Dipnot Yayınları, 2010).

34. Murat C. Yalçıntan, "Kentsel Muhalefetin Halleri ve Halsizlikleri", Planlama.org, February 2009, http://www.planlama.org/index.php/planlamaorg-yazlar6/planlamaorg-yazlar/57-planlamaorg-yazlar/murat-cemal-yalcintan/489-kentsel-muhalefetin-halleri-ve-halsizlikleri.

35. Murat C. Yalçıntan, and Erbatur Çavuşoğlu, "Kentsel Dönüşümü ve Kentsel Muhalefeti Kent Hakkı Üzerinden Düşünmek", in *Kentsel Dönüşüm ve İnsan Hakları*, by Senem Zeybekoğlu Sadri, Mustafa Ökmen, Kıvılcım Akkoyunlu Ertan, Birol Ertan, Hossein Sadri, Murat Cemal Yalçıntan, Erbatur Çavuşoğlu, Dikmen Bezmez, Sibel Yardımcı, Ayten Alkan, and Ezgi Tuncer Gürkaş (Istanbul: İstanbul Bilgi Üniversitesi Yayınları, 2013), 87–106.

36. Erbatur Çavuşoğlu, "Kentsel Muhalefetin Akademik ve Aydın Aktörlerinin Değerleri ve Kapasite Sorunları", Planlama.org, October 2011, http://www.planlama.org/index.php/haberler/59-planlamaorg-yazlar/erbatur-cavuolu/2693-kentsel-muhalefetin-akademik-ve-aydn-aktoerlerinin-deerleri-ve-kapasite-sorunlar.

37. Erbatur Çavuşoğlu, Kumru Çılgın, and Julia Strutz. "Kentsel Dönüşüm Baskısı Altındaki Mahallelerdeki Güç İlişkilerinin Bourdieucu Bir Okuması", paper presented at the 7th Urbanism Congress, YTÜ, Istanbul, November 2011, www.academia.edu/6265664/Kentsel_Donusum_Baskisi_Altindaki_Mahallelerdeki_Guc_Iliskilerinin_Bourdieucu_Bir_Okumasi.

38. An affinity group, which will be elaborated in the thesis, is defined by Trapese Collective (2007) as a small group of activists who work together on direct action using non-hierarchy and consensus. They are often made up of friends or like-minded people and provide a method of organization that is responsive, flexible and decentralized. In *The Ecology of Freedom*, Bookchin (1982) explains groups of affinity not as a means to gather people for action, but as an ecological entity which is a permanent, humanist, communitarian, un-hierarchical and un-patriarchal group of relations which develop emancipatory relations. Bookchin's argument could be an appropriate one with the libertarian and communitarian movements which find their roots in affinity groups as a permanent, intimate and decentralized community. For Bookchin (in Clark 1984, 207), the ecological society—libertarian, communitarian society—is formed from these affinity groups as cellular tissues, since it is based on unity-in-diversity, mutual interdependence and non-domination. For Clough (2012, 1673), affinity as a complex concept and opposed to hegemony, domination, and inequality refers to a political organization but also a particular kind of emotive connection/relationship betwen comrades in the way of an egalitarian, non-hierarchical, grassroots democracy. In terms of anarchist affinity, it is a feeling of trust, closeness, and respect for a society of free and equal individuals. Clough (2012, 1673) recalls what Brown and Pickerill underlined; this requires a critical reflexivity and openness towards comrades.

39. Colin McFarlane, *Learning the City: Knowledge and Translocal Assemblage* (London: Wiley-Blackwell, 2011).

40. Jeff Goodwin and James M. Jasper, *The Social Movements Reader: Cases and Concepts* (Oxford: Blackwell, 2009).

41. Harvey, *Rebel Cities*.

*Chapter Six*

# As Barriers Fall, Contingency Becomes Possibility

*Protest Resisting and Escaping Containment and Categorization*

## Christian Garland

Protest can be seen as a crystallization of "actually existing" societal discontent and antagonism, which is more or less visible in a specific time and place, becoming an event in the process. Protest as event is, in this sense, one in which barriers fall and the contingency of different agents—none more so than those "in" and "outside" an (anti-)political milieu—are dissolved by collective action, communal endeavour and the shared thrill of opposition and resistance.

This conceptualization of protests as events/events as protests looks at how barriers that may have existed between participants before involvement in an event can, and frequently do, fall; as different subjectivities coalesce and their experience is shared. This chapter will aim to sketch how such confluences create new possibilities for those engaged in them, and how these can be seen as a form of resistance to, and escape from, strategies of containment and categorization, by powers operating against them.

Indeed, the division of those engaged in protest into spurious categories, based on their identifiable affiliations, is the favoured tactic of the state and media. Deployed to contain and isolate protestors within this same arbitrary categorization of the "protestor" who is politicized, but whose concerns and discontent are otherwise something completely separate from the general population. When, however, protest becomes an event, in which barriers fall and common linkages are made, it becomes far more difficult for those involved to be isolated by categorization, contained and neutralized as harmless. Crucially, participation is opened up to all those previously "outside" (anti-)political activity, newly emboldened and "politicized" by their involvement, so further dissolving former separations. This chapter will aim to sketch how protest as event can enter an uncharted realm of event as protest, resisting categorization and escaping containment.

## ANTAGONISM BECOME VISIBLE/ DISCONTENT MADE MANIFEST

It is possible to speak of protest "at" an existing state-of-things, "against" this same dismal "fact", that is "actually existing" social reality, one or another aspect of it, whether that be an institution, political party, policy, law, past or present event, or capitalism itself. So, from protests as events/events as protests, it can be understood that a specific space-time of a *particular* protest/ event may be identified with a specific group, or coalescence of groups. However, the indefinite and unknown temporality of the experiences that *give rise to* them, and the breaking of arbitrarily imposed boundaries that the event can be seen to be part of *are an ongoing process*. Indeed, as many of us will be aware, the developmental stages of specific mobilizations, their planning, and all of the networking and organization involved will frequently be undertaken by activists or militants—those already politicized and who are more or less conscious of what they are involved in and what effect they hope it will have. In this, there can of course be seen a radical difference between what remains of the traditional Left—the ultra-Left and anarchist movements—in the "theory" they apply and the practice this reflects. Orthodox Marxism, and what in the UK context is familiarly known as Trotskyism, takes the role of activist or militant—that is, *cadre*—as given; it does not see as problematic a separation between specialists and the untutored masses. However, *unorthodox* Marxist accounts of "practice"—as with other libertarian communist perspectives, taking up Marx's original maxim, "The emancipation of the proletariat must be the work of the proletariat itself"—see such a division as *inherently* problematic, and one that should, as far as possible, be overcome.

The inherent problematic of protests as events being *something separate from those not already involved*, and so *becoming self-enclosed*, is, of course, an always-pressing difficulty, but one many activists/militants have sought to address. On a "macro" scale, this can be seen in the "summit crashing" of the alter-globalization movement at the very end of the twentieth century, and the first few years of the twenty-first. That movement had been around far longer than the worldwide public visibility the protests at the WTO summit in Seattle and subsequent mobilizations brought, and it remains unbowed, despite the necessarily ephemeral nature of the tactic. Those major mobilizations have had an effect far beyond the actual, immediate physical protests/ events. Subsequent mobilizations against the WTO, IMF, World Bank, G8, and others—the supra state political institutions facilitating capitalist globalization (at least into the middle of last decade, and before 2008)—have helped refocus and shift popular understanding of what globalization actually is, and the effects this has, and is having. Such an observation should not be taken to mean unqualified support for the alter-globalization movement, which needs to understand, as *Aufheben* noted at the time,[1] that it was somewhat eclipsed by the "War on Terror" and that "connections need to be made with the struggles of the wider proletariat". The many different participants of "the movement" include as many different perspectives, some simply at the radical limits of left-leaning liberalism—that is, far from radical and severely limited. This chapter is not the place for a long, critical excursus into the different, sometimes quite fractious, tendencies present in the alter-globalization movement, but they are touched on here to give an example of some of the problems involved in the specifics of protest.

Writing at the time of the protests organized against the "Summit of the Americas" of the FTAA in Quebec (2001), Naomi Klein noted,

> Sure there were well-organized groups in Quebec City: The unions had buses, matching placards and a parade route; the "black bloc" of anarchists had gas masks and radio links. But, for days, the streets were also filled with people who simply said to a friend, "Let's go to Quebec," and with Quebec City residents who said, "Let's go outside". They didn't join one big protest, they participated in a moment.[2]

The participation in "a moment" is the nature of protests/events; the above quote is neatly illustrative of that and the way that, in the example it cites, a very "activist" or "movement"[3] event became much more open-ended and "unparticularized" by absorbing the interest and participation of wider society in the city in which it occurred. Klein's article also summarizes well how protests as events can and do radicalize. Both elements are already involved, but much less radical and far less aware of exactly what they are up against. More significantly, those "outside" the movement are thus not seen as "politicized" by many within it. Indeed, "Many good people have come from Trot and liberal backgrounds",[4] as has been noted in the published reflections on Genoa, but as the same author also rightly notes, "We have to dare to dream, we have to dare to step outside the established boundaries". This stepping outside of established boundaries is what can make protests so energizing, and it is the same radicalizing force which overwhelms their containment and categorization. The point at which "events" overtake the temporality of "protests" as specific and clearly defined outlets for limited discontent (clearly defined and limited by the state, but also participants sometimes) is when they spread beyond any spatial confinement, because they are "everywhere", meaning that the specific discontent that is crystallized among relatively few participants becomes manifest *generally* among many. Again, this can and does happen, but sadly it doesn't take place much of the time; to take the UK example here:

> Certainly, in the UK there have been only a few links with struggles around and against wage labour. Of course, the impulse of many taking part in the mobilizations springs from their everyday disgust at the dull compulsion of a world dominated by capital: a world of work, ecological destruction, poverty etc. But the "movement" still does not exist as an everyday effort to resist the conditions of life determined by wage labour.[5]

The same "isolated" or "contained-as-protest" nature of "movement"-oriented events may be especially apparent in the United Kingdom, but it is observable in the United States and Continental Europe, too, with the caveat that to make that observation is not to undermine the efforts of those activists involved; rather, that resisting and escaping containment and categorization is best attained when it is no longer a matter of "just" militants, because that definition is rendered largely irrelevant by the activity of many. Quoting the same article from *Aufheben* is once again apt here:

> It is police action, again, that has sometimes contributed to the breaking down of this kind of separation. Mayday 2001 in London, was promoted as an anti-capitalist event, and pre-hyped by the police to such a degree that otherwise "non-political" working class youth saw it as an opportunity to have a go at property and the hated cops—much more noticeably than at Mayday 2000.[6]

The particular example used here is not to emphasize "violence" as somehow preferable or always needed; as Massimo De Angelis argues, it is important for those "in" the movement *not* "to take a clear position, to draw lines in the sand, to define, to classify, and to be precise".[7] There are a whole raft of issues on tactics, reflection, and debate on differences within "the movement"—even among the most radical elements—they are continuous and ongoing, but what is under discussion here is a movement event responding to the experience of a section of wider society (in this case, that of working-class youth) and the experience of objectification by day-to-day capitalist social relations: property relations upheld and protected by the state.

We have defined "protests as events/events as protest" as being about the breaking down of the limits of clearly demarcated "political" or "movement" events, of little concern to the general population. When these limits are overcome, the "event" becomes one in which participation is no longer exclusively that of "activists" but of anyone sufficiently aware and responsive to what the said "event" can offer them. They become an active participant, and the fact that it involves "protest" means that a rapid and escalating politicization and radicalization—at least potentially—becomes apparent: one such very contemporary UK example is the campaign against what is broadly termed "workfare".

"Workfare" is the umbrella term referring to any scheme targeting the unemployed, using an element of compulsion. Although such schemes have been in existence in one form or another since at least the mid-1980s,[8] the incumbent Conservative-led coalition government has accelerated and intensified them on a scale previously unseen, in spite of the fact that, according to the DWP's own findings, "There is little evidence that workfare increases the likelihood of finding work. It can even reduce employment chances by limiting the time available for job search and by failing to provide the skills and experience valued by employers. . . . Workfare is least effective in getting people into jobs in weak labour markets where unemployment is high".[9]

Of the five variants, perhaps the most notorious is "Mandatory Work Activity",[10] although the "flagship" "Work Programme" and "Work Experience" schemes have come under at least as much fire. "Workfare",[11] with origins in the United States but now widespread in Continental Europe, seeks to shift the burden of unemployment back onto the shoulders of the individual, so a social, societal problem such as unemployment becomes an individual moral failing for which the individual must be continuously held to account. The current campaign against such punitive schemes could be said to have properly begun at the end of 2011 and the first months of 2012,[12] when two claimants, Cait Reilly and Jamison Wilson, who had been sent to work unpaid as a condition of still being able to claim Job Seeker's Allowance (JSA), launched a court case against the DWP,[13] arguing that this amounted to forced labour and was therefore unlawful.[14] Appeal Court judges agreed that such schemes were legally flawed, quashing the regulations underpinning them. Reilly had been compelled to give up her volunteering role at a museum—something closely related to her chosen field—and been made to "accept the help that is offered"[15] in the form of another of the punitive schemes, a "Sector-Based Work Academy".[16] Separately, in May 2013, the DWP tried, again unsuccessfully, in the courts to prevent the public disclosure of the names of participating organizations in the three major variants of workfare, despite the fact that these are already widely known.

> At the end of a freedom of information challenge that has lasted 15 months, Judge David Marks QC ruled that the DWP must publish the names of businesses and charities hosting hundreds of thousands of unemployed people who, in some cases, must undertake weeks of unpaid work as a condition of receiving benefits.
>
> Marks, sitting with two others in the first-tier tribunal, said the DWP had offered "a paucity of compelling economic evidence" to back its claims that organizations involved would be seriously financially damaged by negative publicity campaigns should their identities become public.[17]

Employed labour is also disciplined by the threat of "workfare", through the direct or indirect threat of having benefits withdrawn for noncompliance[18]: the threat of actual destitution being what underlies it. Workfare is also supported by the Victorian workhouse ideology of the "deserving and undeserving poor" and "self-help", receiving a twenty-first-century gloss of "empowerment" aimed at "fulfilling potential" by "overcoming barriers to employment", with "positive thinking" apparently being the deciding factor. Indeed, the lucrative workfare industry specializes in such "positive thinking" to explain its own role in claimants being "helped into work". However, "workfare" really has nothing to do with "helping" anyone "into work"; instead, it is used to "reclassify" claimants who are no longer counted in unemployment statistics, just as those under "sanction" are also omitted. By deploying such tactics, the unemployment total can *appear* to fall without in fact having done any such thing. [19]

Additionally, there is the media propaganda war making use of a narrative of imaginary "lazy-feckless-workshy-scroungers", who have "chosen" the "lifestyle" of unemployment. From the initial media flurry in late 2011 and early 2012,[20] there followed many "Big Name" companies and charities suspending their involvement, and indeed the first two actual withdrawals, these being the national supermarket chain Sainsbury's and the bookshop retailer Waterstones.[21] From this point on, the campaign against workfare really got going, both on the streets and, of crucial significance, on *social media*.

The ongoing campaign against workfare can be seen as a key illustrative example of "protests as events"; barriers falling and contingency becoming possibility especially in its "virtual" form. The highly effective campaign against workfare has thus far resulted in the withdrawal of more than thirty[22] "Big Name" companies and charities, using a range of tactics by anti-workfare activists, but also of *major significance*: ex-customers and ex-donors directly addressing those organizations on Facebook and Twitter.[23] Using the power of "branding" to turn "going viral" into something wholly unintended, image-conscious organizations have been quick to grasp the maxim that they should "never underestimate the power of negative publicity". Less astute organizations have continued to remain participants in the workfare "supply chains", in many cases attempting to give the *appearance* of cutting ties with workfare, while continuing to profit from it. The fact is that while activist groups like Boycott Workfare[24] have played—and continue to play—a crucial role in helping to undo workfare, the campaign to hasten its demise cannot be attributed to any one factor or group. When a campaign becomes *generalized* and not "just" activist based, the previous barriers separating the activist from the rest of society *fall*, and the effectiveness of social media more than facilitates that.

The anti-workfare campaign became generalized when former customers and donors of an organization recognized in the campaign *their own interests*.[25] As much as their existing opposition to de facto forced labour, no activist "leaders" being necessary or desirable, there no longer existed any division separating those "doing" the action from the passive observers watching it "get done". Former customers and donors informing companies and charities directly on social media of their dislike of the organizations' decision to participate in the variants of workfare can be understood as the recognition—however intuitive—that the unwelcome tightening of the screw made by both state and capital (that is, workfare) is also the *pacification* of employed labour. Since the most basic rudiments of capitalism are to cut costs—none being costlier than wages—and to increase profits, the employer can do no better than eliminating the cost of wages altogether by using unpaid labour mandated to do the same work.[26]

> Capitalistic accumulation itself . . . constantly produces, and produces in the direct ratio of its own energy and extent, a relatively redundant population of workers, i.e., a population of greater extent than suffices for the average needs of the valorisation of capital, and therefore a surplus-population. . . . It is the absolute interest of every capitalist to press a given quantity of labour out of a smaller, rather than a greater number of labourers, if the cost is about the same. . . . The more extended the scale of production, the stronger this motive. Its force increases with the accumulation of capital.[27]

As such, the many opposed to companies and charities participating in the variants of workfare create protest as an event and the event as protest through their own activity. "Virtual" or "actual", the effect can be the same—barriers fall, contingency becoming possibility: protest resisting and escaping containment and categorization. The example of the campaign against workfare, and the "virtual" event of online criticism on social media connecting and multiplying dissident voices, is especially useful in offering one of the most contemporaneous examples of "protest as events/events as protests". What is offered in the anti-workfare example is the crucial resistance to, and escape from, containment and categorization that "protests as events/events as protests" can become.

As has been contended in this chapter, the barriers that may have existed between participants before involvement in the event of protest frequently fall; they are deleted for the virtual context. As different subjectivities coalesce, their experience is shared to become an actual "power-from-below". The use of the term "power-from-below" is the recognition that power exists, material force must meet material force after all, as Marx was well aware,[28] and as such, in opposition and resistance to something as apparently "given" as workfare and the actual and many victories this has won, it is possible to speak of a different kind of power. Indeed, this can be observed in the opposition to workfare and what is one very definite aspect of capitalism and the "post-political" nature of the state overseeing it. The understanding that in a capitalist society the overwhelming majority are made dependent on wage labour, workfare being a response by capital and the state aimed at reducing, if not eliminating, this "cost", is present in spontaneous and diffuse critical responses[29]—even if sometimes only implicitly. The mass opposition and resistance to workfare resulting in immeasurable damage being inflicted[30] recognizes the material reality that unemployment can and does befall anyone and it is not the fault of the individual, just as it is simply *wrong* for companies to profit from free labour veiled as "training", and charities to claim they are using "volunteers", who are really anything but.

The virtual event that is the campaign against workfare on social media cannot be categorized as a wholly "activist" event or protest, because it is not limited to the actions of any one group or group of individuals any more than it can be contained as their exclusive preserve. That "non-political" people become involved and frequently "politicized" through their own activity is indicative of the (anti-)power such diffuse protests carry.

## STILL TO COME: "THE REAL MOVEMENT WHICH ABOLISHES THE PRESENT STATE OF THINGS"[31]

In the last five to six years, we have entered a crisis—of capitalism—unseen before. The crisis of capital is, of course, easily identified as an "economic crisis", or, worse, a "financial crisis"; both terms may well be applicable and are. However, the crisis we are living through is much more than that and would indeed seem to be "The Breakdown of a Relationship"[32]—that is, the capital-labour relationship, the class relationship. When this is considered, the apparent lack of sustained and coherent response from the side of labour is better understood, and meaning one which convincingly poses a threat to capital. The last thirty or so years of capital's re-composition and restructuring have fragmented and atomized labour to the point at which any kind of collective action becomes very difficult, if not impossible. That is not meant as some nostalgic longing for unionized full-employment, or social democracy or bureaucratized sectional "struggles", but to understand that *class struggle* has never gone away, nor could it (however much capital wishes it could bring that about). Indeed, the "now hidden now open fight"[33] takes on a character unfamiliar to both sides, and for the side of labour, the proletariat, *ways of contesting* the class relation are, in very many ways, as yet unknown.

What, then, is the point of this in relation to protest; to protest as events? Explaining the uncertain and seemingly tentative nature of movements of opposition and resistance to capital in crisis can be seen as authentic expressions of efforts at contestation, with "the best weapons" (so far) that are available. An example would be, in austerity-scarred Europe, unionized strike actions that only reach stalemate or riot, combusting across cities in the Mediterranean countries—that burn out or are extinguished as fast as they appear, but the misery of austerity continues unabated. While the misery of austerity may continue, it is *lessened* by contestation of the conditions giving rise to it, those being of *capitalism*, austerity being the political orientation towards making capitalism profitable again. Unemployment and structural *underemployment* are the precarious terms of existence for a sizeable, and indeed growing, number of the population; "workfare" is a recognizable political measure to support and advance both unfortunate material realities, as are opposition and resistance measures to counter and undo them.

Indeed, the fact that something such as "workfare" even exists—any-where—can be seen as an inherent component of capitalist restructuring and class re-composition, specifically the fact that labour must be put to use— *pacified*—without, of course, this needing to mean employment or wage labour, let alone wage labour at least relative to its own reproduction. As such, the continuous and ongoing crisis of capitalism finds in workfare the punitive mining of its surplus reserve army of labour—something both useful and profitable.

It can be contended that the inchoate and fragmented nature of the re-sponse from the side of labour to the crisis can also be seen as defined largely by the dispersed and fragmented nature of the social subject, something closely related to capital's decades-long restructuring and re-composition. What cannot be removed from the capital-labour relation is *class struggle* and the underlying antagonism that it embodies. To be sure, the indetermi-nate but recurrent nature of class struggle, being the side of labour contesting the capital-labour relation itself, reappears in new forms and finds these out of necessity.

Contestation of the conditions of existence manifested in protests as events/events as protest, defined and shaped by those involved has been termed "networked" protest, and the particular example of anti-workfare protests—especially the "virtual" event on social media—lives up to this definition well, as the participants recognize themselves and their own direct interests in taking action. Similarly, the earlier example of working-class youth in the UK finding reasons from its own experience for participation in Mayday 2001 is a useful concluding comparison. That working-class youth responded to the "event" in the way that it did was because the protest as event/event as protest responded to the firsthand experience of working-class youth, being the daily misery of life defined by capital and policed by the state; something that on a *generalized scale, a social scale*, remains as yet unseen, but which will indeed "result from the premises now in existence".[34]

# REFERENCES

Anonymous. "Anti-Capitalism as an Ideology . . . and as a Movement?" *Aufheben*, no. 10, 2002 http://libcom.org/library/anti-capitalist-aufheben-10.

*Aufheben*. "Unemployed Recalcitrance and Welfare Restructuring in the UK Today". Stop the Clock! Critiques of the New Social Workhouse. 2000. http://libcom.org/library/aufheben/pamphlets-articles/stop-the-clock-critiques-of-the-new-social-workhouse/unemployed-recalcitrance-and-welfare-re.

*Aufheben*. "Editorial: The 'New' Workfare Schemes in Historical and Class Context". No. 21 (2012). http://libcom.org/library/editorial-%E2%80%98new%E2%80%99-workfare-schemes-historical-class-context.

BBC News. "Graduate 'Made to Stack Shelves' Seeks Judicial Review". 5 December 2011. www.publicinterestlawyers.co.uk/news_details.php?id=200.

Crisp, Richard, and Del Roy Fletcher. *A Comparative Review of Workfare Programmes in the United States, Canada and Australia*. 2008. http://webarchive.nationalarchives.gov.uk/20130128102031/http://research.dwp.gov.uk/asd/asd5/report_abstracts/rr_abstracts/rra_533.asp.

De Angelis, Massimo. "From Movement to Society". In *On Fire: The Battle of Genoa and the Anti-Capitalist Movement*. London: One Off Press, 2001.

Garland, Christian. E-mail response to Wilkinson's statement on workfare participation, 19 May 2013.

Grice, Andrew. "Voters 'Brainwashed by Tory Welfare Myths', Shows New Poll". *Independent*, 4 January 2013. Accessed 25 March 2014. www.independent.co.uk/news/uk/politics/voters-brainwashed-by-tory-welfare-myths-shows-new-poll-8437872.html.

Harper, Stephen, and Christian Garland. "Combat Channel 4's 'Tricks of the Dole Cheats'". Blog post sharing e-mail to Channel 4, 13 August 2012. www.relativeautonomy.com/2/post/2012/08/combat-channel-4s-tricks-of-the-dole-cheats.html.

Klein, Naomi. "The Bonding Properties of Tear Gas". 25 April 2001. Naomi Klein's blog. www.naomiklein.org/articles/2001/04/bonding-properties-tear-gas.

Malik, Shiv. "Young Jobseekers Told to Work without Pay or Lose Unemployment Benefits". *Guardian*, 16 November 2011. Accessed 26 March 2014. www.theguardian.com/society/2011/nov/16/young-jobseekers-work-pay-unemployment?guni=Article:in%20body%20link.

Malik, Shiv. "Waterstones Ends Unpaid Work Placements after Investigation". *Guardian*, 12 February 2012. Accessed 25 March 2014. www.theguardian.com/society/2012/feb/03/waterstones-ends-unpaid-work-placements?guni=Article:in%20body%20link.

Malik, Shiv. "Thousands of Unemployed People Made to Work without Pay". *Guardian*, 15 February 2012. Accessed 25 March 2014. www.theguardian.com/society/2012/feb/15/thousands-unemployed-work-without-pay.

Malik, Shiv. "Government Blocks Publication of Names of 'Workfare' Employers". *Guardian*, 9 November 2012. Accessed 26 March 2014. www.theguardian.com/politics/2012/nov/09/mandatory-work-activity-names-witheld.

Malik, Shiv. "Poundland Ruling 'Blows Big Hole' through Government Work Schemes". *Guardian*, 12 February 2013. Accessed 25 March 2014. www.theguardian.com/society/2013/feb/12/poundland-ruling-government-work-schemes.

Malik, Shiv. "Workfare Placements Must Be Made Public, Tribunal Rules". *Guardian*, 13 May 2013. Accessed 26 March 2014. www.theguardian.com/society/2013/may/19/workfare-placement-published-court-rules.

Marx, Karl. "Introduction to Contribution to the Critique of Hegel's *Philosophy of Right*". (1844). www.marxists.org/archive/marx/works/1844/df-jahrbucher/law-abs.htm.

Marx, Karl. "Development of the Productive Forces as a Material Premise of Communism". In *The German Ideology* (1845). www.marxists.org/archive/marx/works/1845/german-ideology/ch01a.htm.

Marx, Karl. "The General Law of Capitalist Accumulation Section 2. Relative Diminution of the Variable Part of Capital Simultaneously with the Progress of Accumulation and of the

Concentration That Accompanies It". In *Capital*, vol. 1 (1867). www.marxists.org/archive/marx/works/1867-c1/ch25.htm#S2.

Marx, Karl, and Friedrich Engels. "Bourgeois and Proletarians". In *Manifesto of the Communist Party*. www.marxists.org/archive/marx/works/1848/communist-manifesto/ch01.htm#007.

Poundland. "Poundland Work Experience" statement. www.poundland.co.uk/press-release/poundland-work-experience-programme/.

Ramesh, Randeep. "Data Shows Work Programme Failures". *Guardian*, 27 November 2012. Accessed 26 March 2014. www.theguardian.com/news/datablog/2012/nov/27/data-work-programme-failures?guni=Article:in%20body%20link.

Ramesh, Randeep. "'Scrounger' Stigma Puts Poor People Off Applying for Essential Benefits". *Guardian*, 20 November 2012. Accessed 26 March 2014. www.guardian.co.uk/society/2012/nov/20/scrounger-stigma-poor-people-benefits.

Reilly, Cait. "Why the Government Was Wrong to Make Me Work in Poundland for Free". *Comment Is Free, Guardian*, 12 January 2012. Accessed 26 March 2014. www.theguardian.com/commentisfree/2012/jan/15/unemployed-young-people-need-jobs.

Screamin' Alice. "The Breakdown of a Relationship? Reflections on the Crisis". *Endnotes*, 2008. http://endnotes.org.uk/articles/15.

Tommy. "Trots and Liberals". In *On Fire: The Battle of Genoa and the Anti-Capitalist Movement*. London: One Off Press, 2001.

Wintour, Patrick. "Jobseekers and Benefits Data Release Postponed by DWP". *Guardian*, 19 May 2013. Accessed 25 March 2014. www.theguardian.com/society/2013/may/19/benefits-unemployment.

# NOTES

1. "Anti-Capitalism as Ideology . . . and as a Movement?" *Aufheben* no. 10 (2002), http://libcom.org/library/anti-capitalist-aufheben-10.

2. Naomi Klein, "The Bonding Properties of Tear Gas", 25 April 2001, Naomi Klein's blog, www.naomiklein.org/articles/2001/04/bonding-properties-tear-gas.

3. The "movement" referred to here is not "just" the one of anti-capitalist alter-globalization but also, broadly speaking, the anti-political ultra left.

4. Tommy, "Trots and Liberals", in *On Fire: The Battle of Genoa and the Anti-Capitalist Movement* (London: One Off Press, 2001), 108.

5. "Anti-Capitalism as Ideology".

6. Ibid.

7. Massimo De Angelis, "From Movement to Society", in *On Fire*, 109.

8. See "Unemployed Recalcitrance and Welfare Restructuring in the UK Today", Stop the Clock! Critiques of the New Social Workhouse, *Aufheben* (2000), http://libcom.org/library/aufheben/pamphlets-articles/stop-the-clock-critiques-of-the-new-social-workhouse/unemployed-recalcitrance-and-welfare-re; see also "Editorial: The 'New' Workfare Schemes in Historical and Class Context", *Aufheben*, no. 21 (2012), http://libcom.org/library/editorial-%E2%80%98new%E2%80%99-workfare-schemes-historical-class-context.

9. Richard Crisp and Del Roy Fletcher, *A Comparative Review of Workfare Programmes in the United States, Canada and Australia*, 2008, http://webarchive.nationalarchives.gov.uk/20130128102031/http://research.dwp.gov.uk/asd/asd5/report_abstracts/rr_abstracts/rra_533.asp.

10. Shiv Malik, "Thousands of Unemployed People Made to Work without Pay", *Guardian*, 15 February 2012, accessed 25 March 2014, www.theguardian.com/society/2012/feb/15/thousands-unemployed-work-without-pay.

11. "How to Avoid Workfare", http://consentarchive.files.wordpress.com/2012/11/how-to-avoid-workfare-full.jpg.

12. Cait Reilly, "Why the Government Was Wrong to Make Me Work in Poundland for Free", *Comment Is Free, Guardian*, 12 January 2012, accessed 25 March 2014, http://www.theguardian.com/commentisfree/2012/jan/15/unemployed-young-people-need-jobs.

13. "Graduate 'Made to Stack Shelves' Seeks Judicial Review", BBC News, quoted by Public Interest Lawyers, www.publicinterestlawyers.co.uk/news_details.php?id=200.

14. Shiv Malik, "Poundland Ruling 'Blows Big Hole' through Government Work Schemes", *Guardian*, 12 February 2013, accessed 25 March 2014, www.theguardian.com/society/2013/feb/12/poundland-ruling-government-work-schemes.

15. This is the insipid wording of the existing legislation.

16. Sector-Based Work Academies are one of the current existing five workfare schemes, the other four being: the "Community Action Programme", "Mandatory Work Activity", the "Work Programme" and "Work Experience". All such schemes are indeed compulsory—more or less—*pace* the DWP's claims of their "voluntary" nature—and operate using different interpretive trip wires. The Job Centre advisor and/or workfare third-party having rather more space to "interpret" whether or not a claimant is "engaging", with the "help" being "offered" to them, than the harried claimant. Should the claimant be deemed not to be "engaging", they can be and usually are "sanctioned", meaning their JSA—and only income—is withdrawn, sometimes for up to three years.

17. Information Tribunal, www.informationtribunal.gov.uk/DBFiles/Decision/i1016/EA-2012-0207%28+2%29_Judgment_17-05-2013.pdf.

18. Patrick Wintour, "Jobseekers and Benefits Data Release Postponed by DWP", *Guardian*, 19 May 2013, accessed 26 March 2014, www.theguardian.com/society/2013/may/19/benefits-unemployment.

19. Randeep Ramesh, "Data Shows Work Programme Failures", *Guardian*, 27 November 2012, accessed 26 March 2014, www.theguardian.com/news/datablog/2012/nov/27/data-work-programme-failures?guni=Article:in%20body%20link.

20. Shiv Malik, "Young Jobseekers Told to Work without Pay or Lose Unemployment Benefits", *Guardian*, 16 November 2011, accessed 26 March 2014, www.theguardian.com/society/2011/nov/16/young-jobseekers-work-pay-unemployment?guni=Article:in%20body%20link.

21. Shiv Malik, "Waterstones Ends Unpaid Work Placements after Investigation", *Guardian*, 12 February 2012, accessed 25 March 2014, www.theguardian.com/society/2012/feb/03/waterstones-ends-unpaid-work-placements?guni=Article:in%20body%20link.

22. Companies known to have withdrawn as of February 2014: BHS, The Body Shop, Boots, Burger King, HMV, Holland & Barrett, Holiday Inn, Maplin, 99p, Pizza Hut, Sainsbury's, Shoe Zone, Superdrug, TK Maxx and Waterstones. Charities known to have withdrawn as of February 2014: Age UK*, Blue Cross, Cancer Research UK*, The Children's Society, Marie Curie, Mind, Oxfam, PDSA, Red Cross, Scope, Sense, Shelter, Single Homeless Project, St Mungo's and Sue Ryder. *Known to have withdrawn from MWA and the "Work Programme" but remain participants in "Work Experience" workfare. Argos issued the following statement on 24 May 2013: "As we work to becoming a digital retail leader we have been reviewing our recruitment programme for this financial year. As a result we are reviewing the skills needed to take us forward and after careful consideration we have decided to halt any further recruitment of colleagues through the work programme with Job Centre Plus". https://mobile.twitter.com/shivmalik1/status/337966244827385856. Homebase—also owned by Home Retail Group—issued the following statement: "We have run a few small scale work experience schemes on a local level which has provided valuable experience to the unemployed, many of whom have obtained positions as a result. Towards the beginning of April, following a review of the skills required for our new proposition, we have decided not to recruit from this particular Job Centre Plus scheme going forward. We will continue to work hard with Job Centre Plus to help those out of work into meaningful careers". www.facebook.com/photo.php?fbid=453837754707955&set=a.222209914537408.52394.222201111204955&type=1. In addition to all those large organizations known to have withdrawn from all versions of workfare, the British Heart Foundation withdrew from MWA but remains involved in the "Work Programme". Shiv Malik, "Government Blocks Publication of Names of 'Workfare' Employers", *Guardian*, 9 November 2012, accessed 26 March 2014, www.theguardian.com/politics/2012/nov/09/mandatory-work-activity-names-witheld. On a more regional level, Scarborough Council, previously enthusiastic workfare participants, cancelled involvement as of 12 January 2014, www.boycottworkfare.org/?p=3260, while Volunteer Centre Knowsley CVS issued an

unequivocal statement on Twitter, on 10 January 2014: "We are urging social value organizations to not take part in workfare placements". https://twitter.com/KnowsleyCVS/status/421587385772564480.

23. Below is Poundland's Work Experience statement, www.poundland.co.uk/press-release/poundland-work-experience-programme/.

*Social Media Response 13/2047, Work Experience Schemes:*

When we learned of concerns over these schemes, we said we would never use any scheme of this kind to profit from participants, to avoid the need to recruit or to involve individuals who had not voluntarily agreed to join such a scheme.

To make sure we couldn't unwittingly participate in claims of "exploitation", we then stopped accepting new work placements and this is still in place as a precaution while we await further developments.

If we do decide to recommence working locally with job centres, it will be with individuals who have voluntarily agreed without any threat of losing benefits and only on the basis of joining our formal eight week training programme which we've structured to give individuals the real skills and solid experience needed to return confidently to employment.

Our long established family business believes in open, honest, fair and responsible dealings with its customers, suppliers and team members.

18 February 2013

And following is Christian Garland's e-mail response to Wilkinsons, including their statement on workfare participation, 19 May 2013:

Dear Wilkinsons,

The above statement issued in February, certainly is textbook PR-speak: refute criticism of something you have not in fact been accused of, or rather take the actual, real advantage you can gain from choosing to be involved in workfare, and say how that "would never" be the reason for your involvement—weasel words indeed.

Again, in the language of PR, your statement is deliberately very ambiguous, making use of the infinitive to mean everything and nothing. It certainly appears that Wilkinsons is still involved with workfare—the umbrella, generic term used to refer to any kind of scheme using an element of compulsion—it really does. In spite of the disingenuous nonsense of the DWP, workfare certainly does "exist in the UK", and to clarify for you, the five variants are as follows: so-called "Work Experience", the so-called Work Programme, Mandatory Work Activity, Sector-Based Work Academies, and the Community Action Programme.

Workfare, of whatever kind is not "voluntary" but involves *compulsion* more or less, and you "involve individuals who had not voluntarily agreed to join such a scheme", by making use of their *unpaid labour*, when they are sent to you by either the job centre or a third party from the lucrative welfare-to-work industry. If you are using people on "Work Experience", then you can pay them wages can't you, and they will no longer have to have dealings with the punitive benefits system at all?

Until you decide to do that, you look sadly, very much like you prefer "to avoid the need to recruit", since you have JSA claimants, who are more or less *compelled to work unpaid*, as a "condition" of still receiving their king's ransom *Job Seeker's Allowance because they are unemployed*. So-called "Work Experience" is the form of workfare targeted at youth, who "need experience", but is really not about providing any experience which will be of use to securing paid employment—of whatever kind.

The "interpretative" tripwires of the different variants of workfare, allow for greater or lesser compulsion, not just the uncharacteristically candid "Mandatory Work Activity", which goes against the starry eyed positivity of the titles of the other four variants, all of which amount to the same thing: coercion with a smile.

It is certainly to be welcomed that you "stopped accepting new work placements and this is still in place as a precaution", however it remains unclear whether you have decided to make this permanent three months later.

If you "use individuals who have voluntarily agreed without any threat of losing benefits and only on the basis of joining [y]our formal eight week training programme", then it must be asked why you are not paying them actual wages, and why they are being expected to work as a condition—indirectly stated of course— of not having "refused the help that is offered"—the DWP loves euphemisms like that as do third-party workfare outfits.

A claimant is "technically" "voluntarily" agreeing to so-called "Work Experience", or the so-called "Work Programme", but they really don't have much of a choice. Should someone decline involvement in one of the "suggested" schemes you are involved in, then they risk being "sanctioned", or moved onto one of the more openly punitive schemes, where sure enough, "sanctioning" is used much more easily and freely.

The current Tory workfare regime has a spectacular failure rate of *96.5%*, meaning that percentage of people forced into supposedly "improving job prospects", did not secure paid employment as a result. While hardly being impressive, such a dismal rate of "success" figures, since workfare of whatever kind has nothing to do with creating properly paid employment for anyone, but using *material compulsion*, that is, the threat—usually implicit—of losing your only income if you don't play ball.

The workfare regime is also supported by the Victorian workhouse ideology of the "deserving and undeserving poor", and "self-help" which likes to shift the burden of unemployment onto the shoulders of the individual, so social, societal problems, become individual moral failings, something emphasized by Duncan Smith, Hoban and co, and fought using a 24/7 propaganda war.

Please bring an end to participating in such a tawdry sham, which certainly doesn't "give individuals the real skills and solid experience needed to return confidently to employment", your own training scheme may do that, but if it does, then it has no need of so-called "Work Experience", or the so-called "Work Programme".

If you do indeed believe "in open, honest, fair and responsible dealings with customers, suppliers and team members" you should issue a statement announcing your withdrawal from all variants of workfare, as have *28* other "Big Name" companies and charities—thank you. CG.

24. www.boycottworkfare.org/.

25. "Workfare third-party" refers to the booming and lucrative workfare industry, a sector specifically charged with imposing measures that were originally the preserve of the state: punitive measures to "make the unproductive productive", and impose market discipline through the threat of withdrawal of benefits. With an absurd irony, private companies tasked with imposing workfare on the unemployed and also the sick and disabled, now make up what is a growth industry. In a society based on precarious and "flexible" wage labour, which demands that the overwhelming majority of the population *work* at all costs, even if there is not in fact enough actual wage labour to be had, "work" assumes once again, a virtuous "ethic" of (self)-discipline, pious resolve, and thrift, comprising an ideological narrative of "self-help" and "individual responsibility". The franchisees of workfare are these for-profit "partners" of the state, running what remain state functions, and with the legal blessing to act accordingly. A continuous media campaign—especially in certain tabloid newspapers, and in reality TV programmes on Channel 4—have done much to promote the increasingly punitive regime facing claimants, and in so doing helped spread disingenuous myths very much fulfilling the classical definition of "Moral Panics" and "Folk Devils". See Andrew Grice, "Voters 'Brainwashed by Tory Welfare Myths', Shows New Poll", *Independent*, 4 January 2013, accessed 25 March 2014, www.independent.co.uk/news/uk/politics/voters-brainwashed-by-tory-welfare-myths-shows-new-poll-8437872.html; Randeep Ramesh, "'Scrounger' Stigma Puts Poor People Off Applying for Essential Benefits", *Guardian*, 20 November 2012, accessed 26 March 2014, www.guardian.co.uk/society/2012/nov/20/scrounger-stigma-poor-people-benefits; and Stephen Harper and Christian Garland, "Combat Channel 4's 'Tricks of the Dole Cheats'", blog post sharing e-mail to Channel 4, 13 August 2012, www.relativeautonomy.com/2/post/2012/08/combat-channel-4s-tricks-of-the-dole-cheats.html.

26. "Instead of offering paid work to people, they seem to be able to staff their stores with a constant flow of work placements. Meanwhile, despite having applied to the store for a job as soon as it opened, I ended up working longer hours than staff for no pay. If companies can keep getting staff and not paying them, how are people like me ever meant to find paid work?" (anonymous claimant quoted by Boycott Workfare, http://www.boycottworkfare.org/?p=3200).

27. Karl Marx, "The General Law of Capitalist Accumulation, Section 2: Relative Diminution of the Variable Part of Capital Simultaneously with the Progress of Accumulation and of the Concentration That Accompanies It", in *Capital*, vol. 1 (1867), www.marxists.org/archive/marx/works/1867-c1/ch25.htm#S2.

28. Karl Marx, "Introduction to Contribution to the Critique of Hegel's *Philosophy of Right*" (1844), www.marxists.org/archive/marx/works/1844/df-jahrbucher/law-abs.htm.

29. Shiv Malik, "Workfare Placements Must Be Made Public, Tribunal Rules", *Guardian*, 13 May 2013, accessed 26 March 2014, www.theguardian.com/society/2013/may/19/workfare-placement-published-court-rules.

30. Ibid. "In a battle with the Information Commissioner the DWP has said that the government's mandatory work programme would 'collapse' if the names were made public due to the likelihood of protests against the organisations involved".

31. Karl Marx, "Development of the Productive Forces as a Material Premise of Communism", in *The German Ideology* (1845), www.marxists.org/archive/marx/works/1845/german-ideology/ch01a.htm.

32. Screamin' Alice, "The Breakdown of a Relationship? Reflections on the Crisis", *Endnotes*, 2008, http://endnotes.org.uk/articles/15.

33. Karl Marx and Friedrich Engels, "Bourgeois and Proletarians", in *Manifesto of the Communist Party*, www.marxists.org/archive/marx/works/1848/communist-manifesto/ch01.htm#007.

34. Ibid.

## Chapter Seven

# "It's a Beautiful Thing, the Destruction of Wor(l)ds"

## The Script

## Aylwyn Walsh and Myrto Tsilimpounidi

This chapter takes a rather different format from a traditional academic article in that it comprises the text of a performance lecture developed by the two authors. The text arose in response to a growing helplessness at the sudden social and economic decline of Greece, in the wake of the financial crisis (since 2008). That was underscored by a frustration at the limitations traditional academic forms took when colleagues discussed such themes and events as protests at conferences. It seemed to us that pontificating about protests (which are, after all, highly affective and embodied) developed a disjunction between form and content. It was as if, in the era of Tahrir Square, Syntagma Square, and growing social unrest across the Mediterranean, scholars were attempting to quantify the extent of movements' "success", and justify why they were necessary.

That *justificatory* position was perpetuated through a strange mixture of pride, urgency and defeat, as if the presenters realized that parading a set of images which evidenced clashes between "the public" and increasingly brutal police was a tactic that served to highlight protests as events worthy of scholarly analysis. More often than not, however, there was a sensation, as audiences witnessed the extent of revolutionary affect, that academic discourse was struggling to articulate its role in effecting change. We realized that if we began from our respective academic disciplines (sociology and performance studies), in our own version of a street battle, we could attempt to deal with the feelings related to the incessant erosion of what we each considered "home".

## PERFORMANCE AS METHODOLOGY

Johnny Saldaña[1] discusses the value of presenting research in the form of a written script; consisting of "dramatized, significant selections of narrative, collected through interviews, participant observation, field notes, journal entries, and/or print and media artifacts such as diaries, television broadcasts, newspaper articles, and court proceedings".[2] This form of research output can lead us to move beyond mere participant observation, or standard interviews in the field, in order to collect different modes of data: feelings, dynamics, images, metaphors and moments of performance. Such modes can yield complex and rich data, which allow analysis to move beyond "subjective" or "objective" binaries to an intersubjective creative map of words and gestures. Standard ethnographic models of "participant observation" in social sciences[3] become augmented by the fieldwork process, reframed as and by performance.[4] The suggestion that performance offers alternatives to the ethnography of the "static other" has been largely taken up by performance studies as a field.[5] Jane Bacon asserts the need for a "performative imagination" that cuts across field-based practices and reflexive practices, while Hare states that ethnodramas "should show, instead of tell. They should unsettle the status quo and taken for granted assumptions. The performance text makes space for multiple, multi-layered voices, experience and attitudes to be expressed".[6] In short, the presentation of research on protests and events itself becomes staged as an "event".

Norman Denzin and Yvonna Lincoln call performance ethnography "the single most powerful way for ethnography to recover yet interrogate the meanings of lived experience".[7] Denzin has also insisted that research should be pedagogical, political and performative.[8] The intersections of ethnography and performance set the ground for a challenging and vital research experience. This is not least because audiences apply different logics to "serious" presentations and the mode of "performance".

The script we present here moves between the expected discussion of ideas to the presentation of a subjective relationship with the research field, as expressed in a "love letter" to Athens. Myrto's letter is accompanied by her photographs of the city, augmenting the audience's experience of the marble city by including images of some of the decay and erosion of the social fabric. As she confesses to ambiguous feelings about her home city, the audience also experiences the contestation over space and sudden loss, and they are witnesses to the effects of economic austerity on the city. Images dialogue with the letter in an autoethnographic conversation with the city. Wendy Chapkis provides a clear rationale for the use of autoethnographic reflections, suggesting they become a means of revealing one's own "investment in debates . . . while exposing deeply conflicted reactions to the practice".[9] She adds that proximity and engagement can be seen as resources and not impediments to good research.[10]

The script was first presented by Aylwyn Walsh and Myrto Tsilimpounidi, produced by Ministry of Untold Stories, at the 2012 Berlin Biennale; it has subsequently been performed in England, Turkey and the Netherlands. In the eighteen months of presenting it, we have encountered a wide range of reactions—particularly from people who articulate shock at feeling moved in an academic context. While there are some elements of the performance lecture that always elicit strong reactions (such as Myrto's love letter to Athens), other stagings have resulted in questions: "Why does the costume contain a tiny German flag—are we explicitly blaming Angela Merkel for her insistence on harsh austerity measures?" "Why did we put Athens on trial?" Despite framing the scene as ironic, some audiences struggled to understand that the performative frame allows us to work with creative layering. Unlike strictly academic papers, we were able to use satire to undermine hegemonic thinking and, in certain scenes, we could draw attention to corruption without needing to say explicitly that we do not condone clientelism or police brutality. We did not ever intend to demonstrate that Athens ought to be on trial, but rather that this is what people have experienced over the course of the last five years. We hope that the script provides some access to the emotional landscape of a city's protests following the economic, social and political crises it has experienced since 2008.

## NOTES ON CONVENTIONS

As it is the convention in performance texts, stage directions are indicated in italics. Sections indicate the name of the speaker, but do not necessarily correspond with who wrote the text, since it was developed collaboratively. As a matter of convention, we would not ordinarily include footnotes as explanations, but in some places we wanted to indicate the veracity of the data. This is because material conditions are constantly changing, and the data in the performance lecture were constantly updated to reflect some of the most recent figures.

## IT'S A BEAUTIFUL THING,
## THE DESTRUCTION OF WOR(L)DS: THE SCRIPT[11]

*The audience enters. House music plays, with the sound of a crowd during a protest and the tinny re-recorded sound of the protest song "Which Side Are You On?"*

*While the music plays, and we hear the crowd discussing, planning, laughing and shouting, the two presenters hand out gas masks and use cream to paint a protective talisman on others' skin. While some audience members get the props, others receive large counterfeit currency bills with statistics about the current economic crisis printed on them.*

*There is a washing line suspended across the stage, which holds several hundred euros' or pounds' worth of money hung up to dry. There are also different speeches/statements on the washing line.*

*Myrto stands, as if presenting a standard academic paper.*

*Ally sits off centre, listening.*

## Myrto

*Scene 1: The Frame*

The singular compelling imagery of "occupying" as a form of resistance is its multiplicity of voices—the collective mobilization of the "multitude". Yet the force and urgency of a collective resistance lies in the individual untold stories of its proponents. Rather than glorify the movement as a faceless entity, we embrace the daily stories, struggles and wounds of occupation.

Resistant performances in Athens have gathered momentum over the last years, transforming the fixed landscape of a city into a platform for negotiation and dialogue. These performances are connected with existing social conditions: austerity measures, mass immigration and "crisis". Such narratives of globalization and empire building are transforming central areas and traditional notions of Athenian identity, giving birth to a new street-level language that has twisted, innovated, and filled in the gaps of a culture's hegemonic discourse. In this presentation, protests appear as visual markers of the complex discourses of power struggles, marginality and countercultures, that establish a new reality that must be seen and heard.

According to Henri Lefebvre,[12] the city is always related with society in total: its history, main elements, functions and the synthesis thereof. Thus, the city changes whenever society shifts. However, the transformation of the city is not the passive result of social cycles. It is also dependant on the direct connections between persons and groups that form society.[13] The central Athens of previous years is now a terrain of conflict and metamorphosis. Urban identity has been inevitably affected by the current socio-political transformations, and can be witnessed in daily performances of resistance; particularly in the uncanny and imaginative ways people occupy city spaces.

We are arguing that resistance is a space of radical openness, in which the self is re-imagined in relation to its landscape—and in turn, the landscape is remapped.

"Occupation" is not a risk-free activity; it is underscored by the need for resistance to counter multiple forms of domination and exploitation. Yet resistance must acknowledge the need for personal transformations in order to make a claim for wider social change.

In our continuing explorations of Athens in crisis, both on the ground and from a position of exile, we have found it necessary to foreground our subjectivities; our dreams and desires, fears and experiences shape our understanding, help inform expectations and define hopes for how city spaces can be shifted through the repeated performances of protest and revolt.

The city's streets are political. In Athens, in the current milieu, time is marked out not by changing seasons, but between installments of debt relief from the IMF and the EU. It is also mapped by politically motivated protests, gatherings and events.

*Ally takes paper to hang up on the washing line.*
*Returns to centre.*

## Ally

*Scene 2: The Methods*

I'm interrupting your frame with a methodological announcement.

In this section, we unsettle the norms of presentations; ask you to join us in a more embodied trip to discover the streets and squares of Athens and how everyday moments of resistance are performed. We ask you to witness our stories; we ask you to join hands to find words for your own resistance (related or not to the stories of economic crisis in Europe), to add to our growing line of enquiry.

There are many forms of occupation and different pathways to social change. Nothing exists in an absolute state. Yet, through small gatherings and everyday gestures, we hold the power to destroy the hegemonic blueprint of social order. To paraphrase Orwell, "It's a beautiful thing, the destruction of worlds".

We invite you to join us for three performative moments:

In the first, you witness Myrto's confession of her love affair with Athens. The post punk protester cracks out some of her photographs.

In the second section we work towards getting you ready to participate in protests with us in the square. Some of you have gas masks, and some protective cream against tear gas.

In the final performance moment, Athens goes on trial for her unruly lifestyle and continued protests.

*Hang up paper, collect Myrto's letter to be read.*

**Myrto**

*Scene 3: Love Letter to Athens*

*Myrto sitting in a chair.*
  *Ally hands her a letter.*
  *Opens it, reads; reflecting on the images.*
Athens, you urban bitch of cement dreams, we have been apart for so long, but still I call you "home".

I grew up in your shadows, or, more correctly, I grew up with you—so our relationship follows the Freudian notion of family ties: I've embraced you, only to reject you a few years later. Now, from a distance, I am in danger of becoming nostalgic. Bear with me. Sometimes, I could see myself reflected within your cityscapes and I think now we're in the process of resolving the Oedipus complex between us. But let me be a bit more explicit.

Throughout my first steps, you breast-fed me with your urban grand narratives, and in turn I was spellbound by the "birthplace of democracy and civilization". I sat on marble steps overlooking Acropolis reading Plato and Socrates, overwhelmed by an idealistic assurance that this was part of my history.

It's true that every form of nation-building evokes the sentiments of a glorious past, but you, Athens, believed you had the admiration and acceptance of the whole world. Who was I to question such a great heritage? My urban playground of broken marble pillars and identities.

It took me some years to read the small letters and the invisible footnotes to this grand story: Acropolis was the product of slavery; in the great Athenian democracy only upper-class males had the right to vote. In short, whoever was not an Athenian was a barbarian. You xenophobic snob!

During my adolescent urban explorations I understood that, like many capital cities, you are a city of strangers. Refugees, survivors, displaced people and revolutionaries came to call you home. Stories from the civil war and the dictatorship were commonplace in family gatherings. So many war stories and different names for "the barbarians", I lost count. In modern Greek history we were the first generation who did not experience a war (civil war or military coup). Thirty-five years of peace—enough to create a dream of *la dolce vita*.

But, Athens, cities are like living organisms; they do not explicitly tell their past but contain it in the small alleys and cracks on the buildings. And your maps signify a thousand stories: not all of them glorious and genteel. Anyone could have predicted something like the social crisis you have experienced over the last two years, if they just understood the bubble:

For the last fifteen years Athenians experienced the Cinderella phenomenon: a sense of prosperity, an increasing job market related to the Olympic

Games of 2004, new infrastructure. People were lulled into a sense of financial security, driving fancy cars; this was a generation of Ray Bans, nightlife, opa!

We lived our myth of Europeanization and Western lifestyle to the extreme. We had achieved our pumpkin chariot: a European profile and a happily-ever-after capitalistic lifestyle. And the clock struck midnight . . . and Cinderella transformed . . .

Us: a generation implicated in bribery, clientelism, corruption and mismanagement.

You: A city still looking for the Barbarians—like a mythic heroine blinded by hubris, yet to wake up to the realities of your present situation.

**Audience Members**

*Scene 4: Context Using Statistics*

*There is an improvised invitation for people to read statistics, and then place them on the washing line.* [14]

The official unemployment rate is 25.1 percent: for the age group eighteen to thirty, that figure stands at 62.5 percent. [15]

The riot forces have trebled in ranks since 2009, although exact data are not provided by the government.

One out of three Greeks lives below the poverty threshold. [16]

There has been a 45 percent increase in the use of antidepressants. [17]

There have been twenty thousand new homeless people in Athens alone since 2011. [18]

The suicide rate doubled in 2011, almost tripled in the first months of 2012. [19]

5 April 2012: Dimitris Christoulas committed suicide in Syntagma Square as a result of the economic crisis.

3 June 2012: There is a shortage of medication. People with cancer cannot access treatment; state-run hospitals made a call to stop nonessential surgical interventions because of a critical shortage of gloves, syringes and gauze, [20] Medicins du Monde have declared this a humanitarian crisis. [21]

June 2012: second-round elections granted far-right Golden Dawn 7 percent, which means parliamentary representation by fascists. This also grants them MP Asylum.

But every "state of emergency" is also a "state of emergence". [22] In Athens, there is a hopeful, creative, and generative sense to the ways people have protested against austerity measures, racism and corruption. Our dreams painted like graffiti tags on your walls. Our desires marching on your streets, occupying your squares—deporting the barbarians within ourselves.

# Ally

*Scene 5: Taking to the Streets*

*Use Bullhorn:*

> Welcome to Athens. I'm your host in this central square. I'm going to ask
> you to learn part of a common slogan: *le-le-leftheria! (Repeat)*

Protests are a means for people to explore common grievances, expose
new concerns, and collaborate in order to represent issues. Questioning the
norms of appropriate acts of citizenship, they attempt to create a more inclusive and participatory space. Protests that disrupt everyday activities open up
opportunities for those who are usually on the periphery to be seen and heard.
By creating a march in the midst of the city space, the protesters achieve a
subversion of the hegemonic uses of space.

The march transforms into a transgression of the daily roles and levels of
visibility as, side by side, protesters claim their right to the city by demanding how the city should accommodate them all.

The return to street politics meant people were talking about the need to
overcome individual isolation and the obligation to reclaim their lives and
their city.

Many innovative resistance techniques are displayed in the streets of
Athens, all with the common target of interrupting the everyday conditions of
oppression and awakening people's consciousness.

Yet this emergence of street politics is hardly peaceful.

*(Bullhorn) Le-le-leftheria se osous einai sta kelia!*

*Put on hat:*
Could those with masks please wear them now?
The protesters have become targets for tighter surveillance measures; the
official answer to such mobilization has been the intensification of police
control and violence, transforming central streets into urban battlefields. Police continued to demonize the protesters and counter their arguments with
tear gas, plastic bullets and unjust prosecutions. Intimidation, fear and the
curtailment of freedoms are the new order.

People are gathering in public spaces to have their outrage and grievances
spoken out loud, shared through banners, slogans, chants and formations of
bodies in squares and circles.

These strange and compelling dances of solidarity, new ways of being
together in spaces in which bonds of care are not forged through political
affiliations, but through proximity and common experiences. These are performances of civic participation. Some theorists have called it direct democ-

racy; some have become enthusiastic about the agora similar to the general assemblies of Occupy, where, instead of shouting slogans, people gather together to discuss issues. [23]

Now.

Those with masks on? You have been arrested, you will be on trial for participating in riots and destruction of public property. You face three years. Those with Maalox, you face arrest for subversive civil disobedience. Those without, and who have not been hospitalized, you get to go home, make calls to lawyers, publicize the arrests.

In Athens 2012, time is not marked out by the changing of seasons, but mapped by economic haircuts; ordinary people have pinned their hopes onto electing the "right" officials to deliver the country from sure ruin; the seasons of bureaucracy and its failures have remapped the city. Dystopia is unfolding.

*Sit down.*

*Count money.*

## Myrto

*Scene 6: Remapping*

If we consider maps as representations that chart known terrains, and always underpinned by certain discourses—namely, power, territory and politics—then we might also conceive of the destruction of these maps as a process of remapping the terrain and providing new symbols for charting it.

When we imagine the erosion of boundaries and the creation of new territories of dialogue, we should be able to remap our indigenous landscapes in order to include those who remained invisible and marginalized because they could not fit the cognitive, moral or aesthetic map of the dominant world. To paraphrase Bauman, [24] the chance of human togetherness depends on the rights of the marginalized, not on the question of who is entitled to decide who the marginalized are.

The "occupations" are neither crushed nor quelled; they are transformed into new ways of being in the city, with a new mode of examining the frames governing our behaviours. There is a call, then, in navigating street politics and performances of resistance to rework "the right to the city" as the ability to transform the self and imagine the city to come. The existing order is

> not something which can be destroyed by a revolution, it is a condition, a certain relationship between human beings, a mode of behaviour; we destroy it by contracting other relationships, by behaving differently. [25]

*Ally—rounds up Myrto: she is dragged to the chair.*

Ally: Enough—you're being charged with inciting civil disobedience.

## Ally

*Scene 7: Athens Herself Is on Trial*

We have collected a dossier with testimonies and have expert witnesses here
to testify on her behalf.
    *Bends down, patronizingly to Myrto—who is personifying Athens.*
    The charges are:

tenacious non-compliance;
fraternizing with international bankers;
clientelism;
unrepentant laziness;
handing out early pensions;
tax evasion;
sun-baked decadence;
the list goes on.

I know, I know, some people say this trial has a foregone conclusion.
Athens, they say, will be held for a rather large ransom (I mean bailout
package). This package, or MEMORANDUM, was signed by the government with no parliamentary discussion about its terms.
    At the moment, that is set at 321 billion euros.[26] Since that is quite a high
sum, it translates to about ten years of hard times.[27] Some economists have
estimated it's likely to stretch to twenty to thirty years.[28]
    As it stands, no-one else can post bail except your own people. This is
being collected through pensions, cuts in services, solidarity tax. And, in the
fine print, the elites are exempt from paying up.
    Before we hear the statement from the defendant, any objections? (*To
audience.*)
    I didn't think so.

## Myrto

*Testimony from Athens[29]*

Like my comrades, who have been detained on trumped up charges, I am on
    hunger strike, in solidarity with all those people who are starving on my
                                behalf.

This is not a passive resistance; or a peaceful protest
Enacted in order to gain sympathy from those in power.
This is a way to redefine our own corpus;
Outside of the authority this memorandum has placed on us.

The price of freedom has been great.
But the struggle will continue
Until sovereignty is restored.
Until my people can gather freely in streets and squares
Without fear of violence and criminalization.
Until I am able to define the terms of my own recovery.
Until people are aware of the power of their participation in making change
possible.

I am guilty.
And yet, I resist.

## Ally

*Scene 8: The Making of the Agora*

*Distanced from the satirical position of "the trial" scene.*

We've seen and heard some of the untold stories that have resulted in Athens and Greece in a precarious social and political position, teetering on the brink of humanitarian crisis. We have looked at different ways the economic crisis is much more than disappearing capital, the greediness of banks fuelled by corruption and mismanagement. "The crisis", we feel, is symptomatic—in Greece, as elsewhere—of the urgent need for change. From individuals, to local practices, through policies and reforms.

We don't have enough time to conduct a full assembly now, but we would like to include your voices in the new memorandum of social change.

We invite you now to add your own clause to the memorandum of social change: a statement of your own ways of resisting/referring to your own national/transnational context/local issues/identity-or-embodied resistance.

Add your line/statement/thoughts to our washing line. The sentences will hang together and form a map of how we can creatively and collaboratively destroy this world and imagine anew.

*Silence.*

*The audience is typically encouraged to write a statement.*

*The performers do not leave the stage, but engage with questions or reflections on the experience.*

## REFERENCES

Bacon, Jane. "It Ain't What You Do, It's the Way That You Do It". *Studies in Theatre and Performance* 25 (2005): 215–27.
Bauman, Zygmunt. *Postmodernity and Its Discontents.* Cambridge: Polity, 1997.
Bhabha, Homi K. *The Location of Culture.* London: Routledge, 1994.

Chapkis, Wendy. "Productive Tensions: Ethnographic Engagement, Complexity and Contradiction". *Journal of Contemporary Ethnography* 39 (2010): 483–97.

Chatzistefanou, Aris. "Greece's Biggest Hospital Struggles as Austerity Cuts Bite"—Video. *Guardian*, 15 June 2012. Accessed 1 December 2013. www.theguardian.com/world/greek-election-blog-2012/video/2012/jun/15/greece-hospital-austerity-cuts-video.

Denzin, Norman K. *Performance Ethnography: Critical Pedagogy and the Politics of Culture.* Thousand Oaks, CA: Sage, 2003.

Denzin, Norman K., and Yvonna S. Lincoln, eds. *Handbook of Qualitative Inquiry.* Thousand Oaks, CA: Sage, 2002.

Douzinas, Costas. *Philosophy and Resistance in the Crisis: Greece and the Future of Europe.* Cambridge: Polity, 2013.

Douzinas, Costas. "Greece's Lines Are Now Clear". *Guardian*, 20 October 2011. Accessed 1 December 2013. www.theguardian.com/commentisfree/2011/oct/20/greece-lines-clear-elite.

*Ekathimerini*. "Olympic Stadium Opens Doors to Athens Homeless". 1 February 2012. Accessed 1 December 2013. www.ekathimerini.com/4dcgi/_w_articles_wsite1_1_01/02/2012_425521.

Ellis, Carolyn, and Arthur P. Bochner. "Autoethnography, Personal Narrative, Reflexivity: Researcher as Subject". In *Handbook of Qualitative Research*, edited by Norman K. Denzin and Yvonna S. Lincoln, 733–68. Thousand Oaks, CA: Sage, 2000.

Goffman, Erving. *The Presentation of Self in Everyday Life.* London: Penguin, 1990.

Hare, June D. "Review: Johnny Saldaña Ethnodrama: An Anthology of Reality Theatre". *Forum: Qualitative Social Research* 9 (2008): 1–7.

Henley, Jon. "Meeting the EU's Lost Generation". *Guardian*, 6 June 2013. Accessed 1 December 2013. www.theguardian.com/world/blog/2013/jun/06/meeting-eu-lost-generation-jon-henley.

Landauer, Gustav. "Weak Statesmen, Weaker People". In *Anarchism: A Documentary History of Libertarian Ideas, Volume One: From Anarchy to Anarchism*, edited by Robert Graham. Montreal: Black Rose Books, 2005.

Lefebvre, Henri. *The Production of Space.* Translated by Donald Nicholson-Smith. Oxford: Blackwell, 1991.

Lemert, Charles, and Ann Branaman, eds. *The Goffman Reader.* Oxford: Blackwell, 1997.

Mason, Paul. "Love or Nothing: The Real Greek Parallel with Weimar". BBC News, 20 October 2012. Accessed 1 December 2013. http://www.bbc.co.uk/news/world-20105881.

Medecins du Monde. "Athens: A City in Humanitarian Crisis". MDM, 7 November 2010. Accessed 1 December 2013. http://mdmgreece.gr/en/Δελτία-Τύπου/Athens-a-city-in-Humanitarian-Crisis.

Mienczacowski, Jim. "The Theatre of Ethnography: The Reconstruction of Ethnography into Theatre with Emancipatory Potential". *Qualitative Inquiry* 1 (1995): 360–75.

"National Debt Exceeds 321 Billion Euros". *To Vima*, 26 August 2013. Accessed 1 December 2013. www.tovima.gr/en/article/?aid=527437&wordsinarticle=321.

Pelias, Ronald. *Writing Performance, Poeticizing the Researcher's Body.* Carbondale: Southern Illinois University Press, 1999.

Saldaña, Johnny, ed. *Ethnodrama: An Anthology of Reality Theatre.* Walnut Creek, CA: AltaMira Press, 2005.

Schechner, Richard. *Performance Studies: An Introduction.* 2nd ed. New York: Routledge, 2006.

Traynor, Ian. "Crisis Over in the Eurozone? Not in the Real World". *Guardian*, 9 October 2013. Accessed 1 December 2013. www.theguardian.com/business/2013/oct/09/crisis-over-eurozone-not-real-world.

Tsilimpounidi, Myrto. "Performances 'in Crisis': What Happens When a City Goes Soft?" *City* 16 (2012): 546–56.

Turner, Victor. *From Ritual to Theatre.* New York: PAJ Publications, 1982.

Varoufakis, Yannis. "Six Years Have Passed since the Shanghai Crash of 2032, and Europe's Architecture Is Incapable of Responding". *Europe's World*, 1 October 2013. Accessed 1 December 2013. http://europesworld.org/2013/10/01/six-years-have-passed-since-the-shanghai-crash-of-2032-and-europes-architecture-is-incapable-of-responding/#.UpuHj6X7VFI.

Walsh, Aylwyn, and Myrto Tsilimpounidi. "Reflections of an Urban Revolution". In *Sarai Reader 09: Projections*, 210–16. Delhi: Sarai Media Lab, 2013.

## NOTES

1. Johnny Saldaña, ed., *Ethnodrama: An Anthology of Reality Theatre* (Walnut Creek, CA: AltaMira Press, 2005).
2. Ibid., 2.
3. See Erving Goffman, *The Presentation of Self in Everyday Life* (London: Penguin, 1990); Charles Lemert and Ann Branaman, eds., *The Goffman Reader* (Oxford: Blackwell, 1997).
4. See Jim Mienczakowski, "The Theatre of Ethnography: The Reconstruction of Ethnography into Theatre with Emancipatory Potential", *Qualitative Inquiry* 1 (1995): 360–75; Ronald Pelias, *Writing Performance, Poeticizing the Researcher's Body* (Carbondale: Southern Illinois University Press, 1999); Victor Turner, *From Ritual to Theatre* (New York: PAJ Publications, 1982).
5. Richard Schechner, *Performance Studies: An Introduction*, 2nd ed. (New York: Routledge, 2006).
6. Jane Bacon, "It Ain't What You Do, It's the Way That You Do It", *Studies in Theatre and Performance* 25 (2005): 215–27; June D. Hare, "Review: Johnny Saldaña Ethnodrama: An Anthology of Reality Theatre", *Forum: Qualitative Social Research* 9 (2008): 1–7.
7. Norman K. Denzin and Yvonna S. Lincoln, eds., *Handbook of Qualitative Inquiry* (Thousand Oaks, CA: Sage, 2002), 182.
8. Norman K. Denzin, *Performance Ethnography: Critical Pedagogy and the Politics of Culture* (Thousand Oaks, CA: Sage, 2003).
9. Wendy Chapkis, "Productive Tensions: Ethnographic Engagement, Complexity and Contradiction", *Journal of Contemporary Ethnography* 39 (2010): 489.
10. Ibid., 491.
11. Please note that certain ideas of the following text have been published in the following: Myrto Tsilimpounidi, "Performances 'in Crisis': What Happens When a City Goes Soft?", *City* 16 (2012): 546–56; and Aylwyn Walsh and Myrto Tsilimpounidi, "Reflections of an Urban Revolution", in *Sarai Reader 09: Projections* (Delhi: Sarai Media Lab, 2013).
12. Henri Lefebvre, *The Production of Space*, trans. Donald Nicholson-Smith (Oxford: Blackwell, 1991).
13. Ibid., 63.
14. Please note these statements change to reflect up-to-date information on a day-to-day basis.
15. Jon Henley, "Meeting the EU's Lost Generation", *Guardian*, 6 June 2013, accessed 1 December 2013, www.theguardian.com/world/blog/2013/jun/06/meeting-eu-lost-generation-jon-henley.
16. Ian Traynor, "Crisis Over in the Eurozone? Not in the Real World", *Guardian*, 9 October 2013, accessed 1 December 2013. www.theguardian.com/business/2013/oct/09/crisis-over-eurozone-not-real-world.
17. Paul Mason, "Love or Nothing: The Real Greek Parallel with Weimar", BBC News, 20 October 2012. Accessed 1 December 2013. http://www.bbc.co.uk/news/world-20105881.
18. "Olympic Stadium Opens Doors to Athens Homeless", *Ekathimerini*, 1 February 2012, accessed 1 December 2013, www.ekathimerini.com/4dcgi/_w_articles_wsite1_1_01/02/2012_425521.
19. Mason, "Love or Nothing".
20. Aris Chatzistefanou, "Greece's Biggest Hospital Struggles as Austerity Cuts Bite"—Video, *Guardian*, 15 June 2012, accessed 1 December 2013, www.theguardian.com/world/greek-election-blog-2012/video/2012/jun/15/greece-hospital-austerity-cuts-video.
21. Medecins du Monde, "Athens: A City in Humanitarian Crisis", MDM, 7 November 2010, accessed 1 December 2013, http://mdmgreece.gr/en/Δελτία-Τύπου/Athens-a-city-in-Humanitarian-Crisis.

22. Homi K. Bhabha, *The Location of Culture* (London: Routledge, 1994).

23. Costas Douzinas, "Greece's Lines Are Now Clear", *Guardian*, 20 October 2011, accessed 1 December 2013, www.theguardian.com/commentisfree/2011/oct/20/greece-lines-clear-elite.

24. Zygmunt Bauman, *Postmodernity and Its Discontents* (Cambridge: Polity, 1997).

25. Gustav Landauer, "Weak Statesmen, Weaker People", in *Anarchism: A Documentary History of Libertarian Ideas, Volume One: From Anarchy to Anarchism*, ed. Robert Graham (Montreal: Black Rose Books, 2005), 165.

26. "National Debt Exceeds 321 Billion Euros", *To Vima*, 26 August 2013, accessed 1 December 2013, www.tovima.gr/en/article/?aid=527437&wordsinarticle=321.

27. Douzinas, "Greece's Lines Are Now Clear".

28. Yannis Varoufakis, "Six Years Have Passed since the Shanghai Crash of 2032, and Europe's Architecture Is Incapable of Responding", *Europe's World*, 1 October 2013, accessed 1 December 2013. http://europesworld.org/2013/10/01/six-years-have-passed-since-the-shanghai-crash-of-2032-and-europes-architecture-is-incapable-of-responding/#.UpuHj6X7VFI.

29. This extract has been modelled on a statement from hunger-striking political prisoners CCF.

*Chapter Eight*

# The Logic of Movement Practice

*An Embodiment Approach to Activist Research*

Raphael Schlembach

Methodologies of activist research are very much born out of a dilemma: many activist researchers find themselves in a social space located somewhere between academic and activist circles, yet they often feel rejected by both. On the one hand, academia demands political neutrality and rejects the researcher's involvement in social movements. In activist circles, on the other hand, researchers—as engaged as they might be—are frequently accused of turning the movement into a talking shop.[1]

In this chapter I outline and contribute to activist research methodologies that try to break with this dilemma and dichotomy by melting the boundaries between activism and academia, between object and subject and between theory and practice. I use Pierre Bourdieu's theory of practice and his reflexive sociology as a basis for my argumentation.[2] It will constitute the link between the archetype of pure thought—academia—and the archetype of action—movement activism. Going beyond Bourdieu, however, the chapter outlines a methodology of theory *as* practice. Using Bourdieu's theoretical tools, I aim to show how the subject and object of study become blurred in social movement practice, and conclude that theory can be considered to constitute a practice in itself (at least in the social movement context). The chapter brings together Bourdieusian sociology with the practice of activist research to show how the distinction between theory and practice, or thought and action, limits our grasp of the logic of social movement realities.

## ON MOVEMENT "THEORY"

In many ways, the philosophical focus on epistemology in this paper runs counter to the intention of Bourdieu's sociology. For Bourdieu, methodological and epistemological concepts are instruments at the hands of sociologists with which to explore social reality. Time and again, he has taken issue with his critics for separating his theoretical from his empirical work and for discussing his texts without a practical research programme in mind:

> But the clearest misunderstanding stems from the fact that the *lector's* reading is an end in itself, and that it is interested in texts, and in the theories, methods or concepts they convey, not in order to do something with them, to bring them, as useful, perfectible instruments, into a practical use, but so as to gloss them, by relating them to other texts.[3]

Theories, in Bourdieu's sense, are not meant to provoke philosophical discussions, but must underpin empirical research projects and practical social science. This anti-philosophical attitude manifests itself in the rejection of theory for theory's sake.[4] "Theoreticism" divides the social sciences into methodological specialisms and forces an empirical-philosophical dualism into the discipline. Instead, Bourdieu points to the practical side of the pursuit of theory, which, just as empirical work, produces its own knowledge. Research, he contends, is always based on practical, pre-intentional academic dispositions, which at every moment in the research process force themselves into the contextualization and conceptualization of social observations.

He thus argues against the autonomy of philosophical thought. Philosophy, in his view, fails to ponder the relationship between thought and thinker.[5] Bourdieu's own empirical work, ethnographic and sociological, has developed and re-applied concepts not outside of specific social contexts, but with the intention of utilizing them as tools in the analysis of social phenomena. It objectifies sociological analysis in its relation to social philosophy.[6]

However, Bourdieu's anti-theoreticism is not entirely justified. Not all research can rely on its own empirical data and make use of already developed theoretical concepts. Concepts, classifications and theories all need to undergo constant critical examination. The uncritical acceptance of Bourdieu's methodological and epistemological assumptions would lead to an unscientific "methodologism".[7] What is needed is not the neglect of theory in favour of a more practical orientation of research. Theory and practice should not be considered the opposite poles of a one-dimensional spectrum on which all research has to be situated. Instead, what a Bourdieu-inspired critical sociology should call for is the overcoming of the theory-practice dualism altogether.

The "construction of the object of research" is the key to understanding Bourdieu's rejection of what he calls "theoreticist theory".[8] Bourdieu wants to see the object of research at the forefront of every research project. In short, he renounces theory without object. His "theory of practice" allows him to be a practitioner of theory, engaged and involved in the construction of the object of research beyond mere participant observation. As he explains with reference to his field work in Algeria:

> It was absolutely necessary to be at the heart of events so as to form one's opinion, however dangerous it might have been—and dangerous it was. To see, to record, to photograph: I have never accepted the separation between the theoretical construction of the object of research and the set of practical procedures without which they [sic] can be no real knowledge.[9]

In many ways, Bourdieu did thus break with the theory-practice dualism in his work. He criticizes the separation of intellectual thought from practical experience. What he called for was not more "interaction" between, but rather a "fusion" of theory and practice in research,[10] maintaining that every research effort is at the same time empirical *and* theoretical. Nonetheless, his is a "theory *of* practice"; a formulation that leaves no doubt over the continued gap that lies between thought and action. This chapter shall show how this gap can be closed—melting the boundaries between theory and practice—by using Bourdieu's very own concepts.

## EMBODYING PRACTICAL KNOWLEDGE

Protest can sometimes appear as a spectacle from the outside: thousands of bodies dancing to electronic music on a motorway; hundreds of hands digging in Parliament Square to transform the manicured lawn into a vegetable allotment; a carnival procession turning to occupy international financial institutions and stock exchanges; brass and samba bands leading the marches of youths in black balaclavas; anarchists wearing pink and silver fairy dresses and revolutionaries in camouflaged clown costumes chasing and being chased by hordes of riot police.

Yet a movement does not exist merely as events in such "moments of excess".[11] The movement's ideas and realities persist when activists leave the sites of protest and dissent behind. The pink and silver fairies, the guerrilla gardeners, the protesters are also mothers and fathers, friends and colleagues, students and teachers. They continue to campaign, to communicate and to network. The cuts and bruises that some will have received in confrontations with police might heal quickly. However, the incorporated experiences they have made mark a permanent shift in their realities.

The bodily experiences that activists make during direct actions or large protest mobilizations are important in shaping a social movement's reality. The human body is in many ways central to much of a movement's activity, be it in going on protest marches, pushing through police lines, blockading roads or dancing at Reclaim the Streets parties. The Clandestine Insurgent Rebel Clown Army (CIRCA) is a popular direct-action group which has repeatedly stressed the significance of using body image, emotions and physical appearances as strategic tools in the movement. [12] Founded in November 2003 at the time of George W. Bush's visit to the United Kingdom, it was originally perceived as another direct-action tactic, similar to the ones of pink and silver samba bands or carnivals against capitalism. In fact, as two Rebel Clowns write:

> It was meant to be a lot more than a tactic. The methodology of rebel clowning was developed as a way of trying to overcome what we perceived as some of the deeper problems in the way we behave as radicals towards each other, ourselves and our world. [13]

Rebel Clowns dress in a mix of clown costume and camouflaged army wear. For a few years, they had become a common feature of radical protest and direct action against neo-liberal globalization. Where they appear, they provoke a variety of emotions, from laughter to annoyance, sometimes diffusing violent police reaction to protest situations, sometimes provoking it. Whatever tactic is used, body and emotions always play an important role in Rebel Clowning. During the anti-G8 actions in Scotland, a group of Rebel Clowns persuaded half a dozen policemen to play a game, which ended in police and protesters hugging each other. The Rebel Clowns described the game as such:

> Known as "Dwarfs, Wizards and Giants" it's a version of paper-scissors-stone, but played in teams with the whole body. One of the rules is that if both teams choose the same character, no one wins and they all have to hug. This is exactly what happened as clown and cop teams simultaneously chose to be "wizards". [14]

The Rebel Clown Army aims to bring out the very emotions and feelings that have led many activists to become political radicals in the first place. Feelings of anger or sadness, or the firsthand experience of violence, climate chaos or poverty, are a major factor in the emergence of protest. [15] Yet, in combination with police repression and criminalization, such emotions can also lead to depression, frustration and burnout. Many activists, the Rebel Clowns argue, have built up protective armour against such feelings by escaping their bodies and focusing on cognitive, strategic ways of overcoming their fear. With a return to bodily experiences, the Rebel Clowns thus aim to break down dichotomies. When they imitate police behaviour—standing stern-faced with arms crossed in front of their chests as a second reinforcing police line, for example—they effectively challenge our dichotomous thinking in terms of authorities and protester, or activist and non-activist. Rebel Clowning melts the border between what is a premeditated protest strategy and the repetitive imitation of lived experiences and emotions. [16]

Research into movement realities has to take the incorporated knowledge that activists reproduce into account. Alain Touraine has attempted to do just this when he calls for a methodology of "sociological intervention". [17] His method aims at understanding movements better by not only engaging in participant observation but also being an active contributor to the movement's formation and reproduction. However, his method falls short of blurring the boundaries between a movement activist and a movement researcher. Touraine's "intervention" is a sociological instrument to objectify and generate knowledge about the movements he studies. He thus remains at the epistemological outside of his "objects"—witnessing, participating and intervening, while, nonetheless, the very relationship between the researcher and the researched, between theory and practice, is still not subjected to a critical analysis. Those in the movement who go to summit mobilizations or large protests and direct actions, on the other hand, know that they are not witnessing a spectacle. They are involved and caught up in a social reality that at the very moment of its manifestation generates knowledge about itself. They do not act in order to feed into theory, and they do not think simply in order to develop their practice. Instead, their bodies are the epistemological basis for feeling, experiencing and thinking the world, while their thoughts and ideas are the practice of a radical critique of the Social. What they take home are the manifold (bodily) experiences of the event.

## BODILY PRACTICE AND PRACTICAL KNOWLEDGE

Issues of embodiment and incorporation are also central to Pierre Bourdieu's theory of practice. He analyses all practice as embodied practice. Embodiment transcends the Cartesian dualism of mind and body, which assumes the primacy of intellectual judgement over bodily practice. The mind, in the dualist account, takes a leading role in interpreting and judging sensual perceptions and in planning and reflecting on bodily actions. The dualism of mind and body is derived from a view of the body from the outside. It assumes the externality of the intellect or mind from the Social. Bourdieu counters with a Pascalian claim, which he turns into an epistemological cornerstone of his sociology of sociology: "I know the world *because* I am a part of it". An individual's understanding of her reality is precisely derived from her physical and social position in the world. We are all immersed in a physical and social space—often unnoticed and non-reflected upon—and it is through this encompassing position that we gain knowledge of our surroundings. We are not *atopos*, but our biological bodies occupy material and social space in the world. The knowledge we gain is thus derived from a position of internality—internal to worldly practice. What we gain is *practical* knowledge of the world.

Bourdieu's is of course not the only epistemological attempt to break with the dualism of mind and body. His theory of practice does nonetheless present a very practical solution to the problem.[18] Practice is understood as habitual and precognitive. Rather than on intellectual reflection, it is based on bodily experiences that shape the individual self. It is through the exposure of the body—that is, our brain and our senses—to the world that we gain a comprehension of our surroundings. It is thus a *corporeal* comprehension, and not a conscious understanding, of the world that influences our actions within it. Our bodily experiences, from the moment of our birth and repeated over and over again, become the foundation of our practical knowledge of the world. The worldly structures that we learn to understand become *incorporated* in our selves. The instruments of practical knowledge of which we dispose are thus not arrived at through conscious reflection on our sensual experiences, but rather are constructed by the very fact that we are actors in the world. Knowledge, therefore, is a direct result of the practical intervention in the Social.

Just as the Rebel Clown Army does not appeal to a cognitive understanding of its activities, but rather to our emotions, feelings or instincts, Bourdieu embodies our understanding of the world by basing it on habitual dispositions of practice. These dispositions, in turn, are based on the bodily exposure to emotions and sensual experiences.

The body serves as an instrument of knowledge production, just as the laughing or crying face of a Rebel Clown serves as an instrument of communication. Equally, it is the exposure to emotions and experiences of laughter, violence, misunderstanding, fear and so on that shapes an activist's practical knowledge of a situation and that determines her practice. However, it is more than just bodily exposure to repeated worldly experiences that produces knowledge. As Bourdieu has it,[19] every agent is also an actor in the Social. The world encompasses her, but she is also engaged in it; she has a stake in the world. Moreover, it is not just the social movement actor who has a stake in the field of her action. As researchers, theorists or social scientists, we are also encompassed by and implicated in the world that we aim to investigate. Embodied, practical knowledge is generated through the academic's involvement in worldly practice. Again, understanding of the world is attained not despite, but *because* of the theorist's bodily exposure to the Social. The idea that our mind or intellect can remain on the outside of investigative practice, that it can assume a position of objectifying distance, is firmly rejected by

Bourdieu's sociology of embodiment. In it, there is no place for a distant, objective gaze onto the social world.

In his discussion of Bourdieu's reflexive sociology, Loïc Wacquant warns of "[t]he *intellectualist bias* which entices us to construe the world as a *spectacle*, as a set of significations to be interpreted rather than as concrete problems to be solved practically".[20] The supposed virtues of the externality of the mind, Bourdieu writes himself, have "condemned [the social scientist] to see all practice as a spectacle".[21] This has important methodological implications that are taken up by activist research. Research is bound by the incorporated scientific dispositions towards the field of study. Being part of this world means being situated in-the-world, not external to it. Activist research situates itself in the field of investigation. Just as the immanence of the Social in ourselves and the immanence of ourselves in the Social determine the logic of practice for Bourdieu, the active engagement with and within the object of study is a necessary precondition for the practical comprehension of the logic of action in movements.

However, the lack of an objective gaze, the lack of an objectifying distance, represents a methodological problem of non-reflected familiarity. As Bourdieu puts it, the theorist

> knows [the world], in a sense, too well, without objectifying distance, takes it for granted, precisely because he is caught up in it, bound up with it; he inhabits it like a garment or a familiar habitat. He feels at home in the world because the world is also in him, in the form of habitus.[22]

Bourdieu describes this familiarity with the Social as a "necessary coincidence",[23] the coincidence of one's habitual dispositions and one's field of action. It is not, however, this familiarity with the object of study that presents the methodological challenge to social research. Rather, it is the illusion of the possibility of distance from the Social that creates a bias in research. Social theory itself is thus subjected to certain academic habitual dispositions; a scientific habitus. As Brubaker explains, "As a social practice like others, social research is governed and informed by internalized dispositions, not by codified propositions, by the practical logic of the habitus, not by the theoretical logic set forth in treatises and textbooks".[24] Brubaker here argues against a logocentric view of theory, instead basing the production of knowledge on Bourdieu's sociological *sens pratique*. The craft of social research is thus regulated by scientific dispositions which have been acquired through the constant exposure to bodily experiences. This equally applies to social theory: "it is not only sociological perception that is governed by the ingrained dispositions of the sociological habitus, but even, to a considerable extent, the sort of general and abstract thinking called theorizing".[25] The incorporated worldly structures that grant us access to a practical comprehension of practice are the very foundations on which theories are built. More-over, the theories and conceptualizations *of* the Social are, at the same time, *part of* the Social. They are embedded within a world which, constructed as a spectacle, generates the illusion of distance, or of an objectifying boundary, between the theorist and the practitioner. The separation of the mind from the body, of the investigator from the investigated, of thought from action, how-ever, can no longer be maintained within the epistemological framework of Bourdieu's sociology of embodiment. Instead, the embodied structures of the Social—embodied through the repetition of worldly experiences—form the basis for a practical knowledge of practice.

## EPISTEMIC REFLEXIVE SOCIOLOGY

Bodily experiences and emotions all play a central role for the practical comprehension of movement practice. However, the double immanence—of the Social in the self and of the self in the Social—seldom receives a critical appraisal in the investigative process of movement theorists. Instead, one can witness a clear break between the collaborative practice of engaged research and the individualist moment of interpretation. While research "on the ground" is politically committed, engaged and practical, the researcher all too often resumes her intellectualist role in an attempt of a hermeneutic understanding of her practical experiences. From this latter position, the movement is constructed as an object to be observed and analysed. Participa-tion and collaboration then come to mean no more than seeking assistance in the mapping and interpretation of activist practices. Movement activists are, at best, assigned the role of "helpers" in the interpretative process of re-search. The theorist assumes that collaboration in research can enable acti-vists to objectify their own practices without a practical sense and derive, rather than practical knowledge, a hermeneutic understanding of activist practice from it.

What, then, does reflexivity signify for activist research? For the editors of one project, "the concern(s) at hand are the ways in which social research (re)-creates the distance between the researcher (as subject) and researched (as object), in so doing silencing the voices, needs, concerns, knowledges, and practices of the researched".[26] The same authors argue that "'critical' endeavors must take the paradox of their existence seriously if the claim towards criticality is not to be sneered at".[27] The paradox of activist research is a result of its location in a space, which is neither the neutral academic setting nor the non-reflected moment of activist practice. It is the objectifica-tion of this paradox that lies at the heart of a reflexive activist research methodology.

The epistemological foundation of all theory, Bourdieu contends, is situated in-the-world. Theory can never assume a contemplative position outside of its object of study. Therefore, being "implicated in the world . . . there is implicit content in what we think and say about it".[28] Just as activist research objectifies the production of knowledge within a social movement context, Bourdieu's *reflexive sociology* offers to account for the implicit in the realm of theory. The implicit, unconscious presuppositions that are entailed in our mode of thought entice us to construct a subjective agent, a model of the theorist who has taken refuge from the objective world and contemplates it from a distance. Every time, Bourdieu says, when we "pause in thought over our practice . . . [when] we turn back to it to consider it, describe it, analyse it, we become in a sense absent from it".[29] The objectification of this presumption of absence, which Bourdieu calls, borrowing a term from Austin, the *scholastic fallacy*, is at the heart of his programme of reflexivity.[30]

The scholastic fallacy is a bias that denies what Bourdieu's sociology of embodiment upholds: the incorporation, within us, of worldly structures in the form of the habitus. This bias reproduces the Cartesian dualism of mind and body inasmuch as it constructs the world hermeneutically, as an object to be decoded, deconstructed and interpreted, rather than experienced and understood in practical terms. Bourdieu thus calls it a *theoreticist* or *intellectualist* bias, reinforcing the paradigm of the spectacle and the primacy of thought over practice. The scholastic fallacy tempts the theorist to adopt an epistemological position that is removed from practical knowledge. The theorist comes to objectify her object of study without a reflection on her objectifying position.

When participatory movement research answers the academic demand for objectivity with the inscription of political commitment into the research process, this is barely enough to understand the epistemological structures that keep subject and object of research firmly apart. As Bourdieu puts it:

> What [has] to be done [is] not to sweep away the distance magically through spurious primitivist participation, but to objectify this objectifying distance and the social conditions which make it possible, such as the externality of the observer, the objectifying techniques that he uses, etc.[31]

Bourdieu identifies a second set of dispositions that interfere with sociological work and creates a bias in research. It derives from a researcher's location in a specific field. In most cases, the sociologist occupies a specific location within the institutions of academia, which results in the adaptation of certain dispositions that form her *scientific* or *academic habitus*. This is what Bourdieu describes in *Homo Academicus*.[32] Bourdieu's study of academic institutional sociology analyses how the habitus of conflicting academic interest groups played a role in the transformation of the French higher education system in the wake of the May 1968 student protests. Academic knowledge is, just as activist experiences, incorporated into a scientific habitus, and thus becomes embodied knowledge (embodied cultural capital). University elites are formed and their agendas shaped by social demographics and their social origins. The resulting divergent forms of cultural capital led to tensions in the university sector and subsequently to its transformation. Moreover, the embodied scientific habitus does more than simply influence an academic's view on the organization of scholarly activity. Scholarly activity itself is carried out with constant and unconscious reference to acquired academic dispositions. Research itself is then a manifestation of this habitus and of the researcher's embodied beliefs. This leads to a second research bias, which is derived from the researcher's cultural and social background. A reflexive return onto this bias thus objectifies the academic (social) location from which the research is carried out. Membership in specific intellectual circles accordingly limits our understanding of how and what we study. Our intellectual position within the academic field must therefore become an object of analysis.

It is the *intellectualist* or *theoreticist bias*, however, that is most difficult to account for, and which is the focal concern of Bourdieu's reflexive sociology. Activist research asks, "How, if at all, can research be a process of co-constitution rather than one of objectification?"[33] Bourdieu's reflexive sociology offers as an answer the "objectification of the objectifying subject". The reflexive return should go beyond a narcissist inscription of oneself into the research. Auto-ethnography simply reinstates the authority of the subject through a reflexive return of sociological instruments of analysis onto the self. It continues to distinguish between the researcher's authorship and the movement's practice. Reflexivity should also go beyond the recognition of the researcher's position in a microcosmic field (i.e., the academic or activist field). Instead, for Bourdieu, a reflexive sociology is one that objectifies the very relationship between the subject and object of research. In other words, reflexivity aims at tackling the "intellectualist bias" or "scholastic fallacy". This fallacy entices us to take a step out of the world in order to think:

> There is a sort of incompatibility between our scholarly thinking and this strange thing that practice is. To apply to practice a mode of thinking which presupposes the bracketing of practical necessity and the use of instruments of thought constructed against practice . . . is to forbid ourselves from understanding practice as such.[34]

The scholastic fallacy thus occurs when we fail to objectify the presuppositions that guide our thinking of the Social. Reflexivity in this sense has its task in tackling the "unthought categories of thinking that delimit the thinkable and predetermine the thought".[35] A number of methodological writings have based ideas on reflexivity on the work of Bourdieu in order to break with the dichotomy between objectivist and subjectivist understandings of the Social.[36] For activist research methodologies as well, Bourdieu's concept of situating reflexivity in-the-world can play a role. This is so in particular when reflexivity comes to mean a critical confrontation with the academic setting of (sociological) knowledge production and with the practical involvement in movement activities.

## EXPLORING THEORY *AS* PRACTICE

The focus on collective action within social movements, and its clear separation from thought, has been maintained by social movement analysts. Social movement participants have self-generated an image of the "activist" and defined much of its contentious politics as "direct action". In parts of the alter-globalization movement this has gone so far that any attempt at theorizing or reflecting about one's actions is dismissed. Ideological and political analysis has been replaced as the cornerstone of progressive movements by pragmatism and the perceived need to "do something". Writing about the American left at the time of the Iraq war, Liza Featherstone, Doug Henwood and Christian Parenti described this new unifying "ideology" at the forefront of the alter-globalists as "activistism". "Activistists", in this sense, hold the common belief that "the one who acts is righteous",[37] but they are indiscriminate about the effectiveness and strategic relevance of their actions. This criticism does not, however, favour intellectual analysis over political practice. Rather, Featherstone et al. contend that "ideas don't belong on pedestals. They belong in the street, at work, in the home, at the bar and on the barricades".[38] The authors only stop short of advocating the abolition of the boundary between thought and action when they write that "thinking, after all, is engaging".[39]

Activist researchers see a certain urgency in doing away with this distinction. It is an urgency that is derived from the contemporary organization of the Social, from the organization of social relationships reproducing exploitation and domination, and from a system that produces poverty and war. As activists, they work towards sustainable social change; however, the answers to the questions of war and terror, poverty and environmental destruction, are less clear. Can the response from the global justice movement be based on the same morality as the one that drives the aggressive policies of the world's leaders? Do we already have the answers to the world's problems and only need to implement our practical solutions? Those questions are urgent; yet the urgency does not lie in the need to act for action's sake. As Steffen Boehm has put it:

> What seems to be urgent to me then is a conception of the relationship between
> theory and practice that does not privilege either, and, by keeping room for a
> relative autonomy of theory, as practice, is able to intervene in contemporary
> discourses and practices. [40]

The movement's response, he argues, should thus not mean the celebration
of practice at the expense of theory, but should be conceptualized as "theoretical practice" instead. [41]

This is exactly where Bourdieu does not go far enough in his analysis.
Where is the space for agents to question their dispositions to a particular
practice, and thereby to be able to criticize contemporary societal practice?
How can Bourdieu's theory be applied to his own work, completely breaking
down any border between the object and subject of research, and between
structure and agency? How can Bourdieu develop an objective analysis of the
Social if he himself is "situated in-the-world" and his own epistemological
foundation of thought is "embodied practical knowledge"? There have been
some criticisms of his theory of practice from this angle. Jenkins [42] and Alexander, [43] for example, have accused Bourdieu of not achieving the departure
from determinism and for not leaving enough room for agency. Alexander
has gone so far as to call his theory of practice a "deterministic retelling of
structure as practice". [44] Jenkins describes it as having finalistic tendencies, in
which the objective conditions for habitual dispositions are generated by the
subjective experiences of the actor, which, in turn, have been determined by
the objective structures of the Social. [45] Whereas Crossley [46] considers this
interplay to be circular *ad infinitum*, Jenkins maintains that it represents
nothing more than "another form of determination in the last instance". [47]

The question seems to be whether there is room for a subjectively created
condition of active resistance against the determining dispositions and generating structures of practice in Bourdieu's work. Bourdieu seems to consider
the possibility for this to occur in three instances: [48] First, the habitus is the
objective outcome of a continuous historical struggle of subjectivities, so that
subjectivity and objectivity coexist at any moment in time. Second, there are
moments of crisis (such as the political situation in May 1968) during which
the subjective expectations of actors and the objective possibilities for their
realization appear to clash. During such moments of misfit between agency
and structure, agents become aware of their subjectivity and can bring their
traditional dispositions into the realm of open, public discourse. The question
remains, however, whether a crisis situation is not merely another manifestation of an objective structure that determines an actor's subjective experience. In this sense, aren't some actors disposed by their habitus to challenge
their (and society's) traditional mode of practice in such situations? Third,
Bourdieu seems to grant an increased awareness of subjectivity to the profession of social scientist—or academia in general. [49] Within the field of the

sociology of knowledge in particular, Bourdieu says, actors have attained the ability to think reflexively and objectively about human practice without being caught up in the Social themselves. This is interesting, as it potentially undermines the thorough application of the concept of habitus. Clearly, it would mean that the theory of practice does not apply to the "craft of sociology". This point has been raised by Hans-Herbert Kögler. [50] For him, either the sociology of knowledge is exempt from the impossibility of observation from the outside or Bourdieu defeats himself and his profession.

Bourdieu, as discussed above, advocates a form of epistemic reflexivity— a sort of sociology of sociology—non-narcissistic, non-autobiographical. Reflexivity, for Bourdieu, cannot rid sociology of its inherent academic bias, but it can free the researcher of her illusion that she has none. Yet is this epistemic reflexivity only achievable for professional social scientists? Bourdieu answers with a certain pragmatism of social knowledge. As Crossley puts it, scientists also "must see the world from 'somewhere'". [51] However, this "somewhere", this location in the academic field, Bourdieu contends, grants the sociologist a special objective disposition to reflexivity. In a sense, then, reflexivity is (or ought to be) inscribed in the researcher's habitus. This scientific habitus does not, of course, appear out of "nothing", but rather is a result of learning and training to be part of academia. The sociologist is trained in the use of methods which make her particularly suited to assume the role of objective analyst.

There seems to me to be a fundamental incoherence in Bourdieu's argument. Only when the sociologist is trained in removing herself in some way from the practice of the Social can she devise a theory *of* practice. At the same time, however, Bourdieu argues that all theory is also "situated in-the-world" and cannot assume a superior role of externality. At best, I would argue, theory could thus be regarded to come *from* practice, or be generated *by* practice. Crossley [52] very helpfully compares the sociologist's involvement in the world to a match of football. (Social movement) actors could be said to be the players in the game. They do understand the rules and have a sense of the strategy that they use to win. However, they are not at every moment conscious of them. Rather, they have a practical, instinctive knowledge of the rules of the game, or, expressed differently, they have a "feel" for the game. Sociologists, in Bourdieu's theory of practice, Crossley concludes, have a different role to play. They do not score points, or win the game, in the same way the other actors do. Sociologists "win" by describing, analysing and critiquing the other players, and by thinking reflexively about their observations. For Bourdieu, this is how science can be both part of the Social and thinking objectively about it.

While the analogy of the football match is insightful, I think that the wrong conclusions have been drawn from it. What sociologists do when they analyse and criticize is to *play* the game, not simply observe it. They are not sitting on the stands observing the other players from an external position. Thinking and theorizing are an integral part of the game, and as players, sociologists *act* in it. Theory, then, cannot simply be understood as *of* practice, or *from* it. Theory comes to mean practice itself: theory *as* practice.

Participation in movement activities provides us with a practical knowledge of the logic of activist practice, with a "feel for the game". For activist research, theory becomes practice when it is viewed as a movement activity itself. Theorizing, as we have argued above, is an important part of activist praxis, generating identities, realities and knowledge.

## REFERENCES

Adkins, Lisa. "Reflexivity: Freedom or Habit of Gender?" *Theory, Culture & Society* 20 (2003): 21–42.

Alexander, Jeffrey C. "The Reality of Reduction: The Failed Synthesis of Pierre Bourdieu". In *Fin de Siècle Social Theory: Relativism, Reduction and the Problem of Reason*, edited by J. C. Alexander, 128–217. London: Verso, 1995.

Barker, Colin, and Laurence Cox. "What Have the Romans Ever Done for Us?" Accessed 7 February 2014. www.iol.ie/~mazzoldi/toolsforchange/afpp/afpp8.html.

Bevington, Douglas, and Chris Dixon. "Movement-Relevant Theory: Rethinking Social Movement Scholarship and Activism". *Social Movement Studies* 4 (2005): 185–208.

Boehm, Steffen. "Movements of Theory and Practice". *ephemera: Theory and Politics in Organization* 2 (2002): 328–51.

Bourdieu, Pierre. *Pascalian Meditations*. Cambridge: Polity Press, 2000.

Bourdieu, Pierre. *Practical Reason*. Cambridge: Polity Press, 1998.

Bourdieu, Pierre. *In Other Words: Essays towards a Reflexive Sociology*. Cambridge: Polity Press, 1994.

Bourdieu, Pierre. *Sociology in Question*. London: Sage, 1993.

Bourdieu, Pierre. *The Political Ontology of Martin Heidegger*. Oxford: Polity Press, 1991.

Bourdieu, Pierre. *The Logic of Practice*. Cambridge: Polity Press, 1990.

Bourdieu, Pierre. "The Scholastic Point of View". *Cultural Anthropology* 5 (1990): 380–91.

Bourdieu, Pierre. *Homo Academicus*. Cambridge: Polity Press, 1990.

Bourdieu, Pierre. *Outline of a Theory of Practice*. Cambridge: Cambridge University Press, 1977.

Bourdieu, Pierre, and Loïc Wacquant. *An Invitation to Reflexive Sociology*. Chicago: University of Chicago Press, 1992.

Brubaker, Rogers. "Social Theory as Habitus". In *Bourdieu: Critical Perspectives*, edited by Craig Calhoun, Edward LiPuma, and Moishe Postone, 215–35. Cambridge: Polity Press, 1993.

Cox, Laurence, and Alf G. Nilsen. "Social Movements Research and the 'Movement of Movements': Studying Resistance to Neoliberal Globalisation". *Sociology Compass* 1 (2007): 424–42.

Crossley, Nick. *Making Sense of Social Movements*. Buckingham, UK: Open University Press, 2002.

Crossley, Nick. *The Social Body: Habit, Identity and Desire*. London: Sage, 2001.

Dunne, Stephen, Eleni Karamali, and Stevphen Shukaitis. "Inscribing Organized Resistance". *ephemera: Theory and Politics in Organization* 5 (2005): 562–67.

Featherstone, Liza, Doug Henwood, and Christian Parenti. "Action Will Be Taken: Left Anti-Intellectualism and Its Discontents". *Radical Society: Review of Culture and Politics* (2004). Accessed 7 February 2014. www.marxsite.com/Activistism.htm.

Haluza-DeLay, Randolph. "A Theory of Practice for Social Movements: Environmentalism and Ecological Habitus". *Mobilization* 13 (2008): 205–18.

Husu, Hanna-Mari, "Bourdieu and Social Movements: Considering Identity Movements in Terms of Field, Capital and Habitus". *Social Movement Studies* 12 (2013): 264–79.

Jasper, James. "The Emotions of Protest: Affective and Reactive Emotions in and around Social Movements". *Sociological Forum* 13 (1998): 397–424.

Jenkins, Richard. "Pierre Bourdieu and the Reproduction of Determinism". *Sociology* 16 (1982): 270–81.

Kögler, Hans-Herbert. "Alienation as an Epistemological Source". *Social Epistemology* 11 (1997): 141–64.

Kolonel Klepto and Major Up Evil. "The Clandestine Insurgent Rebel Clown Army Goes to Scotland via a Few Other Places". In *Shut Them Down! The G8, Gleneagles 2005 and the Movement of Movements*, edited by David Harvie, Keir Milburn, Ben Trott, and David Watts, 243–54. Leeds, UK: Dissent!, 2005.

Lash, Scott. "Reflexivity as Non-linearity". *Theory, Culture & Society* 20 (2003): 49–57.

Lash, Scott. "Reflexivity and Its Doubles: Structure, Aesthetics, Community". In *Reflexive Modernization: Politics, Tradition and the Aesthetic in the Modern*, edited by Ulrich Beck, Anthony Giddens, and Scott Lash, 110–73. Cambridge: Polity Press, 1994.

Mason, Kelvin. "Becoming Citizen Green: Prefigurative Politics, Autonomous Geographies, and Hoping against Hope". *Environmental Politics* (2013). Accessed 7 February 2014. doi:10.1080/09644016.2013.775725.

Rootes, Christopher. "Theory of Social Movements: Theory for Social Movements?" *Philosophy and Social Action* 16 (1990): 5–17.

Routledge, Paul. "Sensuous Solidarities: Emotion, Politics and Performance in the Clandestine Insurgent Rebel Clown Army". *Antipode* 44 (2012): 428–52.

Shepard, Benjamin. *Play, Creativity, and Social Movements: If I Can't Dance, It's Not My Revolution*. London: Routledge, 2011.

The Free Association. "What Is a Life? Movements, Social Centres and Collective Transformations". In *Moments of Excess: Movements, Protest and Everyday Life*, edited by the Free Association, 66–81. Oakland, CA: PM Press, 2011.

Touraine, Alain. *The Voice and the Eye: An Analysis of Social Movements*. Cambridge: Cambridge University Press, 1981.

# NOTES

1. For examples of discussions on research for movements see Christopher Rootes, "Theory of Social Movements: Theory for Social Movements?", *Philosophy and Social Action* 16 (1990): 5–17; Colin Barker and Laurence Cox, "What Have the Romans Ever Done for Us?" accessed 7 February 2014, www.iol.ie/~mazzoldi/toolsforchange/afpp/afpp8.html; Douglas Bevington and Chris Dixon, "Movement-Relevant Theory: Rethinking Social Movement Scholarship and Activism", *Social Movement Studies* 4 (2005): 185–208; Laurence Cox and Alf G. Nilsen, "Social Movements Research and the 'Movement of Movements': Studying Resistance to Neoliberal Globalisation", *Sociology Compass* 1 (2007): 424–42.

2. For previous efforts to bring Bourdieu's relational sociology into dialogue with social movement theory, see, for example, Nick Crossley, *Making Sense of Social Movements* (Buckingham, UK: Open University Press, 2002); Hanna-Mari Husu, "Bourdieu and Social Movements: Considering Identity Movements in Terms of Field, Capital and Habitus", *Social Movement Studies* 12 (2013): 264–79; or Randolph Haluza-DeLay, "A Theory of Practice for Social Movements: Environmentalism and Ecological Habitus", *Mobilization* 13 (2008): 205–18.

3. Pierre Bourdieu, *Pascalian Meditations* (Cambridge: Polity Press, 2000), 62, emphasis in the original.

4. Pierre Bourdieu and Loïc Wacquant, *An Invitation to Reflexive Sociology* (Chicago: University of Chicago Press, 1992), 30–32.

5. Pierre Bourdieu, *The Political Ontology of Martin Heidegger* (Oxford: Polity Press, 1991).

6. Bourdieu and Wacquant, *Invitation to Reflexive Sociology*, 152–58.

7. Ibid., 28–30.

8. For example, ibid., 224.

9. Quoted in Ibid., 33.

10. Bourdieu and Wacquant, *Invitation to Reflexive Sociology*, 34–35.

11. A term borrowed from the Free Association, "What Is a Life? Movements, Social Centres and Collective Transformations", in *Moments of Excess: Movements, Protest and Everyday Life*, ed. the Free Association (Oakland, CA: PM Press, 2011).

12. For recent engagement with clowning as a protest form, see, for example, Paul Routledge, "Sensuous Solidarities: Emotion, Politics and Performance in the Clandestine Insurgent Rebel Clown Army", *Antipode* 44 (2012): 428–52; Kelvin Mason, "Becoming Citizen Green: Prefigurative Politics, Autonomous Geographies, and Hoping against Hope", *Environmental Politics* (2013), accessed 7 February 2014, doi:10.1080/09644016.2013.775725; and Benjamin Shepard, *Play, Creativity, and Social Movements: If I Can't Dance, It's Not My Revolution* (London: Routledge, 2011). I should insert here a sort of disclaimer regarding my own emotions towards clowning as a form of protest. I have had experiences in which I found "playful" protest severely lacking in judgement. In a particular instance, several protesters found themselves contained in a police kettle with several Rebel Clowns during a demonstration. Their attitude towards the Clowns shifted markedly when playful modes of interaction were directed towards fellow activists—for example, when activists were spoken to in silly voices or otherwise made fun of. In contrast, as the group of Clowns began taking on a negotiating role with the police, they began acting in a "normal" and "serious" way towards senior police officers. This was perceived by other activists as a legitimating function of police authority over their protest, and experienced by bystanders as a reduction to a spectacle involving Clowns and police.

13. Kolonel Klepto and Major Up Evil, "The Clandestine Insurgent Rebel Clown Army Goes to Scotland via a Few Other Places", in *Shut Them Down! The G8, Gleneagles 2005 and the Movement of Movements*, ed. David Harvie et al. (Leeds, UK: Dissent!, 2005), 245.

14. Ibid., 244.

15. See, for example, James Jasper, "The Emotions of Protest: Affective and Reactive Emotions in and around Social Movements", *Sociological Forum* 13 (1998): 397–424.

16. However, a cognitive dimension to protest cannot be underestimated. Protesters do attend protest events with premeditated political convictions, which cannot be written or "play-acted" out of existence.

17. Alain Touraine, *The Voice and the Eye: An Analysis of Social Movements* (Cambridge: Cambridge University Press, 1981).

18. Pierre Bourdieu, *Outline of a Theory of Practice* (Cambridge: Cambridge University Press, 1977); and Bourdieu, *Pascalian Meditations*.

19. Bourdieu, *Pascalian Meditations*, 142.

20. Bourdieu and Wacquant, *Invitation to Reflexive Sociology*, 39, emphasis in the original.

21. Bourdieu, *Outline*, 1.

22. Bourdieu, *Pascalian Meditations*, 142–43.

23. Ibid., 143.

24. Rogers Brubaker, "Social Theory as Habitus", in *Bourdieu: Critical Perspectives*, ed. Craig Calhoun et al. (Cambridge: Polity Press, 1993), 213.

25. Ibid., 215.

26. Stephen Dunne et al., "Inscribing Organized Resistance", *ephemera: Theory and Politics in Organization* 5 (2005): 562.

27. Ibid., 563.

28. Bourdieu, *Pascalian Meditations*, 9.

29. Ibid., 51.

30. Pierre Bourdieu, "The Scholastic Point of View", *Cultural Anthropology* 5 (1990): 380–91; Pierre Bourdieu, *Practical Reason* (Cambridge: Polity Press, 1998), 127–41; and Bourdieu, *Pascalian Meditations*, 9–93. See also Bourdieu and Wacquant, *Invitation to Reflexive Sociology*, 36–47.

31. Pierre Bourdieu, *The Logic of Practice* (Cambridge: Polity Press, 1990), 14.

32. Pierre Bourdieu, *Homo Academicus* (Cambridge: Polity Press, 1990).

33. Ibid.

34. Bourdieu, "The Scholastic Point of View", 382.

35. Pierre Bourdieu, *In Other Words: Essays towards a Reflexive Sociology* (Cambridge: Polity Press, 1994), 178.

36. For example, Lisa Adkins, "Reflexivity: Freedom or Habit of Gender?" *Theory, Culture & Society* 20 (2003): 21–42; Scott Lash, "Reflexivity and Its Doubles: Structure, Aesthetics, Community", in *Reflexive Modernization: Politics, Tradition and the Aesthetic in the Modern*, ed. Ulrich Beck et al. (Cambridge: Polity Press, 1994); Scott Lash, "Reflexivity as Nonlinearity", *Theory, Culture & Society* 20 (2003): 49–57.

37. Liza Featherstone, Doug Henwood, and Christian Parenti, "Action Will Be Taken: Left Anti-Intellectualism and Its Discontents", *Radical Society: Review of Culture and Politics* (2004), accessed 7 February 2014, www.marxsite.com/Activistism.htm.

38. Ibid.

39. Ibid.

40. Steffen Boehm, "Movements of Theory and Practice", *ephemera: Theory and Politics in Organization* 2 (2002): 332.

41. Ibid.

42. Richard Jenkins, "Pierre Bourdieu and the Reproduction of Determinism", *Sociology* 16 (1982): 270–81.

43. Jeffrey C. Alexander, "The Reality of Reduction: The Failed Synthesis of Pierre Bourdieu", in *Fin de Siècle Social Theory: Relativism, Reduction and the Problem of Reason*, ed. J. C. Alexander (London: Verso, 1995).

44. Alexander, "The Reality of Reduction", 149.

45. Jenkins, "Pierre Bourdieu", 272; see also Nick Crossley, *The Social Body: Habit, Identity and Desire* (London: Sage, 2001), 110–115.

46. Crossley, *The Social Body*, 112.

47. Jenkins, "Pierre Bourdieu", 272.

48. Crossley, *The Social Body*, 113.

49. Pierre Bourdieu, *Sociology in Question* (London: Sage, 1993); Bourdieu, *Practical Reason*.

50. Hans-Herbert Kögler, "Alienation as an Epistemological Source", *Social Epistemology* 11 (1997): 141–64.

51. Crossley, *The Social Body*, 114.

52. Ibid., 114.

*Part III*

# Events as Dissent

So far we have concentrated on developing our understanding of an emerging research field that crosses protest with events management and leisure studies by focusing on the ideas of protests as events. In this section that conjunction is flipped over and as we consider how events can be conceptualized as protests.

Elsewhere, Spracklen has described how both rugby league and rugby union are important in the production and maintenance of hegemonic masculinity, a way of being a man that has been culturally defined through its hegemony historically over residual and emergent masculinities.[1] This hegemonic masculinity has defined a particular gender order, and hence this gender order is created inside the imaginary communities. In this sense, rugby league and rugby union serve as important sites for the defence of hegemonic masculinity even though both games seem to be in conflict in an economic and cultural sense. However, there is a hegemonic struggle over how this masculinity is expressed: these expressions have contested versions that relate to localized and globalized discourses. Inside rugby league the contest between the expansionists and the traditionalists is a contest to exert hegemony over "the game". What one has is a popularized, localized working-class game being recast in a globalized, commercialized form. Hence, when Spracklen discusses "what the game means", what this implies is a hegemonic struggle over the heart and soul of the imaginary community. This struggle over hegemony is also apparent between the amateur pastime and the commercialized form in rugby union. As suggested by Williams, hegemony is never total; hence, debate over interpreting invented traditions, symbolic boundaries and expressions of hegemonic masculinity has been possible.[2]

What this application of dominant but not total hegemony means is a more flexible interpretation of the structure-agency divide. Just as structures are not binding, so agency is limited by the meanings created by those structures. We are social beings who use structures as tools to understand our everyday life, but we also have the capacity to change meanings through discussion, debate and action. Giddens suggests that the social is created through a similar process of interaction between structure and agency that creates a structuration, a fluid set of meanings and rules which can be acted upon by humans.[3] Following this, one can see that events, culture and leisure become sites where hegemonic meaning is contested and continually (re)applied. Hence, although a large, professional sports event such as the soccer World Cup produces hegemonic masculinity, and is caught in a hegemonic struggle between exclusionist local discourses and capitalist global discourses, it cannot be given a simple value judgement because it can be the focus of dissent and counter-hegemonic action. Events become protests, and protest is communicative agency and serious leisure at work.

We can see this in all the chapters presented here. Events, protests and the people involved in them are only sites that exist in larger, contested networks of power and control. We can think of events as imaginary communities of a kind, and we can think of protests as imaginary communities of another kind. The first sort of imaginary community is more likely to be exclusionary in nature, conformist and part of the hegemonic apparatus of culture making. The second will be counter-hegemonic, communicative, and resistive. We are not suggesting that either imaginary community or space is isolated from issues of identity surrounding place or nation, or any other social issue. Obviously the people inside the imaginary communities also go to work, have families and homes, watch television, have other interests and have all the attendant highs and lows of life. No doubt many people will belong to a number of imaginary communities, as leisure supposedly becomes a matter of choosing various commodified options available to us in a de-centred, postmodern culture. This relationship with the wider society, however, is explicit in a number of ways in this section's chapters. Events are places of belonging and exclusion: they exert a social power over who is inside and who is outside. Following Foucault, it can be argued that events act as interstices of power, with their own discourses of control.[4] Hence one can be a powerful official within a club with a high degree of control over the imaginary community and the event, but powerless in the wider socio-political processes. The imaginary communities of events become a way of negotiating power, and if they become sufficiently stable, they can act, as in the case of sports, as part of the Establishment with a powerful voice.

Where events—and their imaginary communities—stand in relation to the established, dominant culture of society is as fluid as the definition of that dominant culture. Postmodern theorists suggest that there is no dominant culture. In terms of leisure, Rojek claimed in the 1990s that any kind of power analysis had been discarded and we are all at liberty to enjoy any number of postmodern leisure pursuits.[5] Here we have to disagree. It is clear that there is an unequal power relationship in society, and this implies that access to choice is limited by lack of power. Hence there is a dominant culture, even if what that entails is continually contested. The authors of the chapters in this section describe this tension between protest and event as dissent, and event as commodified leisure, in a number of case studies that provide thought-provoking questions and ways forward for thinking about the extent to which protest and activism can successfully counter hegemonic forces.

## REFERENCES

Foucault, Michel. *Power/Knowledge: Selected Interviews and Other Writings.* New York: Pantheon, 1980.
Giddens, Anthony. *The Constitution of Society.* Cambridge: Polity, 1984.
Rojek, Chris. *Decentring Leisure.* London: Sage, 1995.
Spracklen, Karl. "Playing the Ball: Constructing Community and Masculine Identity in Rugby". Unpublished PhD thesis, Leeds Metropolitan University, 1996.
Williams, Raymond. *Marxism in Literature.* Oxford: Oxford University Press, 1977.

## NOTES

1. Karl Spracklen, "Playing the Ball: Constructing Community and Masculine Identity in Rugby" (unpublished PhD thesis, Leeds Metropolitan University, 1996).
2. Raymond Williams, *Marxism in Literature* (Oxford: Oxford University Press, 1977).
3. Anthony Giddens, *The Constitution of Society* (Cambridge: Polity, 1984).
4. Michel Foucault, *Power/Knowledge: Selected Interviews and Other Writings* (New York: Pantheon, 1980).
5. Chris Rojek, *Decentring Leisure* (London: Sage, 1995).

*Chapter Nine*

# Sounds of Dissent

*Music as Protest*

Craig Robertson

> Musicking is an activity in which all those present are involved and for whose
> nature and quality, success or failure, everyone present bears some responsibil-
> ity. . . . The act of musicking establishes in the place where it is happening a
> set of relationships, and it is in those relationships that the meaning of the act
> lies. They are to be found not only between those organised sounds that are
> conveniently thought of being the stuff of musical meaning but also between
> the people who are taking part, in whatever capacity, in the performance; and
> they model, or stand as metaphor for, ideal relationships as the participants in
> the performance imagine them to be: relationships between person and person,
> between individual and society, between humanity and the natural world.
> —Christopher Small*

Music has long been associated with social movements and protests, especially during the civil rights movements in the 1960s but also in more recent
events such as protests and social change that began in North Africa in
earnest in 2011 and continues there still. Most research in this area has thus
far been concerned with three aspects: first, the social activity that surrounds
musical activity in these settings; secondly, the lyrical and semiotic content
of protest songs; or thirdly, musicological studies of the musical and lyrical
content of protest songs independent of the social interactions involved. This
chapter builds on Christopher Small's concept of active musicking and suggests that music can be seen as both an act of protest in itself and a form of
social control, dependent on the specific contexts and a dynamic, reflexive
relationship between musicking, memory, identity, emotion and belief. Using
research conducted in Bosnia as part of my PhD, this chapter will attempt to
demonstrate these processes in terms of this matrix of interdependent influ-

ences and how they influence social behaviour, both positive and negative, but will also suggest that music has a greater potential to improve conflicted social space than is currently generally utilized.

First, I will attempt to unpack some of the overlapping and conflicting terminologies involved in this context. How are protests, social movements, social change, social control and conflict transformation defined, linked and related? Secondly, I will examine the role of music in the context of several social movements, some more explicitly associated with protest than others, and some from the past while some are more contemporary. These include the hip-hop movement, which began in New York in the 1970s and is now a global phenomenon that links the disaffected urban youth diaspora from many different cultures while increasing tensions and prejudices between subgenres and cultures, and the civil rights movement in the 1960s, which has long been associated with protest, anti-war and other socially conscious songs from the rock and folk traditions in the West. [1] This will be followed by a discussion on what music is or is not actually doing or accomplishing in these contexts as opposed to non-musical interactions. Once purely musical activity has been identified, the issue of how to effectively analyse the process arises. A currently common manner in sociology is to utilize semiotic analysis. I will suggest that this critical analysis turn in sociology is less effective when investigating musical experience due to its phenomenological nature and the fact that music simply is not a language, despite some obvious commonalities. Musicological analysis has thus far been equally ineffective for focusing entirely on the musical materiality itself rather than the social meanings and interactions that led to its creation or the behavioural influences musical events have had. A more effective method of understanding musical experience was suggested by Christopher Small's musicking concept, and I have built upon this with my own research to suggest a reflexive musical meaning-making process matrix which I have applied to the contexts already discussed. The results show that music itself has no intrinsic meaning without a social context, yet this process of meaning making makes music particularly powerful at altering or stabilizing social behaviour. Thus, music is at its core an event that protests against the status quo or else strengthens it.

## PROTEST, MOVEMENT, CHANGE AND CONFLICT

Lo[2] and Schwartz and Paul[3] elegantly illustrated the connections between protests, social movements and conflict by pointing out the shortcomings of social movement theory. Lo pointed out the link between social movements and local protest dynamics, while Schwartz and Paul noted that conflict movements are generally more successful at mobilization than consensus movements. In other words, small, localized protests can lead to a wider social movement, and movements built upon open conflict are demonstrably better at mobilizing forces than peaceful consensual movements. In all cases, however, those involved in the protests and movements desire a social change of some description. The important thing to remember here is that social change is usually conflictual to some degree and often violent, and that small local protests are often an indicator of a potential larger social movement. The implied flip side of such a conflict-based change-driven movement is those in favour of maintaining the status quo. Any challenge, therefore, to the status quo is likely to be perceived by such negatively, as a threat.

Conflict theory has attempted to address this dynamic, but there is no unified theory as yet, and Azar has suggested that this is because the field, until recently, primarily focuses their research efforts on inter-state conflict rather than identity, ideology or inter-factional conflicts. [4] It is this new prevalent form of conflict that forms the basis for motivation for protests that lead to social movements and, ultimately, social behaviour that may lead to social change. For the purposes of this chapter, social change refers to structural social changes usually for the benefit of a marginalized or oppressed, clearly defined social group, although it can also refer to cases in which a minority group has managed to impose control over other groups.

## EXTRA-MUSICAL SOCIAL ACTIVITIES

Much sociological analysis of music and conflict has thus far focused on extra-musical social activities or a semiotic analysis of the lyrical content. For the former, the focus has been on the actors' activities outside of engaging with the music itself, the outward appearances of those involved, such as their clothing, their physical movements and gestures and their verbal and written discussions about the music. A common theme in this research suggests that the music is an important feature in social change or maintenance, and yet the music itself is rarely discussed.

Music is part of every society but it is not aesthetically isolated, being forever associated with a myriad of extra-musical parameters such as gesture, customs, settings and power relations. It has thus far been difficult for scholars to ascertain just what music accomplishes in the social world, since any analysis ends up being similar to analyses of other social activities. Bergh has raised the point: What makes music as a social activity any different from knitting? [5] Despite this, the belief in the special status and power of music proliferates within the professional musician classes—those who consume music and those with the means to organize social music programmes. In the literature review it was illustrated how music strongly interacts with memory, identity, emotion and belief, so it should be no surprise that music is believed to have such power regardless of any evidence shown.

Ruth Adams, for example, has discussed how the punk music scene in England has influenced and continues to inform the English sense of national identity.[6] The Adams example illustrates how a sense of national identity can be fostered from the bottom up, as opposed to top down; punk was a grassroots movement based largely around music, but also a common attitude and frustration with the status quo, not to mention art and fashion. Punk therefore formed a cultural identity that influenced the English national identity and, arguably, the international punk diaspora.[7]

Ansdell and DeNora have pointed out that the very notion of health and well-being is socially constructed and that musicking can help to reorient someone from the dichotomy of illness/cure towards that of human flourishing.[8] DeNora and Ansdell have researched how active musicking is performative of an embodied consciousness in relation to "an ecology of people, places and things",[9] which demonstrates the influence of the social on the personal and how this process is embodied in the entrainment of physical response. Just how the influence flows from the personal to the social still needs to be considered in order to understand how music can effect social behaviour via its affect on the beliefs of an individual.

While the above illustrates that there appears to be outward evidence of how music affects a myriad of social aspects, such as identity, which is at the core of any social movement, it does not explain what is particular about music specifically as a social activity that is believed to work so well in these contexts. Other social researchers have looked to the lyrics for further answers.

## SEMIOTIC ANALYSIS

Music attracts audiences, and where audiences gather, messages can be spread, but music itself does not spread literal messages; the lyrics do. Any discussion about peace protest songs, for example, is really about the lyrics, with galvanizing messages being helped to spread on a musical vehicle. Music for peace includes any usage of music as a platform for lyrics to promote certain ideologies centred on peace and nonviolence such as anti-war activists and human rights social movements.[10] Another factor in these cases is that fame and notoriety increase the likelihood of a message being heard, not the music itself.[11] This has been confirmed by Kruse in his study of the peace campaign of John Lennon and Yoko Ono, in which the music played only a small part in their peace activism when compared to the role that their fame and public access played.[12]

In the case of Turbofolk, a Serbian nationalist music that combined traditional Serbian folk music with commercial dance music, the lyrics were not overtly political. Instead, they focused on topics of love and relationships, and the visual representation of Turbofolk artists was glamorous. [13] Essentially, Turbofolk disseminated the message to Serbs wherever they are that they were connected by this music to their homeland and that their homeland, if unified, was the "Promised Land".

None of the above explains what the music itself adds, if anything, to the understanding of music and social change. Luzha has suggested that music provides a mode of attention that is different from the everyday, and this heightened awareness enables the information contained within the lyrics to be processed on a deeper, more meaningful level. [14] He does not, however, explain what might be happening in the music itself, so the question remains: What is happening in the music during social change contexts?

## MUSICOLOGICAL ANALYSIS

Musicological and ethno-musicological approaches to conflict have examined musical influences, instrumentation, novel musical attributes and replication as means of understanding, but do they help us understand how music affects social change in protest or conflict environments? Ethnomusicology has been very influential on the thinking found within music and conflict transformation, although there has been little in the way of direct engagement with conflict transformation within ethnomusicology itself. One exception was the book *Music and Conflict*, [15] which collected the first attempts within ethnomusicology to address these connections between music and conflict observed around the world. Despite the book's title, many of the chapters primarily examine the peaceful roles and potential of music, from Sugarman's look at the role of songs and the Internet as a peaceful means in Kosovo to Cooper's examination of how traditional music in Northern Ireland has crossed sectarian divides. This is an important step for two reasons: first, musicology and ethnomusicology still tend to focus on the material aspects of music, even as they have since begun to incorporate the multitude of possible meanings following the emergence of the New Musicology in the 1980s. This book has a focus on the social aspects and meaning of musical actions rather than the specificity of notation, recordings or particular performances. Secondly, it unpacks perhaps for the first time just what is happening in the music itself when music and conflict situations occur.

In *Music and Dictatorship in Europe and Latin America*, edited by Roberto Illiano and Massimiliano Sala, [16] there is much ethno-musicological discussion about what music was supported and popularized during times of dictatorship; yet, as with most musicological discussions of this topic, the focus is too much on the music itself or how the social situations affected the music rather than the interplay between musical creation, proliferation, ideological and identity construction and so on. What it does cover, in several languages, is how dictatorships have affected music and musicians in various contexts, including Nazi-controlled France, Germany, Greece and Serbia; fascist Italy, Portugal, Spain, Serbia, Hungary, Argentina, Brazil and Chile; and communist Poland, Russia, Serbia and Cuba. Unfortunately, there was no consideration about how the process flows the other way: how music created, performed and listened to during these periods and places affected the society which had to deal with such circumstances.

Ethnomusicologist Timothy Rice has observed that many musicologists view both music as an emotional response and music as social behaviour as metaphors.[17] In other words, neither the emotional response nor the behaviour is the music itself, and, therefore, they are both of lesser importance when attempting to understand the music itself. Rice continues to point out that many totalitarian states have been interested in controlling music production due to their belief in music's affective power to alter the public's behaviour in a manner that might be antagonistic towards the state. He suggests that totalitarian leaders might understand "better than even some scholars do, music's affective power and therefore the emotion that goes along with its interpretation".

In other words, totalitarian leaders believe in the power of music to alter and influence the behaviour of others through the emotions that it evokes, which in turn affects the behaviour of the leaders when they attempt to control its production. Rice suggests that music has multiple possible meanings laden with emotions

> rich with possibilities for ideological modelling and control and yet able, in many instances, to wiggle free of that control, either because of the uncontrollability of the electronic technologies in which it is disseminated, the multiplicity of references inherent in music as a semiotic form, or the claim by its makers and listeners that it is, after all, not a sign that signifies at all but an art.[18]

Direct emotional connections to sound and therefore music are deeply rooted in human instinct, therefore, but more complex meanings are derived from repetition of sounds and any repetition implies a memory of what has happened before.

I will now briefly examine two cases of music, protest and social change—hip-hop and the civil rights and peace movements—and how they have been analysed using the extra-musical, semiotic and musicological methods mentioned above.

## HIP-HOP

Hip-hop is an example of a social movement encompassing music, poetry, dance, art and ideology. [19] Many commentators over the years have claimed that this movement was largely successful in reducing conflict between gangs in New York. However, gang violence continues and, furthermore, some hip-hop has taken violence as its message across the disenfranchised urban youth diaspora. Hip-hop did succeed in developing a new shared sense of cultural identity in New York and this has spread across the world and has been reinforced through performances and the spread of recorded music. Johnson and Cloonan have pointed out, however, that hip-hop is now associated with violence as much as it is with peaceful culture, if not more so. [20]

Hip-hop music itself was a hybrid art form that combined the large sound systems of dancehall reggae with the technological advances in turntables which enabled DJs to insert "breaks" of Latin percussion, funk or soul. The rapping that is readily identified with hip-hop is claimed to have evolved from reggae "toasting", Gil Scott Heron's performance poetry, and African oral traditions. [21] Certain social values transmitted through hip-hop, such as the feeling that the music represented Bronx youth culture and spoke on their behalf, can be traced back to the values transmitted through reggae in Jamaica, such as national identity and the common struggles of the people. [22]

Hip-hop provided an alternative to gang violence, and it is through this capacity that the music reduced the level of violence by removing some gang members from violent interactions. It helped to create a new shared cultural identity that is considered to be a prerequisite for resolving conflict, but in this case, there was no resolution to the conflict between gangs. One reason is possibly due its organic nature. There was no third party to guide the participants towards resolving the conflict. An opportunity to feel empathy with each other was lost since no further action was taken to negotiate lasting peace.

Hip-hop succeeded in helping to create a strong new cultural identity for a certain social group that had been in conflict, and this new identity was successfully propagated and reinforced through performances. Despite reducing the level of violence in the area, it ultimately failed to resolve the conflict from which it came for several reasons: there was no third party to guide the conflicting groups towards a mutually beneficial solution; the organic nature of the movement meant that there was no common goal to resolve any conflict; and as it travelled beyond the geography from which it originated, the music propagated the ideology of defiance rather than peace. Hip-hop as a social movement did not seem to have been able to resolve conflicts, but it does demonstrate how a social movement and music can consolidate identities. While this consolidation is a necessary step towards social cohesion, it can strengthen identity borders and increase difference.

Furthermore, commodification of the music involved can further strengthen these identity borders.

## CIVIL RIGHTS MOVEMENTS

Musicians have long been involved in peace movements, from Pete Seeger to Bono; yet there is very little, if any, evidence to suggest that the music in these cases actually helped positively transform any conflict, at least directly. In the cases in which song was the musical form, music provided the scaffolding on which to hang certain messages; it provided an amplification system for communication purposes. Furthermore, the commodification of the songs of the civil rights and peace movements led to many consumers feeling that they were part of a movement without doing much more than purchasing records.

A collection of peace songs assembled by the Workers Music Association in the UK entitled simply *Peace Songs* illustrates that the idea of singing for peace is not by any means a new one. The songs are listed in chronological order with the oldest, "Christe d Beistand", dating from the mid-1600s during the Thirty Years' War. The topics covered ranged from the Thirty Years' War in seventeenth-century England, the American Civil War, the Cold War, World Wars I and II and the Vietnam War, among many other conflicts, but by far the most represented was a conflict that did not actually occur: the threat of nuclear war, with roughly one in six songs having that as the explicit topic.[23] There is no social analysis included in this case, but it is a fine illustration that the notion is not new, nor is it a geographically specific phenomenon. It also illustrates that potential conflict, such as the threat of nuclear war, was as much as, if not more of, an inspiration for peace songs as actual conflict. The one thing that all of these music-for-peace examples have in common is that the medium may have been music, but the message is clearly in the lyrical content.

William Roy's research on social movements, race and music[24] is one of the only books of its kind that has established the link between active musical production and social change. He concluded that the lyrical content was secondary in the civil rights movement singing of peace songs, but the physical act of singing together in a group with a perceived common purpose was key in breaking down barriers of race and difference. This confirms the theories proposed by Christopher Small that musical production is a more effective means of strengthening a shared sense of identity than the consumption of music.[25]

Similar to the case of hip-hop, the civil rights movement combined a social movement with music, and the engagement with certain types of music demonstrated and reinforced group identity. On one hand, the movement intended to break down borders and differences between people, but, on the other hand, it could be considered antagonistic towards the authorities or to people who did not share its views. Even if from today's perspective it seems that this form of antagonism was worthwhile for the expansion of human rights and dignity, this illustrates that it is very difficult, if not impossible, to include everyone equally in any social movement, musical experience or identity-building exercise.

## THEMES DERIVED FROM HIP-HOP AND
## THE PEACE MOVEMENT CASES

In all of the above cases, four aspects of music and social movements can be observed: musical activity in a protest environment can help consolidate separate identities, at least temporarily; these consolidated identities often strengthen the borders between their own and other identities by focusing on difference; the consolidated identities can have at their core a shared hatred as much as a shared love for another group of people; the commodification of the music associated with a social movement or protest may propagate a particular message, but it may also encourage weak participation.

### Consolidated Identities and the Case of Turbofolk

Musical experiences in hip-hop and peace movements have demonstrably helped to consolidate the group identities of those involved, as explored above, and there are other instances of this process. Attali has pointed out that music is an activity that helps to consolidate identities and cement group cohesion,[26] and Kent concludes that this could mean a group with a common feeling of hatred for another group. Thus musicking within this group would be a hateful application of music.[27] Others who have illustrated how music can be used in hateful ways and to foster conflicts through consolidation of nationalism and hatred include Pettan[28] and Hogg.[29] The usage of Turbofolk, the dominant musical genre in Serbia in the early 1990s, by the Serb nationalists is a prime example of unpeaceful music.[30]

Turbofolk was originally a type of Balkanized "Europop", carrying more or less conservative family values. As the nationalist regime of Milosović took hold, it became transformed, in the words of Jelena Subotić, a presenter of Belgrade's independent Radio B-92, into "a perfect channel for disseminating the poisonous seeds of hatred".[31] Turbofolk not only helped consolidate Serbian national identity but also projected it wherever it was played.[32] Hogg argues that this is akin to CCTV, where the technology is visible (audible) and it attempts to control society by letting them know that the authorities are near and they are being watched—not that their space will be invaded, but rather that it already is occupied because the air is already

dominated. Hogg argues that this musical space occupation expresses ownership, authority and exclusivity over the space in which it occupies. He argues
that this ties in with Dandeker's writings on surveillance, that strategies for
sanctions to be mobilized in surveillance include the coercive, which recorded music could be: "to devise mechanisms of excluding potential rule
breakers from the opportunity to disobey instructions".[33]

While superficially it appears that a new cultural identity was formed by
Turbofolk, it was more about finding an old style that appealed to the greatest
proportion of the population who were too poor to search elsewhere for new
music. Other forms of internal conflict were decreased by economic circumstances, and then music from the poor of the past was uncovered to create a
renewed sense of cultural identity.

But what else happened? Was this music listened to while ethnic cleans-
ing of the Bosnians occurred? What do the other Balkan people think of this
music and this new sense of identity? What about Serbs still in other Balkan
states? Do they feel attached to this music as well? What happened to the
Yugoslav identity that the Serbians liked so much? Has there been any music
making with Croats or Bosnians? Are there any shared musical experiences?
Is it possible for a resurgence of Turbofolk to occur in order to bring about a
renewed sense of togetherness among the Balkan people? Does music even
need to be good in order to be useful? These questions were completely
unanswered by Jovanović, and much of the available literature on this topic
is written in Serbian and remains untranslated. What can be said here is that
music appears to help people feel a connection and a shared sense of identity,
but this process is not inherently positive.

## Strengthened Identity Borders and Difference

While consolidated identities are necessary for the development of a coherent
social movement, they simultaneously tend to accentuate the identity borders
and highlight the differences between in and out groups. Bergh observes that
music used in this way is unlikely to produce harmonious results, as it highlights differences rather than similarities.[34] One of Bergh's research sites was
the Norwegian Resonant Community project, which was an attempt to reduce indigenous Norwegian prejudice against immigrants in schools by presenting concerts of traditional music from the immigrant countries at schools.
The project was deemed by Bergh to have ultimately failed to reduce conflict
between native Norwegians and the immigrant community since it utilized
music as a representation that strengthened cultural boundaries. Another reason for the relative lack of success could have been that the children were
passive recipients of performances rather than actively engaged in producing
music themselves. This ties in with the suggestion by both Small and Attali[35]
that musical production and active participation is more likely to produce

stronger group cohesion than passive consumption of music, although Small does point out that even music consumption is a form of active musicking. Despite this apparent failure, the project had been reported as a success and continues to be referenced as such. Bergh suggests that this is due to the original report being focused on abstract attitudes towards the idea of another culture existing somewhere else rather than within their own community.[36] This highlights a common problem with music and conflict transformation projects such as the West-Eastern Divan Orchestra, which is often reported as successfully illustrating how Israelis and Palestinians can work together, when, in actuality, the orchestra has not changed the daily lives of those involved outside of the orchestra, and it has had even less effect on the rest of Israel and Palestine. If anything, that particular project has had a negative effect on the conflict, since it has satisfied some observers that the situation is improving if such a project can exist, when in fact the situation is the same or worse. Bergh suggests that these large media-savvy music and conflict-transformation projects are driven by the favoured Western discourses on music which assume the greatness of music and use big festivals and professional musicians, and that these discourses are driven by the musicians themselves,[37] although this attitude is slowly changing and this has been documented and discussed at great length.[38] Furthermore, none of these studies have discussed the internal conflicts found within the projects themselves, as observed by both Bergh and myself. The Resonant Communities project, for example, contained within it some conflicting goals that were never addressed: the organizers wished to reduce prejudices between immigrant school children and indigenous Norwegians, the musicians wanted to demonstrate their culture(s) to the children as well as earn a living and the children for the most part just enjoyed participating in an event that enabled them to leave the classroom.

## Commodification

While in the hip-hop and peace movements music has been used to consolidate identities within the groups and highlight differences between those in and out of the groups, the commodification process has lessened the impact of both processes. This is one reason why those interested in maintaining the status quo often support the commodification of music associated with challenging social movements. In addition to the hateful applications of music already mentioned, George Kent also categorized "music as commodity" to be unpeaceful in nature, since readily available commercial music can divert the attention of a public away from challenging or controversial topics. Indeed, many dictatorships have supported easy-to-digest commercial music and hindered the spread of music that challenges the status quo. The real reason for this is due to the potential uncontrollable and unpredictable aspect of musical affect on a population, since things that affect behaviour in uncontrollable and unpredictable manners are dangerous at worst or at the very least risky for any state. Western democratic states lack the explicit powers available to dictators and despots, but they at least attempt to control music's power through the encouragement of the commodification of music in the capitalist system. Music that embodies a challenge to the state, once commodified, can satisfy people's desire to challenge without their actually challenging the state; commodification of music can effectively neuter the change potential of musical experience. This is a form of conflict management but not of a mutually beneficial variety, since one or more sides to the actual and potential conflict are circumvented, suppressed, diverted or otherwise prevented from equalities.[39] This is a whole topic in itself and it is not within the scope of this chapter to address the commodification of music as social control apart from noting it here.

Adorno was perhaps the first to discuss music in terms of what groups of people believed it meant to them and therefore how it informed their behaviour. He believed that habitualizing music consumption objectivized music and commodified it. Objectification defeats dialecticism, as it is oriented around recognition and reproduction rather than interrogation. It makes assumptions about the world and classes and categories of people and the nature of things rather than engaging with the "intimate experience of things".[40] DeNora has pointed out that Adorno viewed this objectification as preventing challenging cognitions and being easily subjected to external controls. Adorno calls this belief in the stable connection between ideas and reality "ontological ideology",[41] and he believed that this was conducive for actors to relate their specific experiences to general concepts. In other words, by consuming music for pleasure habitually (the fetishization of music),[42] the public was reinforcing the social status quo and was less able to engage dialectically with music in an effort to affect change within society; they would avoid challenging music that might raise their consciousness through negative dialectics.[43] New structures in music would be meaningless to them unless value was placed on challenging the structure of society. If the current social structure provides commodified music that is habitually consumed for pleasure, there is little or no incentive to engage in any other manner with music. Lilienfeld has pointed out that Adorno was not alone at the time in this view, as Ernst Bloch and Georg Lukács also believed in this connection between the objectification of music, capitalism and consumption.[44]

Music appears to link directly with basic emotions, both reflecting and evoking them. These emotions then combine cognitively to produce complex emotions connected with memories and a sense of identity. These, in turn, provide meanings to attach to this music that are believed to be true and real. Finally, certain modes of attention and behaviour are afforded by these beliefs in the meanings attached to music through this process. Unfortunately, capitalism is very adept at the commodification of beliefs. Attali has noted that the fetishization of music and how it de-ritualizes a social form can "repress an activity of the body, specialise its practice, sell it as a spectacle, generalise its consumption, then see to it that it is stockpiled until it loses its meaning".[45]

Nevertheless, how music interacts with a social group's identities, memories, emotions and beliefs can be seen to influence group behaviour in some way, and this is the manner in which music can affect social change or suppress it.

## REFLEXIVE MEANING CREATION THROUGH MUSIC: THE CASE OF PONTANIMA

The idea that music has this relationship with belief, identity, emotion, memory and behaviour is not completely without precedent. Adorno mentioned how music interacts with belief, emotion and behaviour in his book *Quasi una Fantasia*.[46] This was never fully explored by him, however, nor any of his dedicated followers and detractors. The evidence for this process came from my own research on Pontanima, an inter-religious choir in Sarajevo. Pontanima is made up of roughly equal members of the cultures involved in the Bosnian war and they exclusively sing liturgical music from those cultures in places of worship, primarily around Bosnia. The findings from this research have demonstrated how music interacts with individual and group identity, memories, emotions and beliefs, and, ultimately, behaviour.[47]

Within Pontanima there is a common belief that choral music singing helps people to feel normal while they are doing it, while simultaneously helping them to remember a time when there was less conflict. Because of the memories associated with singing, the memories associated with oppression and relative lack of freedoms were not retrieved in the same way. These selected memories were brought to the foreground with fondness and then afterwards, while the memory of the musical experience lingered, there was a feeling and belief that this state of harmony could be achieved—if for no other reason, then because it is now conceivable. Due to this ongoing reflexive process, beliefs were altered and strengthened and memories were selected and foregrounded over others. Past emotions influenced this selection process, and current emotions strengthen the selections and beliefs. Finally, those in Pontanima continue to sing the mission, even though an ongoing reflexive relationship between these aspects continues to threaten the very existence of Pontanima.

## CONCLUSION

This chapter has drawn on a number of different contexts to illustrate how music has been used in a variety of different forms of protest and conflict transformation scenarios, and how protests can lead to social movements. But what ultimately is the difference between music and conflict transformation and music and protest? Conflict transformation requires relatively equal or acceptable perceived access to status, basic needs and rights. In order for music to be a successful part of conflict transformation, all sides of the conflict would need to engage in musical activity as equal partners, sharing the identity, memory and emotions that result. Over time and repeated instances of such activities, it is possible for a new shared belief system about the participants to emerge.

Protests, by contrast, highlight inequalities and demonstrate the level of displeasure felt by those with the lesser status. Music in this context operates with the same set of processes, but on a different scale. Music consolidates the identities of the protesters in the same manner as conflict transformation, but there is little or no attempt to build a shared identity with those they are protesting against. As such, protest is a form of conflict rather than conflict transformation, although a necessary step, since conflict transformation is not possible without a relatively equal access to needs and rights, as mentioned before.

Music can be used in protest and in conflict transformation, and the processes of interacting with identity, memory, emotion, belief and behaviour are the same. The difference is a question of scale and order; protests require a form of conflict in order to obtain a more equal access to resources and rights before a process of conflict transformation can begin. Therefore, the processes of musicking are the same regardless of purpose, scale and outcome. In most peaceful cases, these processes are felt rather than understood and, as such, are haphazardly applied with a limited level of quantifiable evidence. There is more evidence that supports how conflictual and violent protests and movements use these processes, but this is a question of the level of understanding of the processes involved rather than any inherently positive or negative attributes associated with musical interventions. Ultimately, the better the understanding of these processes, the more focused the application, and this is something that peaceful protesters and movements can improve upon.

## REFERENCES

Adams, Ruth. "The Englishness of English Punk: Sex Pistols, Subcultures, and Nostalgia". *Popular Music and Society* 31, no. 4 (2008): 469–88.

Adams, Terri M., and Douglas B. Fuller. "The Words Have Changed but the Ideology Remains the Same: Misogynistic Lyrics in Rap Music". *Journal of Black Studies* 36, no. 6 (2006): 938–57.

Adorno, Theodor. *Quasi una Fantasia: Essays on Music.* Translated by Susan H. Gillespie. London: University of California Press, 2002.

Ansdell, Gary, and Tia DeNora. "Musical Flourishing: Community Music Therapy, Controversy, and the Cultivation of Wellbeing". In *Music, Health and Wellbeing*, edited by Raymond MacDonald et al., 97–112. Oxford: Oxford University Press, 2012.

Attali, Jacques. *Noise: The Political Economy of Music.* Manchester, UK: Manchester University Press, 1985.

Azar, Edward E. *The Management of Protracted Social Conflict: Theory and Cases.* Aldershot, UK: Dartmouth, 1990.

Becker, Howard S. *Art Worlds.* Berkeley: University of California Press, 1982.

Bergh, Arild. "I Am What I Am: Music and Representation in Conflict Transformation". Paper presented at the annual IPRA conference, Calgary, Alberta, Canada, June 29–July 3, 2006.

Bergh, Arild. "I'd Like to Teach the World to Sing: Music and Conflict Transformation". PhD diss., University of Exeter, 2010.

Chang, Jeff. *Can't Stop Won't Stop.* New York: St. Martin's Press, 2005.

Collin, Matthew. *This Is Serbia Calling: Rock 'n' Roll Radio and Belgrade's Underground Resistance.* London: Serpent's Tail, 2001.

Dandeker, Christopher. *Surveillance, Power, and Modernity: Bureaucracy and Discipline from 1700 to the Present Day.* Cambridge: Polity Press, 1990.

DeNora, Tia. *Music in Everyday Life.* Cambridge: Cambridge University Press, 2000.

DeNora, Tia. *After Adorno: Rethinking Music Sociology.* Cambridge: Cambridge University Press, 2003.

DeNora, Tia. "Practical Consciousness and Social Relation in MusEcological Perspective". In *Music and Consciousness: Philosophical, Psychological and Cultural Perspectives*, edited by David Clarke and Eric Clarke, 309–26. Oxford: Oxford University Press, 2011.

Dyson, Michael Eric. "The Culture of Hip-Hop". In *That's the Joint! The Hip-Hop Studies Reader*, edited by Murray Forman and Mark Anthony Neal, 61–68. New York: Routledge, 2004.

Eyerman, Ron, and Andrew Jamison. *Music and Social Movements: Mobilizing Traditions in the Twentieth Century.* Cambridge: Cambridge University Press, 1998.

Forman, Murray. "Represent: Race, Space and Place in Rap Music". In *That's the Joint! The Hip-Hop Studies Reader*, edited by Murray Forman and Mark Anthony Neal, 201–22. New York: Routledge, 2004.

Gordy, Eric D. *The Culture of Power in Serbia: Nationalism and the Destruction of Alternatives.* University Park: Pennsylvania State University Press, 1999.

Hesmondhalgh, David. "Towards a Critical Understanding of Music, Emotion and Self-Identity". *Consumption Markets & Culture* 11, no. 4 (2007): 329–43.

Hogg, Bennet. "Who's Listening?" In *Music, Power and Politics*, edited by Annie J. Randall, 211–30. London: Routledge, 2005.

Illiano, Roberto, and Massimiliano Sala, eds. *Music and Dictatorship in Europe and Latin America.* Turnhout, Belgium: Brepols, 2009.

Johnson, Bruce, and Martin Cloonan. *Dark Side of the Tune: Popular Music and Violence.* Farnham, UK: Ashgate, 2009.

Jordan, John, ed. *Peace Songs.* London: Workers' Music Association, 1989.

Jovanović, Jelena. "The Power of Recently Revitalised Serbian Rural Folk Music in Urban Settings". In *Music, Power and Politics*, edited by Annie J. Randall. London: Routledge, 2005.

Kent, George. "Unpeaceful Music". In *Music and Conflict Transformation: Harmonies and Dissonances in Geopolitics*, edited by Olivier Urbain, 104–14. London: I. B. Tauris, 2008.

Kruse, Robert J., II. "Geographies of John and Yoko's 1969 Campaign for Peace: An Intersection of Celebrity, Space, Art and Activism". In *Sound, Society and the Geography of Popular Music*, edited by Ola Johansson and Thomas L. Bell, 11–31. Farnham, UK: Ashgate, 2009.

Lilienfeld, Robert. "Music and Society in the 20th Century: Georg Lukács, Ernst Bloch, and Theodor Adorno". *International Journal of Politics, Culture, and Society* 1, no. 2 (1987): 310–36.

Lo, Clarence Y. H. "Communities of Challengers in Social Movement Theory". In *Frontiers in Social Movement Theory*, edited by Aldon D. Morris and Carol McClurglueller, 224–48. New Haven, CT: Yale University Press, 1992.

Luzha, B. "Music Brings People Together in Post-War Kosovo". *International Journal of Music Education* 23, no. 2 (2005): 149–51.

Moore, Allan F. *Rock: The Primary Text: Developing a Musicology of Rock*. Aldershot, UK: Ashgate, 2001.

O'Connell, John Morgan, and Salwa Castelo-Branco, eds. *Music and Conflict*. Champaign: University of Illinois Press, 2010.

Pettan, Svanibor, ed. *Music, Politics and War: Views from Croatia*. Zagreb: Institute of Ethnology and Folklore Research, 1998.

Rice, Timothy. "Reflections on Music and Meaning: Metaphor, Signification and Control in the Bulgarian Case". *British Journal of Ethnomusicology* 10, no. 1 (2001): 19–38.

Robertson, Craig. "Singing to Be Normal: Tracing the Behavioural Influence of Music in Conflict Transformation". PhD diss., University of Exeter, 2014.

Roy, William. *Reds, Whites, and Blues: Social Movements, Folk Music, and Race in the United States*. Princeton, NJ: Princeton University Press, 2010.

Schwartz, Michael, and Shuva Paul. "Resource Mobilization versus the Mobilization of People: Why Consensus Movements Cannot Be Instruments of Social Change". In *Frontiers in Social Movement Theory*, edited by Aldon D. Morris and Carol McClurglueller, 205–23. New Haven, CT: Yale University Press, 1992.

Small, Christopher. *Musicking: The Meanings of Performing and Listening*. Middletown, CT: Wesleyan University Press, 1998.

Thomas, Calvin. "A Knowledge That Would Not Be Power: Adorno, Nostalgia, and the Historicity of the Musical Subject". *New German Critique* 48 (Autumn 1989): 155–75.

Toksoz, Itir. "Do You Hear the People Sing? Music as a Means of Peaceful Protest in Turkey". In *Music, Power and Liberty*, edited by Craig Robertson and Olivier Urbain. London: I. B. Tauris, 2014.

Toop, David. "Uptown Throwdown". In *That's the Joint! The Hip-Hop Studies Reader*, edited by Murray Forman and Mark Anthony Neal, 233–46. New York: Routledge, 2004.

## NOTES

\* The opening quote is from Christopher Small, *Musicking: The Meanings of Performing and Listening* (Middletown, CT: Wesleyan University Press, 1998), 10, 13.

1. I was part of a research team that investigated the role of music and the arts in the events in North Africa between 2011 and 2012 that are beyond the scope of this chapter to explore. There is as yet little academic research on the recent protests in Turkey around Gezi Square, although observations of YouTube clips clearly show that music has played a significant role. See Itir Toksoz, "Do You Hear the People Sing? Music as a Means of Peaceful Protest in Turkey", in *Music, Power and Liberty*, ed. Craig Robertson and Olivier Urbain (London: I. B. Tauris, 2014).

2. Clarence Y. H. Lo. "Communities of Challengers in Social Movement Theory", in *Frontiers in Social Movement Theory*, ed. Aldon D. Morris and Carol McClurglueller (New Haven, CT: Yale University Press, 1992), 224–48.

3. Michael Schwartz and Shuva Paul, "Resource Mobilization versus the Mobilization of People: Why Consensus Movements Cannot Be Instruments of Social Change", in *Frontiers in Social Movement Theory*, ed. Aldon D. Morris and Carol McClurglueller (New Haven, CT: Yale University Press, 1992), 205–23.

4. Edward E. Azar, *The Management of Protracted Social Conflict: Theory and Cases* (Aldershot, UK: Dartmouth, 1990).

5. Arild Bergh, "I'd Like to Teach the World to Sing: Music and Conflict Transformation" (PhD diss., University of Exeter, 2010).

6. Ruth Adams, "The Englishness of English Punk: Sex Pistols, Subcultures, and Nostalgia", *Popular Music and Society* 31, no. 4 (2008): 469–88.

7. Allan F. Moore, *Rock: The Primary Text: Developing a Musicology of Rock* (Aldershot, UK: Ashgate, 2001).

8. Gary Ansdell and Tia DeNora, "Musical Flourishing: Community Music Therapy, Controversy, and the Cultivation of Wellbeing", in *Music, Health and Wellbeing*, ed. Raymond MacDonald et al. (Oxford: Oxford University Press, 2012), 97–112.

9. Tia DeNora, "Practical Consciousness and Social Relation in MusEcological Perspective", in *Music and Consciousness: Philosophical, Psychological and Cultural Perspectives*, ed. David Clarke and Eric Clarke (Oxford: Oxford University Press, 2011), 310.

10. Ron Eyerman and Andrew Jamison, *Music and Social Movements: Mobilizing Traditions in the Twentieth Century* (Cambridge: Cambridge University Press, 1998).

11. Craig Robertson, "Singing to Be Normal: Tracing the Behavioural Influence of Music in Conflict Transformation" (PhD diss., University of Exeter, 2014), 112.

12. Robert J. Kruse II, "Geographies of John and Yoko's 1969 Campaign for Peace: An Intersection of Celebrity, Space, Art and Activism", in *Sound, Society and the Geography of Popular Music*, ed. Ola Johansson and Thomas L. Bell (Farnham, UK: Ashgate, 2009), 11–31.

13. Eric D. Gordy, *The Culture of Power in Serbia: Nationalism and the Destruction of Alternatives* (University Park: Pennsylvania State University Press, 1999), 134; Jelena Jovanović, "The Power of Recently Revitalised Serbian Rural Folk Music in Urban Settings", in *Music, Power and Politics*, ed. Annie J. Randall (London: Routledge, 2005), 134.

14. B. Luzha, "Music Brings People Together in Post-War Kosovo", *International Journal of Music Education*, 23, no. 2 (2005): 149–51.

15. John Morgan O'Connell and Salwa Castelo-Branco, eds., *Music and Conflict* (Champaign: University of Illinois Press, 2010).

16. Roberto Illiano and Massimiliano Sala, eds., *Music and Dictatorship in Europe and Latin America* (Turnhout, Belgium: Brepols, 2009).

17. Timothy Rice, "Reflections on Music and Meaning: Metaphor, Signification and Control in the Bulgarian Case", *British Journal of Ethnomusicology* 10, no. 1 (2001): 23.

18. Rice, "Reflections on Music and Meaning", 36.

19. Terri M. Adams and Douglas B. Fuller, "The Words Have Changed but the Ideology Remains the Same: Misogynistic Lyrics in Rap Music", *Journal of Black Studies* 36, no. 6 (2006): 938–57.

20. Bruce Johnson and Martin Cloonan, *Dark Side of the Tune: Popular Music and Violence* (Farnham, UK: Ashgate, 2009).

21. Michael Eric Dyson, "The Culture of Hip-Hop", in *That's the Joint! The Hip-Hop Studies Reader*, ed. Murray Forman and Mark Anthony Neal (New York: Routledge, 2004).

22. Jeff Chang, *Can't Stop Won't Stop* (New York: St. Martin's Press, 2005), 23, 32.

23. John Jordan, ed., *Peace Songs* (London: Workers' Music Association, 1989).

24. William Roy, *Reds, Whites, and Blues: Social Movements, Folk Music, and Race in the United States* (Princeton, NJ: Princeton University Press, 2010).

25. Small, *Musicking*.

26. Jacques Attali, *Noise: The Political Economy of Music* (Manchester, UK: Manchester University Press, 1985), 6.

27. George Kent, "Unpeaceful Music", in *Music and Conflict Transformation: Harmonies and Dissonances in Geopolitics*, ed. Olivier Urbain (London: I. B. Tauris, 2008), 108.

28. Svanibor Pettan, ed., *Music, Politics and War: Views from Croatia* (Zagreb: Institute of Ethnology and Folklore Research, 1998).

29. Bennet Hogg, "Who's Listening?", in *Music, Power and Politics*, ed. Annie J. Randall (London: Routledge, 2005), 211–30.

30. Gordy, *The Culture of Power in Serbia*; Jovanović, "The Power of Recently Revitalised Serbian Rural Folk Music".

31. Matthew Collin, *This Is Serbia Calling: Rock 'n' Roll Radio and Belgrade's Underground Resistance* (London: Serpent's Tail, 2001), 80; Hogg, "Who's Listening?", 223.

32. Hogg, "Who's Listening?", 224.

33. Christopher Dandeker, *Surveillance, Power, and Modernity: Bureaucracy and Discipline from 1700 to the Present Day* (Cambridge: Polity Press, 1990), 38–39.

34. Arild Bergh, "I Am What I Am: Music and Representation in Conflict Transformation", paper presented at the annual IPRA conference, Calgary, Alberta, Canada, June 29–July 3, 2006, 2.

35. Small, *Musicking*; Attali, *Noise*.

36. Bergh, "I Am What I Am", 4.

37. Bergh, "I Am What I Am", 5.

38. See Small, *Musicking*; Howard S. Becker, *Art Worlds* (Berkeley: University of California Press, 1982); Tia DeNora, *Music in Everyday Life* (Cambridge: Cambridge University Press, 2000); Tia DeNora, *After Adorno: Rethinking Music Sociology* (Cambridge: Cambridge University Press, 2003).

39. Attali, *Noise*; David Hesmondhalgh, "Towards a Critical Understanding of Music, Emotion and Self-Identity", *Consumption Markets & Culture* 11, no. 4 (2007): 329–43.

40. DeNora, *After Adorno*, 5.

41. Ibid., 6.

42. Ibid., 17.

43. Calvin Thomas, "A Knowledge That Would Not Be Power: Adorno, Nostalgia, and the Historicity of the Musical Subject", *New German Critique* 48 (Autumn 1989): 161.

44. Robert Lilienfeld, "Music and Society in the 20th Century: Georg Lukács, Ernst Bloch, and Theodor Adorno", *International Journal of Politics, Culture, and Society* 1, no. 2 (1987): 310–36.

45. Quoted in Kent, "Unpeaceful Music", 110.

46. Theodor Adorno, *Quasi una Fantasia: Essays on Music*, trans. Susan H. Gillespie (London: University of California Press, 2002), 59, 158, 270.

47. Robertson, "Singing to Be Normal".

*Chapter Ten*

# Rave Culture

*Freeparty or Protest?*

## Rev. Ruth Dowson, Dan Lomax and Bernadette Theodore-Saltibus

In this chapter we argue that rave culture can be classified as a form of protest. As a youth-oriented subculture, or "tribe",[1] based around social ideas, music and art, raves emerged from the era of Thatcher's children, whose "cultural heroes came in the form of radical young entrepreneurs who started up clubs and record labels, rather than the politicians and poets of yesteryear".[2] Furlong views raves as "a mix of hedonism, consumerism and escapism",[3] a sanctuary away from education and work, in which participants are free from boundaries and controls, in an environment that involves active protest and consumption of drugs. In examining criteria that might shed light onto this discussion, we explore the narratives of rave organizers and find elements of shared values, activities and motivations, and common processes as utilized by more conventional event organizers.

Having previously sidelined raves to the realms of "unplanned events", Getz's typology now recognizes the existence of "events at the margins",[4] that encompass elements of planning, but which might have an "anti-establishment"[5] flavour, instigated by "agitators . . . or social activists".[6] While now acknowledging that protests involve some planning, Getz argues that there is "no real organisation or responsibility"[7] for such events. In this research, we explore the role and contents of an event planning process for raves and freeparties, as evidenced by their organizers.

191

## HISTORICAL ORIGINS OF RAVES

Although the role of popular music in social protest is well recognized, Peddie[8] debates Lahusen's assumption that pop music in and of itself "is inherently oppositional",[9] but recognizes "that popular music does, at times, define itself through opposition".[10] In this study, it is argued that rave culture can be classified as a form of protest. In the late 1980s, raves known as "warehouse parties"[11] were met by police control and confiscation of PA equipment, sometimes resulting in full-scale riots and, on one occasion, "the arrest of 836 people at a single party".[12]

In part, a response to the "yuppie lifestyle and laissez-faire economics"[13] of Thatcherism and Reaganism,[14] raves emerged from and for the youth of this era, youth influenced by a spirit of entrepreneurialism, to develop their own alternative entertainment industry.[15] These events led to the development of a youth-oriented subculture or "tribe",[16] originally based around a combination of social and political ideas and music. The "grassroots organized, anti-establishment"[17] rave, in which "drug use is portrayed as the defining characteristic",[18] is examined here through the lens of protest, in 2014's political environment, as compared to its Thatcher-era origins, when most rave attendees today might have been toddlers, or even unborn.

### Raves or Freeparties?

Having been treated historically as forms of symbolic protest, raves have evolved into what are now known as "freeparties", which still take place on a weekly basis. The former term "rave", with its negative connotations, is shunned by organizers, who prefer the term "freeparty", defined by one organizer as follows: "A gathering of like-minded people. An all-night or longer event where people go to dance, socialize and have fun in an uninhibited way", in what they call a "temporary autonomous zone", a reference to Bey's poetic phrase that declines to be defined, yet is "understood without difficulty . . . understood in action".[19] The perception that freeparty organizers aim to project is that these events are parties of freedom, where attendees are free to have fun, away from the constraints of everyday life, in the context of what is viewed as a restrictive and controlling society.

### PRIMARY RESEARCH—FREEPARTY ORGANIZERS

This research has been undertaken through in-depth interviews with organizers of freeparties. These organizers adhere to perceptions of a freeparty as a sanctuary, away from constraints and restrictions, yet in doing so, they appear to create their own constraints and restrictions. Some of these restrictions might be made apparent through the development of a manifesto which states their shared organizational values, their rationale for freeparties, and instructions for behaviour. These rules for freeparties define acceptable behaviour, imposing their own societal values, some of which could be viewed as "restrictive and controlling", in some instances exceeding that of "normal" society.

In addition, the interviewers have identified organizations that run politically related freeparties, including a freeparty following the death of a prominent political figure. The publicity for this event announced the organizers' interpretation of the political standpoint that this figure embodied, compared to their own ideals and values, which led to a decision to celebrate this death. The event itself was popular, and held in a countryside location. As with any rave, the invitation text from the organizers provided a phone number and instructions which should only be passed on to trusted and known people; these instructions, grounded in secrecy, instituted a high level of accreditation. Further instructions included warnings against the use of any social media, and to delete the text immediately.

However, once the event was over, a media frenzy began. As the hashtag on Twitter fed into Facebook and Instagram, the event reached the local press and was then picked up by a national newspaper, and a peaceful event with police cooperation was characterized by news media as wanton destruction. Meanwhile, the pictures of the freeparty organization's successful post-event cleanup operation were copied from the organizers' own website and rebranded with a newspaper's copyright, with headlines accusing organizers of damaging a beauty spot, which would require a costly cleaning operation. It was notable that the same article quoted an organizer confirming that litter had been bagged up and removed by them, with a promise to return the site to its original state. In this report it was evident that the press showed bias towards the event, positioning it negatively, within their definition of a rave. The photographs posted on the newspaper's website showed refuse that had been collected and bagged by individuals attending the freeparty. On the organizers' website, photographic evidence shows that at the end of each event, all rubbish is collected and removed. Such media response to an event underlines Tepper's observed construction of "a 'cultural frame' that links an activity . . . to a lifestyle, a category of people, and a social problem, thereby constructing notions of deviance and harm in the public's imagination".[20] Meanwhile, Martin argues, "Raving, as a worldwide phenomenon, does pose a significant challenge to many aspects of dominant western values".[21]

## LEGAL AND REGULATORY ASPECTS OF PLANNING AND
## MANAGEMENT OF RAVES AS EVENTS

With limited academic research and literature on the planning and management of raves from an events management perspective, contextualizing even the fundamentals of the Event Planning Process and key areas of Health and Safety when planning, managing and implementing raves, becomes almost paradoxical.[22] Research into the seemingly spontaneous, instantaneous and secretive underground world of the implementation of rave events challenges not only the fundamental conventions of events management itself but also, by extension, the conventions of the management of the traditional event space. We have sought to focus on the seemingly unplanned[23] nature of the rave event and aim to clarify the processes that support this unusual event type, best described as an anti-commercial, utopian, egalitarian, apolitical escape.[24]

It is noteworthy that even attempting to define a rave is problematic, as trying to normalize the concept of a rave itself can become exclusionary and, in some sense, an oxymoron—that is, attempting to provide a definition for the indefinable. Attempts to provide academic definitions for a rave range from an "event space where people dance to electronic music"[25] to the very basic definition of "a party".[26] While sizes of raves range from thirty to forty people up to thirty thousand attendees, they are capable of attracting a diverse demographic, transcending class, gender, ethnicity and sexual orientation, and they are usually characterized by a sense of escapism and an almost "evangelical passion for the empathogenics",[27] in which patterns of consumption include drugs rather than alcohol, and a mixture of house, reggae, ska, garage, grime, dub, and techno music. Most ravers would argue that they share a sense of community which, according to Presdee, stems from the creation of a sense of "hyperreality",[28] which defines the rave space as an area devoid of a fixed authenticity (a free space) and is empty of authority. Thornton notes that the location or event space itself provides a key context for legality, and the un-regulation and lack of official or regulatory approval provides the appeal and a sense of "forbidden and unpredictable sense of place"[29] for the ravers. This seemingly unpredictable and forbidden space provides the context of the perceived loose legal parameters for operational and logistical elements of the rave event. In this context, it is necessary to define the regulatory framework within which legal events are required to conform, and to establish to what extent raves, as events, adhere to such frameworks.

Premises Licences and Temporary Event Notices are key to establishing a legal framework for operating safe events. The Health and Safety Act 1974[30] provides the foundation and requirements for safe events within Section 2 (which alludes to a duty of care towards anyone affected by the execution of the work itself). Derivative regulations to support the implementation of the law, ranging from the Six-Pack Regulations[31] and beyond, provide an operational framework for core aspects of the implementation of the event.

The Health and Safety Executive[32] also provide extensive guidance documents in the form of the Purple, Green, Red and Yellow Safety Guides, along with other approved Codes of Practice to supplement and provide support for operating within the context of the law. Such codes exist in order to enable the provision of a safe and healthy environment, not only for the event attendees but also for anyone else involved in the implementation of the event itself, such as employees, sub-contractors and volunteers.

The Licensing Act 2003[33] requires that, prior to the staging of any event, organizers apply for either a Premises Licence or a Temporary Event Notice. Applications for either licence require that the applicant provide key information in terms of the size and date of event, event location and venue. There are four key areas, known as the Licensing Objectives, which include:

the prevention of crime and disorder
public safety
the prevention of public nuisance
the protection of children from harm[34]

Enforcement agencies and licence holders also have a duty to do all that is reasonably practicable in reducing and preventing crime and disorder in their area under the following legislation:

- Crime and Disorder Act 1998
- Violent Crime Reduction Act 2006
- Anti-Social Behaviour Act 2003
- Health Act 2006
- Clean Neighbourhoods and Environment Act 2005

The essential purpose of a licence holder taking responsibility under these objectives is to regulate behaviour on their premises that have access to licensable activities. The licence holder can only seek to manage the behaviour of customers inside and in the immediate vicinity around their premises as they seek to enter or leave, but beyond that point, they do not have any control.

Despite a perception that raves are only subversive because they are an illegal trespass (under the Criminal Justice and Public Order Act 1994[35]), Alwakeel argues that "a specific political currency lies precisely in its very persistence in the face of regulation".[36] We would argue that the protest aspect of raves is more than an illegal trespass, as attendees physically embody subversive action, and the media coverage from such events provides evidence that this continues to be the case.

The Criminal Justice and Public Order Act also banned the playing of music during the night. In relation to raves, important parts of the Act include the following: Sections 61 and 62 (trespassers); Sections 63, 64 and 65 (raves); and Sections 66 and 67 (seizure of equipment). Sections 63–65 of the Criminal Justice Act are aimed at preventing and stopping raves. Section 63-1(b) states, "Music includes sounds wholly or predominantly characterized by the emission of repetitive beats".[37] The Act enables the police to seize equipment being used, and empowers them to stop people within a five-mile radius. If a police demand is ignored and people do not leave, it could result in three months' imprisonment for organizers, as well as a £2,500 fine.[38]

## PARTICIPANT AND ORGANIZER MOTIVATION

If raves and freeparties are taken as those dance events that exist outside of the licensing and legal spheres, then it is important to understand why both organizers and attendees take safety and legal risks in order to participate, even though legal alternatives exist in abundance. Certainly, from the perspective of the production available at legal events, dance events provide more extensive lighting, special effects, visuals and facilities than those that are covertly organized. As a result, it is likely that the meaning and motivations associated with attendance will differ, with Martin identifying two key areas of thought, based around resistance to the position individuals and subcultures have in society and a postmodern stance that there is no defined meaning and that behaviour is "nothing but style".[39] Furthermore, there are the key concepts of community and freedom, in which the freeparty gives the space in which attendees can express alternative behaviours and ideologies, in an environment supported by others, without interference from corporate interest or judgemental individuals.[40]

Obviously there are many reasons why raves and freeparties are organized. At one extreme, illegal sound systems and parties form part of events related to wider protest movements such as Occupy, anti-G8 and Reclaim the Streets. For example, anti-G8 protests in Germany in 2007 included the Resistance Art Festival, whose stated aim was "to offer people a place to rest and to find a new energy to go back to the barricades",[41] while sound systems were set up in Piccadilly Circus in December 2011 as part of the Occupy Everywhere day of action.[42] Carmo calls such events the "Protestival"[43] and highlights the importance of the usually nonviolent, creative behaviour rooted in everyday activities, such as dance, as a means of retaking urban spaces and "subverting and liberating them from their conventional uses".[44] Carmo also cites Bey's "Temporary Autonomous Zones",[45] with the freeparty serving as a physical manifestation of free space in which political and social norms are free to be challenged.

This desire for free spaces goes beyond the direct protest and confrontation, and can be found in both legal and illegal events. The festival has traditionally been a source of free space,[46] but over time, for some, the experience of organized events has become more commercialized and formulaic.[47] In the UK in the last fifty years there has been a trajectory from commercial events such as the 1970 Isle of Wight festival, which was criticized by some as against the prevailing spirit of the time for its "free music", through a growth of free festivals in the 1970s and 1980s, to the commercial festivals of the last twenty years. Anderton argues that the politicization of free festivals in the 1980s, alongside the right-wing moral panic when the movement coalesced with the new rave scene in the late 1980s to early 1990s, led directly to the Criminal Justice Act 1994.[48] This act, in turn, made promoters more accountable and thus required major additional funding to ensure legality, leading to the commercialization of such events. As a result, the free spaces and behaviour they promise may still be invoked by legal festivals, but in many ways legal festivals are limited, and it is into this gap that freeparty organizers have leapt. In addition, the sanitization of the festival experience has attracted a great many new attendees, for whom the new-found security in the ordered environment of the legal festival is a positive, and it is the presence of these less adventurous individuals which has driven away those seeking a greater sense of difference.[49]

Free space is, therefore, a place in which to escape the commercialization and conformity of legalized parties, and to be surrounded by people sharing similar attitudes to freedom. As a result, a liminal space is created in which existing preconceptions of personality, behaviour and legality can be explored.[50] Indeed, for some, the experience is seen as a spiritual one.[51] However, many legal club and festival experiences, especially in smaller and more underground subgenre-specific events, give the opportunity for free expression and illegal behaviour, such as recreational drug use, which is similar to the freeparty experience. The question, then, is this: How different are legal events from freeparties? And is there something else, in addition to the freedom created by the liminal space of the freeparty?

Martin identifies the nature of resistance in rave attendees in that the very act of taking that step into a space created outside the accepted framework of society is a major part of the appeal.[52] By taking oneself outside of legal controls and society acceptance, there is a personal step towards free expression, and one which is at the limit of possible experience not achievable in legal club surroundings. In addition, the very nature of the spaces used, being temporary, means that each experience is unique and unknown.[53]

It may be that this unknown quality will attract attendees whose primary motivation is thrill seeking, subcultural capital or cool hunting,[54] rather than the freedom as discussed before. As a result, the fundamental motivation of attendees is a concern for those staging the event, as confrontations between those of different intrinsic motivations may well impact on the freedom and free space which was the original intention of the event. As such, control of information and accreditation by direct invitation are key to ensuring the right atmosphere.[55]

## SACRED SPACE

Another lens through which we explore this narrative is by examining the concept of sacred space under criteria proposed by Ostwalt, who declared that "holiness is the otherness of place—powerful, seductive, and challenging to human being".[56] For those who attend raves, the place takes on a special meaning, and attendees report that they get "lost in the music", that they lose all "concept of time" and are filled with a "euphoric" feeling.[57]

Sacred spaces are seen as "dangerous and provocative",[58] where it is possible to apply Grimes's concept of "ritual partitions" as "abstract ideas or mental images"[59] that might be found in woodlands, as well as physical barriers, such as those provided by the walls of empty warehouses or underground bunkers. For freeparties, the danger lies in the likelihood of police intervention, as well as in physical activities such as the "wall of death" or "mosh pits", and the consequences of illegal drug use, where "a temporal utopia or spatial, sacred places tend to attract like-minded individuals" in the search for a "utopian element".[60] Individuals who attended freeparties said they even experienced collective euphoria.[61]

The location is created to be sacred and "foundational".[62] A freeparty can be compared to a place of religious worship, a space for individuals to gather communally. Some people perceive freeparties as a "spiritual" gathering,[63] in which participants might actively demonstrate their beliefs when congregated. Just as sacred places "assume and promote a participatory element",[64] this experience is also found in freeparties. Whether places are sacralized by actions (according to Grimes[65]) or act as sacred in and of themselves (Jonathan Z. Smith[66]), the question arises as to whether spaces such as freeparty locations become sacred to attendees through the activities that take place within them[67] or through the people attending the raves.

## RAVE ORGANIZERS' NARRATIVES

The individuals interviewed belong to a range of organizations that plan and deliver events which they describe as "freeparties"; they "never use the word 'raves'", viewing a "freeparty" as "an event that is innately political", although some freeparties might also have an explicitly political theme. This change in terminology results from the desire to distance the organizers and their events from past negative connotations associated with raves (still perceived by those in the judicial system and the media), and also because they argue that raves have evolved into brands and legal club nights, commercialized and "homogenized" within today's entertainment industry, part of a "bingeing culture" in which people are "essentially rotting themselves from the inside". Such heavy criticism of the current culture of the legal nighttime economy highlights their distance in terms of values and motivations, as they challenge the conformity of providers of mainstream festivals and club nights, partly on the basis of commercialization, as well as with a sense of morality in rejecting the norm:

> Going into town with all the bouncers, with all the drunk people, with all the girls with skirts up to here, I find that far more immoral than what we do. You know, what we do actually has a sense of community.

In establishing the motivations of freeparty organizers, their values are very much to the fore, with the aim of "showcasing that embracing the principles of mutual aid and solidarity can have tremendous and real societal impact". Their events are literally free to attendees—that is, no charge is made to participants, although some organizers will send out a bucket for donations to cover their costs (which are not insignificant, such as fuel for generators or the inevitable "collateral damage" to their own sound systems), while others may provide cups of tea or bottles of water for a small charge. The purpose of the freeparty is to provide an environment in which people can be "free" to act as they will, with

> freedom to conduct yourself in a reasonably hedonistic manner, but also an attitude of self-policing; this is increasingly prevalent, or else it's not sustainable, there would be no event. It's not a "free-for-all", it's a "look out for everybody"!

The organizers' use of language implies that any hedonism is controlled within specific performance parameters, which is a contradiction, in that the experience is not free of structure, nor of free will, but it operates within implied organizational boundaries, which delineate a caring community with enforced rules and codes of acceptable behaviour, in stark contrast to many of the realities of Saturday-night club and street culture. The organizers recognize that these illegal events provide a liminal space in which a "sense of mass euphoria is cultivated, which can lead people to act irrationally, or out of societal norms". And yet, at the end of the freeparty, when the sun nudges its way over the horizon, party-goers will awake to a surprise, meticulously planned by the organizers, when they find themselves "on a beach, or . . . in the woods, or . . . looking over a massive reservoir. It has to be pretty, it has to be 'fluffy' . . . it sets the vibe".

The freeparty collaborative organizations often have explicit statements of intent, expressing their values and motivations

> to remind people that actually we have their best interests at heart, but specifically that it's not a profiteering or drug-based exercise, it's a social enterprise. And that the people involved are principled people, and that the people who propagate it are principled.

Such value-laden views are common across all the organizations we encountered, engendering an environment in which attendees are encouraged to explore new concepts, with an explicitly educational purpose, with or without a political connection. Even those freeparty organizers who self-identify as "fluffy" rather than explicitly "political" wish to provide an alternative to the values experienced in town and city centres every Friday and Saturday night.

From our interviews, we identified two types of freeparty organizers: those who work professionally in events, usually experienced in event production or event tech roles, and those with a full-time day job, not in events, but who are experienced enthusiasts for whom running freeparties is a serious and highly treasured hobby. In many ways, this reflects the reality of events delivery generally, with a split between those who are professionals doing a job and those whose jobs or other interests cause them to choose or to have to run events.

Freeparty organizers' initial motivations, however, are shared, aiming for excitement, mental and emotional stimulation, and "adrenaline". In contrast, while attendees are likely to go to freeparties for the excitement, the organizers perceive that many attendees do not share their deeper values, recognizing that although they may want to attract people "like us", their events (some more than others) may also attract "wrong 'uns" and the very young, excluded from the legal events scene by age restrictions. All the organizations we encountered have in place strict controls on those connected with them, using social media platforms to accept and reject prospective freeparty attendees. The smaller the contact list, the more controls there are in place, and the more likely the organizers are to reject applications they deem unsuitable. For example, the number of shared contacts with the applicant and the organization may be helpful in enabling an aspiring member, but, equally, who those shared contacts are will have a greater influence on their acceptability for accreditation, and in enabling organizers to maintain a balance of people who are known and trusted to receive information about an upcoming event. There is a level of secrecy about the profiles of these organizations on social media sites; indeed, it was commented that the most obvious and explicit "rave" organizations online are among the least likely to have any organizational part to play in the running of such events and, in some cases, even attending them. Accreditation is, therefore, a key activity within the event planning process that takes place prior to the event. Interviewees spoke of receiving a minimum of fifty to sixty requests to join their social media profiles each week. The age profile of organizers is largely reflected in the age profile of their own freeparty attendees, with some notable exceptions, and these exceptional events are generally much bigger (with thousands of attendees rather than hundreds), with many more attendees in younger age groups, while the average age of attendees at smaller freeparties might be over thirty, and include people in their fifties and sixties.

Asked about their event planning processes, it was notable that those involved in events on a professional level take a more structured approach, including keeping detailed minutes of planning meetings. A key requirement of successful negotiations with police on-site is the ability to communicate and explain event planning processes, especially regarding health and safety. This aspect of health and safety was of paramount importance to all the groups interviewed, and all demonstrated in-depth knowledge of legal and regulatory frameworks and requirements, able to quote specifics. Again, this is in contrast to many organizers of traditional events, and is perhaps because, having brushed up against the law, freeparty organizers know to their cost what is required.

Through our discussions about the roles undertaken at their events, we have identified a typology of core organizational roles for freeparty organizers on-site:

- *The Problem Solver-Negotiator*: a troubleshooter who spends his or her time searching out problems and issues to resolve, also takes responsibility for negotiating with police. May also play the roles of peacekeeper, facilitator and mediator. A diplomat, seen by some as the "*Schmoozer*".
- *The Soundboy-DJ*: usually male, responsible for ensuring the sound system is up and running as quickly as possible once the team arrives on-site; enjoys playing with technical equipment before, during and after the event. In smaller organizations will also be the DJ, keeping the sound system alive until the party ends.
- *The Welfare Angel*: usually female, offering tea and sympathy, as well as compassion and care for those who are unable to care for themselves—the "fluffy" ones.
- *The Creative-Designer*: whether installing lighting in trees or decorating the site with fairy lights and signage, responsible for setting the "vibe" and enhancing the atmosphere.
- *The Volunteer*: not a core member of the crew, but ready to don a hi-vis jacket in order to contribute to the wider objectives of the freeparty, whether organizing the "Wall of Death" or physically defending the party from uninvited and unwelcome guests.

These roles are common to all the organizations we met, although the smaller the organization, the more likely an individual is to undertake more than one role.

Venue search is another key element of the event planning process that plays a vital role in the success of freeparties. In the past, many parties were held inside, in buildings accessed via illegal means, resulting in some organizers being charged with burglary. Another limitation of holding indoor events arises from security concerns. According to one organizer, they moved to holding freeparties outdoors, because

> a paramount concern is public safety, which we generally found in inner-city indoor venues; they are genuinely a lot more dangerous, because you can light up large outdoor spaces. The term we use is: "leaving no dark spaces for dark shit to happen", because if you have dark corners, bad things can happen in it . . . and lighting up a whole warehouse can be tricky. There was an event once in a 75,000-square-foot warehouse . . . in an industrial area . . . and that's an immensely large area to keep well lit and well safe. Whereas outdoors you've got the contributing factor of natural lights, and large floodlights can be put up in trees and generally larger areas can be lit up quite well.

The move to outdoor venues prompted a different range of criteria for venue selection:

- Accessibility: In order to assemble a large number of people at short notice, the location needs to be a large site that is easily accessible; however, to restrict numbers of uninvited people, the location also needs to be hidden. While some organizers we spoke to select their venue based on proximity to public transport, others prefer a more out-of-the-way location, creating "a balance between easily accessible, to get the most number of people in as short a time as possible to create a sustainable atmosphere where the police can't shut it down easily, to allow as many people to access it as possible, but also creating a barrier in that it should be inaccessible to the general public, and not particularly bother them".
- Distance from neighbours: Sound travels across the countryside for miles, and causes disturbances that are taken into account by local authorities and organizers of legal festivals. Care is taken to select a location that is as far off as possible and has "no residential premises nearby", so that party-goers will not appear "too obnoxious in creating residential noise pollution issues".
- Car parking: Because the venue selected is away from causing noise disturbance to neighbours, the larger the freeparty, the more car-parking space is required, because "if it is in the middle of nowhere the only way of getting there is by car". Usually, freeparty attendees will car-share, putting into practice the organizers' principled approach to sustainability.

- Environment: The surprise element that transforms the end of the party: "Everybody turned up when it was dark, and it was just a concrete car park, but when they woke up in the morning there were hundreds of people sitting in the dunes, surrounded by dunes and they didn't know it— until the sun came up". Setting the scene for the end of the event is an important feature of the venue selection process, adding to the anticipation of organizers and repeat attendees.

The importance of each of these criteria may vary from one organizer to another, depending on preference and the size of the event. However, the move from indoor to outdoor venues means that the weather plays an important part in the timing of parties, notably moving freeparties into the summer, but even then, taking account of temperature fluctuations, ensuring that

> it's warm enough so people don't get cold and ill. Environmental conditions
> are really important—it needs to be *warm*. We have certainly put off events to
> the detriment of our professional reputation, based on people could get rained
> on and get ill. You don't want people to get hypothermia, or get ill.

In their contact with police, organizers observed that the initial approach by the police set the tone for each encounter, noting that an aggressive police manner would usually result in the early closure of the freeparty, sometimes with confiscation of rigs and vehicles. Perceived inexperience and youth of police officers were seen as detrimental factors in such meetings, leading to aggressive behaviour, countered by organizers with cups of tea and well-practiced negotiation skills. In contrast, organizers recounted many more positive examples of responding to police arrival on-site, including having "had police dancing on my dance floor", and even developing "a certain understanding now . . . the local police are like 'oh it's these guys'. You know they come do their thing, tidy up, they're courteous and respectful and they are off".

The range of responses from police varied from positive encouragement, as organizers "wander down, have a chat with them and invite them up" to police deception, arrests and, occasionally, prosecution.

So, what of Getz's assertions regarding the level of planning for such events?[68] Each freeparty organization had identified and communicated a clear purpose to their events, fitting with Getz's stipulation, with objectives that were more deeply considered and held than those of many professional managers of traditional events. Freeparty organizers have a programme for the event, clearly seeking to create an "experience"—again, having given much thought and planning to choosing the venue, and developing the style, structure and content of the event. The controls imposed by freeparty organizers, not only on methods of communication and accreditation but also on permissible behaviour on-site, are in many respects much stricter than those used in traditional planned events. Getz's final criteria is that event producers are held accountable as individuals; our research concludes that many free-party organizers have had their equipment impounded, and some have been arrested and even charged with a range of offenses, demonstrating a higher level of accountability than would be observed in legal events.

## CONCLUSION

In conclusion, the research identifies the renaming of raves to freeparties as an effort to move away from the negative connotations associated with rave culture. The language of freeparty attempts to distance and differentiate itself from rave culture. Meanwhile, mainstream commercialized festivals and events in the nighttime economy now reflect the original rave concept. For example, within the current context of legal mainstream commercial events, evidence suggests that empathogenics and hallucinogenics play a key role, combined with high levels of alcohol consumption, which is not always consistent with the freeparty ethos.

Getz notes that "events at the margin" do not appear to follow any formal event planning process.[69] Our research suggests that, rather than following a traditional format for event management, freeparty organizers have developed a complex system of processes, catering to shorter timelines. With less time for contingency planning, health and safety planning and attendee communication, the impacts of these aspects on the critical path are key features of the freeparty planning process.

We conclude that Getz's assumption that there is no organizational responsibility is inaccurate, as the organizational structures we have identified (unlike a more formalized event management structure) take a decentralized collaborative approach, with no single event manager identified. Lines of responsibility include organizational responsibility from the planning team, as well as community and collective responsibility that all attendees have towards each other. This feature is not as explicit within the formalized event context. Team roles are allocated according to skill sets, with the identification of roles such as the "problem solver" responsible for logistical elements and health and safety issues; "Soundboy DJ", the entertainment provider; and "welfare angel", welfare management, food and beverage, responsible for first aid and emergency responses as well as attendee well-being. The "Schmoozer", often assigned to interact with local authorities while the event is live, takes police on site visits, and is the main point of contact for non-attendees on-site, and also serves as the mediator within and among the wider event team.

The objectives and motivations of attendees differ from those of organizers, although it was observed that many freeparties served as political protests, which was a greater motivation for organizers than for attendees. It was evident that other motivations included protests against certain elements within the societal framework, such as the pursuit of an alternative lifestyle, involvement in subcultural activity, as well as wishing to engage in what is perceived as anti-establishment activities. Key concepts and philosophies within the freeparty community include the freedom of ideas and the "Protestival" nature of such events.

Despite the accurate perception that raves operate outside the formalized legal framework, the freeparty institutes high levels of health and safety and security, with these elements forming key logistical considerations in both venue selection and event implementation. Risk assessments are conducted, with hazard identification and risk assessment and mitigation forming core elements of the event management process. The use of in-house volunteer stewards and security ensures that acceptable levels of behaviour are enforced, and inappropriate behaviour results in ejection from the event, reinforcing the philosophy of mutual aid, safety and self-policing.

If sacred space is deemed as "dangerous and provocative",[70] a clear area of danger for this type of event is more externally focused on police intervention and ensuring that the "wrong 'uns", or non-members, do not gain access to the event. Another key criterion for maintaining this sacred space is to ensure that there is no violence or antisocial behaviour. This is clearly evidenced in codes of behaviour or organizational manifestos. High levels of accreditation and very strict control of access to the freeparty event minimizes the perceived danger of the event. Although there is some encouragement of hedonistic behaviour, there is clear evidence that codes and parameters of behaviour are enforced and the paradox of definite levels of control exist within this "free space" environment.

The planning process of events such as freeparties is questioned by some academics; however, from our research, it is clear that the event planning process is evident. A key area of difference is the critical path of the event, which creates a much shorter timeline for the planning, coordination and implementation process. Shared with a formal events context, aspects such as venue search and selection, health and safety issues, and entertainment and logistical elements are all clearly part of the freeparty planning process, with aspects such as security clearance or accreditation being carefully managed as a priority. Marketing the event and attendee communication become critical to the success of the event in establishing a viable number of attendees prior to the possible arrival of police. Police intervention can include termination of the freeparty, based on a manageable number of attendees leaving the freeparty, thereby causing police to assess the risk cost of terminating the event versus allowing it to continue. The rapport built between the organizers and the potential impact on the local community and the police can also influence such decisions.

Overall, it is clear that the common perception of the rave (now freeparty) can be reframed within a context of high levels of planning and organization, with many elements of event organization being implemented at equal if not higher levels than their legal counterparts. With the added complexity of operating within significantly shorter timelines, it is evident that the freeparty event itself meets all the specific characteristics of a formal event planning process.

Freeparty organizers might engage in this activity to meet a variety of political objectives—whether linked to explicitly political themes, or through implicit anti-capitalist or social enterprise values and principles. As to whether freeparties are free, while attendees are not required to contribute financially to gain entry, in terms of the freedom to participate in hedonistic behaviour, very specific boundaries exist to facilitate control within the party itself. While embodying subversion and disdaining official approval, in creating value-driven communities that care, freeparty organizers demonstrate a sense of responsibility that reaches beyond that of many conventional event organizers—a political act in itself.

## REFERENCES

Alwakeel, Ramzy. "The Aesthetics of Protest in UK Rave". *Dancecult: Journal of Electronic Dance Music Culture* 1, no. 2 (2010). Accessed 31 May 2013. http://dj.dancecult.net/index.php/journal/index.

Anderson, Tammy L., and Philip R. Kavanaugh. "A 'Rave' Review: Conceptual Interests and Analytical Shifts in Research on Rave Culture". *Sociology Compass* 1, no. 2 (2007): 499–519.

Anderton, Chris. "Music Festival Sponsorship: Between Commerce and Carnival". *Arts Marketing* 1, no. 2 (2012): 145–58.

Bell, Catherine. *Ritual Theory, Ritual Practice*. Oxford: Oxford University Press, 1992.

Bey, Hakim. *T.A.Z.: The Temporary Autonomous Zone, Ontological Anarchy, Poetic Terrorism*. 2nd ed. Brooklyn, NY: Autonomedia, 2003.

Carmo, Andre. "Reclaim the Streets, the Protestival and the Creative Transformation of the City". *Finisterra* 48 (2012): 103–18.

Christopher, Stanley. "Teenage Kicks: Urban Narratives of Dissent Not Deviance". *Crime, Law and Social Change* 23, no. 2 (1995): 91–119.

Cloonan, Martin. *Popular Music and the State in the UK: Culture, Trade or Industry?* Aldershot, UK: Ashgate, 2007.

Duff, Cameron. "The Importance of Culture and Context: Rethinking Risk and Risk Management in Young Drug Using Populations". *Health, Risk & Society* 5, no. 3 (2003): 285–99.

Furlong, Andy. *Youth Studies: An Introduction*. Oxford: Routledge, 2013.

Furlong, Andy, and Fred Cartmel. *Young People and Social Change*. 2nd ed. Maidenhead, UK: Open University Press, 2007.

Garratt, Sheryl. *Adventures in Wonderland: A Decade of Club Culture*. London: Headline, 1998.

Gauthier, François. "Orpheus and the Underground: Raves and Implicit Religion—from Interpretation to Critique". *Implicit Religion* 8, no. 3 (2005): 217–65.

Getz, Donald. *Event Studies*. 2nd ed. Abingdon, UK: Routledge, 2012.

Goulding, Christina, Avi Shankar, and Richard Elliott. "Working Weeks, Rave Weekends: Identity Fragmentation and the Emergence of New Communities, Consumption". *Markets & Culture* 5, no. 4 (2002): 261–84.

Grimes, Ronald L. *Rite Out of Place: Ritual, Media and the Arts.* Oxford: Oxford University Press, 2006.

Hemment, Drew. "Dangerous Dancing and Disco Riots: The Northern Warehouse Parties". In *DIY Culture: Party and Protest in Nineties Britain*, edited by George McKay, 208–27. London: Verso, 1998.

Hutson, Scott. "The Rave: Spiritual Healing in Modern Western Subcultures". *Anthropological Quarterly* 73, no. 1 (2000): 35–49.

Martin, Daniel. "Power Play and Party Politics: The Significance of Raving". *Journal of Popular Culture* 32, no. 4 (1999): 77–99.

Meashom, Fiona. "Play Space: Historical and Socio-Cultural Reflections on Drugs, Licensed Leisure Locations, Commercialisation and Control". *International Journal of Drug Policy* 15, no. 5 (2004): 337–45.

Merchant, Jacqueline, and Robert MacDonald. "Youth and Rave Culture, Ecstasy and Health". *Youth and Policy* 45 (1994): 16–38.

Newcombe, Russell. *Raving and Dance Drugs: House Music, Clubs and Parties in North-West England.* Liverpool, UK: Liverpool Rave Research Bureau, 1991.

O'Grady, Alice. "Spaces of Play: The Spatial Dimensions of Underground Club Culture and Locating the Subjunctive". *Dancecult: Journal of Electronic Dance Music Culture* 4, no. 1 (2012): 86–105.

Ostwalt, Conrad. *Secular Steeples: Popular Culture and the Religious Imagination.* 2nd ed. London: Bloomsbury Academic, 2012.

Peddie, Ian. *The Resisting Muse: Popular Music and Social Protest.* Guildford, UK: Ashgate, 2006.

Presdee, Mike. *Cultural Criminology and the Carnival of Crime.* London: Routledge, 2000.

Reynolds, Simon. *Energy Flash: A Journey through Rave Music and Dance Culture.* London: Picador, 1998.

Riches, Gabrielle. "Embracing the Chaos: Mosh Pits, Extreme Metal Music and Liminality". *Journal for Cultural Research* 15, no. 3 (2011): 316–32.

Roberts, Katherine. "The Origins of Raves and Their Expression Today". Unpublished undergraduate thesis. Leeds Metropolitan University, 2013.

Siokou, Christine, and David Moore. "This Is Not a Rave! Changes in the Commercialized Melbourne Rave/Dance Party Scene". *Youth Studies Australia* 27, no. 3 (2008): 50–57.

Smith, Jonathan Z. "Birth Upside Down or Right Side Up?" *History of Religions* 9, no. 4 (1970): 281–303.

Stranks, Jeremy. *Health and Safety Law.* 5th ed. London: Prentice Hall, 2005.

Tepper, Steven J. "Stop the Beat: Quiet Regulation and Cultural Conflict". *Sociological Forum* 24, no. 2 (2009): 276–306. Accessed 31 May 2013. http://onlinelibrary.wiley.com/doi/10.1111/j.1573-7861.2009.01100.x/abstract.

Thornton, Sarah. *Club Cultures.* Cambridge: Polity Press, 1995.

## NOTES

\* We would like to acknowledge here the input of Katherine Roberts, whose undergraduate events management dissertation and collaboration on the initial conference presentation inspired us to dig deeper.

1. Andy Furlong and Fred Cartmel, *Young People and Social Change,* 2nd ed. (Maidenhead, UK: Open University Press, 2007), 82.

2. Andy Furlong, *Youth Studies: An Introduction* (Oxford: Routledge, 2013), 154.

3. Ibid., 154.

4. Donald Getz, *Event Studies*, 2nd ed. (Abingdon, UK: Routledge, 2012), 66.

5. Ibid., 66.

6. Ibid., 48.

7. Ibid., 67.

8. Ian Peddie, *The Resisting Muse: Popular Music and Social Protest* (Guildford, UK: Ashgate, 2006).

9. Ibid., xvii.

10. Ibid., xvii.

11. Drew Hemment, "Dangerous Dancing and Disco Riots: The Northern Warehouse Parties", in *DIY Culture: Party and Protest in Nineties Britain*, ed. George McKay (London: Verso, 1998), 208–27.

12. Ibid., 209.

13. Ibid., 210.

14. Tammy L. Anderson and Philip R. Kavanaugh, "A 'Rave' Review: Conceptual Interests and Analytical Shifts in Research on Rave Culture", *Sociology Compass* 1, no. 2 (2007): 499–519.

15. Furlong, *Youth Studies*, 154.

16. Furlong and Cartmel, *Young People and Social Change*, 82.

17. Anderson and Kavanaugh, "A 'Rave' Review", 500.

18. Ibid., 507.

19. Hakim Bey, *T.A.Z.: The Temporary Autonomous Zone, Ontological Anarchy, Poetic Terrorism*, 2nd ed. (Brooklyn, NY: Autonomedia, 2003), 97.

20. Steven J. Tepper, "Stop the Beat: Quiet Regulation and Cultural Conflict", *Sociological Forum* 24, no. 2 (2009): 279, accessed 31 May 2013, http://onlinelibrary.wiley.com/doi/10.1111/j.1573-7861.2009.01100.x/abstract.

21. Daniel Martin, "Power Play and Party Politics: The Significance of Raving", *Journal of Popular Culture* 32, no. 4 (1999): 77–99.

22. Sheryl Garratt, *Adventures in Wonderland: A Decade of Club Culture* (London: Headline, 1998); Stanley Christopher, "Teenage Kicks: Urban Narratives of Dissent Not Deviance", *Crime, Law and Social Change* 23, no. 2 (1995): 91–119; Fiona Measham, "Play Space: Historical and Socio-Cultural Reflections on Drugs, Licensed Leisure Locations, Commercialisation and Control", *International Journal of Drug Policy* 15, no. 5 (2004): 337–45.

23. Getz, *Event Studies*.

24. Garratt, *Adventures in Wonderland*; Russell Newcombe, *Raving and Dance Drugs: House Music, Clubs and Parties in North-West England* (Liverpool, UK: Liverpool Rave Research Bureau, 1991); Mike Presdee, *Cultural Criminology and the Carnival of Crime.* London: Routledge, 2000; Simon Reynolds, *Energy Flash: A Journey through Rave Music and Dance Culture* (London: Picador, 1998); Cameron Duff, "The Importance of Culture and Context: Rethinking Risk and Risk Management in Young Drug Using Populations", *Health, Risk & Society* 5, no. 3 (2003): 285–99.

25. Jacqueline Merchant and Robert MacDonald, "Youth and Rave Culture, Ecstasy and Health", *Youth and Policy* 45 (1994): 16–38. See also Measham, "Play Space"; and Christopher, "Teenage Kicks".

26. Merchant and MacDonald, "Youth and Rave Culture"; Measham, "Play Space"; and Christopher, "Teenage Kicks".

27. Merchant and MacDonald, "Youth and Rave Culture".

28. Presdee, *Cultural Criminology*.

29. Sarah Thornton, *Club Cultures* (Cambridge: Polity Press, 1995).

30. Ibid., xxxii; see also Jeremy Stranks, *Health and Safety Law*, 5th ed. (London: Prentice Hall, 2005).

31. Health and Safety Guidance (HSG) publications, accessed 19 January 2014, www.hse.gov.uk/.

32. Health and Safety at Work Act, 1974.

33. The Licensing Act, 2003.

34. The Licensing Act 2003, Explanatory Notes, accessed 19 January 2014, www.legislation.gov.uk/ukpga/2003/17/notes/contents.

35. Criminal Justice and Public Order Act 1994, accessed 31 May 2013, www.legislation.gov.uk/ukpga/1994/33/part/V/crossheading/powers-to-remove-trespassers-on-land.

36. Ramzy Alwakeel, "The Aesthetics of Protest in UK Rave", *Dancecult: Journal of Electronic Dance Music Culture* 1, no. 2 (2010), accessed 31 May 2013, http://dj.dancecult.net/index.php/journal/index.

37. Criminal Justice and Public Order Act 1994.

38. Martin Cloonan, *Popular Music and the State in the UK: Culture, Trade or Industry?* Aldershot, UK: Ashgate, 2007.

39. Martin, "Power Play and Party Politics", 78.

40. Christine Siokou and David Moore, "This Is Not a Rave! Changes in the Commercialized Melbourne Rave/Dance Party Scene", *Youth Studies Australia* 27, no. 3 (2008): 50–57; Chris Anderton, "Music Festival Sponsorship: Between Commerce and Carnival", *Arts Marketing* 1, no. 2 (2012): 145–58; Gabrielle Riches, "Embracing the Chaos: Mosh Pits, Extreme Metal Music and Liminality", *Journal for Cultural Research* 15, no. 3 (2011): 316–32; Christina Goulding, Avi Shankar, and Richard Elliott, "Working Weeks, Rave Weekends: Identity Fragmentation and the Emergence of New Communities, Consumption", *Markets & Culture* 5, no. 4 (2002): 261–84.

41. "Rave Against the G8: Resistance Art Festival TAZ", *Indymedia UK*, last modified 31 March 2007, www.indymedia.org.uk/en/2007/03/366655.html.

42. "Occupy Everywhere—Piccadilly Circus Street Party (London)", YouTube, last modified 15 December 2011, www.youtube.com/watch?v=-UnDn0JwMXo.

43. Andre Carmo, "Reclaim the Streets: The Protestival and the Creative Transformation of the City", *Finisterra* 48 (2012): 103–18.

44. Ibid., 115.

45. Bey, *T.A.Z.*

46. Alice O'Grady, "Spaces of Play: The Spatial Dimensions of Underground Club Culture and Locating the Subjunctive", *Dancecult: Journal of Electronic Dance Music Culture* 4, no. 1 (2012): 86–105.

47. Anderton, "Music Festival Sponsorship".

48. Ibid.

49. Siokou and Moore, "This Is Not a Rave!"

50. Riches, "Embracing the Chaos". See also O'Grady "Spaces of Play".

51. François Gauthier, "Orpheus and the Underground: Raves and Implicit Religion—from Interpretation to Critique", *Implicit Religion* 8, no. 3 (2005): 217–65. See also Scott Hutson, "The Rave: Spiritual Healing in Modern Western Subcultures", *Anthropological Quarterly* 73, no. 1 (2000): 35–49; and Martin, "Power Play and Party Politics".

52. Martin, "Power Play and Party Politics".

53. Ibid.; see also Carmo, "Reclaim the Streets".

54. Hutson, "The Rave"; also Siokou and Moore, "This Is Not a Rave!"

55. Siokou and Moore, "This Is Not a Rave!"

56. Conrad Ostwalt, *Secular Steeples: Popular Culture and the Religious Imagination*, 2nd ed. (London: Bloomsbury Academic, 2012), 90.

57. Katherine Roberts, "The Origins of Raves and Their Expression Today" (unpublished undergraduate thesis, Leeds Metropolitan University, 2013).

58. Ostwalt, *Secular Steeples*, 90.

59. Ronald L. Grimes, *Rite Out of Place: Ritual, Media and the Arts* (Oxford: Oxford University Press, 2006), 94.

60. Ostwalt, *Secular Steeples*, 90.

61. Roberts, "The Origins of Raves and Their Expression Today".

62. Ostwalt, *Secular Steeples*, 90.

63. Roberts, "The Origins of Raves and Their Expression Today".

64. Ostwalt, *Secular Steeples*, 90.

65. Grimes, *Rite Out of Place*.

66. Jonathan Z. Smith, "Birth Upside Down or Right Side Up?" *History of Religions* 9, no. 4 (1970): 281–303.

67. Catherine Bell, *Ritual Theory, Ritual Practice* (Oxford: Oxford University Press, 1992), 15.

68. Getz, *Event Studies*, 48.

69.  Ibid.
70.  Ostwalt, *Secular Steeples*.

## Chapter Eleven

# Events of Emancipation and Spectacles of Discontent

*How the Tea Party and Occupy Wall Street "Happened"*

## Nils-Christian Kumkar

On 19 February 2009, Rick Santelli, a CNBC editor, while reporting from the floor of the Chicago board of trade, had an angry outburst: speaking about the "Homeowners Affordability and Stability Plan", he complained about the government not helping those who "carry the water instead of drink the water" and called for a new "Tea Party".[1] Over the next few days, the video of this "rant heard round the world" was replayed on all major cable-news networks and available on various web pages.

And even though the number of people attending the first Tea Party protests in cities all over the country on 27 February was rather small,[2] this quickly changed in the following weeks: after newly formed or already existing conservative networks and organizations worked on publicizing the event, on 15 April, commonly referred to as "Tax Day", protests in about 750 cities drew more than half a million participants.[3] Over the next two years the Tea Party dominated the headlines. Only one year after Obama's stunning victory in the 2008 presidential election, the tide seemed to have shifted: polls indicated around a third of all Americans supported the Tea Party in early 2010,[4] and the Republican Party scored a "historic victory" in the 2010 congressional election. The passing of a number of central pieces of legislation of the Obama administration, perhaps most prominently the health care reform dubbed "Obama-care", was slowed down considerably by blockades in Congress and accompanied by sharp popular protest.

Two and a half years later *Adbusters*, a Canada-based magazine, sent a tweet to its 90,000 subscribers[5] and called for an occupation of Wall Street, to start a "new social dynamic" (and, interestingly, to go a "step beyond the Tea Party movement").[6] On 17 September, between two thousand and five thousand people protested around several locations in Manhattan and finally came together for the first General Assembly (GA) in Zuccotti Park, which they declared as the beginning of a permanent occupation.[7] After controversial measures taken by the NYPD against Occupy protesters in the following weeks had caused outrage in parts of the public, 15 October, a "global day of action" called for by the Spanish "Indignados" movement, saw an explosion of the movement: protests in 911 cities in eighty-two countries led to numerous new occupations.[8]

And even though the encampments and continuous mass-protests were relatively short-lived, with most camps in the United States being raided in October and November 2011, the protests nevertheless also seem to be connected to a shift in the overall discourse by emphasizing social inequality as a major problem[9] and connecting it to the question of democracy and representation as it is captured in the most prominent slogan of Occupy Wall Street: "We are the 99 percent". It is debatable what impact Occupy Wall Street really had on the reelection of Barack Obama in 2012 or on the landslide victory of the left-wing Democrat Bill de Blasio in New York City's mayoral race in 2013, but it had engraved itself enough into the public discourse to be considered an important factor in the equation.

Already this very rough sketch of the protest mobilizations shows a number of similarities between the two: both exploded onto the scene seemingly out of nowhere. Both seemed to have difficulty transforming these explosions into sustainable political structures (although to different degrees, and on different levels). And, not least for this reason, in both cases opinions on the lasting impact of the protests differ greatly. In the case of Occupy, they range from sweeping claims that "This Changes Everything"[10] to the very circumscribed judgements, which, for example, argue that "measured in terms of words published per political results . . . OWS may be the most over-described historical event of all time".[11] It is this tension between their sudden and stunning unfolding and its ambivalent traces that make it a promising endeavour to approach them from the angle of the "event". That is, to ask the seemingly naïve question, "What just happened?", and, rather than aiming at dissolving the paradox, try to reconstruct the different forces that shaped it.

This chapter does so in three steps: After stating a little more precisely how the in itself ambivalent notion of the event can be understood as framing the analysis, the first part will explain why Bourdieu's concept of the *critical event*, and, implicated in this, the concept of the *habitus,* are suitable tools for addressing the questions raised. The second part will review the results of my ongoing research on both movements in the light of these categories. In the concluding third part, the results for the Tea Party and Occupy Wall Street will be discussed.

## EVENTS, SPECTACLES, AND THE CONCEPT
## OF THE CRITICAL EVENT

The range of concepts of the event that circulate, especially in the parts of the social sciences and humanities that occasionally call themselves "critical", clusters around two opposing poles, which we could call the emphatic and the distanced notion of the event. The first defines the event in its difference to structure and, by doing so, posits itself in opposition to structuralism as the science of "business as usual". This is maybe most prominent in the writings of Alain Badiou, who invests the concept with almost chiliastic verve: the event is seen as intervening in a given state of affairs, disrupting and transcending the situation seemingly out of nowhere. [12] But the more "modest" conceptions in this debate also tend to see the event as encapsulating that which at least theoretically escapes the structure—this notion can be seen as documented, for example, in the debates around the relation between event and structure that have taken place in historiography since the 1970s. [13] The second defines the event in almost the exact opposite terms: it collapses into the structure itself—the contrast is maybe nowhere as sharp as in the German discourse, where the English word "Event" is almost exclusively used to describe some kind of spectacle, [14] while "Ereignis" (as part of the Heideggerian legacy) is used in the emphatic sense described above.

When it comes to analysing protest mobilizations that consider themselves as being anti-systemic to a certain degree, [15] this polarization enforces itself as a decision the researcher cannot escape: either identify with the self-perception as openers of new horizons or miss the reality effect that this opening of horizons might have had. Pierre Bourdieu's concept of the *critical event*, which he developed in his writings on the May 1968 events in France, offers a promising starting point in analysing protests as events, in that he fully acknowledges the tension as one between different interpretative predispositions, capturing a certain truth of the object which has to be understood in a to-be-reconstructed model encompassing them both:

> Those who pay instant attention to the instant, which, drowned in the event and the emotions it arouses, isolates the critical moment, and thus constitutes it as a totality containing within itself its own explanation, introduce thereby a philosophy of history: they tend to presuppose that there are in history moments which are privileged, in some way more historical than others. . . . The scientific ambition, on the other hand, aims to reinsert the extraordinary event into the series of ordinary events within which it finds its explanation. It does so in order to further examine how to locate the singularity of what remains a

moment like any other in the historical series, as we can clearly see with all threshold phenomena, qualitative leaps where the continuous addition of ordinary events leads to a singular, extraordinary instant. [16]

This *extraordinary instant,* the *critical event,* is defined by the breaking down of the normal expectations and experiences of time and social order— caused by the synchronization of various crises or critical states of tensions in different social fields. The actual catalysing event that triggers this synchronization might be seemingly external, even accidental. But the emerging conjunctural crisis furthermore synchronizes and collectivizes the experience of inhabitants of the different social fields and thereby renders them "practically contemporaneous". [17] Last, and maybe most important, this coincidence of breaking down the symbolic order as "ordinary experience of time as presence in an already present future", [18] opens the horizon of expectations: everything seems, and, via the reality effect of expectations in social reproduction, to a certain degree actually *is,* possible.

What makes this concept so fruitful is not only the complex modelling of the embeddedness of the event in a *multi-layerdness* of structures but also the importance it attributes to seemingly minor developments and occasions. Key in understanding the synchronizing and explosive nature of the critical event is the *habitus* of the actors that has to resonate with the crisis in a double sense: On the one hand, the system of generative structures that the protestors are equipped with is itself in crisis, since normal expectations do not seem to fit the reality surrounding them anymore. On the other hand, the social crisis also gets framed and structured by ways these very generative structures process the crisis of their field—a dialectic that goes beyond the conventional opposition between macro- and micro-sociology in acknowledging their mutual constitution.

> [I]t goes without saying that the provisional indeterminacy of options is very differently perceived and appreciated. It engenders more or less "crazy" hopes in some, notably all those who hold intermediate positions in the different fields, claimants tempted to project on to the old order, which they continue to recognize implicitly, the new aspirations which it excluded and which become possible once that order is undermined. For those on the contrary who are involved in maintaining and reproducing the status quo, therefore with the "normal" future of this economy in which they have invested everything and from the beginning, the sudden appearance of an objective discontinuity . . . seems like the end of the world. [19]

The dialectical relationship between the structuring of the actions of the subject yet in turn being structured by these very actions, so central in understanding social movements in general, [20] gains importance in these critical moments, since the openness of the crisis allows for practical consequences of theoretical decisions. Decisions, which in the normal course of social reproduction would seem "crazy", and therefore would be eliminated by spontaneous adjustments of the interpretative patterns, can unfold as adjustments of praxis. It is in these very situations that "[spontaneous] theory can immediately and adequately intervene in praxis", as Georg Lukács puts it in his famous essays in "History and Class Consciousness".[21]

To analyse the protest mobilizations as critical events therefore means to, first, identify and reconstruct the long-term dynamics that built the tensions in the various fields that erupted in the synchronized crisis and, second, to ask what homologies between these different areas of conflict made this synchronization possible. The interpretation and experience of the very critical event by the participants in the protests should allow them, third, to further accentuate the dynamics of the synchronization, but also, fourth and even more important, to ask if the unfolding dynamics really led to an opening of new imagined-as-real possibilities for social and/or individual developments. This last point is considered a sine qua non for a point of potential rupture in the reproduction of "business as usual".

## TEA PARTY

An important part of the crises in the different fields that erupted in the Tea Party as well as in Occupy Wall Street is frequently summed up as the decline of the U.S. middle class and the income polarization in the United States in general.[22] But the catch-all term of "the middle class"—90 percent of all Americans describe themselves as "lower-middle", "upper-middle" or plain "middle class"[23]—veils (rather than illuminating) the different crises that the constituencies of the respective movements experienced both according to their socio-demographic vulnerability and the interpretative patterns they could mobilize to cope with them.

The position of the early constituency of the Tea Party groups in social space can be sketched out using the available surveys on Tea Party support that were conducted during the first years of their activity:[24] According to their reported income, the constituency of the Tea Party belongs mainly to the upper third strata of the U.S. population. Most of them, since they do not belong to the highest quintile, nevertheless experienced stagnating or falling income during the years after 2008 and only a very modest growth in income in the two decades before. That they were not hit nearly as hard as the bottom two quintiles of the income distribution is documented in that the majority of them described their own economic situation as "fairly good".

However, this "fairly good" financial situation can also be a precarious one: since 2000, when the growth in income really slowed down or even reversed,[25] the level of indebtedness, especially of households over fifty-five years old, which make up the largest part of the Tea Party's constituency, increased substantially.[26] This process, for many, had shock-like qualities when the mounting rate of foreclosures of 2007–2009 hit their neighbour-hoods: The decline in the median household wealth from 2000 to 2011 is to a large part due to the decline in the real-estate prices[27]—that is, in the value of the very same assets that secured the debts of exactly the age cohorts[28] that tended to support the Tea Party. Studies on the geographical patterns of Tea Party activism find it to be concentrated especially in regions that were hit particularly hard by foreclosure waves.[29]

In the political field, the years leading up to the Tea Party were also characterized by a crisis of the Republican Party—on the one hand, the defeat in the presidential election and the legacy of political conflict of the Bush presidency seemed to point towards a necessary "reinvention" of the party. On the other hand, the polarization of the party itself in a "fundamen-talist" wing that blamed the defeat on the "moderate" positions of the party's presidential candidate McCain and a moderate wing that interpreted the elec-tion of Barack Obama as a signal for a changing tide in public opinion seemed to make this very reinvention improbable,[30] especially because the "fundamentalist" current was gaining more and more influence at the party's base.[31] This constellation allowed for a set of actors to use the rise of the Tea Party as an opportunity to advance their position in the political apparatus of the Republican Party.

In the economic field, the "financial crisis" and the election of Barack Obama as one of the proponents of the so-called Green New Deal[32] stoked fears in actors of the economic field—namely, the fossil-fuel industries and the inflation-sensitive owners of wealth: Would they have to accept at least a temporary loss due to the structural reforms necessary for initiating such a new cycle of accumulation? These groups were later among those financing the Tea Party groups that from the very beginning attacked important corner-stones of the Green New Deal and contributed heavily to the failure (or underachievement) of the American Recovery and Reinvestment Act of 2009.[33] Today, this antagonism is documented, for example, in the staunch opposition many Tea Party groups take towards so-called sustainable poli-cies—in my observations at Tea Party meetings, the very word "sustainable" itself is often treated as a hint towards a hidden plan to transform the United States into a "totalitarian, planned economy".

The Tea Party arose as an effect of the synchronization of these crises, the eroding of the economic base of the petty bourgeoisie, the conflict in the political apparatus of the Republican Party, and the conflict about how to reverse the falling of the rate of profit in the U.S. economy into one. One way of observing this synchronization is to look how different slogans, such as calling Obama a "socialist", were able to resonate with different sets of actors in different fields and gave them the impression of a common fight.

The fear of *socialism* as the hidden goal of Obama's presidency and the developments of the last years and decades could, in this sense, be understood as a metaphor expressing an experiential homology in the different fields: in the GOP, where this motive started to circulate early on but gained traction during the run-up to the presidential election, it allowed for a polarizing rhetoric of originally rather peripheral candidates such as Sarah Palin, implicitly denouncing the more centrist, leading actors in the party as deviators in the struggle against "tyranny". The small shop- and homeowners felt "betrayed" when they, despite all the middle-class rhetoric of the Bush and Obama administrations, saw assistance flowing into the pockets of those they considered "undeserving" (it is worth keeping in mind that the Homeowners Affordability and Stability Plan, against which Rick Santelli had protested, was an assistance program promising assistance to "unreasonable"—that is, poorer—homeowners threatened by foreclosure). Both located at the rather dominated end of the dominating pole of their respective field, they felt exposed to anonymous forces devaluing their capital and undermining their position in the field. Obama's promise of *Change*, however vague it remained, gave these processes a face and reframed it as a hidden agenda. It is this projection of the inner dynamics of their respective field onto the conscious actions of a shared enemy that also allowed for the alliance with the actors at the dominating pole of the economic field for whom change and socialism were synonyms simply because the first seemed to imply a restructuring of their field at their expense.

But an analysis of first-person accounts of activists in the Tea Party and a more detailed reconstruction of its development point at some limitations or difficulties for understanding it as a critical event.[34] First of all, the alleged catalyst, the rant heard round the world, even though referenced by almost all my interviewees, seems to be a rather more mythical starting point than an actual triggering event. In their stories of their way into the Tea Party the speech gets usually only mentioned as an event of importance for the mobilization of *other* people, while their own politicization is described as related to other experiences—mostly the emergence of the Tea Party as it was witnessed via the media. This seems to validate the observation already sketched out in the beginning: while the speech was immediately promoted heavily and the call for a Tea Party dispersed through television and the blogosphere and backed by conservative think tanks and advocacy groups, it did not in fact mobilize larger numbers of people. It took the effort of a number of agents, maybe most importantly Fox News, which ran about 100 promotional clips for its coverage of the 15 April rallies,[35] and six nationwide organizations, three of them newly founded,[36] to portray the movement as already existing before it actually materialized. The synchronization effect was rather the outcome of a coordinated attempt to further polarize an already existing conflictual political landscape than the organic and unforeseeable outcome of a conjuncture of semi-autonomous fields.

But even more important, since a coordinated campaign can still have unpredicted outcomes, is the question of the other, maybe most central element of the critical moment: the opening of the horizon of the possible. And, indeed, some of my interviewees described a feeling of rush and liberation when they described their encounters with the Tea Party—for example, Patricia's story in this discussion I had with three activists:

Patricia: But everybody embraced me, everybody came over, they *talked*, we got on the bus, and we, we rode for the five hours, and it was, it was like, it was like—

Marcos: Liberating.

Patricia: Yeah! And it, it was almost, ahm, like being around *long* lost relatives—

Marcos: Yeah.

Patricia: that you didn't know exist. You know, 'cause we, we, we talked *non-stop*, the *entire* bus ride. Nobody slept on the way there; nobody slept on the way back. And we, we just, we, we talked about everything that we had bottled up inside us, or of our political views, what we thought about every topic we could possibly cover in, in six hours. And nobody got tired of talking. Because it was just like, somebody had took a bottle of seltzer, shook it up and the cap was untied.

Marcos: Mhm

Patricia: And somebody just let it loose.

Patricia: Because it was, it was a sense of like *freedom*. You know, it was awesome.

Marcos: Yeah.

Patricia: And even once we *got* there. And we were in D.C., everybody had that same energy. Everybody. I mean, ah, people from California, from, from Texas, from Tennessee, from Florida, from, just every state. Everybody had that same feeling of wow. You know, I'm, I'm not by myself, I'm not here alone; there is other people who feel the way I feel. And it was, it was pretty awesome. It was pretty awesome.

But this feeling did not correspond with any positive horizon of social or individual potentiality. That is, while the narratives and discussions are permeated with a deep-seated anxiety about the decline of U.S. society and one's position in it, they are also remarkably *passive*. Neither the individual nor the group seemed to see any desirable and feasible direction that society could take from this point onwards.[37] And, what is even more surprising, given the fact how active and engaged they are in their respective groups, they also don't see any space for political agency on their side (other than appellative hopes such as "the States are going to take back their rights. And that's where it's gonna start").

On the part of the rank-and-file members of the Tea Party groups I spoke to, political action is limited to communicatively validating one's interpretation of the current developments as the decline of U.S. society. This practice, labelled "education" by the activists, is an important part of the group's meeting culture. Communication to the outside seems to mostly take the form of face-to-face conversations permeated by the pleasure of "convincing" people that have been "asleep" rather than confrontations with the public, which are experienced as frustrating and disempowering. The outward politics of the group are centred on collective expressions of anger and disagreement in settings where opposition is improbable, such as protests along major roads or taking part in patriotic parades.

## OCCUPY WALL STREET

The constituency of Occupy Wall Street had lived through a different complex of crises in the years following the beginning of the financial crisis than that of the Tea Party.[38] They are younger, and a lot of them experienced the economic downturn as a personal reality when they left high school or university. They had experienced unemployment or were unemployed at the moment of the surveys in considerably higher numbers than the Tea Party constituency—no surprise, since young people were disproportionally hit by unemployment.[39]

The material vulnerability is especially high, since the income of most of them barely allows for savings: the income of the largest part fell into the lowest two quintiles of the U.S. income distribution, a situation that gets aggravated by the extraordinary high cost of living in cities and particularly New York.[40] Even if the degree of indebtedness seems at first sight to be comparable to that of the Tea Party constituency, one should be aware that the kind of debt they held is very different: the lion's share of the debts of their age-cohort is unsecured medical and educational debt,[41] which both became important issues in the public debate after the rise of Occupy Wall Street, since the protestors drew attention to the dire circumstances that these kinds of debt created for poorer households. In particular, educational debt can be problematic, since defaulting on it has very serious repercussions for the rest of the individual's biography, not only a threat to one's already-achieved living standard but also "mortgaging the future".[42]

Interrelated with and sharpened by these developments is the crisis in the field of education/cultural reproduction: while obtaining a college or university degree became significantly costlier in the last decades (the average cost of a university education rose from 23 per cent of median annual income in 2001 to 35 per cent in 2010), the median expected income stayed the same since 1979 if adjusted for inflation. That the number of students enrolled during these years nevertheless increased might be due not least to the fact that the wages of those who only hold a high school diploma actually decreased.[43]

The crisis in the political field that contributed to the rise of the Tea Party and that, in the following years, had led to an increasingly polarized political landscape, also had an impact on Occupy Wall Street, albeit in a mediated way. It expressed itself rather as a crisis of the relation of the political field to the "audience" that later became Occupy Wall Street's constituency. This audience had for a large part been successfully mobilized in Obama's grassroots campaign in the presidential election of 2008, but felt abandoned rather quickly afterwards. Their alienation from the realm of political representation turned to frustration when the right wing of the Republican Party seemed to be able to successfully dictate the agenda and to hinder the already very modest remnants of Obama's campaign promises that had motivated them in 2008: a conflict that in early 2011 manifested in the mass protests and the occupation of the capitol in Madison, Wisconsin, against anti-union legislation proposed by the state governor Scott Walker (legislation that was supported by the national Tea Party organizations).

The call released by *Adbusters* therefore met a receptive audience: the political and social frustration at home mixed with euphoria about the mass protests around the Mediterranean Sea, which a lot of my interviewees[44] followed closely over the Internet, sometimes even with envy.[45] Maybe one of the most important actions taken by the preparatory committee that was formed and met throughout the summer was to set up the *we are the 99 percent tumblr-blog* on which people could share their grievances and proclaim why they are part of "the 99 percent". The sentiment of belonging to the largest part of society that had been unduly sidelined allowed for different experiences of social deprivation and biographical disappointment to be articulated as part of a single, if vaguely defined, social conflict between the *1 percent* and the *99 percent*. This act of interpretative collectivization is also documented in one of the very few "authorized" declarations of Occupy Wall Street: the Declaration of the Occupation of New York City, which states that "all our grievances are interconnected" and, after a long list of diverse grievances, remarks, "These grievances are not all inclusive".[46]

Nevertheless, the first days of the encampment in Zuccotti Park didn't reach out beyond a relatively small activist base that itself was not really convinced that any kind of new dynamic could develop out of this setting—it was "just . . . these silly anarchists, like chanting the same anarchist things", as one of my interviewees put it—and the media only reported reluctantly: "Wall Street Protestors, Protesting Till Whenever" was the title of a short article the *New York Times* published on 30 September.[47]

Both changed after the widely publicized repressive actions by the New York police that generated solidarity declarations from prominent intellectuals like Noam Chomsky,[48] mobilized greater numbers of supporters on the street and facilitated alliances with other actors in the political realm of New York's civil society, such as unions and civil rights groups. In tandem, the national and international media coverage exploded,[49] turning Occupy Wall Street into the perceived centre of a worldwide phenomenon that understood itself as "Occupy",[50] thereby rendering "practically contemporaneous" different social groups over a whole array of different socio-spatial settings.

In the first-person accounts of Occupy Wall Street I collected, the unfolding events are described as a rush-like experience, sometimes employing religious vocabulary—one interviewee described the concrete floor of Zuccotti Park as "awaiting" and "warm" when one lay down for sleeping; another one spoke of the "weight" that was "lifted off the shoulders" when one entered the park. At this level the experience of my interviewees in Occupy Wall Street can, as the rush of overcoming a feeling of isolation and powerlessness, be compared to that of my interviewees from the Tea Party.

One can point out relevant differences already on the very basic level of the political interpretations of this experience by the actors. The occupiers tended to interpret the events around the occupation of Zuccotti Park as something that changed them and everyone involved, especially in that it gave them a sense of collective agency. And even if some expressed fears that Occupy Wall Street might have presented a window of opportunity that is now closing in on them again, the prevailing sentiment seemed to be more optimistic towards one's own strategic and tactical potential and the general historical situation:

Peter: And we've, I think we've come up with tactics, and learned from the opposition, how we can actually, you know, sort of outsmart them anytime. Both in actions, like direct actions, like zig-zag.

Leila: I mean, that it's interesting, I mean honestly, is that, like actually, I think the world is kinda changing, we're, like, the masses have more of a political voice.

Peter: Mhm.

Leila: And I mean, I mean, you know, all these people protesting, I mean this wasn't around like ten years ago. You know, so even that we're talking about like gay marriage . . . you know, anyways, ahm, but the fact that protestors are having this kind of publicity, and voice, I think is pretty amazing.

Maybe the most striking example of this "activism" (as opposed to the Tea Party's "passivism") is documented in the already mentioned declaration: in its somewhat original interpretation of *Adbusters'* suggestion to formulate a central demand, the declaration addresses not those in power, but rather the 99 percent itself, as the actual agents of possible change. This kind of optimism, however, contrasts sharply with the difficulties in translating the real and imagined alliances that formed behind slogans such as "we are the 99 percent" into structured agents with defined political goals. Passages dealing with these questions tended to be the most tense, conflictual interactions in the group discussions, echoing the "shouting matches" as one of my interviewees described the meetings of the Spokes Council, the institution that was formed by Occupy Wall Street to deal with these issues of coordination and "scaling up", but quickly fell apart.[51]

These discussions—in the "artificial" group discussions I conducted, just as in the meetings I took part in, or in the recordings of the actual meetings of the Spokes Council and debates in blogs and leaflets—often centred on the question of what Occupy is (or was) "really about". One reoccurring motive was the feeling that more and more issues had covered over the root problem that Occupy Wall Street was built to resolve (to "get money out of politics" and not to "save the polar bears"). The other position rather saw Occupy in danger of being "corrupted" by abandoning its principles of all-inclusiveness and entering into all too close, pragmatist coalitions with institutionalized political actors. In the absence of political structures that could settle this conflict by guaranteeing certain standards or to exclude certain positions ("some kind of mechanism for purging people", as one of my interviewees somewhat, but only somewhat, ironically put it), these fears tended to lead to mutual blockades of the involved fractions and surely accelerated Occupy Wall Street's disintegration after it lost its geographical centre at Zuccotti Park.

## CONCLUSION

So what can comparing these two waves of protests under the lens of Bourdieu's concept of the critical event teach us? Even if the results of this study are necessarily very broad-brushed, I would argue that it allows us to reevaluate standard notions of the two protests and their constituency, as they are captured in the somewhat ironic title of this chapter.

In the popular discourse on comparing the two movements, two figures seem dominant. They are loosely linked to the diverging assessments of the movements' outcomes sketched out in the beginning of this chapter. One of them heavily emphasizes the "authenticity" of the protests. Seen in this light, the Tea Party, because of the funding it received from wealthy donors and advocacy groups (most prominently the Koch brothers), is portrayed as "Astroturf",[52] a mere spectacle staging the anger of embittered parts of the white middle class. The other, focusing more on questions of impact and strategy, tends to take the opposite approach: now it is the Tea Party that successfully has engrained itself in the political apparatus and effectively and permanently challenged the administration, while Occupy Wall Street is seen as mere moral outrage.

Both of these views capture important aspects of these protests, but also distort the image of them: they tend to ignore, or at least bracket, the diverse critical tensions that surfaced in and through these movements as well as their respective subjectification of these tensions—that is, the way the participants themselves made sense of the developments according to their own socially structured interpretative dispositions or habitus.

The very accusative nature of the term "Astroturf" for the Tea Party might serve as an illustrative example in that regard: what my interviewees from the Tea Party seemed to reject about that term was not so much the top-down character of the metaphor, but rather the implication that they in some regard would be directed from "behind the scene", which was something that they rather associated with the imagined practices of their political opponent. That is, they interpreted the metaphor in the very same logic that structured their own experience of the crisis and therefore something that is quite unfairly projected onto them.[53] That the Koch brothers had indeed financed some of the groups was in turn nothing that they considered problematic, but rather understood as a transparent alliance between people that together fought against "socialism". In that sense, calling the Tea Party a "spectacle" in a lot of ways could be said to rather express the researcher's normative assumption of where in the social hierarchy movements should emerge. Yet, as the mentioning of the very passive nature of the Tea Party participants' approaches to politics suggested, it also captures a certain reality: the passiveness and resignation that is documented in the first-person accounts of the Tea Party activists and that springs from the dialectics of the very alliance of actors and the objective social position of the mobilized rank-and-file of the Tea Party.

This might be illustrated via a detour through the second aforementioned figure, that is the impression, often combined with a certain "Tea Party envy", especially when articulated from the left, that Occupy Wall Street is rather to be understood as mere moral outrage. This impression draws on the difficulties to develop structures or engrain oneself into existing institutions to develop some kind of agency in the political field itself. That it gained such permanent virulence in the debates in Occupy Wall Street itself points to the fact that it is not sufficient to understand it as a pure "neglect" of political pragmatism on the side of the activists. As the reader probably noticed in the sketches on the constellation of different fields at the outset of the two mobilizations, the homologically positioned actor in the political field was missing in the case of Occupy Wall Street (nobody started an Occupy caucus in Congress, as opposed to the Tea Party caucus which was initiated by Senator Michele Bachmann[54]). This from the very outset limited the space for rapid institutionalization, but also blocked the simple delegation of agency.

It is this delegation that can be seen as explaining a part of the frustration and passivity that one encounters in conversations with Tea Partiers: the permanent fear of "treason" by their elected representatives springs from the fact that they have been used as mobilized audience for the inner conflicts of the political field at least as much as they have engrained themselves in this very political field, but have, since this very engraining went so smoothly from the outset, barely formed any independent structures to resist this "cooptation".[55] It is to be seen in how far Occupy Wall Street, or parts of its constituency, will be able to form structures without relying on such institutionalized actors in the political field. But my observations suggest that this question is still vividly discussed in most groups that formed out of the remains of Occupy Wall Street.

But the strength of the concept of the critical event in that regard is not so much to finally decide which of the mobilizations is or is not to be seen as a truly "critical event". Rather, it in this case allows for pointing at the very openness of the processes giving rise to both of them. Since none of the social conflicts that synchronized in the respective moments seems to have been resolved, and many of them even escalated further, it is all but improbable that they will surface again and with force.

## REFERENCES

Abramowitz, Alan. "Partisan Polarization and the Rise of the Tea Party Movement". Paper presented at the Annual Meeting of the American Political Science Association, Seattle, Washington, 2011. Accessed 12 March 2014. http://faculty.washington.edu/jwilker/353/AbramowitzTea.pdf.

*Adbusters*. "#OCCUPYWALLSTREET A Shift in Revolutionary Tactics". 2011. Accessed 13 March 2014. https://www.adbusters.org/blogs/adbusters-blog/occupywallstreet.html.

Badiou, Alain. *Being and Event*. London: Continuum International Publishing, 2007.

Bourdieu, Pierre. *Homo Academicus*. Stanford, CA: Stanford University Press, 1988.

————. "Die politische Repräsentation: Elemente einer Theorie des politischen Feldes". In *Politik: Schriften zur Politischen Ökonomie 2*, by Pierre Bourdieu, edited by Franz Schultheis and Stephan Egger, 43–96. Berlin: Suhrkamp Verlag, 2013.

Burghart, Devin, and Leonard Zeskind. *Tea Party Nationalism: A Critical Examination of the Tea Party Movement and the Size, Scope, and Focus of Its National Factions.* Kansas City, MO: Institute for Research & Education on Human Rights, 2010. Accessed 13 March 2014. http://www.naacp.org/page/-/TeaParty/TeaPartyNationalism.pdf.

Carr, David. "Cable Wars Are Killing Objectivity". *New York Times*, 20 April 2009. Accessed 13 March 2014. http://www.nytimes.com/2009/04/20/business/media/20carr.html.

Cho, Wendy K. Tam, James G. Gimpel, and Daron R. Shaw. "The Tea Party Movement and the Geography of Collective Action". *Quarterly Journal of Political Science* 7 (2012): 105–33.

Chomsky, Noam. "Noam Chomsky Announces Solidarity with #occupywallstreet". *Occupy Wall Street*, 2011. Accessed 13 March 2014. https://occupywallst.org/article/noam-chomsky-solidarity/.

CNBC's Rick Santelli's Chicago Tea Party, 2009. Accessed 13 March 2014. http://www.youtube.com/watch?v=zp-Jw-5Kx8k&feature=youtube_gdata_player.

CNN Opinion Research Corporation. *CNN Opinion Research Poll*, 2010. Accessed 13 March 2014. http://i2.cdn.turner.com/cnn/2010/images/02/17/rel4b.pdf.

Cordero-Guzman, Hector R. "Main Stream Support for a Mainstream Movement: The 99% Movement Comes from and Looks Like the 99%". Working Paper. New York: School of Public Affairs, Baruch College PhD Programs in Sociology and Urban Education, City University of New York, 19 October 2011. Accessed 13 March 2014. http://occupywallst.org/media/pdf/OWS-profile1-10-18-11-sent-v2-HRCG.pdf.

————. "Profile of Users of the Occupy Wall Street Website: A Window into the Demographics of an Evolving Movement". Working Paper. New York: City University of New York, 18 November 2011. Accessed 13 March 2014. http://bjsonline.org/wp-content/uploads/2011/12/OWS-profile2-wave2-10-21-22-fin-out11.pdf.

Crossley, Nick. "From Reproduction to Transformation: Social Movement Fields and the Radical Habitus". *Theory, Culture & Society* 20, no. 6 (12 January 2003): 43–68.

Debord, Guy. *Society of the Spectacle*. Detroit: Black & Red, 1983.

*Economist*. "Not What It Used to Be". December 2012. Accessed 13 March 2014. http://www.economist.com/news/united-states/21567373-american-universities-represent-declining-value-money-their-students-not-what-it.

Foster, James E., and Michael C. Wolfson. "Polarization and the Decline of the Middle Class: Canada and the U.S." *Journal of Economic Inequality* 8, no. 2 (1 June 2010): 247–73.

Frank, Thomas. "To the Precinct Station: How Theory Met Practice . . . and Drove It Absolutely Crazy". *The Baffler* 21 (2012). Accessed 13 March 2014. http://www.thebaffler.com/past/to_the_precinct_station.

Gebhardt, Winfried. "Feste, Feiern und Events: Zur Soziologie des Außergewöhnlichen". In *Events: Soziologie des Außergewöhnlichen*. Opladen: Leske+Budrich, 2000.

Gelder, Sarah Ruth van. *This Changes Everything: Occupy Wall Street and the 99% Movement*. San Francisco: Berrett-Koehler Publishers, 2011.

Gilcher-Holtey, Ingrid. "'Kritische Ereignisse' und 'Kritischer Moment': Pierre Bourdieus Modell der Vermittlung von Ereignis und Struktur". In *Struktur und Ereignis*, edited by Andreas Suter and Manfred Hettling, 120–37. Göttingen: Vandenhoeck & Ruprecht, 2001.

Gottschalck, Alfred, Marina Vornovytsky, and Adam Smith. *Houshold Wealth in the US: 2000 to 2011*. United States Census Bureau, 2012. Accessed 30 January 2014. http://www.census.gov/people/wealth/files/Wealth%20Highlights%202011.pdf.

Kleinfield, N. R., and Cara Buckley. "Wall Street Occupiers, Protesting Till Whenever". *New York Times*, 30 September 2011. Accessed 13 March 2014. http://www.nytimes.com/2011/10/01/nyregion/wall-street-occupiers-protesting-till-whenever.html.

Kraushaar, Wolfgang. *Der Aufruhr der Ausgebildeten: Vom Arabischen Frühling zur Occupy-Bewegung*. Hamburg: Hamburger Edition, 2012.

Krugman, Paul. "Tea Parties Forever". *New York Times*, 13 April 2009. Accessed 13 March 2014. http://www.nytimes.com/2009/04/13/opinion/13krugman.html.

Lukács, Georg. "Was ist orthodoxer Marxismus?" In *Geschichte und Klassenbewusstsein—Studien über marxistische Dialektik*, 2. Aufl., 13–38. Schwarze Reihe 2. Amsterdam: De Munter, 1967.

Mannheim, Karl. "A Sociological Theory of Culture and Its Knowability (Conjunctive and Communicative Thinking)". In *Structures of Thinking*. London: Routledge, 1997.

Milkman, Ruth, Stephanie Luce, and Penny Lewis. *Changing the Subject: A Bottom-Up Account of Occupy Wall Street in New York*. New York: Joseph S. Murphy Institute for Worker Education and Labor Studies, 2013.

Mishel, Lawrence R., Josh Bivens, Elise Gould, and Heidi Shierholz. *The State of Working America*. Ithaca, NY: ILR Press, 2012.

Motel, Seth. "A Third of Americans Now Say They Are in the Lower Classes". *Pew Social & Demographic Trends*, 10 September 2012. Accessed 13 March 2014. www.pew socialtrends.org/2012/09/10/a-third-of-americans-now-say-they-are-in-the-lower-classes/.

*New York Times*. *Polling the Tea Party*. New York Times/CBS News Poll, 14 April 2010. Accessed 13 March 2014. http://www.nytimes.com/interactive/2010/04/14/us/politics/20100414-tea-party-poll-graphic.html.

NYCGA. "General Assembly Minutes 9/17/11". 17 September 2011. Accessed 13 March 2014. http://www.nycga.net/2011/09/general-assembly-minutes-91711/.

NYCGA. "Declaration of the Occupation of New York City". 29 September 2011. Accessed 13 March 2014. http://99.occupymediawiki.org/wiki/Declaration_of_the_Occupation_of_New_York_City.

NYCSC. "NYC Operational Spokes Council 03/12/2012". NYCGA, 12 February 2012. http://www.nycga.net/2012/03/nyc-operational-spokes-council-03122012/.

Robbins, Liz. "Tax Day Is Met with Tea Parties". *New York Times*, 16 April 2009. Accessed 13 March 2014. http://www.nytimes.com/2009/04/16/us/politics/16taxday.html.

Rosenthal, Lawrence, and Christine Trost. "Epilogue: A Tale of Two Movements". In *Steep: The Precipitous Rise of the Tea Party*, 275–81. Berkeley: University of California Press, 2012.

Ross, Andrew. "Mortgaging the Future Student Debt in the Age of Austerity". *New Labor Forum* 22, no. 1 (1 January 2013): 23–28.

Solty, Ingar. "The Crisis Interregnum: Considerations on the Political Articulation of the Global Crisis: From the New Right-Wing Populism to the Occupy Movement". *Studies in Political Economy* 91 (2013): 85–112.

Tea Party Patriots. "Fire the Speaker! It's Time for Real Leadership". Tea Party Patriots, 2014. Accessed 30 January 2014. http://www.firethespeaker.com/tpp/slider.

Trost, Christine, and Lawrence Rosenthal. "Introduction: The Rise of the Tea Party". In *Steep: The Precipitous Rise of the Tea Party*, 1–22. Berkeley: University of California Press, 2012.

Tseng, Terence, Mark Esposito, and Jorgo Chatzimarkakis. "Youth Unemployment after the Financial Crisis: 'Quo Vadimus?'" *World Financial Review*, 2013. Accessed 13 March 2014. http://www.worldfinancialreview.com/?p=3622.

Velsey, Kim. "Brooklyn Is the Second Most Expensive Place to Live in the U.S." *New York Observer*, 28 January 2014. Accessed 28 February 2014. http://observer.com/2012/09/brooklyn-is-the-second-most-expensive-place-to-live-in-the-u-s/.

Vornovytsky, Marina, Alfred Gottschalck, and Adam Smith. *Houshold Debt in the US: 2000 to 2011*. United States Census Bureau. Accessed 30 January 2014. http://www.census.gov/people/wealth/files/Debt%20Highlights%202011.pdf.

Williamson, Vanessa, Theda Skocpol, and John Coggin. "The Tea Party and the Remaking of Republican Conservatism". *Perspectives on Politics* 9, no. 1 (2011): 25–43.

# NOTES

1. CNBC's Rick Santelli's Chicago Tea Party, 2009, accessed 13 March 2014, http://www.youtube.com/watch?v=zp-Jw-5Kx8k&feature=youtube_gdata_player.

2. Vanessa Williamson, Theda Skocpol, and John Coggin, "The Tea Party and the Remaking of Republican Conservatism", *Perspectives on Politics* 9, no. 1 (2011): 25–43.

3. Liz Robbins, "Tax Day Is Met with Tea Parties", *New York Times*, 16 April 2009, accessed 13 March 2014, http://www.nytimes.com/2009/04/16/us/politics/16taxday.html.

4. CNN Opinion Research Corporation, *CNN Opinion Research Poll*, 2010, accessed 13 March 2014, http://i2.cdn.turner.com/cnn/2010/images/02/17/rel4b.pdf.

5. Wolfgang Kraushaar, *Der Aufruhr der Ausgebildeten: Vom Arabischen Frühling zur Occupy-Bewegung* (Hamburg: Hamburger Edition, 2012), 71.

6. "#OCCUPYWALLSTREET A Shift in Revolutionary Tactics", *Adbusters*, 2011, accessed 13 March 2014, https://www.adbusters.org/blogs/adbusters-blog/occupywallstreet.html.

7. NYCGA, "General Assembly Minutes 9/17/11", 17 September 2011, accessed 13 March 2014, http://www.nycga.net/2011/09/general-assembly-minutes-91711/.

8. Kraushaar, *Der Aufruhr der Ausgebildeten*, 88–92.

9. Ruth Milkman, Stephanie Luce, and Penny Lewis, *Changing the Subject: A Bottom-Up Account of Occupy Wall Street in New York* (New York: Joseph S. Murphy Institute for Worker Education and Labor Studies, 2013).

10. Sarah Ruth van Gelder, *This Changes Everything: Occupy Wall Street and the 99% Movement* (San Francisco: Berrett-Koehler Publishers, 2011).

11. Thomas Frank, "To the Precinct Station: How Theory Met Practice . . . and Drove It Absolutely Crazy", *The Baffler* 21 (2012), accessed 13 March 2014, http://www.thebaffler.com/past/to_the_precinct_station.

12. Alain Badiou, *Being and Event* (London: Continuum International Publishing, 2007).

13. Ingrid Gilcher-Holtey, "'Kritische Ereignisse' und 'Kritischer Moment': Pierre Bourdieus Modell der Vermittlung von Ereignis und Struktur", in *Struktur und Ereignis*, ed. Andreas Suter and Manfred Hettling (Göttingen: Vandenhoeck & Ruprecht, 2001), 120–37.

14. Winfried Gebhardt, "Feste, Feiern und Events: Zur Soziologie des Außergewöhnlichen", in *Events: Soziologie des Außergewöhnlichen* (Opladen: Leske+Budrich, 2000). This school of thought can at least be traced back to the writings of the Situationist International and their understanding of late capitalism as the society of the spectacle. See Guy Debord, *Society of the Spectacle* (Detroit: Black & Red, 1983).

15. The term *anti-systemic* is used to describe the non-single-issue nature of the two mobilizations that, despite all their differences, both see themselves as fighting a society-wide, structured development—be it the decline into socialism and tyranny, in the case of the Tea Party, or capitalism, in the case of Occupy Wall Street. It is nevertheless important to keep in mind that the imagined nature of this system diverges greatly between the two, not at least in what emphasis they put on structural dynamics vis-à-vis the agency of their opponents. The term has been chosen, furthermore, to avoid adopting the vocabulary deployed by the movements themselves, since they tend to have vastly different conjunctive meanings in the two *Lebenswelten*—the term *radical*, for example, was considered an insult by my Tea Party interviewees, while it was treated as a defining element of the self-perception by Occupy activists, who sometimes accused themselves of not being "radical enough". For the meaning of the term *conjunctive*, see Karl Mannheim, "A Sociological Theory of Culture and Its Knowability (Conjunctive and Communicative Thinking)", in *Structures of Thinking* (London: Routledge, 1997).

16. Pierre Bourdieu, *Homo Academicus* (Stanford, CA: Stanford University Press, 1988), 160.

17. Ibid., 180.

18. Ibid., 182.

19. Ibid., 183.

20. Nick Crossley, "From Reproduction to Transformation: Social Movement Fields and the Radical Habitus", *Theory, Culture & Society* 20, no. 6 (12 January 2003): 43–68.

21. Georg Lukács, "Was ist orthodoxer Marxismus?", in *Geschichte und Klassenbewusstsein—Studien über marxistische Dialektik* (Amsterdam: De Munter, 1967), 13–38.

22. James E. Foster and Michael C. Wolfson, "Polarization and the Decline of the Middle Class: Canada and the U.S.", *Journal of Economic Inequality* 8, no. 2 (1 June 2010): 247–73.

23. Seth Motel, "A Third of Americans Now Say They Are in the Lower Classes", *Pew Social & Demographic Trends*, 10 September 2012, accessed 13 March 2014, http://www.pewsocialtrends.org/2012/09/10/a-third-of-americans-now-say-they-are-in-the-lower-classes/.

24. The demographic data on the Tea-Party supporters in this chapter is mainly drawn from a poll conducted by the *New York Times* and CBS News in April 2010, *New York Times*/CBS News Poll, 14 April 2010, accessed 13 March 2014, http://www.nytimes.com/interactive/2010/04/14/us/politics/20100414-tea-party-poll-graphic.html, if not specifically stated otherwise.

25. Lawrence R. Mishel et al., *The State of Working America* (Ithaca, NY: ILR Press, 2012).

26. Marina Vornovytsky, Alfred Gottschalck, and Adam Smith, *Household Debt in the US: 2000 to 2011* (United States Census Bureau), accessed 30 January 2014, http://www.census.gov/people/wealth/files/Debt%20Highlights%202011.pdf.

27. Alfred Gottschalck, Marina Vornovytsky, and Adam Smith, *Household Wealth in the US: 2000 to 2011* (United States Census Bureau, 2012), accessed 30 January 2014, http://www.census.gov/people/wealth/files/Wealth%20Highlights%202011.pdf.

28. Vornovytsky, Gottschalck, and Smith, *Household Debt in the US: 2000 to 2011*.

29. Wendy K. Tam Cho, James G. Gimpel, and Daron R. Shaw, "The Tea Party Movement and the Geography of Collective Action", *Quarterly Journal of Political Science* 7 (2012): 105–33.

30. Lawrence Rosenthal and Christine Trost, "Epilogue. A Tale of Two Movements", in *Steep: The Precipitous Rise of the Tea Party* (Berkeley: University of California Press, 2012), 275–81.

31. Alan Abramowitz, "Partisan Polarization and the Rise of the Tea Party Movement", paper presented at the Annual Meeting of the American Political Science Association, Seattle, Washington, 2011, accessed 12 March 2014, http://faculty.washington.edu/jwilker/353/AbramowitzTea.pdf.

32. The Green New Deal is a slogan covering varying reform suggestions by many different actors. But all of them can be described as suggesting a shift to so-called green technologies as the groundwork for initiating a new cycle of accumulation, replacing the petrochemical and automobile industries that had this role in the Fordist accumulation regime.

33. Ingar Solty, "The Crisis Interregnum: Considerations on the Political Articulation of the Global Crisis: From the New Right-Wing Populism to the Occupy Movement", *Studies in Political Economy* 91 (2013): 85–112.

34. During my fieldwork in the United States between the fall of 2012 and summer of 2013, I conducted fifteen in-depth interviews and three group discussions with activists from four Tea Party groups and participated in and observed several meetings and protest events of various Tea Party groups. The materials in the following pages are drawn from transcriptions of these conversations. The names of persons and groups as well as their geographical locations have been changed.

35. David Carr, "Cable Wars Are Killing Objectivity", *New York Times*, 20 April 2009, accessed 13 March 2014, http://www.nytimes.com/2009/04/20/business/media/20carr.html.

36. Devin Burghart and Leonard Zeskind, *Tea Party Nationalism: A Critical Examination of the Tea Party Movement and the Size, Scope, and Focus of Its National Factions* (Kansas City, MO: Institute for Research & Education on Human Rights, 2010), accessed 13 March 2014, http://www.naacp.org/page/-/TeaParty/TeaPartyNationalism.pdf.

37. Explicitly asked for the "best world" they could imagine, the participants in one group discussion, at first visibly irritated, described a romanticized version of the past, without the political and cultural conflicts they detested—a world with more "wholesome TV shows" and in which, "rather than saying, ah, Thanksgiving is the start of the genocide upon the indigenous population of native Americans, it would be an understanding that Thanksgiving is an opportunity to thank our creator".

38. The data used in the following is drawn from a survey conducted at the May Day rally of OWS in 2012 and from two online surveys at the OccupyWallst.org home page if not indicated otherwise. Milkman, Luce, and Lewis, *Changing the Subject*; Hector R. Cordero-Guzman, "Main Stream Support for a Mainstream Movement: The 99% Movement Comes from and Looks Like the 99%", Working Paper (New York: School of Public Affairs, Baruch College PhD Programs in Sociology and Urban Education, City University of New York, 19 October 2011), accessed 13 March 2014, http://occupywallst.org/media/pdf/OWS-profile1-10-18-11-sent-v2-HRCG.pdf; Hector R. Cordero-Guzman, "Profile of Users of the Occupy Wall Street Website: A Window into the Demographics of an Evolving Movement", Working Paper (New

York: City University of New York, 18 November 2011), accessed 13 March 2014, http://bjsonline.org/wp-content/uploads/2011/12/OWS-profile2-wave2-10-21-22-fin-out11.pdf.

39. Terence Tseng, Mark Esposito, and Jorgo Chatzimarkakis, "Youth Unemployment after the Financial Crisis: 'Quo Vadimus?'", *World Financial Review*, 2013, accessed 13 March 2014, http://www.worldfinancialreview.com/?p=3622.

40. According to a recently published study, Manhattan and Brooklyn are the two most expensive places to live, since the cost of living in Brooklyn has now even overtaken that of San Francisco. Kim Velsey, "Brooklyn Is the Second Most Expensive Place to Live in the U.S.", *New York Observer*, 28 January 2014, accessed 28 February 2014, http://observer.com/2012/09/brooklyn-is-the-second-most-expensive-place-to-live-in-the-u-s/.

41. Vornovytsky, Gottschalck, and Smith, *Household Debt in the US: 2000 to 2011*.

42. Andrew Ross, "Mortgaging the Future: Student Debt in the Age of Austerity", *New Labor Forum* 22, no. 1 (1 January 2013): 23–28. This might also explain why David Graeber's *Debt: The First 5000 Years* (Brooklyn, NY: Melville House, 2011) was, by some, proclaimed to be the manifesto of Occupy Wall Street, even though only a very small portion of the book actually deals with the current developments in the United States.

43. "Not What It Used to Be", *Economist*, December 2012, accessed 13 March 2014, http://www.economist.com/news/united-states/21567373-american-universities-represent-declining-value-money-their-students-not-what-it.

44. I conducted three group discussions and more than twenty in-depth interviews with participants in Occupy Wall Street between fall 2012 and spring 2013, as well as several participant observations at protests and meetings.

45. Activists mentioned the protests in Egypt, Tunisia, Greece, and Spain and sometimes referred to a feeling of frustration they had because they felt that "something like this" wouldn't be possible in the United States. The *Adbusters* call also mentioned the events in Egypt and Spain.

46. Occupy Wall Street, "Declaration of the Occupation of New York City", 29 September 2011, accessed 13 March 2014, http://99.occupymediawiki.org/wiki/Declaration_of_the_Occupation_of_New_York_City.

47. N. R. Kleinfield and Cara Buckley, "Wall Street Occupiers, Protesting Till Whenever", *New York Times*, 30 September 2011, accessed 13 March 2014, http://www.nytimes.com/2011/10/01/nyregion/wall-street-occupiers-protesting-till-whenever.html.

48. Noam Chomsky, "Noam Chomsky Announces Solidarity with #occupywallstreet", *Occupy Wall Street*, 2011, accessed 13 March 2014, https://occupywallst.org/article/noam-chomsky-solidarity/.

49. Research on LexisNexis shows sixteen newspaper articles worldwide for the period from 17 September to 23 September featuring "Occupy Wall Street", most of them smaller side notes; there were 76 from 24 September to 30 September, 225 from 1 October to 7 October, and 229 for 14 October to 20 October, including front-page coverage and extensive commentary.

50. A map of the worldwide protests in the first weeks after the Global Day of Action can be found at "Map: Occupy Wall Street, a Global Movement", *Mother Jones*, accessed 13 March 2014, http://www.motherjones.com/politics/2011/10/occupy-wall-street-protest-map.

51. The last available minutes of OWS Spokes Council date from 12 March 2012 and end with the following sentences: "a few violent, vocal disruptors come in and commence yelling at everyone. After some time of trying to deal with this commotion, Facilitation steps down and declares the meeting over. The live-tweeter and livestreamer also walk out. End of meeting". NYCSC, "NYC Operational Spokes Council 03/12/2012", 12 March 2012, accessed 13 March 2014, http://www.nycga.net/2012/03/nyc-operational-spokes-council-03122012/.

52. "Astroturf" is an American brand of synthetic turf and was in April 2009 used by prominent opponents of the movement such as Paul Krugman in the *New York Times* to designate the Tea Party as not being a grassroots movement. The term quickly caught on and was mentioned in nearly all my interviews with Tea Party activists and in many articles on the Tea Party. Paul Krugman, "Tea Parties Forever", *New York Times*, 13 April 2009, accessed 13 March 2014, http://www.nytimes.com/2009/04/13/opinion/13krugman.html.

53. This projection took on varying forms in the interview. But the most central elements of it were the idea that power over the media allowed the political adversary to skew the picture of one's political goals and practices while orchestrating OWS, and the accusation that George Soros was the true financier behind Occupy Wall Street.

54. See http://teapartycaucus-bachmann.house.gov/, accessed 13 March 2014.

55. To a certain degree, this delegation can be seen as constitutive of the political field as a whole, as Bourdieu suggests. The frustration of the Tea Partiers could then be understood as resulting from a projection of the (necessary) gap separating them from the representatives onto an outside force intervening into the "right" working of the political system. The youngest document of this probably being the campaign by the Tea Party Patriots against the Republican Speaker of the United States House of Representatives, John Boehner, calling for "real leadership" (Pierre Bourdieu, "Die politische Repräsentation. Elemente einer Theorie des politischen Feldes", in *Politik: Schriften zur Politischen Ökonomie 2*, by Pierre Bourdieu, ed. Franz Schultheis and Stephan Egger [Berlin: Suhrkamp Verlag, 2013], 43–96; cf. Tea Party Patriots, "Fire the Speaker! It's Time for Real Leadership", Tea Party Patriots, 2014, accessed 30 January 2014, http://www.firethespeaker.com/tpp/slider).

*Chapter Twelve*

# Emotional Construction of Identities in Protest Spaces

## Tatiana Golova

When Italian scholar of social movements Alberto Melucci stated in a paper published in 1988 that protest events represent just visible aspects of the collective action, and the "constructivist view cannot limit itself to consider the action as an event",[1] he challenged one then prevailing, often implicit, interpretation of collective action as an action by an already-existing collective subject. His main focus was a question of how a "collective" actor is formed and maintained,[2] and how, in latency periods, networks "submerged in everyday life" work beyond visible protests. Our understanding of individual and collective identities has changed a lot since the late 1980s. However, the underlying question of how short-lived protest events and the construction of a more sustainable collective action system are connected, analytically and empirically, still deserves more attention.

In this chapter I address one under-researched aspect of that connectivity: the emotional. In the course of the so-called emotional turn, "emotions of every sort have reappeared in research on social movements, in a still-growing flow of articles and books".[3] However, the interplay between different emotions is a still relatively unexplored field, as stated by Jasper.[4] The interconnections between different kinds of emotions—transient at the one side and more sustainable at another side—are of particular interest for me. Protest actions are usually associated with transient, reflex emotions. That focus goes back to the crowd behaviour approach and reflects an important, easily observed, quality of protest actions to elicit shared emotions and *We-feelings* by participants.[5] Further, activists foster the solidarity, and enhance the development, of collective identity by participating in protest events.

One under-researched aspect of this process is how affective solidarity, which is typically directed "towards people with whom one is not, in most cases, linked by direct personal contacts",[6] transcends temporal and spatial limits of a protest event, as well as limits of interactions with physically co-present participants. The durable affects and "medium-term" moods shape goals, tactical tastes, and reflex emotions.[7] This chapter is based on the assumption that short-time emotions can be transformed into more sustainable ones, but not straightforwardly or unconditionally. Reflex emotions of protests are fluid and, soon after, are little more than memories.[8] The long-lasting emotions connected with certain protest events do not necessarily reproduce the short-term experiences at the new level, but could in fact be very different.[9]

Such transformation requires *emotion work*—or, more broadly speaking, emotion management[10]—by activists, participants, and organizers; happening before, during, and after the events. I prefer to conceptualize this activity as *emotional framing*, because it is more flexible than "management", without being as positive-normative as "emotional achievement".[11] The notion of framing allows cognitive, emotional, and practical aspects of identity construction to combine, which is necessary to explain the transformation of affective solidarity. Shared participation experiences are, in fact, interactively shared with a relatively small number of other participants, because of the constraints of human perception and limits of embodied engagement with the world and the others.[12] A participant can intensify affective bonds to the co-protesters from her "small group", whom she knows personally. However, the affective solidarity goes beyond this level of co-presence and personal ties and includes abstract groupings and non-human objects as well. It would not be possible without cognitive mediation and symbolic structuration. As Jasper suggests, "In the constructionist view, emotions are constituted more by shared social meanings than automatic psychological states".[13] At the individual level, participants are becoming "politically active", and their possible political socialization, through the protest event, has a direction and an identity potential. To sum up, meanings and emotions in protest events should both be considered in the interdependence of short-term and long-term perspectives.

I am particularly interested in the spaces as a focus of such emotional framing in the context of collective identity. The collective identity is considered as a shared definition of orientations (ends and means) of action, and the context (opportunities and constraints) in which it is performed. The identity is, first of all, a process of constructing and not a static outcome. It is interactively produced and negotiated by several individuals and groups.[14] This choice has two main reasons, one empirical and the other theoretical. I started my research of the spaces of the autonomous left-wing scene in Berlin with a cognitive-oriented understanding of identities and space production.

During the field research, however, I learned that for participants in, and organizers of, contentious actions, spatial strategies and imaginaries are highly emotional matters, and that they play an important part in the overall emotional dynamics of protest. Thinking about conceptualization of that evidence/practice, I have realized that emotions and spaces are both about embodiment and materiality of human action and society; it would thus be worthwhile to explore and theorize their potential interconnections and disparities.

As Pierre Bourdieu notes about the riots in the banlieues, there "are compelling reasons to believe that the essential principle of what is lived and seen on the ground—the most striking testimony and the most dramatic experiences—is elsewhere".[15] Protest events cannot be explained in their own empirical limits. If they can mobilize the support of activists or sympathizers, the attention of the general public, the reactions of antagonists or of state actors, then it is partly because of being short-lived and spatially limited—that is, tangible. Still, the unique dynamics of an event are structured by the factors that are not that short-lived: mobilizing networks, their specific interpretation of problems, discontent, repertoires of action, resources of activists, traditions of protest policing, and so on. Yet the argument can be reversed: we can better understand what happens at a site of protest if we consider its relations with symbolic, temporal and spatial orders exceeding its boundaries. In what follows, I will apply this approach to protest spaces. Constructing protest spaces, social movement actors experience ideas and identities as embodied. On the other hand, the protest event spaces are more than a material form of the meanings and relations produced "somewhere else". The construction of space is an identity mechanism in its own right.

The remaining part of this chapter is organized around two main sections. The first offers a review of concepts of social occasion, frames and framing, especially emotional framing, and space. I propose a combination of these concepts for the study of spatialized identity processes in protest events. The second focuses on the field study of collective identity construction among the autonomous left scene in Berlin, which I conducted between 2000 and 2004, with a follow-up from 2008 to 2010. Here, I implement an analytical distinction between two levels of protest event spaces: interactive spatial arrangements and symbolic non-landscapes. Further, I identify the main spatial frames of marches and principal tensions between the frames as symbolical structures and resources of collective action, at the one side, and the activities of participants framing certain events, on the other. As I will show, the emotional framing brings different temporal and spatial levels together.

## PROTEST EVENTS AS RITUALS AND SOCIAL OCCASIONS

The sociological accounts of collective emotions in rituals go back as far as to Emile Durkheim, who developed the idea of "collective effervescence".[16] Ritual gatherings generate emotional arousal from the collective performance of ritual practices, such as music and shared rhythmic movements. This arousal is focused at symbols and individuals representing the group, and, consequently, at its beliefs and moral values.[17] Collective effervescence and its key ingredient—collective emotional arousal—are experienced mentally and physically and bind people to the values of their social group. Some of Durkheim's insights are still useful, despite the old-fashioned vocabulary and a partly esoteric view of collective dynamics. In particular, he assumed that beliefs and symbols which are imbued with emotions during rituals keep their functions—and affective charging—for a group in everyday life as well.[18] According to von Scheve, evidence for such a position can be found in modern psychological and neuroscience research.[19]

Referring to Durkheim, Randall Collins develops a concept of "emotional energy" as a main motivational force.[20] Individual and collective emotional dynamics of protest are interwoven: "social movements periodically gather, in smaller or larger collective occasions, sometimes to recreate the effervescence that launched the movement, and sometimes to infuse new emotions".[21] Occasions that combine a high degree of mutual awareness of participants and a high degree of emotional "entrainment" are high points for both individual lives and groups.[22] Successful rituals transform short-term emotions and allow the development of "distinctively collective emotions, the feelings of solidarity, enthusiasm, and morality".[23] As an aspect of this transformation, the feelings of membership are attached to certain cognitive symbols.[24] The co-presence together with collective movements is, for both Durkheim and Collins, a central condition for physical and psychological synchronization between participants and the experience of solidarity.[25] This account is especially relevant for protest forms based on locomotion, such as marches and walking picket lines. In other words, co-present individuals, doing the same movements, focusing their attention at the same symbols, and sharing reflex emotions, tend to feel like members of a *We-group* and consequently to (re-)create that group.

The notion of protest ritual is certainly well known, and the insights of Collins are useful. However, for a better understanding of spatial mechanisms of identity construction, another vocabulary is needed, one that would pay more attention to the spaces as parts of (ritual) social settings. I refer to protest events as social occasions, a term introduced by Erving Goffman (with reference to "standing behaviour patterns" by Roger Barker[26]). *Social occasion* is a wider social affair, undertaking or event, temporally and spatially situated in such a way that it forms into a unit that can be looked forward to and back upon.[27] It provides a structuring social context for many different interactions, setting the tone for what happens during and within it. This idea does not imply that the participants just follow a once-established pattern of appropriate behaviour. The opposite seems to be true: it is people who determine what actually happens, which kind of event is taking place here and now, through their actions; the negotiating of rules and reality is part of negotiating the occasion.

I consider protest events as social occasions. The protesters as well as others—police officers, journalists, bystanders—are negotiating the character of the gathering, and its political meaning, by their actions. The answer to the question of whether a certain event is a political assembly has far-reaching consequences. These consequences differ widely and are influenced by specific legal contexts and political cultures in which various manifestations of protest take place. Since the 1960s and under the influence of the new social movements, the dominant interpretation of public protests in the German law, and public discourses, has gradually changed: they are considered as worthy of protection, because they allow the individuals public articulation of meaning and active political participation—that is, they have a serious democratic function.[28] A milestone for such reframing was the "Brokdorf ruling", set by the Constitutional Court in 1985 in connection with anti-atom protests in Brokdorf in 1981. The ruling had an enormous influence on the policing of protest events, with repression focusing on allegedly "violence-affined" parts of participants, and not on a whole demonstration.[29] The street protest in general has become an accepted form of participation, with the authoritarian framing and policing reserved for the politically marginal and more direct-action-oriented actions.[30] "Political assemblies" can be prohibited, or dissolved by the police forces, only on certain conditions, and their realization can even be enforced by police despite counter-mobilization. Consequently, the definition of a situation as a political assembly, or street protest—and not, for instance, as a riot or carnival—is highly relevant, not only for the identity construction by participants but also for the kind of policing to be deployed.

## FRAMES AND FRAMING OF PROTEST OCCASIONS

Emotions of a protest event are varied, fluid, and neither entirely prescribed nor sufficiently described by the definition of an event as a "social occasion". Different interactions/interactional chains during one and the same march can generate various emotional engagements and responses—especially shifts from one emotional state to another—and the constantly changing, open-ended character of actions enhance affective solidarity.[31] Kemper's objection should be taken seriously: "If emotions depend on the interpretation of the situation, it seems that all who define the situation similarly ought to experience the same emotion. The problem, in part, comes down to whether or not it is possible to have a standard set of categories for defining situations which will link them logically and empirically with emotions".[32] But when a social occasion sets a tone for interactions, for appropriate and inappropriate behaviour patterns, it sets a tone for moods and for emotional states as well, defining which emotions and emotional displays (such as "self-control") are appropriate. The (competent) participants have more or less realistic expectations about the emotional states of a certain march or a rally (and according to the kind of street protest). Emotional socialization of activists, their appropriation of a "toolkit" of a certain protest culture, implies learning of accepted emotional displays of protest.[33] In this sense, protest routines are emotional routines as well.

A breach of an appropriate behaviour pattern can result in an emotional response. Laughter and humour are probably the best-known case of an emotional reaction to dealing with conflicts and tensions of a defining situation. The negative emotional reactions are a part of corrective responses to the breach of interactional rules, analysed in detail by Goffman.[34] Further, participants can play with definitions of situation, by bringing in some "inappropriate" theatrical and creative moments and provoking emotional reactions of participants, possible antagonists, and spectators. Doing so, they refer to the frame of rallies, marches and other demonstrations of protest. According to Goffman, frames are interpretative structures which guide perception and representation of reality—that is, enable individuals to answer the usually implicit question, "What is it that's going on here?" The answer is "presumed by the way the individuals then proceed to get on with affairs at hand".[35] Consequently, the answer can not only be discursive but also exist on the level of practical consciousness (see below). Frames enable an individual or group "to locate, perceive, identify, and label" events within their *lifespace* and the world at large.[36] Whereas a frame is a rather stable interpretative structure (a meaning-making machine, according to Willems), framing refers to the actors' interpretative practice, which is active and rather fragile.[37] A gathering becomes a "march", if participants of the gathering—including protesters as well as other persons present, such as police officers—are defining it so by their actions, appropriate for a "march" in a certain socio-historical context. Their situative, occasion-relevant roles vary, and may include controlling or even hindering the march. As such, it would constitute a further response to Kemper's objection: appropriate behaviour in a social occasion is role-specific, and an emotional state of an actor depends partly on his or her own role in the situation.

A frame of a social occasion[38] as larger situative context of different interactions includes, in addition to role-specific behaviour patterns, some equipment, and temporal as well as spatial arrangements.[39] One particularly interesting way to negotiate a situation is through the construction of such appropriate spatial arrangements. I assume that institutionalized spatial arrangements form integral parts of frames of a political march as a social occasion. Before introducing a concept of space necessary for developing this argument, I discuss the relations between Goffman's frame analysis and framing approach in social movement studies.

For the framing perspective on social movements, the notion of mobilization is central: movement actors "frame, or assign meaning to and interpret, relevant events and conditions in ways that are intended to mobilize potential adherents and constituents, to garner bystander support, and to demobilize antagonists".[40] The resulting collective action frames, such as the well-known injustice frame, are more action and conflict oriented than everyday interpretative structures.[41] The research implications outlined by Goffman and the research agenda of a framing approach differ widely, despite Goffman's methodological guidelines being rather indecisive.[42] However, I can see no serious obstacles on either side for a combination of a framing approach with Goffman-oriented frame analysis of protest social occasions. Such analysis would contradict tendencies to reify frames as structures at the expense of framing as process. It would enable a stronger focus on emotional aspects and interactional contexts of interpretative work of movement actors.[43] Cognitive structures dominated the view of framing for a long time. The discussion tended to ignore "[e]motional mechanisms . . . lurking unacknowledged beneath numerous processes otherwise taken as cognitive".[44] Yet in the last ten years it has been increasingly recognized that social movements "offer a radically different emotional (re-)framing of reality".[45] Cognitive, emotional, and moral aspects of reality construction by social movement participants are hardly separate realms of their activities. Therefore, they should be studied in their interplay and using the same concepts.[46]

A framing approach is well suited for studying the collective identity formation in protest events for several reasons. First, it can be combined fruitfully with a constructivist identity concept, which views personal and collective identities as, partly, outcomes of the dialectical interplay between framing as interpretative process and frames as interpretative structures, which are themselves resources and products of framing.[47] During this process, frames defining various identity fields (protagonists, antagonists, and bystanders of contention) and their relations are used, negotiated and re-developed.[48] These attributions are an aspect of the definition of appropriate ends, means and the context of collective action. The collective identity as a process of constructing a collective action system is not purely cognitive; it requires emotional involvement, and individual connections to a *We* for it to be affective (purely cognitive self-identifications are not able to motivate).[49] Secondly, notions of frames/framing take into account plurality and the contested character of interpretative activities. Not only do the views of participants of a protest event differ widely, but their antagonists, as well different publics, also try to re-frame and counter-frame an action and the issues at stake. Thirdly, framing perspectives allow for the combination of short-term and long-term perspectives: the framing of a protest event starts before the ritual itself and goes on beyond it. The frames used here are not restricted to the protest event as such, but refer to wider problems. For example, an anti-racist demonstration against a certain administrative practice, residence re-striction (*Residenzpflicht*), refers to the broader problem of a perceived racist consensus in Germany. Such "situated" frames, and frames of certain situa-tive elements of protest occasions, are interconnected and should be studied in their interplay.

Protest events are a focus of the emotional framing by the social move-ment groups and other public actors. The participation in a demonstration is not restricted to the verbal or visual communication of meaning. Instead, the symbolic representation includes presence and expressivity of the crowd as such.[50] In a demonstration, the bodies are used as means of political action.[51] Thanks to such engagement, moral and cognitive ideas are experienced as embodied.[52] The question of how an emotionalized physicality actually helps to construct a certain collective identity deserves special attention. The spa-tial components of protest events play a significant role here and allow a better understanding of how cognitive elements of identity are being con-nected with feelings of solidarity.

## SPACES OF PROTEST OCCASIONS

Though the "spatialities of contentious politics cannot and should not be reduced to scale or any other spatial 'master concept'",[53] the concept of space plays a major role in my argument and is central for application of other concepts: place and non-continuous symbolic spaces (as introduced below). An explicit sociological, relational concept of space—instead of the often implicit idea of an abstract, endless and empty "container" space filled up with people and objects[54]—is necessary to understand spatial aspects of collective identities. Since Henri Lefebvre's groundbreaking work,[55] the idea of space as socially produced has been widely accepted. Space and other spatial categories, first of all "place", are discussed by social scientists of different disciplines and national (or, in the case of English language, supra-national) discourse fields, and these discussions are mostly independent. I use the concept of social spaces as developed by Martina Löw: relational orderings of people, other living beings and social objects, based on localiza-tions.[56] Löw distinguishes between two basic processes of space constitution: First, the positioning of social objects and people in relation to each other. Examples are the display of books on a shelf, the self-positioning of people or the construction of buildings. Secondly, the constitution of space requires synthesis: the objects and people are connected to form spaces through symbolic processes of perception, imagination or remembering. The positioning and the synthesizing happen simultaneously and are empirically inseparable in the routinized production of space in everyday life.[57] The same can be assumed of emotional protest events. This analytical differentiation allows the putting forward of interpretative and creative work by contentious actors: individuals and groups can construct different spatial arrangements on the same location and from the same set of physical objects using different interpretations.

The relation between the symbolism of spaces and their construction in action can be explained through classification of spatial aspects:[58]

1. The physical-material form of space, including the individuals' bodies in their physicality
2. The system of signs, symbols and representations, which are being attached to the spatial arrangements and their elements in the process of (inter-)action
3. The institutionalized social practice of producing, appropriating and using the material form of space

Through their social practice individuals and groups connect as symbolic and physical elements while creating spatial arrangements. According to Bourdieu,[59] the interpretations objectivized in space orderings have to be explicated through the social practices if they are to be more than dead letters—that is, have some relevance. Some of the symbolic structures, to which spatial arrangements are being connected in the framing process, define the *We-group*. The relationality of space, as stressed by Doreen Massey, means that spaces are shaped mainly by the relations of actors.[60] An additional aspect of relationality of protest space is its organization according to the symbolic relations and antagonisms of identity fields (and not just simultaneity of its physical elements).

The difference between spatial structures and constitution of actual spaces of certain protest events reflects the above-mentioned difference between frames as interpretative structures and the process of framing of social movement issues and protests. In this sense, the construction of collective identity as structuration[61] of collective action system has both spatial and symbolic dimensions, and these dimensions are overlapping. People make their spaces/ spatialities in the process of constructing their various identities.[62] At the same time, identities are formed in spatialized and power-filled social relations. Activists construct a salient collective identity while creating the everyday and protest spaces. In this sense, the construction of collective identities can be considered as spatially structured.

The idea of spatial structuration is based on the assumption that the institutionalized space produced and reproduced in human action is not identical with the built space. Relational orderings of people can be institutionalized if they stay effective beyond the action of an agent and entail normative positioning and synthesizing.[63] This is true not only for the repetitive everyday spaces but also for the spatial arrangements of highly emotional protest events. The interactional protest spaces show structural moments despite being short-lived on certain locations. However, the spaces do not reproduce "themselves"—that is, they are not reproduced mechanically. Instead, the actors refer to different rules and meanings which often contradict and challenge each other. In other words, the production of spaces is not just a question of action but also one of inter-action. The ability to construct *own spaces* can be considered a form of the productive power of collective action. The concept of social occasion helps to understand the interactive construction of contested spaces. Institutionalized spatial arrangements are integral parts of the frames of political event as a social occasion. And the other way round, participants negotiate a social occasion, and its political meaning, partly through the construction of certain spaces. These spaces are not merely a physical blueprint of social phenomena, as supposed in Durkheimian social morphology, but, including symbolic, material, and practical aspects, have their own effects and are integral to the production of the identity.[64]

## PROTEST SPACES OF THE LEFT-WING SCENE IN BERLIN

In the following section, I will apply this outline of emotional spatial framing in protest events to an empirical case. Protest practices, as spatial practices, should be considered in the historical and cultural context of repertoires of collective action.[65] I have studied the demonstrations organized or influenced by groups and individuals of the radical left-wing scene in Berlin between 2000 and 2008. Participant observation was conducted and the texts produced by activists were analysed, along with media coverage and legal regulations. The protest events of the left-wing scene are influenced by other protest cultures from past and present. However, the empirical focus on one collective identity allows the highlighting of the connections between its cognitive and emotional elements and the spatial structures.

To make the study of demonstration spaces easier, I make an analytical distinction between their two levels: the situational spatial arrangements and the more abstract symbolic spaces. Participants and other actors of protest events attach some identity-relevant meanings to the interactive spatial arrangements. At the same time, they refer to the meanings of certain places and objects lying beyond the limits of the event. The situational spatial arrangements are produced through the positioning of protesters in relation to each other and the other persons present, especially police officers, journalists and spectators. The ability to create a good and powerful demonstration instead of a monotonous one, without much expression (described as *slouching demonstration*, or *Latschdemo*), is considered in written and oral scene discourses as an expression of the power of the radical left and its capacity to act. The construction of certain spaces supports the creating of a *good demonstration*. Two main models are *bloc* and *parade*.

The normative order of a *bloc* is oriented towards a spatial unity, which puts in the scene a symbolic unity and the force of the *We-group*. The head of a demonstration is typically formed to a bloc with sides closed by banners designed by involved groups and networks; the frontal banner in particular is colourful and graphically ambitious. The communication of political messages to the outside is accompanied by a clear-cut separation of "inside" and "outside" of political activism. The banners belong to protest practices that are not genuinely spatial, but help to construct protest spaces as well. Each side of a bloc forms a closed front; participants are moving forward in tight rows, eventually in chains by linking arms with each other. The direct and mutual influence on each other helps to synchronize the actions of participants. Their movements are being interactively coordinated, but not minutely prescribed. In this sense, chains work quite differently from Foucault's disciplinary power, which produces docile, simultaneously moving (marching) bodies.[66] The practice of *sprinting* explicates the interactivity of that moving spatial ordering. The sprinting is initiated by the first row of a bloc; next, rows are virtually forced to follow: the bloc stops, jumps to a countdown and then runs as fast as possible. The participants can slow their neighbours down or pull them along behind them if they move arm in arm or hold a banner together. The resulting small confusions are typically resolved by laughter, which reinforce the upheaving emotional effect of a demonstration sprint. The framing of sprinting in terms of fun and autonomy can go beyond the situation itself. An example from my long-term participant observation in a group maintaining an autonomous cultural project (here, the collective members recount a demonstration in support of free spaces, where they actively participated):

X: The first row was really tough—how many times did we run? And quite long distances (laughter).

Y: Amateur sprinting (laughter).

Z: It certainly made an impression, such a mob running down the Unter den Linden [a main street].

The physically demanding sprinting breaks the routine of slow movements and reinforces the emotional effects of collective locomotion. The
mobile ordering of a bloc is often interpreted in the situation itself, and
beyond it relationally, as a way by which the *We-group* resists the intervention of the *Them-Police*; that symbolic opposition reinforces the identiary
boundaries and the emotional loyalty of participants, having a positive effect
on further mobilizations.

The second main spatial form is *parade.* It has become popular in the last
ten years and is clearly oriented towards the techno culture. The appropriation of the parade form by the left-wing scene can be traced back to the so-
called *Fuckparade*, initiated in the 1990s by the counterculture-oriented actors of the techno club scene in Berlin, as an alternative to the Love Parade.
*Parades* construct a unity through the use of electronic music and sometimes
incorporate dance as participation. The participants are far more flexible in
the direction and move without clear lines. Here, the prominent solidarity
mechanisms of ritual gatherings mentioned above, collective locomotion and
rhythmic movements, work together and have synergetic effects. However,
loud music from trucks obstruct another embodied protest practice—the
chanting of protest slogans. The chanting communicates political messages
inside and outside the demonstration and is valued as a possibility for grassroots participation: anyone could start a wave, and what slogans are chanted
and for how long is negotiated by protesters (even if the slogans are well
known and refer to the more stable frames of the collective identity). The
*power* of a demonstration is defined in scene discourses as an achievement of
participants, partly in symbolic opposition to organizing groups, who should
not dominate the march by long speeches or music tracks. Therefore, the
differences between *parade* and *bloc* are not those between a more or less
embodied protest form.

The parade demonstration breaks with the spatial symbolism of the closed
*We-group.* It is a result of searching for the more inclusive and open spaces
that have become popular in the last ten years. Another example is the out-of-
control concept first tried out in Hamburg in 2007 after the critical discussion
of *own* protest practices. [67] The closed container space of a bloc demonstration was considered not freely chosen but forced upon the participants by the
police, surrounding the march by a moving "kettle" [68] and thus making any
direct interaction with the public impossible. A part of the protesters swarms
around, in and out of the demonstration, and the police kettle around this.
"The swarm" is meant to interact with the demonstration and with the public
to offer a more inclusive identity space. [69] The co-existence of open and
closed spaces of demonstration in the same repertoire of protest practices
supports Massey's argument on the opposition between political left and
right: it cannot be reduced, on the level of space construction, to "a simple
opposition between spatial openness and spatial closure". [70] Depending on

context, the left can refer to the greater spatial openness (when deploring the European rules of immigration) or to the greater closure (when protecting a demonstration). A spatial form is never self-explanatory.

To sum up, the interactional spatial arrangements of demonstrations are institutionalized and resources of collective identity. But bloc, parade or out-of-control are rarely seen in a pure form and should be considered as frames, as orientations of practical and symbolic action. Actual demonstrations are more or less closer to them thanks to the framing activities of participants, and according to external factors such as the behaviour of other actors. The realization of a normative space is a matter of pride and joy, especially if it has been contested by the police. Appropriate behaviour patterns have spatial aspects: for example, in the case of police interventions—to link arms, build chains and not run away. As the reaction to such interventions, the leaders of the assembly (using the loudspeaker car), or some groups of participants, would call on the people to build chains and to take care of each other. The control of individual panic reactions to the symbolic and physical threat of running police officers in riot gear should happen by the control of the collective space. The framing of protective spaces takes place beyond the protest situations as well. For example, in a widely known leftist brochure on state repression, chains are interpreted as a way to protect oneself, the dem-onstration and the others:

> In case of attacks: Do not panic. Take a deep breath, stop, and encourage others to do the same. Now it is time to build chains (if not happened yet), and, if nothing else seems possible, retreat slowly and in a group formation. To make regular chains and to remain at your place is often enough to block the attacks by our friends in need and to prevent the demonstration from getting split up, the participants arrested, and the injured left behind. [71]

A resistance to the police practice of picking out individuals from the ranks of participants is an attempt to preserve a unified ordering of a march and to hold the antagonist *We-against-Them*-ordering. Because such resis-tance can be interpreted as prohibited—that is, "obstructing the police"—it comes with bodily and legal risks. Through shared bodily investment, com-mitment to the group and solidarity are fostered. Verbal expressions of anger are more common and have the same symbolic function, even if they are considered as "powerless". The participants that deviate from appropriate behaviour as defined by the group—that is, do not show emotional or practi-cal reaction—put into question not only their own competence but also the whole social occasion; they put the identity resources of other protesters in danger and provoke peer-to-peer correctives. The construction of appropriate spaces and a "powerful demonstration" is seen explicitly as the participants' own responsibility, and not one of the organizers. This is consistent with the imperative of personal responsibility crucial for the (post-)autonomous left.

The construction of a specific social occasion of demonstration, and its spaces, is never a mere reproduction of the relevant frames. The dynamics are interactive and depend on other actors as well; the state actors play a major role. The binary *We-against-Them* space is constituted through interactions between police officers and protesters. In addition to direct interactions mentioned above, already the lining up of police in riot gear or the formation of a "black bloc" implies a threat of physical coercion and has a symbolic effect.[72] The dynamic of protest event is influenced by structural conditions and interactions beyond its temporal limits. Several forms of expressive behaviour during demonstrations are subjected to legal restrictions: according to German law, the organizer of an outdoor assembly must file a notification to a competent body. The authority can impose an order containing conditions or partial prohibitions. In case of violations, a demonstration can be dissolved by police. Legally, such restrictions are discretionary. My observations show that the police indeed use them flexibly—that is, ignoring the visible violations for a long time and then reacting to them. In this sense, the orders constitute legally protected room for police manoeuvring and make its actions less predictable. The restrictions often affect space-relevant practices, such as sprinting and closing off of the sides of a demonstration by banners longer than 1.5 metres. Even if the orders, according to the federal assembly law, have to be considered for each case separately, they are typically pronounced for all of demonstrations, especially of those organized by left-wing groups.[73] The state regulation of demonstrations tends to reduce protests to the public expression of opinion. As I showed in the above, this comes at the cost of bodily engagement, which is crucial for the formation of affective solidarity. It affects the protest culture of the left-wing scene in particular because of its normative orientation towards direct action, valued as a form of prefigurative politics. However, the spreading of legal restrictions on spatial protest practices results in the protesters and the police entering into conflict around the production of the bloc space. Rather unintentionally, such conflicts increase the influence of space production on identity.

Moving through the streets, protest actors—organizers as well as other participants—address the meanings of places that are not primarily connected to the protest event and extend its temporal limits. Political actors are obliged to show their rationality by the choice of protest sites: a demonstration could go practically anywhere on public ground (only certain areas are restricted), but it does not. Instead, organizers choose the places that "make sense" in their own symbolic universe for a certain cause. The object pool of the left-wing scene is clearly divided into *Our Own* (such as former squats or neighbourhoods at risk of gentrification) and *Antagonist* places, connected to their political adversaries (such as the headquarters of the right-wing extremist party NPD or the building of the German Foreign Office). The neutral places associated with the "Public", such as the main streets of Berlin, are seldom chosen for this reason, but rather interpreted as symbol for the *Capitalist city*. Appellative addressing of the state institutions such as Bundestag is rare as well. This constellation is similar to the structure of the left-wing identity field in general, including the orientation to the prevalence of individual ideas (identity) above wide acceptance.

The meanings of places can be experienced not just cognitively but also on the levels of emotions and embodied protest practices, if they are being integrated in the interactive spatial arrangements of a march. It happens only if the places are actively referenced, not merely passed by. This is possible through a symbolic attack (with a glass bottle or a paint bomb) or a speech, followed by emotional reactions such as booing or applauding. The productive collective power of defining reality can be realized through integration of *antagonists'* places into *own* protest spaces. The identity field oppositions between *Us* and *Them*, especially *State* or *neo-Nazis*, are spatially realized— and reproduced—in the protest occasion. The references to the *own* places and areas are well integrated in the studied protest culture as well; the housing projects, for instance, can be put in the scene by the unfolding of huge banners from their roofs, waving black flags and/or pyrotechnics. Therefore, the emotional interactions between a demonstration and other groups involved in the occasion can be positive as well.

Such positive or negative references are highly selective, for each route addresses only a few objects from the identiary pool. Additionally, while the demonstration passes meaningful places the streets between them stay mainly meaningless. Instead of symbolic landscapes of the left-wing scene, I identified discontinuous and relational *non-landscapes of meanings*. They are constituted, or brought together, not by proximity in the physical space, but rather by the collective action. The spatial connections are based on the identity-relevant relations as opposed to the physical objects.

## CONCLUSION

The difference between two levels of protest event spaces is analytical and not empirical. The interplay of situational, interactive arrangements and symbolical non-landscapes is what characterizes these spaces. The protesters position themselves in relation to each other, further actors (for example, police officers), and buildings or places associated with *We-* and *Them-* groups. Protest participants do this not just by appropriating material elements but also by working with meanings. Human action integrates physical objects into a relational arrangement using their symbolism. Some collective-action frames concern the demonstration as social occasion; as such, they include institutionalized spatial orders such as bloc or parade.

The question "What is happening here?" is answered through those framing activities. Such activities are emotionalized because of the shared physical involvement of people exposing themselves to the risks of physical action. The elements of collective identity can be embodied, and lived through, thanks to their integration into interactive protest spaces. In other words, people bring meaning, physicality and action together while constructing protest spaces. Here, symbolic relations and oppositions are experienced on cognitive, emotional and body levels at the same time. Their effects last beyond the limits of an event because of that emotional reinforcement. It is that which makes the spatial construction of collective identity particularly effective. The ability to construct protest spaces as a form of collective power does not require those spatial orderings to be permanent on certain locations. Episodic and emotionalized protest spaces create specific identiary effects.

## REFERENCES

Assall, Moritz. "Demokratie mit Preisschild: Versammlungsauflagen in Theorie und Praxis". In *Grundrechte-Report 2008: Zur Lage der Menschen- und Bürgerrechte in Deutschland*, edited by Till Müller-Heidelberg et al., 111–14. Frankfurt-Main: Fischer, 2008.

Atteslander, Peter, and Bernd Hamm. "Grundzüge einer Siedlungssoziologie". In *Materialien zur Siedlungssoziologie*, edited by Peter Atteslander and Bernd Hamm, 11–32. Köln: Kiepenheuer & Witsch, 1974.

Barker, Roger. *Ecological Psychology: Concepts and Methods for Studying the Environment of Human Behavior*. Stanford, CA: Stanford University Press, 1968.

Benford, Robert D. "An Insider's Critique of the Social Movement Framing Perspective". *Sociological Inquiry* 67, no. 4 (1997): 409–30.

Bourdieu, Pierre. "The Kabyle House, or the World Reversed". In *The Logic of Practice*, 271–83. Cambridge: Polity Press, 1992.

Bourdieu, Pierre. "Site Effects". In *The Weight of the World: Social Suffering in Contemporary Society*, edited by Pierre Bourdieu et al. Stanford, CA: Stanford University Press, 1999.

Brown, Gavin, and Jenny Pickerill. "Space for Emotion in the Spaces of Activism". *Emotion, Space and Society* 2 (2009): 24–35.

Butler, Judith. "Bodies in Alliance and the Politics of the Street". Lecture, 2011. http://www.eipcp.net/transversal/1011/butler/en.

Collins, Randall. "Social Movements and the Focus of Emotional Attention". In *Passionate Politics: Emotions and Social Movements*, edited by Jeff Goodwin, James M. Jasper, and Francesca Poletta, 27–44. Chicago: University of Chicago Press, 2001.

Collins, Randall. *Interaction Ritual Chains*. Princeton, NJ: Princeton University Press, 2004.

della Porta, Donatella, and Mario Diani. *Social Movements: An Introduction*. Oxford: Blackwell, 1999.

Durkheim, Emile. *The Elementary Forms of the Religious Life* (1912). Reprint: London: Allen & Unwin, 1965.

Flam, Helena, and Debra King, eds. *Emotions and Social Movements*. London: Routledge, 2005.

Foucault, Michel. *Discipline and Punish: The Birth of the Prison*. London: Penguin Books, 1991.

Giddens, Anthony. *Central Problems in Social Theory: Action, Structure, and Contradiction in Social Analysis*. Basingstoke: Macmillan, 1979.

Goffman, Erving. *Behavior in Public Places: Notes on the Social Organization of Gatherings*. New York: Free Press, 1966.

Goffman, Erving. *Interaction Ritual: Essays in Face to Face Behaviour*. Chicago: Aldine, 1967.

Goffman, Erving. *Frame Analysis: An Essay on the Organisation of Experience*. Boston: Northeastern University Press, 1986.

Goodwin, Jeff, James M. Jasper, and Francesca Poletta. "Emotional Dimensions of Social Movements". In *The Blackwell Companion to Social Movements*, edited by David A. Snow, Sarah Soule, and Hanspeter Kriesi, 413–32. Oxford: Blackwell, 2004.

Hilfe e.V., Rote. *Was tun wenn's brennt?! Rechtshilfetipps bei Demonstrationen, bei Übergriffen, bei Festnahmen, auf der Wache*. 2011.

Hochschild, Arlie R. "Emotion Work, Feeling Rules, and Social Structure". *American Journal of Sociology* 85, no. 3 (1979): 551–75.

Hunt, Scott A., Robert D. Benford, and David A. Snow. "Identity Fields: Framing Processes and the Social Construction of Movement Identities". In *New Social Movements: From Ideology to Identity*, edited by E. Larana, Hank Johnston, and J. Gusfeld, 185–208. Philadelphia: Temple University Press, 1994.

Jasper, James M. "The Emotions of Protest: Affective and Reactive Emotions in and around Social Movements". *Sociological Forum* 13, no. 3 (1998): 397–424.

Jasper, James M. "Emotions and Social Movements: Twenty Years of Theory and Research". *Annual Review of Sociology* 37 (2011): 14.1–14.19.

Juris, Jeffrey S. "Performing Politics: Image, Embodiment, and Affective Solidarity during Anti-Corporate Globalization Protests". *Ethnography* 9, no. 1 (2008): 61–97.

Läpple, Dieter. "Gesellschaftszentriertes Raumkonzept". In *Stadt-Räume*, edited by M. Wentz, 35–46. Frankfurt/Main: Campus, 1991.

Lefebvre, Henri. *The Production of Space*. Oxford: Blackwell, 1991 (1974: *La production de l'espace*).

Leitner, Helga, Eric Sheppard, and Kristin M. Sziarto. "The Spatialities of Contentious Politics". *Transactions of the Institute of British Geographers* 33, no. 2 (2008): 157–72.

Löw, Martina. "The Constitution of Space: The Structuration of Spaces through the Simultaneity of Effect and Perception". *European Journal of Social Theory* 11, no. 1 (2008): 25–49.

Kemper, Theodor. "Social Constructionist and Positivist Approaches to the Sociology of Emotions". *American Journal of Sociology* 87, no. 2 (1981): 336–62.

Klandermans, Bernd. "Identität und Protest: Ein sozialpsychologischer Ansatz". *Forschungsjournal Neue Soziale Bewegungen* 10, no. 3 (1997): 41–51.

Massey, Doreen. *Space, Place and Gender*. Cambridge: Polity Press, 1994.

Massey, Doreen. "Thinking Radical Democracy Spatially". *Environment and Planning: International Journal of Urban and Regional Research, D: Society and Space* 13, no. 3 (1995): 283–88.

Massey, Doreen. *For Space*. London: Sage, 2005.

Melucci, Alberto. "Getting Involved: Identity and Mobilization in Social Movements". In *From Structure to Action: Comparing Social Movement Research across Cultures*, edited by Bernd Klandermans, Hanspeter Kriesi, and Sidney Tarrow, 329–48. Greenwich, CT: JAI Press, 1988.

Melucci, Alberto. *Challenging Codes: Collective Action in the Information Age*. Cambridge: Cambridge University Press, 1996.

Out of Control. "Out of Control—Demonstrationskultur in der Weite des Raumes". 2007. http://www.gipfelsoli.org/Home/militant_reflection/militant_reflection_deutsch/Ueber_Militanz/4433.html,%2003.10.2008.

Paris, Rainer. "Vermummung". *Leviathan* 19, no. 1 (1991): 117–29.

Poletta, Francesca, and James M. Jasper. "Collective Identity and Social Movements". *Annual Review of Sociology* 27 (2001): 283–305.

Roth, Roland. "'Die Macht Liegt auf der Straße': Zur Bedeutung des Straßenprotests für die Neuen Sozialen Bewegungen". In *Straße und Straßenkultur: Interdisziplinäre Beobachtungen Eines Öffentlichen Sozialraumes in der Fortgeschrittenen Moderne*, edited by Hans-Jürgen Hohm, 195–214. Konstanz: Universitätsverlag, 1997.

Rucht, Dieter. "Soziale Bewegungen als demokratische Produktivkraft". In *Politische Beteiligung und Bürgerengagement in Deutschland. Möglichkeiten und Grenzen*, edited by Ansgar Klein and Rainer Schmalz-Bruns, 382–403. Bonn: BpB, 1997.

Scheve, Christian von. "Collective Emotions in Rituals: Elicitation, Transmission, and a 'Matthew-Effect'". In *Emotions in Rituals and Performances*, edited by Axel Michaels and Christoph Wulf, 78–92. London: Routledge, 2012.

Sewell, William H. "Space in Contentious Politics". In *Silence and Voice in the Study of Contentious Politics*, edited by Ronald Aminzade et al., 51–88. Cambridge: Cambridge University Press, 2001.

Snow, David A. "Framing Processes, Ideology, and Discursive Fields". In *The Blackwell Companion to Social Movements*, edited by David A. Snow, Sarah A. Soule, and Hanspeter Kriesi, 380–412. Oxford: Blackwell, 2004.

Snow, David A., and Robert D. Benford. "Ideology, Frame Resonance, and Participant Mobilization". In *From Structure to Action: Comparing Social Movement Research across Cultures*, edited by Bernd Klandermans, Hanspeter Kriesi, and Sidney Tarrow, 197–218. Greenwich, CT: JAI Press, 1988.

Swidler, Ann. "Culture in Action: Symbols and Strategies". *American Sociological Review* 51, no. 2 (1986): 273–86.

Tilly, Charles. "Spaces of Contention". *Mobilization* 5, no. 2 (2000): 135–59.

Warneken, Bernd Jürgen. "'Massentritt': Zur Körpersprache von Demonstranten im Kaiserreich". In *Transformationen der Arbeiterkultur*, edited by Peter Assion, 64–79. Marburg: Jonas, 1986.

Warneken, Bernd Jürgen. "'Die friedliche Gewalt des Volkswillens': Muster und Deutungsmuster von Demonstrationen im deutschen Kaiserreich". In *Massenmedium Straße: Zur Kulturgeschichte der Demonstration*, edited by Bernd Jürgen Warneken, 97–119. Frankfurt/Main: Campus, 1991.

Willems, Helmut. "Goffman's Qualitative Sozialforschung: Ein Vergleich mit Konversationsanalyse und Strukturaler Hermeneutik". *Zeitschrift für Soziologie* 25, no. 6 (1996): 438–55.

Winter, Martin. *Politikum Polizei: Macht und Funktion der Polizei in der Bundesrepublik Deutschland*. Berlin: Lit, 1998.

Yang, Guobin. "Achieving Emotions in Collective Action". *Sociological Quarterly* 41, no. 4 (2000): 593–614.

## NOTES

1. Alberto Melucci, "Getting Involved: Identity and Mobilization in Social Movements", in *From Structure to Action. Comparing Social Movement Research across Cultures*, ed. Bernd Klandermans, Hanspeter Kriesi, and Sidney Tarrow (Greenwich, CT: JAI Press, 1988), 338.

2. Ibid., 332.

3. James M. Jasper, "Emotions and Social Movements: Twenty Years of Theory and Research", *Annual Review of Sociology* 37 (2011): 14.2.

4. Ibid., 14.7.

5. And not only in protest participants but also in other persons involved in the situation.

6. Donatella della Porta and Mario Diani. *Social Movements: An Introduction* (Oxford: Blackwell, 1999), 88.

7. James M. Jasper, "The Emotions of Protest: Affective and Reactive Emotions in and around Social Movements", *Sociological Forum* 13, no. 3 (1998): 397–424.

8. Gavin Brown and Jenny Pickerill, "Space for Emotion in the Spaces of Activism", *Emotion, Space and Society* 2 (2009): 24–35.

9. Jeffrey S. Juris, "Performing Politics: Image, Embodiment, and Affective Solidarity during Anti-Corporate Globalization Protests", *Ethnography* 9, no. 1 (2008): 61–97.

10. Arlie R. Hochschild, "Emotion Work, Feeling Rules, and Social Structure", *American Journal of Sociology* 85, no. 3 (1979): 551–75.

11. Guobin Yang, "Achieving Emotions in Collective Action", *Sociological Quarterly* 41, no. 4 (2000): 593–614.

12. Such constraints are still present, even if modern communication technologies enable real-time information about other parts of protest event.

13. Jasper, "The Emotions of Protest", 400.

14. Melucci, "Getting Involved", 342.

15. Pierre Bourdieu, "Site Effects", in *The Weight of the World: Social Suffering in Contemporary Society*, ed. Pierre Bourdieu et al. (Stanford, CA: Stanford University Press, 1999), 123.

16. Emile Durkheim, *The Elementary Forms of the Religious Life* (1912; reprint London: Allen & Unwin, 1965).

17. Christian von Scheve, "Collective Emotions in Rituals: Elicitation, Transmission, and a "Matthew-Effect", in *Emotions in Rituals and Performances*, ed. Axel Michaels and Christoph Wulf (London: Routledge, 2012), 78–92.

18. Randall Collins, *Interaction Ritual Chains* (Princeton, NJ: Princeton University Press, 2004), 36: "Collective effervescence . . . carries over into more prolonged effects when it becomes embodied in sentiments of group solidarity, symbols or sacred objects, and individual emotional energy".

19. von Scheve, "Collective Emotions in Rituals".

20. "[S]ituations are attractive or unattractive to [individuals] to the extent that the interaction ritual is successful in providing emotional energy". Collins, *Interaction Ritual Chains*, 44.

21. Randall Collins, "Social Movements and the Focus of Emotional Attention", in *Passionate Politics: Emotions and Social Movements*, ed. Jeff Goodwin, James M. Jasper, and Francesca Poletta (Chicago: Chicago University Press, 2001), 27–44.

22. Collins, *Interaction Ritual Chains*, 42–43.

23. Collins, "Social Movements and the Focus of Emotional Attention", 29. Of course, some gatherings/rituals *fail* to arouse emotions (see below).

24. Collins, *Interaction Ritual Chains*, 42.

25. von Scheve, "Collective Emotions in Rituals".

26. Roger Barker, *Ecological Psychology: Concepts and Methods for Studying the Environment of Human Behavior* (Stanford, CA: Stanford University Press, 1968).

27. Erving Goffman, *Behavior in Public Places: Notes on the Social Organization of Gatherings* (New York: Free Press, 1966), 18–20; Erving Goffman, *Interaction Ritual: Essays in Face to Face Behavior* (Chicago: Aldine, 1967), 144.

28. Roland Roth, "'Die Macht Liegt auf der Straße': Zur Bedeutung des Straßenprotests für die Neuen Sozialen Bewegungen", in *Straße und Straßenkultur*, ed. Hans-Jürgen Hohm (Konstanz: Universitätsverlag, 1997), 195–214; Dieter Rucht, "Soziale Bewegungen als demokratische Produktivkraft", in *Politische Beteiligung und Bürgerengagement in Deutschland. Möglichkeiten und Grenzen*, ed. Ansgar Klein and Rainer Schmalz-Bruns (Bonn: BpB, 1997), 382–403.

29. Martin Winter, *Politikum Polizei: Macht und Funktion der Polizei in der Bundesrepublik Deutschland* (Berlin: Lit, 1998), 199–200.

30. Roth, "'Die Macht Liegt auf der Straße'", 207.

31. Juris, "Performing Politics", 75.

32. Theodor Kemper, "Social Constructionist and Positivist Approaches to the Sociology of Emotions", *American Journal of Sociology* 87, no. 2 (1981): 352–53.

33. Ann Swidler, "Culture in Action: Symbols and Strategies", *American Sociological Review* 51, no. 2 (1986): 273–86; Brown and Pickerill, "Space for Emotion in the Spaces of Activism", 30.

34. Goffman, *Interaction Ritual*.

35. Erving Goffman, *Frame Analysis: An Essay on the Organization of the Experience* (Boston: Northeastern University Press, 1974), 8.

36. Ibid., 21.

37. Helmut Willems, "Goffman's Qualitative Sozialforschung: Ein Vergleich mit Konversationsanalyse und Strukturaler Hermeneutik", *Zeitschrift für Soziologie* 25, no. 6 (1996): 438–55.

38. "Frame" as an interpretative structure is not identical with "social occasion" as a unit of interaction analysis.

39. Goffman, *Behavior in Public Places*; Goffman, *Interaction Ritual*.

40. David A. Snow and Robert D. Benford, "Ideology, Frame Resonance, and Participant Mobilization", in *From Structure to Action: Comparing Social Movement Research across Cultures*, ed. Bernd Klandermans, Hanspeter Kriese, and Sidney Tarrow (Greenwich, CT: JAI Press, 1988), 198.

41. David A. Snow, "Framing Processes, Ideology, and Discursive Fields", in *The Blackwell Companion to Social Movements*, ed. David A. Snow, Sarah A. Soule, and Hanspeter Kriesi, 380–412 (Oxford: Blackwell, 2004), 385.

42. Robert D. Benford, "An Insider's Critique of the Social Movement Framing Perspective", *Sociological Inquiry* 67, no. 4 (1997): 412–13.

43. Ibid.

44. Jasper, "Emotions and Social Movements", 14.4; see Benford, "An Insider's Critique of the Social Movement Framing Perspective"; Jasper, "The Emotions of Protest", for earlier diagnosis.

45. Helena Flam and Debra King, eds., *Emotions and Social Movements* (London: Routledge, 2005), 12.

46. Jeff Goodwin, James M. Jasper, and Francesca Poletta, "Emotional Dimensions of Social Movements", in *The Blackwell Companion to Social Movements*, ed. David A. Snow, Sarah Soule, and Hanspeter Kriesi (Oxford: Blackwell, 2004), 413–32.

47. Scott A. Hunt, Robert D. Benford, and David A. Snow, "Identity Fields: Framing Processes and the Social Construction of Movement Identities", in *New Social Movements: From Ideology to Identity*, ed. E. Larana, Hank Johnston, and J. Gusfeld (Philadelphia: Temple University Press, 1994), 192.

48. Ibid.

49. Alberto Melucci, *Challenging Codes: Collective Action in the Information Age* (Cambridge: Cambridge University Press, 1996), 71; Francesca Poletta and James M. Jasper, "Collective Identity and Social Movements", *Annual Review of Sociology* 27 (2001): 283–305.

50. Bernd Jürgen Warneken, "'Die friedliche Gewalt des Volkswillens': Muster und Deutungsmuster von Demonstrationen im deutschen Kaiserreich", in *Massenmedium Straße: Zur Kulturgeschichte der Demonstration*, ed. Bernd Jürgen Warneken, 97–119 (Frankfurt/Main: Campus, 1991).

51. Bernd Jürgen Warneken, "'Massentritt': Zur Körpersprache von Demonstranten im Kaiserreich", in *Transformationen der Arbeiterkultur*, ed. Peter Assion (Marburg: Jonas, 1986), 64–79.

52. Judith Butler, "Bodies in Alliance and the Politics of the Street", Lecture, 2011, http://www.eipcp.net/transversal/1011/butler/en.

53. Helga Leitner, Eric Sheppard, and Kristin M. Sziarto, "The Spatialities of Contentious Politics", *Transactions of the Institute of British Geographers* 33, no. 2 (2008): 169.

54. Dieter Läpple, "Gesellschaftszentriertes Raumkonzept", in *Stadt-Räume*, ed. Michael Wentz (Frankfurt/Main: Campus, 1991), 35–46.

55. Henri Lefebvre, *The Production of Space* (1974; reprint Oxford: Blackwell, 1991).

56. Martina Löw, "The Constitution of Space: The Structuration of Spaces through the Simultaneity of Effect and Perception", *European Journal of Social Theory* 11, no. 1 (2008): 25–49.

57. Ibid.

58. Läpple, "Gesellschaftszentriertes Raumkonzept"; Peter Atteslander and Bernd Hamm, "Grundzüge einer Siedlungssoziologie", in *Materialien zur Siedlungssoziologie*, ed. Peter Atteslander and Bernd Hamm (Köln: Kiepenheuer & Witsch, 1974), 11–32.

59. Pierre Bourdieu, "The Kabyle House, or the World Reversed", in *The Logic of Practice* (Cambridge: Polity Press, 1992), 271–83.

60. Doreen Massey, "Thinking Radical Democracy Spatially", *Environment and Planning: International Journal of Urban and Regional Research, D: Society and Space* 13, no. 3 (1995): 283–88.

61. Anthony Giddens, *Central Problems in Social Theory: Action, Structure, and Contradiction in Social Analysis* (Basingstoke: Macmillan, 1979). About spatial structuration, see Löw, "The Constitution of Space".

62. Massey, "Thinking Radical Democracy Spatially", 285. Massey focuses at the individual level and refers rather to the multiple social identities instead of the collective action system. It has implications for the analysis, even if social identity and collective identity tend to be different sides of the same social process. See Bernd Klandermans, "Identität und Protest: Ein sozialpsychologischer Ansatz", *Forschungsjournal Neue Soziale Bewegungen* 10, no. 3 (1997): 41–51.

63. Löw, "The Constitution of Space".

64. Massey, "Thinking Radical Democracy Spatially", 4.

65. William H. Sewell, "Space in Contentious Politics", in *Silence and Voice in the Study of Contentious Politics*, ed. Ronald Aminzade et al. (Cambridge: Cambridge University Press, 2001), 51–88.

66. Michel Foucault, *Discipline and Punish: The Birth of the Prison* (London: Penguin Books, 1991).

67. The tactic of *five fingers* was an important inspiration for the *out-of-control* concept. It was developed during anti-nuclear protests in Wendland and became known as part of the G8 protests in Heiligendamm: arriving at police blockades, a demonstration split in several predefined blocs; those flow around the obstacle and meet again behind it. An important difference is that the five fingers tactic was developed for the rural areas, less controllable by police forces.

68. The police use the *kettling* tactic to control large protests, especially when it considers those as potentially violent or as a threat to the public order. The cordons contain large groups of protesters for several hours, preventing them from leaving. Eventually, the police tighten the grip or direct people from one side of the kettle to another and back again. In a *moving kettle*, the containment is not restricted to a certain area. The demonstration moves forward while surrounded by tight police lines, but the participants are still not autonomous in their movements. In fact, the police can transform the moving kettle into a stationary one at any point.

69. Out of Control, "Out of Control—Demonstrationskultur in der Weite des Raumes", 2007, http://www.gipfelsoli.org/Home/militant_reflection/militant_reflection_deutsch/Ueber_ Militanz/4433.html,%2003.10.2008.

70. Doreen Massey, *For Space* (London: Sage, 2005).

71. Rote Hilfe e.V., *Was tun wenn's brennt?! Rechtshilfetipps bei Demonstrationen, bei Übergriffen, bei Festnahmen, auf der Wache*, 2011, 5–6. "Friends in need" ("dein Freund und Helfer"), a popular ironic description of police officers, goes back to the proclaimed self-image of police in the Weimar Republic and in the NS-state. Translated by TG.

72. Rainer Paris, "Vermummung", *Leviathan* 19, no. 1 (1991): 117–29.

73. Moritz Assall, "Demokratie mit Preisschild: Versammlungsauflagen in Theorie und Praxis", in *Grundrechte-Report 2008: Zur Lage der Menschen- und Bürgerrechte in Deutschland*, ed. Till Müller-Heidelberg et al. (Frankfurt-Main: Fischer, 2008), 111–14.

# Conclusion

## Ian R. Lamond and Karl Spracklen

As we write this concluding chapter events and protests continue to be in the news. In terms of events, there are big film festivals such as Cannes alongside cultural and sports events closer to our homes in the United Kingdom. One of us has just bought tickets to the Bloodstock Festival, a music festival dedicated to heavy metal that is held in Derbyshire, and is planning to support his wife's tribal belly dance group as they perform on a moving float at the 114th Skipton Gala. Another of us has recently participated in a nonviolent direct-action training day for peace activists, including tips on effective ways to blockade a military base, while looking forward to a festival of words in his hometown. The English stages of the Tour de France are heading towards Yorkshire, and some of our colleagues are involved in arts projects, scientific conferences on sports coaching and the planning of finding the best spots to watch the spectacle roll by. Events are so much a part of our everyday work and leisure lives that it is difficult to find something we do that is not an event—indeed, the use of the word *event* to describe things that are planned in work and leisure means just about anything, and everything is in danger of becoming an event. This of course is problematic. If we do use the word *event* in its original signifying way to define things we do in our everyday lives, we also semiotically refer to the other meaning of the word, the commercial practice of instrumental exchange and hegemonic control. Notwithstanding that caution, it is clear that events are happening all around us, both communicative actions (leisure activities) in the Habermasian lifeworld and the products of instrumentality that are associated with modern capitalism.

In terms of protests, these are less easy to find on websites such as the BBC, or even respectable, liberal newspapers such as the *Guardian*. But go beyond the mainstream media channels and there are protests happening all over the world. In Brazil, people protest about the money paid to host the soccer World Cup and the Olympics and the gentrification of working-class districts. In Turkey, people protest about the failures of the Erdogan government in ensuring the safety of workers after a terrible loss of life in a coal mine. Closer to our homes there are local protests of which we are aware, burgeoning campaigns to stop "fracking" on the Bowland Shales, which stretch between the Yorkshire Dales and Blackpool on the Lancashire coast, and ongoing campaigns to get radical and Green politicians elected in the local and European elections. We are both members of our staff union and have joined protests, pickets and marches in the last couple of years to campaign against the marketization of British education. Events and protests, and protests as events and activism as serious leisure, are going on everywhere.

In this concluding chapter, we will draw together the key themes of this book and set out the important ontological, epistemological, political and ethical issues for activists and academics as activists. We will also set out the key messages for the subject fields of social movement studies, political studies and leisure studies. We will then map out the agenda for a new subject field, critical events studies, showing how this might engage with other disciplines to challenge the hegemony of neo-liberalism in the teaching and research of events management.

## KEY THEMES

The book develops and enhances conversations that have been happening since the first Protest as Events symposium we organized. The chapters have gathered together the insights from the most exciting and challenging contributors to that event, giving them an opportunity to explore the ideas they introduced there, in greater depth. The key themes that were initially identified in the introduction continue to frame each chapter, setting out the critical dialogue in the book and setting out the scope for future research and action. The chapters are broken down into three sections: mediatization and the media spectacle; identity, embodiment and categorization; and events as dissent. Although the three parts frame the individual chapters they have much commonality between them; all the chapters exist in dialogue with one another, and all the chapters reflect, to a greater or lesser degree, on the themes that inform the three parts of the book. The key themes, then, are the synergies in politics, globalization, political studies, cultural studies and the growing protest movement with leisure studies and events management.

Our authors cover a broad range of theoretical perspectives and empirical approaches, and come from a diverse and global reach. The chapters address issues of individual and collective identity; relations between protests and social structures; theoretical reflections on the significance of social movements; and spatiality and affective constructions of protest identities and embodiment in activism research. These, coupled with the use of critical case studies in each chapter, and the section introductions that frame the critical and theoretical development of events as protest and protest as events, make this book a key contribution to the emergence of a new subject field: critical events studies. The connection between politics and protest studies and cultural, social and political protest to events studies/events management studies/leisure studies represents an underdeveloped area of research and scholarship. It is an area ripe for development, although it needs increased encouragement. Nascent fields of critical events management studies and critical leisure studies offer a new dynamic that can supplement and enhance the inter-disciplinarity of politics and protest studies, potentially attracting a wider readership for the book. This collection would indicate that drawing such areas of research into politics and protest studies is alive and kicking, and a research domain that is full of potential for expansion and development.

## KEY MESSAGES FOR SOCIAL MOVEMENT STUDIES, POLITICAL STUDIES AND LEISURE STUDIES

For these subject fields, there are some common messages from this book, as well as some particular messages for each. The common message is that understanding events as protest, and protests as events allows protests to be analysed in a richer, critical manner. It becomes possible for each subject field to understand about how humans interact through events and leisure, how humans plan and organize, do identity work, situate themselves in networks and structures, but also how hegemonic power is used to constrain and control the ability of humans to do leisure and do events.

For social movement studies, we hope that this book provides a new and useful way of conceptualizing social movements. Academics exploring the phenomenon of new social movements can better understand what is happening by thinking about social activists as engaging in serious leisure, and about protests as forms of events. But we hope this book will show to academics studying social movements that it is naïve to pretend to be disinterested in the morality and politics of those movements. You are either with the activists or against them. We are unashamedly radical in our own politics and believe that academics need to stand up and be counted on countering the evils of hegemony, of racism and sexism, of global capitalism. We believe that climate change is happening and needs to be stopped. We believe that the free market has failed to distribute power fairly. We believe that there is a common ground that needs to be found between radicals inside and outside higher education. Social movement studies provide a way to connect the two spaces of resistance, but for this to happen academics need to declare their politics and their ethics, and activists need to recognize that academics have to balance deep political commitment with other extrinsic motivations.

For political studies the key message is that of engagement. There are many excellent pieces of empirical research on radical activism and radical politics published within the subject field of political studies. But there are too many academics in the subject field who use abstract theory to hide a lack of engagement with the objects of study. Political studies needs to engage with actual humans and human activities. The argument that empirical research is the gathering of factoids and case studies does not hold for social activism. With the mainstream sources of news about radical social activism being biased against reporting "what actually happened", it is essential to go beyond the public sphere and explore these cultures and networks like an anthropologist. This is a crucial political turn that needs a "hands-on" approach to exploring what is going on and reporting back. We need to use our theories and our critical frameworks to make sense of the turn to radical activism and social movements, but we need to generate an evidence base from which we can abstract to the higher levels of political theory.

For leisure studies, there is a dilemma and an opportunity. The dilemma for leisure studies is the decline and fracturing of the subject field. Events management courses and schools have become commonplace in universities that used to provide courses and schools in leisure studies—often, the same staff have been transferred from teaching and researching leisure studies to teaching events management. This eventization of leisure is noted by Spracklen, Richter and Spracklen in their study of the privatization and commodification of leisure spaces in Leeds:

> Leisure, both in terms of spare time and identity-inducing activities, as a modern phenomenon came into existence through capitalist forms of production. Although Veblen (1970 [1925]) was the first sociologist to notice changing patterns and significations of leisure consumption associated with the increasing affluence of Western elites in the first half of the twentieth century, it was only in the period following the Second World War that leisure (in the modern West) started to be associated with the construction of cultural identities. Leisure offered means of social differentiation and tendencies of individualisation and was thus in principle exploitable for business. Parker (1972, 1976) noted the emergence of leisure consumers and leisure choices made within the flux of rapid societal change; Roberts (1978) argued that increasing concern with leisure in a post-industrializing West was leading to the establishment of leisure policies and managers in the private sector. . . . The future of leisure, seen in the third quarter of the twentieth century, was ultimately positive: people would have more leisure time, it was believed, along with the more dispensable wealth to fill that leisure time with worthwhile pursuits. Relatively new courses offered by universities, such as Events Management, Entertainment and Hospitality and Retailing, to name but a few, and their

popularity demonstrate the on-going commodification of leisure and recreation
for which planners and managers are required. This in turn has implications for
the conceptualisations of leisure, the actual uses of leisure spaces and time and
not least the opportunities for alternative cultures and scenes. [1]

Leisure studies has become the study of how to manage and make profit
from leisure activities, and the privileging of words such as *management* in
course titles, along with a proliferation of courses designed around sport,
physical activity, tourism and events all point to the end of leisure studies as
a critical study of leisure as an everyday human activity. But this dilemma is
not necessarily the end of leisure studies or leisure theory. This book shows
that leisure is an important part of our lives, and, with the commodification
of culture and the rationality of work, leisure remains the only space and
activity in our lives in which it is possible to be a deliberative, communicative agent. Following a Habermasian critical lens, leisure studies has the
opportunity to become the study of all spaces, events, activities and interactions that shape identities freely within the lifeworld of human culture. That
is, leisure studies can be the study of the leisure that remains free from
instrumentality and a political critique of the extent of hegemony, capitalism
and other things that structure oppression and marginalization. In the next
section, we look at how these critical studies might be applied to events to
create critical events studies.

## CRITICAL EVENTS STUDIES

As we have already mentioned, events management is one of those areas that
has, in the recent past, emerged out of the fragmentation of leisure studies.
The incorporation of protests into its field of inquiry, with a concomitant
acknowledgement of its origins in a leisure studies discourse, may represent
one of the most radical upheavals since the field's emergence.

In the introduction we noted the two primary axes along which events
management commonly categorizes events, these were scale and content.
While the ubiquity of deploying these metrics, in formulating a typology of
*events*, is evident from their centrality in most event management courses, it
is one that frames protest events as a problem, something to be mitigated; a
risk to the smooth running of those highly marketized, corporately backed
and "cash cow" *events* which are considered a more appropriate bearer of
that label. Events become brands and products to be traded; the emotional,
human response to them (and interactions central to them) are commodified
and often sold back to those that actually produced them as memorabilia and
merchandising. At a band gig I recently attended I was greeted, upon exiting,
with the opportunity to buy a DVD recording of the performance I had *just*
left: a mnemonic artefact to facilitate *my* event experience. When I asked if I

could charge a standard Equity[2] rate for appearing as an extra in the film, I was given a cold look of incomprehension. The standard model for developing an events typology, derived from the scale/content axes, works to bifurcate consumer and producer, while obfuscating the active citizen. Protest undermines that implicit fragmentation, challenging the embedded structures of power and domination such frameworks hide. The division between instigator and participant in protest is not one that is as formally conceptualized, nor does it easily map over onto the consumer and producer frame of the *events industry*. Protest events expose the structures of power that such typologies exert through an acknowledgement of the centrality of contestation which is at the core of the *event*. *Critical events studies* would not shy away from the contested, and energetically active, character of the *event*; it seizes it, and celebrates it, and turns its back on the limiting and ossifying constraints the standard models try to straightjacket events into.

Acknowledging that *event* is contested should not, however, mean we avoid trying to get some purchase on the term. Without any form of purchase we have no hope of trying to develop a *critical* events studies. In our introduction, the conceptualization of *event* in Badiou[3] and Žižek[4] was used to begin re-framing an understanding of *event* that can feed into a fresh articulation of event studies. In developing their thought in a form that attempts to open up the field of events management and events studies, we approach a fuzzy definition of *event* as something like this: *An event is a rupture with the mundane*[5] *that opens up a liminal*[6] *space where there is the potential to encounter the Real.*[7] This working definition compresses a substantial amount of theory; like *Doctor Who*'s Tardis, it is much smaller on the outside. To fully unpack it would require another book (and one that the editors are looking to develop). But let us at least consider some of its implications. Following Habermas,[8] we understand that there are attempts to colonize the event space, and the dominant political hegemony to frame what is to be construed as *the Real*. In many industrially developed nations that hegemony might be the strong cultural political economy[9] of neo-liberalism, and its various machinations, including the exploitation and concretization of concepts around race, sexuality and so forth. In other states that colonization may be from a more totalitarian politico-military regime. Whatever the hegemonic framework is which attempts to colonize the *event*, that should be the primary focus of any critical events studies.

Within the context in which the editors of this book work, this has profound pedagogical implications for the teaching of events management. There is an explicit trajectory within events management education of preparing students to be *fit for purpose* as active members of an "events industry". That trajectory is completely consistent with a dominant discourse of *employability* and models of capitalistic growth. Employability has become so naturalized within our construal of education that it has become a sine qua non for the function of learning. To challenge that construct is to *appear* to be speaking up for mass *un*-employment and a complete disconnection between learning and the social; this is only the case if we consider "industry", like event, to be uncontested. Adorno,[10] Horkheimer,[11] and many others within the tradition of critical theory have challenged such a construal. The pedagogical work of Freire[12] and Boal[13] provide us with a strong lead in suggesting that, instead of a neo-liberal association, learning and emancipation represent the more efficacious combination. Critical events studies, as articulated in the teaching of events management, would need to promote emancipation and highlight the exploitative irony inherent in the conceptualization of an events *industry*.

To summarize, events management, within a critical mode, needs to accept (and relish) the challenge of the contested nature of events, while confronting any dominant hegemony that tries to colonize them.

So what of methodology? The essence of contestation is that no one discipline, research philosophy, area or approach could ever fully encompass it. In order for critical events studies to mature and develop, it must be multimodal. Traditional social science tools ranging from auto-ethnographies to (much to the personal discomfort of this writer) statistically driven positivism, as well as the many hues that lie beyond and between them, need to be brought to bear in expanding the horizons of critical events studies scholarship. But a critical perspective on events need not be purely understood in social scientific terms. While the social sciences and philosophic reflexivity may be operating in the background of this book's editors, the field of critical events studies needs to be open to investigation at a level that goes beyond inter-disciplinarity to accept contributions that can be made from a truly poly-disciplinary domain. At the centre of research into events, there needs to be the project of working with an essentially contested conceptualization of the event, while trying to develop it into a truly emancipatory field.

## CLOSING THOUGHTS

It began as a casual comment, spoken to a colleague over a cup of coffee and an almond croissant in a coffee shop in Leeds. *So why don't we teach our students about the events some anti-cuts groups are organizing?* That conversation grew into the nascent thought that protests are, and should be, a legitimate area of research in events and events management. Professor Rhodri Thomas, head of the International Centre for Research into Events, Tourism, and Hospitality (ICRETH), facilitated a meeting between the two editors. Together, with the support of another two colleagues (Professor Kevin Hannam and Daniela Carl), the idea of hosting a one-day symposium on Protests as Events/Events as Protests grew and started to take shape.

As organizers, we were unsure what to expect from the day. It all felt a little scary. Discussions around protest and social movements were the mainstay of radical geographers, political scientists, sociologists, anthropologists, and others with a long heritage of scholarship around it, and related areas. The Occupy movement, revolutions in the Arab world and riots in some of the big cities in the UK were drawing to the fore inquiring minds from multiple disciplinary areas. What could the incorporation of event studies and events management hope to add? One of the organizers hoped that the symposium would not end in embarrassment: *just half a dozen papers and maybe twenty delegates would be amazing.* On 12 June 2013 the Protests as Events symposium had around seventy attendees, from seven countries, and a programme of thirty papers and three workshops. It was—wonderful. Closing your eyes in the middle of the area used for our midday lunch, listening to those multiple voices animatedly discussing protests as events, catching a soupçon of laughter and a Pierre Schaeffer–esque symphony of accents and languages, was breathtaking.

From that day to working on this book has felt like a long journey, but it has been a pathway well worth walking. The book's editorial team has a mixed level of experience when it comes to moving from an idea to seeing it in a tangible form on a bookshelf; for one it may be another venture—for the other it is a first step of a new adventure. Between us we have grown closer as friends as well as colleagues, and that's been great; it has been part of the *Real*, glimpsed through the liminal space the event of developing this book has opened. Now the end of that walk is coming into view, new paths are opening up. There is a word in classical Greek—νόστος (Nostos). *Nostos* translates as "homecoming". In Homer it relates to the travails of Odysseus as he heads homeward to a world changed from the one he left. Despite that, it is a welcoming world and one where he knows his future lies. The conversations begun that day in June 2013 have not gone. They are continuing, evolving, growing new forms and articulating new approaches. Protests are events. This book firmly plants that seed—let us see what can be grown.

## REFERENCES

Adorno, Theodor W. *The Culture Industry.* London: Routledge, 2005 [1991].
Badiou, Alain. *Philosophy and the Event.* Translated by Louise Burchill. Cambridge: Polity, 2013.
Boal, Augusto. *Theatre of the Oppressed.* London: Pluto Press, 2008 [1979].
Freire, Paulo. *Pedagogy of the Oppressed.* Translated by Myra B. Ramos. London: Penguin Books, 1996 [1970].
Getz, Donald. *Events Studies: Theory, Research and Policy for Planned Events.* 2nd ed. London: Routledge, 2012.
Habermas, Jürgen. *The Theory of Communicative Action, Vol. 2: Lifeworld and System: A Critique of Functional Reason.* Cambridge: Polity, 1992.
Horkheimer, Max. *Critique of Instrumental Reason.* London: Verso, 2013.

Jessop, Bob, and Ngai-Ling Sum. *Towards a Cultural Political Economy: Putting Culture in its Place in Political Economy.* Cheltenham, UK: Edward Elgar, 2013.
Lacan, Jacques. *The Language of the Self.* Translated by Anthony Wilden. Baltimore: Johns Hopkins University Press, 1968.
Lacan, Jacques. *Ecrits: A Selection.* Translated by Bruce Fink. New York: W.W. Norton, 2004 [1966].
Spracklen, Karl, Anna Richter, and Beverley Spracklen. "The Eventization of Leisure and the Strange Death of Alternative Leeds". *City* 17, no. 2 (2013).
Žižek, Slavoj. *Event: Philosophy in Transit.* London: Penguin, 2014.

# NOTES

1. Karl Spracklen, Anna Richter, and Beverley Spracklen, "The Eventization of Leisure and the Strange Death of Alternative Leeds", *City* 17, no. 2 (2013): 165.
2. Equity is the union that represents those working in the performing arts in the United Kingdom. The current minimum rate (as approved by the BBC and ITV) for a walk-on, non-speaking part is about £65.
3. Alain Badiou, *Philosophy and the Event*, trans. Louise Burchill (Cambridge: Polity, 2013).
4. Slavoj Žižek, *Event: Philosophy in Transit* (London: Penguin, 2014).
5. Badiou, *Philosophy and the Event*; and Žižek, *Event.*
6. Donald Getz, *Events Studies: Theory, Research and Policy for Planned Events*, 2nd ed. (London, Routledge, 2012).
7. Jacques Lacan, *Ecrits: A Selection*, trans. Bruce Fink (1966; reprint New York: W.W. Norton, 2004).
8. Jürgen Habermas, *The Theory of Communicative Action, Vol. 2: Lifeworld and System: A Critique of Functional Reason* (Cambridge: Polity, 1992).
9. Bob Jessop and Ngai-Ling Sum, *Towards a Cultural Political Economy: Putting Culture in Its Place in Political Economy* (Cheltenham, UK: Edward Elgar, 2013).
10. Theodor W. Adorno, *The Culture Industry* (1991; reprint London: Routledge, 2005).
11. Max Horkheimer, *Critique of Instrumental Reason* (London: Verso, 2013).
12. Paulo Freire, *Pedagogy of the Oppressed*, trans. Myra B. Ramos (1970; reprint London: Penguin Books, 1996).
13. Augusto Boal, *Theatre of the Oppressed* (1979; reprint London: Pluto Press, 2008).

# Index

# Notes on Contributors

**Jonathan Cable**, Researcher and Lecturer at Cardiff University, completed his PhD in Journalism Studies in 2012. His thesis examined the impact of the media on the protest tactics of three different protest groups, considering the effect those tactics had on the groups' ability to publicize their key messages. Since then he has worked on a number of different projects, including a BBC Trust–funded project, at Cardiff University, investigating BBC impartiality across various forms of programming; an AHRC-funded project focusing on public engagement activities in the Arts and Humanities; and a collaborative research project with a local Cardiff community news website.

**Reverend Ruth Dowson** is Senior Lecturer at the UK Centre for Events Management at Leeds Beckett University (UK). Ruth has over thirty years of experience in events management, both in the public and private sectors. In 2007 Ruth began teaching events management, taking on course leadership at the UK Centre for Events Management in 2009. She was ordained a priest in the Church of England in 2013 and is currently the only full-time events academic who can also perform weddings and funerals. Ruth's research interests include the role of events in the culture of the church, the use of religious heritage buildings for events, the eventization of religious heritage objects, protest events and raves, and the influence of personality on individuals and team development.

**Nezihe Başak Ergin** is Lecturer at Giresun University in Turkey. After finishing her first degree in Urban and Regional Planning at Mimar Sinan Fine Arts University, Istanbul, she continued her studies with a master's of science degree and PhD research in Sociology at Middle East Technical University, Ankara. During her doctoral studies, she was visiting researcher in the School of Geography at the University of Leeds. Since 2009 she has been a teaching and research assistant in the Department of Sociology and the Graduate School of Social Sciences at the Middle East Technical University. Her research interests are social movements, urban struggles, critical and radical geography, participatory and emancipatory research and teaching, art and resistance, and academia.

**Christian Garland** is a doctoral researcher who writes and publishes— broadly speaking—in the tradition of critical theory, the Frankfurt School kind, but his interests beyond that include a consideration of protest and social movements informed by autonomist Marxism and anarchism. He has a BA in Philosophy and Politics (UEA) and an MA in Social and Political Thought (Sussex). Having had a brief hiatus, Christian is hoping to return to his PhD shortly, subject to funding. He has taught—casually and on precarious terms—at the universities of Edinburgh, formerly ECA; Warwick; Bedfordshire; and, most recently, Middlesex.

**Tatiana Golova** is Lecturer at Otto von Guericke Universitat, Magdeburg (Germany).Tatiana studied at the St. Petersburg State University in Russia and received her PhD from the University of Magdeburg. Her publications include *Hate Crime in Russia* (co-author, 2010) and *Räume kollektiver Identität* (Spaces of collective identity, transcript, 2011). Her research specialties are political radicalism and contentious politics.

**Cassandra Kilbride** is a research assistant in protests as events at Leeds Beckett University (UK). After completing her degree in events management Cassandra has offered research support for a number of academics in events studies, leisure studies and cultural policy studies. She is a researcher, freelance artist and event manager. In 2011 she was festival organizer at the Raise Your Banners Festival of Political Song. She is often found engaged in some form of craftivisim.

**Nils-Christian Kumkar** is a PhD candidate with the research group Critical Junctures of Globalization at the University of Leipzig (Germany). After he finished his studies in sociology and economics at the University of Göttingen and the University of California–Los Angeles, Nils worked as a junior researcher at the Institute for Urban and Regional Sociology in Dortmund and at the Institute for Democracy Research in Göttingen, where he started to do research on contemporary conservative social movements, civic engagement and their interpretation of the crisis of the Euro-Zone. His current research focuses on how different social classes in the United States and Germany experience, criticize, and maybe even challenge the politics of crisis through various forms of movements and protests.

**Ian R. Lamond** is Lecturer at Leeds Beckett University (UK). Since completing his PhD at Sheffield Hallam University in 2012, Ian has been lecturing in events management. Prior to that Ian worked in the arts as both practitioner and administrator for almost fifteen years. His academic background is in philosophy, cultural policy studies and political discourse analysis. Ian's research interests include the study of events in contested spaces; media, memory and events; event theory; and critical event studies, with a particular interest in the applications of critical approaches to discourse analysis, critical stylistics and corpus linguistics in the analysis of events. Current research projects include a study of the changing discursive construction of the 2011 London riots in contemporaneous Twitter posts; discourses of environmental sustainability in regional rural businesses; and an inquiry into the mnemonic constitution of Leeds Pride. Ian enjoys working both on his own and in collaboration with colleagues internally and externally. He has presented papers at conferences across Europe and recently returned from a British Council–funded workshop project in Brazil. Ian is a member of the Political Studies Association and the Media, Communications and Cultural Studies Association.

**Dan Lomax** is Senior Lecturer at the UK Centre for Events Management at Leeds Beckett University (UK). Dan has worked in the events sector for almost twenty years. He has been involved with a wide variety of different music and cultural events, focusing on nightclubs, stage shows and music/film festivals. He has extensive experience planning and staging music and club events, both as promoter and professional DJ, performing at more than three thousand shows, and he is a veteran of many club and music scenes in Leeds since the early 1990s. Dan's research interest is in event experience and design. His current research is in how the animation of events and events spaces affects the experience of attendees.

**Angie Ng** is a PhD student in the School of Applied Social Sciences, Durham University (UK). Angie's PhD research is on the sale of sex by women in Hong Kong; she is also currently employed as a research assistant at the University of Bern in Switzerland. In terms of social involvement, she is an organizer with SlutWalk Hong Kong and involved in other progressive movements as well. Her research interests include sex trafficking, women selling sex, social inequality and social attitudes, social movements and the media, and primary health care.

**Henry Rammelt** is a junior researcher currently finishing his PhD at the Institute of Political Sciences, Université Lumiere Lyon 2 (France). Henry's research is focused on social mobilization and social capital in countries with a transition background, especially Eastern Europe. He was a research fellow at the Romanian Academy's Institute for the Quality of Life, and at the Francophone Doctoral School in Social Sciences in Bucharest. Previously he worked as research coordinator for Transparency International Romania. He majored in Political Sciences and Sociology at the University of Dresden and at the Institute of Political Sciences Lyon.

**Craig Robertson** is a researcher at the University of Exeter (UK). Craig has recently completed a PhD in music sociology at the University of Exeter with his thesis "Singing to Be Normal: Tracing the Behavioural Influence of Music in Conflict Transformation". He has an interdisciplinary approach to the social research of musical experience in conflict zones and has conducted empirical research in Bosnia-Herzegovina and Tunisia. He has presented his research at international sociology and peace research conferences in Europe and Asia. He is the co-author and co-editor of a forthcoming book entitled *Music, Power and Liberty*.

**Raphael Schlembach** teaches in the Department of Sociology at Sussex University. His research interests are interdisciplinary with a focus on political sociology, paying particular attention to contemporary critical theories and protest movements. He has recently published his research monograph *Against Old Europe* (2014), in which he looks at the political visions and dead ends of the European alter-globalization movements.

**Karl Spracklen** is Professor of Leisure Studies at Leeds Beckett University (UK). He has held senior officer positions within the Leisure Studies Association, and was its chair until 2013. He is also the secretary of the International Society for Metal Music Studies, the editor of *Metal Music Studies* and a key organizer of the British Sociological Association's Alcohol Study Group. His research interests include leisure theory; communicative leisure; privatization of leisure spaces, tourist spaces and tourist performativity; whiteness and masculinity; class; northernness and national identity; rugby leagues; whisky and real-ale tourism; and various music genres (metal, folk, neo-folk and goth). He researches and writes alone and in collaboration with a range of other people internally and externally. Karl is co-editor (with Professor Karen Fox of the University of Alberta) of a book series entitled Leisure Studies in a Global Era. The books in the series include one he has written, *Whiteness and Leisure*, and one he has co-edited with Leeds Metropolitan University colleagues Brett Lashua and Steve Wagg, *Sounds and the City*. This series will have a huge impact globally on leisure studies, tourism, events and related subject fields.

**Bernadette Theodore-Saltibus** is Senior Lecturer at the UK Centre for Events Management, Leeds Beckett University (UK). Bernadette is a specialist in state and civic events, VIP protocol and event security with over twenty years in the field of events management at all levels. She has worked extensively, planning and managing high-level VIP events ranging from state conferences, parades and state visits, specializing in state protocol. Prior to immigrating to the UK, Bernadette served the head of state of St. Lucia as her aide de camp. She was a lead author on St. Lucia's State Civic Protocol, now widely referred to as the standard guidance for all national/international and political events on the island. Her research interests include event security, event law, risk management and risk mitigation and contingency planning, particularly within non-traditional event typologies.

**Myrto Tsilimpounidi** is a postdoctoral fellow and the Executive Director of Ministry of Untold Stories at the University of East London (UK). Recent publications include "Performances 'in Crisis': What Happens When a City Goes Soft?" for *City* and an article on street art in *Journal of Arts and Communities*. She co-edited *Remapping "Crisis": A Guide to Athens*, a book on crisis and its urban manifestations, and is working on a new book on the sociology of crisis. Myrto is a social researcher and photographer. Her research focuses on the interface between urbanism, culture, and innovative methodologies. Past work explores the impact of migration on societal changes through an empirical investigation of cosmopolitan theory. Current projects focus on street politics, landscapes of belonging and the new aesthetics of crisis in Southern Europe.

**Aylwyn Walsh** is Lecturer and Artistic Director of Ministry of Untold Stories at the University of Lincoln (UK). Recent publications have included work on prison and performance in *Contemporary Theatre Review*; arts in health care for the *Journal for Applied Arts and Health*; and articles in *Total Theatre* magazine, *Women in Prison* magazine, *Prison Service Journal*, and *Theatre Topics*. She co-edited *Remapping Crisis: A Guide to Athens*. Aylwyn is a performance maker/scholar working on the arts and social change. Her work is concerned with exploring the intersections of interdisciplinary methodologies. She has developed practice-led research in women's prisons in the UK and in Greece and is conducting a cross-arts project on containers.